AIR WARS

AIR WARS

The Fight to Reclaim Public Broadcasting

Jerold M. Starr

Beacon Press
Boston

Beacon Press
25 Beacon Street
Boston, Massachusetts 02108-2892
www.beacon.org

Beacon Press books
are published under the auspices of
the Unitarian Universalist Association of Congregations.

05 04 03 02 01 00   8 7 6 5 4 3 2 1

This book is printed on acid-free paper that meets the uncoated paper
ANSI/NISO specifications for permanence as revised in 1992.

Text design by Sara Eisenman and Preston Thomas
Composition by Wilsted & Taylor Publishing Services

Library of Congress Cataloging-in-Publication Data
Starr, Jerold M.
    Air wars : the fight to reclaim public broadcasting / Jerold M. Starr.
        p.   cm.
    Includes bibliographical references and index.
    ISBN 0-8070-4210-2 (cloth)
    1. Public broadcasting—Pennsylvania—Pittsburgh.   2. Freedom of
speech—Pennsylvania—Pittsburgh.   3. Pressure groups—Pennsylvania—Pittsburgh.   I.
Title.
    HE8700.79.U6 S73   2000
    384.54′09748′86—dc21   00-021480

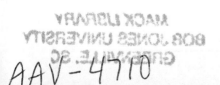

Contents

Introduction

Our democracy requires some space in our vast system of communications that is not controlled by the imperatives of power or profit. This would be space where issues can be explored without censorship, where scripts are not designed around product placements and commercial interruptions, where program ideas are not driven by the selling of audiences to advertisers, where minorities can be served without concern for ratings.

The current trend of increasing concentration of media ownership into the hands of fewer and larger corporate giants makes the need for alternative perspectives and sources of information even more crucial. This was the mission envisioned for public broadcasting by the Carnegie Commission: to serve as "a forum for controversy and debate" and "a voice for groups in the community that may otherwise be unheard," so that we could "see America whole, in all its diversity." In doing so, public broadcasting could act as a watchdog on government and corporate abuses, create space for public discussion, and make it possible for citizen groups to form around the issues of the day.

I have been a friend of public broadcasting all my adult life. I love its mission and cherish many of the programs it has brought me over the years. I believe our ability to support an independent, noncommercial forum for public debate and artistic experimentation is a measure of our maturity as a democracy. So it has been with a great deal of sadness and regret that I have watched as this wonderful service has been attacked by government forces hostile to editorial independence and forced over time to become increasingly beholden to corporate sponsorship in order to survive. At times, it has seemed like the Tories were taking back the commons and replacing the speakers' stands with video billboards.

Over the years, I found myself watching public television less and less as the pursuit of great ideas gave way increasingly to the pursuit of big bucks or flashy productions. There were fewer programs that challenged the mind and more shows on business, investing, and collecting. There were fewer performances of original drama or serious music and more imports, reruns, and overproduced pop. There were more and longer commercials. Several recent books published on the subject tell the story: public broadcasting has been characterized as "for sale," a "vanishing vision," even as dead.

Then something happened to change my grumbling into activism. An editor friend extended an invitation to write a feature piece on local media for her paper. Then came an invitation from the group Fairness and Accuracy In Reporting (FAIR) to testify at a scheduled national hearing in Pittsburgh on PBS programming. The financial troubles of my local station, WQED, became front-page news. I began to ask questions, talk to friends, and think seriously about whether the institution that I cared so much about could be taken off the block, brought back to life, and restored to its original vision.

This is my story and that of others who feel as I do that we have a responsibility to save our friend from hostile forces and itself—to put the public and the public interest back into public broadcasting.

I am a scholar/activist in the humanist tradition. I was recruited to Brandeis in 1964 by Morrie Schwartz (of *Tuesdays with Morrie*) to do graduate study in sociology. As an NIMH fellow, I was thoroughly trained in qualitative research methods by Everett Hughes, Jack Seeley, and other distinguished Brandeis faculty. My dissertation was based on qualitative methods and I have regularly taught courses on the subject at the University of Pennsylvania (with Renee Fox) and West Virginia University over the past thirty years. Thus it is second nature for me to take copious notes on all my professional interactions as well as to maintain large files of documents and clippings on relevant issues. My interest aroused by my participation in the WQED story, I began to read widely in the relevant literature.

Over time, I interviewed dozens of public broadcast officials, communications attorneys, media activists, and others. As I developed insights into the subject, I started presenting papers to colleagues and publishing opinion editorials and short articles. I did not intend to write a book. A few years into the project, however, it seemed inevitable.

My research could be characterized as "participatory" insofar as it represents scholarly activity in the service of members of the community who received and acted on my findings. I followed what scholars in applied sociology call the "advocacy model," utilizing "conflict methodology," which entails recognizing conflicts of interest between various institutions and the public and being willing to use adversarial strategies to secure information about corporate activities that would otherwise be kept secret.

In the final analysis, however, this is a personal book about my efforts to make public broadcasting more accountable to my community. I hope it will inspire as well as inform. I have spent the past six years with other citizen activists fighting for a more democratic and pluralistic public broadcasting service. With limited material resources, my colleagues and I took on

WQED, a $32 million a year public broadcasting complex, and stopped it from cashing in its second station, WQEX, to cover debts incurred from mismanagement and possible embezzlement.

Because of the precedent-setting potential of the case, we played a major role in saving up to seventy other public television stations from being sold off—maybe one in your town. We opened up spaces for labor and public interest groups on our local station's board of directors and community advisory board. We got programming for working people on the station's schedule, where it didn't previously exist. We even produced a program on domestic violence. And we're not done yet.

While much of this book concentrates on our effort to save and improve public service broadcasting in Pittsburgh, I will also tell the stories of activists fighting for accountable public broadcasting elsewhere around the nation. In the process, I will map out the terrain of the U.S. commercial media and public broadcasting systems, and introduce you to weapons that can be used to represent the public interest where it is not being served. Before we're done, you will be alerted to the corporate giants that threaten the public interest in this age of media merger mania. More important, I hope you will be impressed with the thousands of media activists winning small battles for media democracy in cities and towns across America.

Finally, I hope you will support the efforts of public interest organizations gearing up for the major battles over national media policy that loom ahead. This includes an exciting new plan to restructure public broadcasting as an independent public trust, free from undue government and corporate influences.

Chapter 1

Trouble in Three Rivers City:
WQED Debt Comes Due

In April 1993, the front page of my daily newspaper headlined the troubles of Pittsburgh's local public broadcasting corporation, QED Communications, Inc. (now WQED Pittsburgh). Facing a $7.4 million loss of revenues, CEO Lloyd Kaiser had dismissed fifty-four employees (about 25 percent of his staff) and, after twenty-one years, resigned his position. Don Korb, a member of QED's board, accepted board chair Elsie Hillman's offer to serve as acting CEO for the year.

Korb, a former Westinghouse vice president and treasurer, had served for ten years as chair of the QED board's finance committee. Elsie Hillman is the wife of billionaire Henry A. Hillman, one of the forty richest men in America. She has been a major power in the national Republican Party, former chair of the Pennsylvania Republican Party, and widely acknowledged kingmaker for Pennsylvania senator John Heinz, governors Richard Thornburg and Tom Ridge, and former U.S. president George Bush, a distant relative. She was also the power behind WQED.

From Community Station to National Center

Pittsburgh's WQED, VHF channel 13, was reserved in 1952 and launched in 1954, subsidized by 60,000 Pittsburghers who contributed two dollars each.

It was the first community-owned noncommercial television station in the nation. In 1958, the corporation persuaded the FCC that "there was a compelling need for a second educational channel in Pittsburgh." With the granting of UHF channel 16, WQED became the first public station to operate a second station, WQEX.

In the early days, WQED's *Heritage* series featured filmed visits with great artists and scientists. Its portrait of Martha Graham was the first in public broadcasting to win a national award. From 1954 to 1961, WQED produced an hour-long, award-winning program called *Children's Corner,* featuring Josie Carey as host and a young puppeteer named Fred Rogers.

In 1961, Carey left and her show was replaced by *Mister Rogers' Neighborhood,* starring Fred Rogers and produced by his own Family Communications, Inc. In 1968, *Mister Rogers' Neighborhood* became an instant success on the Public Broadcasting Service (PBS) nationwide. The program continues to be broadcast from the studios of WQED.

Carey recalls the early days at WQED: "We went door to door collecting two dollars per family, we collected money from the schools for in-school programming, we did local shows—the Kilty Band concerts, shorthand, remedial reading, game shows, 'Children's Corner.' We never intended to be the equal of networks; we were a community station."

In contrast, Lloyd Kaiser reported in his farewell interview that Elsie Hillman had hired him in 1970 with a mandate from the board of directors to change the city's image from "a dirty little steel town" into a national media production center. The big turning point had occurred in 1975, when Hillman brokered a deal between Bob Dorsey, of Gulf Oil, and the Mellon Corporation to fund WQED production of a new round of *The National Geographic Specials,* a series which had been canceled in 1973 after a nine-year run on commercial television. For the next sixteen years this series brought over $50 million in production and promotion money to WQED.

Other programs followed, and at one point WQED ranked fourth among member stations in supplying programming to PBS. These nationally distributed productions brought WQED more than $3 million a year in additional income from other PBS stations. In the salad days, corporate underwriters would "forward fund" such programs. For example, Gulf would give WQED up to $2 million and let it float for a couple of years while the *National Geographic* programs were in development. The series had high production costs (for example, producers might take multiple shots of "a zebra jumping over a log" until they got one that they thought was perfect), and station officers enjoyed generous expense accounts, including world travel and leases on luxury automobiles.

In the late 1980s, however, it all began to unravel. Corporations generally stopped forward funding shows. In 1988, *National Geographic* decided it would be cheaper to produce its own shows. Subsidies to WQED dwindled from $3 million a year in 1987 to under half a million in 1989.

As the relationship with *National Geographic* was coming to an end, WQED got $10.8 million from Digital Equipment Company (DEC) to underwrite *The Infinite Voyage*, a twelve-part science series. To secure the money, however, WQED and PBS had to permit the show to air with DEC commercials on commercial stations during the same week it played on PBS. After four seasons, the program was dropped in 1991. Similarly, for a time, WQED coproduced a family drama, *Wonderworks*, with the Disney Channel. However, WQED put up only $5 million of the $14 million budget and had to agree to Disney airing the shows several times on its own channel before they were permitted to play on public television. Another show, *Space Age*, was canceled after just six episodes. By 1991, WQED had dropped to eighth in PBS national production.

The WQED boat was leaking fast. Money was coming in, but it was going out faster. The Gulf Oil float covered expenses in the short term, but this only prolonged the day of reckoning. As explained by Ceci Sommers, then vice president of public relations for QED Communications, "We could borrow from ourselves without the encumbrance of making interest payments. But in essence that didn't get us out of debt. We used a loan to offset the deficit, but we still had to pay back those loans."

In July 1990, Lloyd Kaiser pledged all of QED's assets as collateral for a $6 million Mellon Bank line of credit to keep the station operating. Failure to pay up or renegotiate would result in Mellon being able to take over the station, including equipment purchased with federal money. Mellon required that QED keep $1.25 million from its capital fund on deposit as collateral, but QED wasn't able to comply.

In a three-part series in October of 1991, the *Pittsburgh Post-Gazette* reported the corporation's $2.1 million loss over the previous year. Nevertheless, management and board spokespersons dismissed concerns and reassured supporters. Of about 260 employees, only 3 were laid off in 1990, 12 in 1991, and 19 in 1992 (13 percent over three years). There was no public outcry and no evidence that the board increased its scrutiny of management. Moreover, still seeking the big shows, WQED went ahead with productions that weren't fully funded, running up costs not covered by corporate underwriters or by broadcast outlets willing to prepay for the finished product. By June 1993, revenue from national productions had fallen by 60 percent, but national programming still constituted more than 60 percent of the station's budget.

One consequence of this organizational strategy was the decline of locally produced programs addressed to issues of importance to the Pittsburgh area. In October 1991, the *Post-Gazette* reported that according to a Corporation for Public Broadcasting study, the typical public TV station produced 105 hours per year of local programming. At WQED, however, local programming hours had declined from 93.75 in 1988–89 to 78 in 1989–90 to 60.5 in 1990–91.

When questioned by the press, Lloyd Kaiser had responded that local programming was a "poor investment and should be avoided to place more resources into purchasing national programming." At the time of Kaiser's announced retirement, QED Communications was producing only two half-hour local shows a week, and WQED suffered rising costs, declining membership, and a flood of red ink.

The corporation's financial officer, Ron Bencke, later mused, "We thought national programming would come back and this was temporary. We got used to the old lifestyle." Kaiser claimed that such "gambles" were necessary. He argued that if you cut staff while grants are pending you will be unable to deliver on projects if funding comes through. Elsie Hillman went along with the gamble. As she told the *Wall Street Journal* in January 1994, "We all had rosy-colored glasses on, thinking things would come along to replace [*National Geographic*]."

The Plot Thickens

Within days of the April 1993 announcement of major staff cutbacks and Kaiser's resignation, the corporation was awash with more scandal. It was revealed that the top four executives enjoyed retirement pensions valued at well in excess of $100,000 each a year. In addition, they each had received $189,000 in one-time cash-in payments from an insurance fund purchased for them by the board as deferred compensation. Finally, the press uncovered four different for-profit subsidiaries and established that in 1989–90 the same four executives had each received two paychecks—one from QED Communications, Inc., and one from its for-profit subsidiary, Q Productions in Los Angeles. These second paychecks boosted salaries by an average of 30 percent while the officials involved were publicly claiming to have taken 10 percent pay cuts as a public relations gesture.

When the time for sacrifice came, it was imposed mostly on lower-level employees. Don Korb revealed that two-thirds of the fifty-four employees fired were earning less than $40,000 a year; one-third of them earned less than $20,000 a year. One of those fired was my neighbor, a producer. At the time he was on leave at the University of Chicago, completing an M.A. degree program, and his wife was pregnant with their fourth child.

These cuts were projected to save the station about $1.2 million in the 1993–94 fiscal year, only about 15 percent of the shortfall. Some fourteen vice presidents kept their jobs. Adding insult to injury, WQEX station manager Michael Fields linked the fiscal scandal to future program policy: "We can't afford to keep shows on the air that the business community doesn't want to support."

I had been a "friend" of public broadcasting for many years. I had fond memories of the kind of programs that had impressed me deeply and had not been shown on commercial television since the brief "golden age" of live drama and documentaries, in the 1950s and early 1960s. At the same time, I had been long aware of the drift of public television toward more conservative, bland, and commercial programming.

By 1993, PBS on WQED had become little more than insects mating, British people talking, sauces simmering, beltway pundits barking, and corporations hawking. Now it appeared that this corporate culture had also perverted my station's governance and stolen tax dollars and public contributions. Adding insult to injury, they were using this self-inflicted crisis as justification for even more of the same.

Even the affiliated radio station, WQED-FM, had been captured by conservative elites. Having given up National Public Radio news programming years earlier, WQED-FM was almost entirely devoted to classical music; it broadcast no jazz or folk music, no regularly scheduled news or public affairs shows, and only one locally produced weekly show about happenings in the Pittsburgh cultural scene.

Aimed at subscribers, WQED's *Pittsburgh Magazine* was a big glossy publication filled with very upscale advertisements for a yuppie readership. The *Post-Gazette*'s magazine reviewer called it at best attractive but "journalistically timid." It rarely featured investigative journalism or discussion of local problems. Much of it was devoted to celebrity puff pieces, sometimes featuring people WQED would then hit up for money.

The QED Accountability Project

Our movement in Pittsburgh began with four of us in my living room soon after the *Post-Gazette*'s revelations. Joining me were Catholic peace activist Molly Rush, social worker and labor writer Fred Gustafson, and Russ Gibbons, former communications director of the United Steelworkers of America and program coordinator for the Philip Murray Institute of Labor Studies of the Community College of Allegheny County. Gibbons had also directed and cohosted a program, *Labor's Corner*, on WQEX over the period 1989 to 1992.

We were all critical of the drift of public broadcasting away from its founding mission and toward increasing commercialism and pro-corporate conservatism, and we shared a desire to promote more accessible governance and diverse programming at WQED. After three meetings we launched our reform movement on May 19, 1993, calling it the QED Accountability Project. For us the name expressed a value on active citizenship and good government that was nonideological and would make us attractive to a diversity of participants. Within weeks we received formal endorsement from the Alliance for Progressive Action, an umbrella organization for forty-six public interest groups in Pittsburgh.

Kooks with Gripes

Shortly after CEO Lloyd Kaiser's announced resignation, I called his office and interviewed his secretary, Michelle Mora, about WQED's governance. I was especially interested in the idea of subscriber election of board members, as practiced at KQED in San Francisco. Mora didn't think the board had ever considered this, but she offered to consult the WQED legal division and get back to me. Two days later I got a call from board chair Elsie Hillman and took advantage of the opportunity to interview her for publication.

Hillman said the idea of a subscriber-elected board had "never come up," but allowed that "maybe the public could nominate two to three seats to the board." She noted that the board would soon appoint a bylaws committee to review the station's constitution. In apparent ignorance of FCC guidelines, she claimed that board meetings had to be open to the public but the board was not required to announce the dates of the meetings in advance. She went on to say that she didn't consider it appropriate to allow non–board members, even subscribers, to get on the meeting agenda because "we could have some kooks come in with a personal gripe. . . . If we gave the podium to them we would be there the rest of the afternoon." Finally, Hillman told me that subscribers with legitimate concerns should come to her and she would exercise "discretion" as to whether there was "some real purpose" in their concerns and refer them to the appropriate person.

At the invitation of managing editor Pat Barnes, I wrote a long news article for *In Pittsburgh Newsweekly,* headlined "Watchdog Group Demands Reforms at WQED" and announcing formation of the QED Accountability Project. The article quoted colleagues calling for a more "accessible" and "accountable" station and for "a true alternative to commercial broadcasting fare" through bylaws reforms that would start with the board of directors being democratically elected by the station's subscribers. On April 25, before my piece was printed, the *Post-Gazette*'s TV critic, Robert Bianco, had published a column that criticized WQED's "outrageous" executive salaries and the "unraveling string of half-truths." He likened the station to "an entrenched aristocracy" protected by "a dilettante board" and called on the community to "demand an active role in the search for new leadership," so that "this asset will be preserved for future generations."

When my *In Pittsburgh* article was published in late May, I called Bianco and advised him that we planned to send a delegation to the next QED board meeting. Bianco wrote a six-paragraph "late news" report headlined " 'QED: They're Watching You: Project Demands Accountability." He also granted my request to include our post office box number for those interested. (I always made this request of journalists because the addition of this information transformed a news story into a recruitment poster.)

No sooner had these articles appeared than I began to receive a number of anonymous letters alleging various fiscal improprieties at the station—falsification of books for audit, first-class travel and the skimming of travel accounts, the use of station personnel by executives to do personal home remodeling, the use of station facilities to organize meetings for other associations, the sale of jobs, and the theft or rigging of bids for items donated for auction. At the *Post-Gazette,* reporter Sally Kalson said they had been getting such letters for a couple of years but could do nothing with them because they were anonymous and representatives of the station would only deny the allegations. She also indicated that as a member of the press she couldn't be an advocate regardless of her sympathies.

Many also wrote us to inquire about joining the QED Accountability Project. We assumed that at least one person did so on behalf of WQED, because as we developed our campaign they always had copies of our communications and always seemed aware of our plans. Ceci Sommers, the corporation's head of public relations, apparently was given a copy of our flier and called me personally to discuss it. She invited Project representatives to consult on the composition of the station's community advisory board (CAB) and the upcoming Corporation for Public Broadcasting (CPB) national town meeting to evaluate PBS programming.

On June 8 Sommers faxed me information about the next board meeting and invited me to meet with her afterward. She attached a three-page memo with four pages of documentation rebutting the charges in our flier about corporate control of governance and programming at PBS and QED Communications. WQED's vice president for broadcasting, John Cosgrove, had prepared the memo for Hillman and Sommers.

Clearly, we had their attention. Two days later I faxed back, countering Cosgrove's claims and urging "public discussion on WQED of issues we have raised." I pointed out that according to the minutes provided to me by Sommers, the 1993 CAB had twenty-three members but only thirteen cared enough to come to the one meeting and none were from any of the forty-six public interest organizations that were members of the Alliance for Progressive Action. I offered to help in rectifying this "problem." I also indicated that between six and twelve members of our group were coming to observe the board meeting. I asked for five minutes at the meeting "to read and distribute a short statement . . . that describes who we are and what we seek." I added that if granted this time we would "limit our participation" to the speech.

Station officials knew there would be media coverage and certainly could not risk a disruption that would make them look even more unresponsive to public concerns than they already seemed. They also wanted to convey a tone of rational optimism—hard to do in the midst of a public confrontation. They agreed to my request.

Confronting the Board

The QED Accountability Project held an organizing meeting at the offices of Citizen Action on June 9, 1993, and made plans for a contingent to witness WQED's June 15 board meeting. Nine of us attired ourselves in suits and dresses and met at the station for the June 15 board meeting. We gathered in the lobby and were escorted to a side room to wait until the board had finished lunch and got down to business.

A long table in the middle of the room was festooned with fruit, cookies, and punch. I was fairly sure this was the first time Elsie Hillman had catered a protest; we crowded around the table. Robert Bianco's second piece had alerted the media, and reporters from the *Post-Gazette* and the *Tribune-Review* who were covering the board meeting came looking for us, the latter with a photographer in tow. It was a perfect setup. In the thirty minutes or so we were kept waiting, I was interviewed as the Project's spokesperson and photographed by the press.

Afterward, we filed into the boardroom, registered at management's request, and took our seats. Later in the meeting I was introduced and allowed to speak. I expressed alarm over the board's fiscal mismanagement and complained about the domination of programming by "corporate and conservative interests." I stated that our purpose was to honor the original vision of public broadcasting as "a voice for groups in the community that may otherwise be unheard" and a "place for debate and controversy." I compared the station's problems to those of other not-for-profit corporations that had sacrificed their public mission to private greed with the complicity of their boards of directors. I proposed that these problems were rooted in QED's corporate structure and listed my concerns. I suggested that the board's review of its bylaws provided the station with "a unique opportunity to reform itself" and urged "adoption of the model of KQED San Francisco, which has a twenty-seven-member board, all of whom are elected by the station's subscribers."

In the middle of the speech, I departed from my text and referred to the allegations in the anonymous letters, curious about how they would be perceived by the board. I suggested that if true many of these alleged acts would constitute felonies. I closed by requesting, "as a gesture of good faith," two documents that had been refused even to the press—QED's financial report to the CPB and a report they had commissioned from Dr. Myron Joseph.

We had learned about the Joseph report from the anonymous letters. Prompted by employee complaints that eventually became a federal lawsuit, QED had engaged Dr. Joseph, a Carnegie Mellon University professor, to investigate. Joseph interviewed staff about alleged managerial abuses and concluded that the problem was Ceci Sommers's confrontational management style (at the time, she was the manager of the radio station), plus a lack of internal management structure. Although the employee eventually lost the suit, Sommers was removed from her post at the radio station but not fired. By her own account a close friend of Elsie Hillman's, she was transferred to the newly created position of QED vice president for public relations, allegedly with a raise in salary. Since "special reports on employment practices" are specifically mentioned in the FCC guidelines as public documents, in requesting the Joseph report we were making points about both the station's lack of openness and its treatment of employees at the same time.

After the meeting, two members of the board handed me their cards, one without comment, the other with the advice that the board could not get into "micromanaging" the station. No one showed any interest in the charges of embezzlement. I left the building with Project member Dr. Charley McCollester. As we walked to our cars he commented that our contingent of public interest group leaders, professors, and clergy would make a good board in itself. I replied that we certainly couldn't do any worse than QED's.

I was aware that we were being tracked by a small, slight man whom I had seen at the board meeting. He caught up to us and introduced himself as Hugh Nevin. He explained that he had been appointed to head a new corporate governance committee to revise the station's bylaws and wanted to meet with me to evaluate the possibility of my participation. He suggested that we be joined by David Kalson, a colleague of his and the brother of *Post-Gazette* reporter Sally Kalson. We had lunch about a week later and he subsequently called to invite me to serve on the committee.

Our request for the Joseph report triggered a prompt reaction. Elsie Hillman called my home right after the board meeting. (My younger son, well trained, asked her if it was a solicitation call. She said no, she was Elsie Hillman, but of course it *was* a solicitation of sorts.) When I came on the line, Hillman repeated her statement to the press that she had just learned of the report—whereas the anonymous letters had claimed she had personally authorized it—but found that it concerned management practices at WQED-FM that had been since corrected. She also said she was personally concerned not to embarrass Sommers, and I agreed not to press that issue. Concerned not to squander the Project's credibility on potentially libelous claims from anonymous sources who had their own axes to grind, I advised Hillman that we wanted to keep the focus on structural reform, not personalities.

Sommers herself, clearly threatened, began to call me more often and eventually asked if we could meet privately in a food court downtown. She was preoccupied with an alleged conspiracy to get her fired, which she thought was led by Lloyd Kaiser in retaliation for past challenges to his leadership. At our meeting, she gave me a large batch of old memoranda as evidence of these claims. (She lasted another eighteen months at QED, until the end of 1994.)

Both of Pittsburgh's major papers gave our board meeting protest great coverage. The *Tribune-Review* ran my picture opposite that of acting CEO Don Korb, with the caption "No Confidence." We got the headline—"QED Board Told Problems Remain"—and the lead—"A grass-roots watchdog group wants QED Communications, Inc., to be more accountable to the community served by the public television, radio and magazine group." Repeating her attempt at co-optation, Sommers was quoted as recommending that our project become "part of the existing Community Advisory Board," which she described as "a 30-member group of volunteers that meets once a year." The rest of the article dealt with the station's financial problems.

The *Post-Gazette* also referred to us as a "community watchdog group" and noted that my speech constituted "the first time an outside group had been permitted to speak at a QED board meeting." Sally Kalson, who wrote the piece, devoted four paragraphs to summarizing my remarks. Citing Hillman's plan to "use an outside oversight committee to review all corporate operations and make suggestions," Kalson remarked, "As it turned out, eight representatives of such a committee were already in her midst: the contingent from the newly formed QED Accountability Project, a citizens watchdog group."

In Pittsburgh Newsweekly covered the meeting as well, and also referred to us as a "watchdog group." Recognizing that this identity gave us a certain legitimacy, we embraced it. In point of fact, we were a rather diverse group. While the founders were all progressives, many of those later attracted to the campaign through press coverage were not activists but just people who had a special interest and, in some cases, a background in public television. In time this movement would grow to include thousands.

How did so many citizens find a passion for preserving something so apparently pedestrian as public broadcasting? We certainly do not see ourselves as kooks with gripes. Rather, we are alarmed at the threat to democracy posed by the increasing concentration of corporate ownership of our nation's system of mass communications. Accordingly, we treasure the unique and critical role that public broadcasting can play in presenting citizens with alternative sources of information and perspectives on local and national issues. Before we go on with Pittsburgh's story, then, we should consider the broader picture.

Chapter 2

Corporate Media's
Threat to Democracy

In democratic societies, various publics within the citizenry are the basic units of self-government. These publics emerge through discussion of issues promoted by interest groups—people with common concerns—within the community. The process then comes to involve the larger, more initially disinterested body of citizens, as what we call public opinion, in the larger sense, evolves and crystallizes.

In contrast to the early days of the Republic, however, the size and complexity of modern U.S. society does not permit the formation of public opinion through direct participation. The mass media are a necessary vehicle of communication for rational discussion featuring the full range of political and cultural perspectives. Unfortunately, this cannot occur if political or economic authorities are in a position to censor or manipulate dissenting views. Democracy is imperiled when too few interests are allowed to control our information and our discussions.

Media Monopolization

In 1983, a mere fifty corporations controlled more than half of all communications enterprises: CDs, books, newspapers, magazines, radio, television, and motion pictures. By 1992, this number was down to only twenty; today it is less than half that, and dropping, with another dozen or so firms rounding out the system. These include such multimedia giants as Time

Warner, Disney, CBS/Viacom, News Corporation, Bertelsmann, General Electric, AT&T, and Sony. Direct board links and joint ventures are pervasive, further standardizing products and prices.

Eleven thousand magazines are published regularly in this country, but just two firms rake in more than half the magazine revenues. A half dozen companies account for 90 percent of domestic music recordings sales. There are hundreds of independent film producers, but four major movie studios account for more than half of the movie business. Moreover, the studios are again buying up chains of theaters to give their products a competitive advantage at the expense of consumers.

There are twenty-five hundred book publishers, but five produce most of the revenue. Once-distinguished independent publishing houses like Random House, Knopf, Vintage, Harper & Row, Scribner, Viking, Putnam, and Henry Holt are now units under the dominion of media conglomerates like Rupert Murdoch's News Corporation, Newhouse, and Bertelsmann. Publisher Andre Schiffrin comments, "The question is which books will make the most money, not which ones will fulfill the publisher's traditional cultural mission." The Barnes and Noble and Borders chains control nearly one-half of all U.S. retail bookselling, and the share of this market claimed by independent booksellers fell from 58 percent in 1972 to 17 percent in 1997.

As recently as the era of World War II, 80 percent of the nation's daily newspapers were independently owned. The situation is now reversed. Multi-paper chains now own 77 percent of the country's 1,520 dailies. Only fifty-five American cities have more than one daily paper; more than seven thousand have no paper of their own. In addition, all papers depend primarily on two or three news gathering sources like the Associated Press, The New York Times News Service, and Reuters.

In 1999, the Newspaper Association of America petitioned the FCC to suspend its rule that bars daily newspapers from owning radio or television stations in their own circulation areas. Even the small arena of the so-called alternative press is threatened by the trend toward monopolization. In 1999, there were 113 members of the Association of Alternative Newsweeklies, with a combined weekly circulation of almost 7 million and an overall readership of at least twice that. Ad revenues were nearly $400 million.

Jay Walljasper of the *Utne Reader* once observed, "The success of the alternative press reveals that readers do indeed respond to journalism that doesn't edit out human feelings, doesn't rely solely on experts for the truth, and doesn't speak only in the accents of the rich and powerful." Unfortunately, as with the corporate press, new chains are emerging. The Phoenix,

Arizona–based *New Times* owns eight city weeklies with a combined circulation of 743,000. Stern Publishing, owner of the *Village Voice and LA Weekly*, owns seven papers with a combined circulation of 750,000. In September 1999, it put all of them up for sale. These chains have even pursued such monopolistic strategies as buying two weeklies in a town and cutting back to one.

In 1999, New Mass. Media, owner of the *Hartford Courant*, a major daily, acquired the *Hartford Advocate* and four other alternative weeklies. Carly Berwick of the *Columbia Journalism Review* asked, "When your local alternative weekly and the local daily are both part of the same company, to what is the weekly an alternative?"

The 1996 Telecommunications Act, passed overwhelmingly by both houses of Congress, opened the floodgates to even more concentration of ownership in the media. This legislation was written in great part by media lobbyists. In contrast, public interest advocates had limited access; as Kevin Tagland, representing the Benton Foundation, complained, "No one saw the final draft of the bill before it was passed." The story was virtually ignored by the nation's print and broadcast journalists. In what coverage there was, perhaps the most significant provision in the bill was largely overlooked— the reduction of concentration restrictions.

The 1996 act raised the limit on a network's total station ownership from 25 percent to 35 percent signal reach of the total U.S. population. It also doubled the number of local radio stations a single company can operate in large markets, from four to eight; and in smaller markets, two companies are now allowed to own all the stations between them. Finally, all limits were removed on the number of radio stations a single company can own nationwide.

Following passage of the act, a veritable feeding frenzy in radio frequencies swept through the country. Within two years, four thousand of the nation's eleven thousand radio stations changed hands. In just three years, ownership has become concentrated in 22 percent fewer companies. By September 1997, in each of the fifty largest markets, three firms controlled more than 50 percent of radio advertising revenue. According to the *Wall Street Journal*, these deals "have given a handful of companies a lock on the airwaves in the nation's big cities."

Today there are approximately one thousand television stations, but just the top twenty-five television groups control 36 percent of the stations and three networks supply most of the programming. Mel Karmazin, CEO of CBS, made news early in 1999 with his publicized offer to buy NBC. General

Electric, NBC's parent, declined and proceeded to buy a major stake in Value-Vision, the third-largest home shopping cable network, with a view toward combining its TV and internet businesses into one powerful retailer.

On September 8, 1999, Viacom's Sumner Redstone and CBS's Mel Karmazin announced that Viacom would acquire CBS in a $37.3 billion deal. "Content is king," trumpeted Redstone, whose company owns Paramount Pictures and publishing's Simon & Schuster, as well as the UPN Network, the Paramount Television Group, several cable channels, and the Blockbuster video outlet chain. "Distribution is king," added Karmazin, who will become second in command, bringing to the table the CBS television network, the Infinity Broadcasting radio chain, and two country music channels, among other assets. These behemoths squat rent-free on public air space, but the talk was all about challenging Time Warner, not serving the American public.

The Commercialization of the Media

How commercial broadcasters have had their way with Congress is no mystery. The National Association of Broadcasters (NAB) represents 85 percent of network-owned and -affiliated commercial television stations, and 40 percent of all independent and public TV stations in the United States. It has 7,500 members and annual revenues of more than $35 million. NAB president Edward O. Fritts is a former college roommate of Senate Majority Leader Trent Lott. The NAB has given huge fees to other lobbying firms with strong connections to both parties.

Of course, the industry giants don't rely solely on the NAB. According to Common Cause, over the period from 1985 to 1994, communications and media PACs gave almost $38 million to congressional election campaigns. In just the first half of 1996, the corporate parents of three networks—Disney, Westinghouse (now CBS), and General Electric—spent more than $6.7 million on lobbying.

In this game, the media give money to the politicians, who use it to buy media time to solicit votes from the public. Republican Larry Pressler presided over the 1996 telecommunications bill in the Senate and received $103,000 in media and telecommunications PAC money in just the first half of 1995. The bill was shepherded through the House by Republican Thomas Bliley, who took in more than $53,000 the year before. Almost half of all telecommunications firms contributed to President Bill Clinton's reelection campaign. For election year 2000, industry representatives have projected that stations will sell $600 million worth of political ads, a 41 percent increase over 1996.

Meanwhile, concerns for editorial quality have been sacrificed to the quest for higher profits. These days, U.S. television networks broadcast six thousand commercials per week, an increase of 50 percent since 1983, and newspaper advertising revenues are now at an all-time high of $43.9 billion. Despite this, layoffs of from twenty-five to three hundred employees occurred at several papers over 1998–99. With their capacity to cover stories severely impaired, both print and broadcast newsrooms are then forced to rewrite wire-service copy, work the phones, hire freelancers, or buy coverage from other sources. Surveys indicate that press releases and PR-generated material now account for between 40 and 70 percent of the "news" in today's media. A prominent network television newsman recently lamented, "Everything now is dollars and cents," and in 1996, only 14 percent of print journalists expressed satisfaction with the quality of their papers.

A new commercialism is coming to pervade the whole journalistic process. The managing editor of a small Virginia newspaper commented recently that the focus used to be "'Is this a good story?' Now I have to think, 'Is this a story that will connect with my readers' particular lifestyles?'" The Minneapolis *Star Tribune* launched an advertising campaign to change Minnesotans' perception of their enterprise from that of a newspaper to "the brand of choice for information products."

Advertiser Influence

Mainstream newspapers are big business. The average newspaper devotes more than 65 percent of its space to advertisements, which, in turn, provide 75 percent of its revenue. Those who subsidize the press in this way do not leave representation of their interests to chance. A survey of 250 daily newspaper editors by Marquette University's journalism department found that more than 90 percent of U.S. newspapers have experienced pressure from advertisers to change or kill stories. In a follow-up question, almost 90 percent of those surveyed said that advertisers had followed through on threats to withdraw advertising. More than a third (37.6 percent) reported that advertisers' attempts to influence news coverage were successful, with smaller papers more likely than large ones to cave in. More than half (55.1 percent) of the editors reported pressure from within their organizations to write or tailor stories to please advertisers.

In many cases, we are talking here about any content that any group of readers might find offensive. According to a report by G. Bruce Knecht in the *Wall Street Journal,* many large advertisers now demand prior notice when an issue in which their ad appears contains "controversial" stories or opinions. For the recently merged DaimlerChrysler corporation, for instance, this has meant "any and all editorial content that encompasses sexual, political, [or] social issues or any editorial that might be construed as provocative or offensive"; an Ameritech spokesperson has said the company avoids "anything controversial"; and the Young and Rubicam advertising agency has admitted warning publishers about stories that it considers "antisocial or in bad taste."

Television networks and stations make their money by selling audiences to advertisers, doing so, as former FCC commissioner Nicholas Johnson once said, "at a cost per thousand, like cattle." The top one hundred advertisers pay for two-thirds of all network television. To serve big business, the networks cultivate the bland formulas that ensure the largest possible audience at the least possible cost. Their concern to avoid offending any potential consumers of their sponsors' products has led to what Emmy Award–winning producer Rod Serling once called "an objectionable censorship of ideas," which in turn has fostered an "inability to even find a point of view."

A study of 241 investigative reporters and editors employed at commercial television stations found nearly three-quarters of those surveyed reporting that advertisers "tried to influence the content of news" at their stations, even trying to kill stories by threatening to withdraw advertising. Almost half said the advertisers actually followed through on their threats. Almost as many (40 percent) conceded that advertisers "succeeded in influencing a news report" at their station as said that the station had withstood the pressure (43 percent). Fifty-nine percent admitted to "pressure" from *within* their stations "to not produce news stories that advertisers might find objectionable."

Constraints on resources and controversy lead to the prevalence of stories that are easy to get, politically safe, and saleable, like crime, disaster, and celebrity gossip. A survey by the Project for Excellence in Journalism of four thousand lead stories on network news shows and in newsmagazines and major newspapers found that "human interest" (that is, celebrity scandal and gossip) stories increased from 15 percent of the total in 1977 to 43 percent in 1997.

Bias and Censorship in Reporting
National News

The work culture of the news industry provides another source of reporting bias. Sociologist David Croteau's 1998 survey of Washington bureau chiefs and national journalists found that two-thirds were male, 89 percent white, and 95 percent had a college education or more. Some 95 percent had household incomes in excess of $50,000 per year; more than half in excess of $100,000 a year. Although of those who responded most considered themselves to be in the "center" politically, like most educated, typically urban professionals, these journalists tended to be more liberal than the general public on social issues such as racial equality, gay rights, abortion, and gun control.

On the other hand, like most upper-income people, journalists tend to have a middle-class sensibility, with "implicit faith in the conventional wisdom about government spending," trade, taxes, and inflation. Croteau's study shows that, by wide margins, journalists were more likely than the general public to support expanding NAFTA and less likely to support employer-provided health insurance and protecting Medicare and Social Security.

According to Croteau, even the journalists' sources were heavily biased toward the establishment. Government officials and business representatives led the list of those talked to "nearly always," followed by Wall Street analysts. Labor representatives and consumer advocates put together were consulted less than a third as often as were representatives of business. Think-tank analysts, typically conservative, were consulted almost twice as often as university-based academics.

As one network executive advised media researcher Charlotte Ryan, spokespersons for public interest groups "are not covered because they are not players. The news media covers players, decision-makers. We don't care what your spokespeople think and we generally won't report it." In a clear repudiation of the legacy of the "fourth estate," Jeff Gralnick at ABC News states, "The evening news is not supposed to be the watchdog on the government."

In the 1940s there were about a thousand full-time labor-beat reporters and editors on U.S. daily papers. Today there are fewer than ten. A 1989 study of a thousand network evening news broadcasts on the three networks found that business and economic reporting got almost double the time devoted to all workers' issues, including child care, the minimum wage, and workplace health and safety. Bruce Nussbaum explains, "College-educated journalists living in big cities" are "apt to talk with white-collar corporate managers or entrepreneurs but not with blue-collar unionized workers." Howard Kurtz of the *Washington Post* agrees: "Most journalists simply don't know personally anybody whose job might have been threatened by NAFTA." Neither are they likely to be encouraged by their editors to consider the other side. A 1985 *Los Angeles Times* poll found that 53 percent of newspaper editors said that in labor-management disputes they generally sided with management, while only 8 percent said they sided with labor.

Even deeper still, the interests of the media corporations are intrinsically opposed to the interests of labor. David Moberg reports that when *Washington Post* labor reporter Peter Perl went to cover a $325-a-day seminar on union busting, he found four managers and vice presidents from his own paper in attendance. The consultant putting on the seminar hailed the *Post* as "a leader in the field." When Senate Republicans filibustered to block passage of a 1994 measure to prohibit the hiring of "permanent replacements" during strikes, the *Post* gave its editorial approval.

Local TV News

The situation is even worse at the local level. According to studies by the Rocky Mountain Media Watch (RMMW), local TV news generally is being diminished by more and more commercials and dominated by "fluff" and "mayhem" stories that do little to educate or empower viewers. Pittsburgh ABC affiliate news anchor Sally Wiggin confesses, "Our job, first and foremost, is to make money. Then it's to cover the news. We have become a headline service, with stories that used to be two minutes now down to 1:10 to 1:40."

RMMW's many studies are each based on one hundred videotapes of same day and time news telecasts from stations around the country. Three trained observers then view all tapes and code each item for content and duration. News topics are broken down into twenty-six categories. The researchers then calculate the "mayhem index"—the percentage of news time given stories about crime, disaster, and war—and the "fluff index"—the air time given to previews/promos, anchor chatter, soft news, and celebrity stories.

RMMW reports that commercial time has swelled from an average of three minutes per half hour of TV in the 1950s to more than five minutes in the 1970s to more than nine minutes of ads per half hour today. While commercials take up 31 percent of the typical half hour, news stories take up 40 percent, sports and weather 22 percent, and previews/promos and anchor chatter 7 percent. Crime stories, which average more than 30 percent of all stories, dominate the news. Although white-collar crime has a more widespread impact on American society, violent crimes account for more than two-thirds of all crime stories reported on local TV news. The "mayhem index" typically measures 42 percent of all news on all one hundred stations, while fluff accounts for another 39 percent.

By contrast, "solution-oriented" stories are rare. Those are stories that go beyond drama to give viewers context, information, and/or advice about seeking solutions to the problems depicted. They occur most often in the form of health stories (45 percent), which constitute 7 percent of all stories. Only 12 percent of crime stories are solution oriented, and solution-oriented stories of any kind that focus on collective responses are almost nonexistent.

The domination of programming by fluff and mayhem keeps the public ignorant and, according to communications scholar George Gerbner, contributes to a "mean world syndrome." In fact, research shows that those who watch a great deal of TV news tend to perceive their community as more dangerous than it really is and buy more watchdogs and guns for "protection."

In *Harper's* editor Lewis Lapham's view, this is all part of the design: "The bad news is what sells the good news. . . . The good news is the advertising. That's what it's about and the bad news—the dead guys or the crime—is to get the suckers into the tent. . . . First they give you the vision of hell, which is what scares the viewer and sets up the good news, which is the advertising. . . . It's part of the pitch. It's the freak show in order to sell the snow cone."

The Cable "Alternative"

Many have argued that diversity is served because viewers now have many alternatives to the commercial television networks, available on cable. This argument is severely flawed. First, millions of people cannot afford cable. Second, cable systems have undergone the same concentration of ownership as the broadcast media. Only 5 million of the 94 million subscribers have a choice between competing cable companies and whatever channels each happens to offer. In 1995, only two systems controlled half of the eleven thousand or more cable systems in the U.S.: TCI (now AT&T) and Time Warner. In October 1999, the FCC cleared the way for AT&T to own more than a third of the nation's cable franchises as well as large interests in a number of major video producers and television programmers.

Third, typically cable networks are subsidiaries of broadcast companies. Disney, which owns ABC-TV, also owns the cable Disney Channel, ESPN, ESPN2 (80 percent), and shares of Arts & Entertainment (37.5 percent) and the History Channel (37.5 percent). Time Warner owns HBO (75 percent), Cinemax, CNN, and Comedy Central jointly with Viacom and AT&T. General Electric, which owns NBC, also owns CNBC, MSNBC, and significant shares of Court TV, Bravo, American Movie Classics (25 percent), the History Channel (25 percent), and Arts & Entertainment (25 percent). CBS owns Country Music Television and the Nashville Network. When the Viacom acquisition of CBS is approved, concentration will increase. You get the picture—but *they* own it.

The Promise of Public Broadcasting

In 1952, the FCC reserved educational frequencies throughout the nation in the first allocation of television channels. The Ford Foundation served as the major supporter of educational television until 1962, when Congress passed the Educational Television Facilities Act to construct and upgrade educational TV station facilities. By 1967 there were 127 stations, primarily government supported, broadcasting an average of fifty hours a week. Most programming at the time consisted of lectures and other classroom supplements. These stations attracted about 14 million regular viewers and another 6.3 million for instructional programs.

In 1967, by order of President Johnson, the Carnegie Commission issued its report *Public Television: A Program for Action,* introducing the phrase and concept of public television, which members of the commission saw as having a mission far broader and more energetic than that of educational television. The Carnegie Commission recognized that "all that is of human interest and importance" may not be "appropriate or available for support by advertising," and proposed a system free of commercial constraints. The intention is clear: "We seek for the citizen freedom to view, to see programs that the present system, by its incompleteness, denies him."

The market will never be responsive to the full range of people's desires. As media historian Robert McChesney points out, the market gives people "what they want" only within the limits of what is most profitable to produce. Shows with serious content generate smaller audiences than those featuring sex, violence, and celebrity, and thus they are less profitable to produce. Controversy tends to divide the audience for the sponsors' products. Moreover, commercial television places a premium on eighteen- to thirty-five-year-olds, people with rising discretionary income and less developed consumer preferences. As a consequence, the tastes of less commercially desirable audiences—children, seniors, racial minorities, the poor, citizen activists, and others—go begging.

Thus, according to communications scholar Allan Browne, "program diversity in a market is far more enhanced by the addition of a noncommercial channel than by the addition of another commercial station." As Browne explains, "The economic rationale for [public service broadcasting] takes the form of government intervention to address market failure."

Finally, in commercial media the implicit image of the audience is that of a pool of consumers, not citizens or community members serving in any of the other roles that are essential to a healthy society. Given such a system, McChesney asks, "Will the citizen be replaced by the consumer? Will the commercial values of greed, materialism and selfishness tower over all others, weakening our bonds of community and feeding the sense of moral bankruptcy so prevalent already in today's society?"

Journalist Bill Moyers has advised that when he served as press aide to the Johnson administration, helping to push through the legislation for public broadcasting, "We didn't think public broadcasting should serve an audience. We thought it should serve the public." Accordingly, as television critic Les Brown informs us, "Noncommercial television has the virtue of preserving nonmaterialistic values—cultural, philosophical and social—which are the ones that matter to most countries in the long run."

For a nation torn by conflicts over Vietnam, civil rights, and other issues, the Carnegie Commission imagined a public broadcasting service that "could help us see America whole, in all of its diversity" and know "what it is to be many in one." For a society in which communities were being eclipsed by massification and too many citizens were beset by apathy, public television could be a "forum for debate and controversy," providing "a voice for groups in the community that may otherwise be unheard." In the final analysis, the authors of the commission's report stated, public television should create programs "not to sell products or to meet the demands of the marketplace," but to "enhance citizenship and public service." It should televise "occasions where people of the community express their hopes, their protests, their enthusiasms, and their will."

A broad diversity of conflicting interests reached consensus on the plan that ultimately emerged. Economic leaders saw public television as a channel to the educated middle class not served by commercial TV. Political leaders saw it as a tool for defusing militancy by providing radicals with a forum where they might reason together with institutional representatives. Liberals saw it as a modestly financed, idealistic public program. Conservatives thought it might promote America's image abroad. Some radicals, inspired by early educational TV experiments, hoped to use public television as an instrument for protest and reform.

In the federal statute adopting the Carnegie Commission recommendations, Congress called for an "alternative" that would express "diversity and excellence," involve "creative risks," and address "the needs of the unserved and underserved audiences, particularly children and minorities." As he signed the bill into law, President Johnson declared, "Public television will help make our Nation a replica of the old Greek marketplace, where public affairs took place in view of all the citizens."

The experiment began with great promise. There were documentary series like *Public Broadcasting Laboratory* and *The Great American Dream Machine,* which challenged the conventional wisdom of corporate spokespersons and political officials with testimony from public interest advocates and ordinary people. There were dramas by American playwrights like Arthur Miller, Eugene O'Neill, William Soroyan, Wendy Wasserstein, and Thornton Wilder, featuring American performers like Lee J. Cobb, Faye Dunnaway, Dustin Hoffman, Stacy Keach, George C. Scott, and Meryl Streep. There were no commercials.

Chapter 3

The Broken Promise of PBS

In 1997, Ron Hull, former director of the Corporation for Public Broadcasting's Television Program Fund, was asked by PBS executive vice president Robert Ottenhoff to look through the corporation's archives for shows that could be released on home video. Hull read through some 12,000 old folders and came up with 850 programs that might be useful. That averages fewer than 3 programs a month over the previous lifetime of PBS, not a lot but programs that commercial television would likely never have even considered.

Many of the programmers Hull also consulted remembered *The Great American Dream Machine* and other public affairs shows, all of which were deemed "too dated." Among the theater presentations, one of Hull's personal favorites (and mine) was *Steambath* (1973), by Bruce Jay Friedman, featuring Bill Bixby and Valerie Perrine, a penetrating and hilarious black comedy on the absurdity of life and the banality of evil, in which the steambath is a kind of purgatory and God is portrayed as a Puerto Rican attendant. Hull described it as "one of the most talked-about programs we've ever produced." Interviewed in *Current* in 1997, Hull went on to say that he was "concerned that [the play's] portrayal of God as a Puerto Rican towel boy could prove controversial. Nowadays, public TV stations are much more conservative in their programming choices than in 1973."

Notice that Hull is quoted as saying that the *stations* are more conservative, not the public. Notice that controversy, which is what creates a public, is considered by the stations to be bad. This makes the stations anti-public. Finally, notice how old these shows are.

Certainly, public television has continued to distinguish itself with some excellent programs over the years. However, the conclusion seems inescapable—the service has retreated significantly from its most promising beginnings. What happened?

PBS: The "Lemon Socialism" of Mass Communications

In Europe, communications scholar Patricia Aufderheide points out, "public service broadcasting . . . was usually established early on as a government service that either dominated or monopolized the national spectrum." In Europe, public television is independently funded, with revenue raised by such devices as an annual tax on television sets, a license fee on the purchase of a new set, or fees charged to commercial television stations for their use of the public airwaves.

In the United States, the Carnegie Commission originally recommended permanent and independent funding for public broadcasting in the form of a federal trust fund based on a manufacturers' excise tax on television sets. Commission chair James R. Killian Jr. argued that "a free, innovative, creative public television service" would not be possible if it were to be "ultimately dependent" on Congress for its funding. Unfortunately, conservatives and the National Association of Broadcasters persuaded Congress to remove the trust fund from the proposed legislation. As a consequence, public broadcasting in America has followed no rational, coherent plan. Rather it has made a series of adjustments to appease those upon whom it depends for its support: political officials, corporate underwriters, and affluent subscribers.

Congress created the Corporation for Public Broadcasting (CPB) to act as the fiscal agent for the U.S. public broadcasting service. The CPB makes budget submissions directly to Congress and receives such funds as appropriated. In turn, CPB provides funds to the Public Broadcasting Service (PBS), National Public Radio (NPR), and Public Radio International (PRI) for production and operating expenses. Nearly three-fourths of CPB funds are passed through to the individual stations in the form of "community service grants."

The Public Broadcasting Act of 1967 further specified that the CPB would act as a "heat shield" for political fire directed at the system by ensuring "strict adherence to objectivity and balance in all programs or series of programs of a controversial nature." The CPB's governing board consists of ten members, no more than six from the same political party, appointed by the president and subject to confirmation by the Senate.

At least four CPB presidents (including the last two) and the current NPR president have come to their jobs from a background in government service communications, having worked for the Voice of America, the United States Information Agency, and/or Radio Free Europe/Radio Liberty. The term of the CPB board appointment is six years. No one may be appointed for more than two consecutive full terms. Historically, board members have been appointed on the basis of political patronage rather than expertise; this has compromised the CPB's capacity to defend the integrity of its programming.

PBS is a membership organization consisting of all public television stations and controlled by a board consisting of station managers, representatives of the CPB and its forerunner, National Educational Television, and representatives of the public, usually heads of corporations, foundations, and universities. The national office of PBS has the responsibility for scheduling, advertising, and transmitting the programs to the stations. The stations collectively own PBS and pay dues to it out of their CPB community service grants. PBS surveys stations on their programming needs and works with local producers to make programs for national distribution and to provide marketing and other support services.

Spending on all public broadcasting in the United States amounts to about $2 billion a year. About 75 percent of this goes for television and 25 percent for radio. Out of 1,500 television stations in the United States, only about 350 are CPB supported. They are controlled by 177 licensees. Around two-thirds of all public TV stations transmit over UHF frequencies which have a smaller range than VHF.

The prohibition against CPB itself scheduling, advertising, and transmitting programs appeased conservative politicians and commercial broadcasters anxious about Congress establishing a liberal "fourth network." Patricia Aufderheide has characterized this compromised vision of public broadcasting as "the 'lemon socialism' of mass media," modestly funded and highly decentralized.

In terms of ownership and operation, there are four different types of public TV stations: 39 percent are operated by community associations, 35 percent by state governments, 24 percent by universities, and 2 percent by local governments. For public radio, 34 percent of stations are operated by community associations, 9 percent by state governments, 52 percent by universities, and 5 percent by local governments.

National Public Radio is both a production and interconnection system for noncommercial educational ("full service") stations qualified to receive programs funded by the CPB. Of the 11,500 AM and FM stations operating in the United States, only 1,860 FM stations are noncommercial. Moreover, just 699 of these noncommercial stations (359 licensees) qualify for federal support as public radio, and they reach about 86 percent of the American population. Of these, about 330 are NPR members; the other 1,000 or so are college or religious (mostly evangelical Christian) stations.

To facilitate matching grants for program development, public broadcasting is "forward funded" in three-year cycles (a year of appropriations and two years of authorization). However, Congress and/or the White House always has the power to rescind previous authorizations. The CPB budget for the fiscal year 2000 is $300 million.

Almost 60 percent of public broadcasting's income is contributed directly by taxpayers and individual contributors, with another 15 percent donated indirectly through public colleges and universities and tax-exempt foundations. In 1997, overall revenue sources broke down roughly as follows: federal support 17 percent (over 80 percent channeled through CPB), state and local tax-based support (including higher education) 28 percent, and private support 55 percent. Of the latter, the largest components are subscribers (24 percent) and business (14 percent), followed by foundations at 6 percent. These distributions vary slightly each year.

About three-fourths of all money spent on public television goes to cover the operating costs of the local stations—offices, studios, personnel, local programming, and the rescheduling of the national program service to meet local station preferences. Only about a fifth of all money goes to making television programs intended for a national audience, and this type of program production is highly concentrated within the PBS system. Only 4 percent of all public TV programming is local. Three stations provide more than 60 percent of the national schedule while more than three hundred do not contribute anything.

The major producers of national programs are WGBH-TV Boston, WNET-TV New York, and WETA-TV Washington, D.C. The Children's Television Workshop, producer of *Sesame Street,* provides 16 percent of the schedule. The rest is imported or produced independently. In addition, while independents produce nearly 20 percent of all national programming, most of their productions are channeled through the same three "presenting" stations mentioned above—and it is widely recognized that independent producers have difficulty breaking into this system, especially if they live in other parts of the country.

In her very revealing look at public television production, writer/producer B. J. Bullert reports that PBS gatekeepers and staff tend to limit opportunities to a small number of filmmakers who have proven themselves "trustworthy." Even if they are accomplished filmmakers, activists typically are not considered to be "journalists" and are not trusted. Bullert advises, "Public television insiders often label the work of advocacy filmmakers as 'propaganda,'" assuming that their interests will influence their reporting.

PBS: A Short Political History

In the early years, there were two major production centers for PBS programs. One was National Educational Television (NET), created by the Ford Foundation and merged into WNET-TV New York in 1971. The other was the National Public Affairs Center for Television (NPACT), established by the Ford Foundation and the CPB in 1971 and attached to WETA-TV in Washington, D.C.; NPACT produced *Washington Week in Review* and *Thirty Minutes* (with various guests), as well as documentaries and election coverage.

When the Nixon administration took office in 1969, it launched an attack on all media it suspected of "anti-administration" or "liberal" bias. Alarmed by the growing success of the public broadcasting alternative, President Nixon set his sights on reining in PBS. Nixon was especially angered by PBS plans to offer a public affairs show hosted by a critic of his Vietnam policy. At the same time, he sought to curry favor with the big three commercial networks by accusing public broadcasters of deserting "the bedrock of localism" and trying to create a fourth network.

Several PBS member stations then accused NET and NPACT of ultra-liberal programming. PBS responded by establishing a code of standards and practices and monitoring all programming on behalf of the stations. In 1970, PBS cut back the number of documentaries substantially. In his bizarre but revealing justification, PBS president Hartford N. Gunn Jr. said, "The country is suffering from a surfeit of problems, and I'm not sure we'd be doing anything constructive by simply raising more problems."

In June 1972, having appointed eleven of the fifteen CPB board members, Nixon led a campaign to destroy public broadcasting's editorial independence. An immediate goal, according to White House aide Jon Rose, was "to get the left-wing commentators who are cutting us up off public television at once." Another aide, Clay T. Whitehead, conceived the strategy of shifting program authority from the big-city production centers to the many smaller and more conservative stations around the country. Whitehead got help from Antonin Scalia in drafting the Nixon administration's long-term funding bill.

To clear the way for his restructuring of the system, Nixon vetoed a two-year $155 million authorization for the CPB. The CPB, in turn, voted to discontinue all funding of public affairs programming. When CPB went after PBS funds, the latter protested. Out of this conflict there emerged a partnership agreement that placed more constraints on CPB, preserved PBS, and strengthened the local stations. A rising proportion of CPB funds were to be "passed through" to the stations in the form of "community service grants." Thus CPB would have fewer discretionary funds for program development and was expected to consult with PBS on this process. PBS would continue to operate the interconnection on behalf of the stations, subsidized by CPB.

Media researcher Marilyn Lashley considers this a "watershed" in the history of public broadcasting in America. Hereafter, the local stations' influence on public television policy and programming was enhanced while the national organizations became absorbed primarily in maintaining the coalition in order to maximize appropriations. The various formulae subsequently adopted have given the numerous small-town station managers in conservative pockets of the country effective veto power over programs that more sophisticated viewers (even in their own areas) would like to see. As NET president James Day once commented, "The greatest force for blandness is not the government, it's the stations." Even in years when the CPB provided matching funds to stations choosing minority programming, few took advantage of the offer. For example, in 1989 the award-winning *South Africa Now* was carried by only 30 of the 327 public television stations in the country.

After a respite during the Ford and Carter years, the "Reagan Revolution" targeted PBS for assassination. Reagan aides saw this as part of a strategy to "defund the left." Reagan's conservative Congress rescinded appropriations for the 1981–83 cycle, which meant that there were no federal authorizations for 1984–86. This in turn undermined the "matching formula" arrangement used to raise other funds.

It wasn't until 1989 that bipartisan congressional support again reached the level of the $220 million originally authorized, and later rescinded, for

1983. By then the damage had been done. In the first two years of the Reagan administration, 1981 and 1982, the CPB abandoned experimental television and programs for the unserved and underserved members of the public in favor of lighter fare that pandered to wealthier contributors.

About 100 million people, covering 60 percent of American households, tune in to public television at least sometime each week. In 1995, almost half of all households who watched PBS had a total income of less than $40,000 a year, and a recent survey found that only 26 percent are college graduates. Unfortunately, when it comes to programming, these millions of less affluent viewers don't count for very much. In the view of Colorado public television station manager Willard Rowland Jr., financial pressures have led station managers to "orient programs toward a narrowly defined audience of upscale viewer-checkwriters." About 22 percent of all public television revenues come from fewer than 10 percent (that is, 5 million) of its regular viewers.

The check writers are 80 percent college educated, with household incomes more than two-and-a-half times that of the average American family. These viewers can give away money and still afford other sources of information and entertainment. For them, public television is a secondary source of programming, but, as Rowland points out, they "end up substituting for the public as a whole." As one WGBH-TV producer advised media researcher William Hoynes, "You have to do programming for people that are going to fund public television . . . and the viewers that are going to support public television are not . . . very low income people." Another producer acknowledged, "People who can't afford that membership, then they're lost, or they are not as clearly targeted as people who can afford and will be able to devote part of their income to that."

Political Pressure from the Right

In 1992, the conservative Heritage Foundation issued a report that criticized the "liberal bias" of PBS programming and proposed that Congress again cut off its funding over 1993–94. Republican leaders proposed to privatize public broadcasting, forcing even greater reliance on corporate underwriting. Eventually, Congress rescinded $7.1 million already appropriated for the fiscal years 1995 and 1996.

To begin with, supported by Jesse Helms, Orrin Hatch, and others, Bob Dole sought to limit funding for "liberal" programs by holding CPB reauthorization hostage to a statutory requirement that the CPB enforce "balance and objectivity" in controversial programming. In 1993, a series of "ascertainment meetings" were scheduled around the country, at which citizens were to provide testimony on programming. In addition, a post office box and a toll-free telephone number were instituted to receive complaints.

By February 1994, the CPB had received six thousand calls and almost five thousand cards and letters. PBS claimed that 77 percent of the postcards and "a significant number" of the phone calls were identical (orchestrated) complaints about two documentaries critical of agricultural chemicals; most of the people who wrote or called acknowledged that they had not seen the program in question but were calling at the request of an organization with which they were affiliated.

Nevertheless, this pressure achieved its objective. In the same month, the industry trade paper *Current* reported, "After Congress mandated that public broadcasting examine itself for bias in its programming, CPB funded several proposals that feature notable conservatives or deal with issues from a right-of-center perspective."

Indeed, over the next several years, the Corporation for Public Broadcasting funded major projects by former Reagan and Bush speechwriters Peggy Noonan and Tony Snow and by *McLaughlin Group* pundits Morton Kondracke and Fred Barnes, as well as a series based on William Bennett's *Book of Virtues*, a diatribe by black conservatives that blamed welfare and lack of self-reliance for problems in the ghetto, a program on "scientific creationism," and an attack on "political correctness" based on alleged "reenactments." (*New York Times* TV critic Walter Goodman said that the point of the last show was that "white male heterosexuals, particularly those of a conservative bent, are becoming an endangered species.")

Don Marbury, director of CPB's Television Program Fund, explained these developments as consistent with public television's role as "one of inclusion, being responsive to diversity." He described creationism as "very important" to "a great deal of the American populace" and saw public television's role as doing things "that cannot or will not be done anywhere else."

PBS vs. Feminists

In the summer of 1999, America fell in love with its World Cup champion women's soccer team. Through July, the stadium crowds built in anticipation of a final against China that filled the Rose Bowl with 91,500 cheering fans. ABC estimated there were 40 million viewers, making it the most-watched soccer game ever on U.S. television. These women athletes were celebrated on talk shows, magazine covers, and cereal boxes, but there was a reflective side to the media's treatment of their accomplishment as well. ABC sportscasters interviewed some of the players' mothers, who talked about their own youthful athletic prowess and their frustration in lacking opportunities for serious competition: they had come of age before the enactment of Title IX, part of the Education Amendments of 1972, federal legislation designed to ensure equal access to education and extracurricular activities. In the glow of the women's World Cup victory, both President Clinton and Senate majority leader Republican Trent Lott paid tribute to Title IX.

Interestingly enough, just two months earlier, PBS had presented *National Desk,* a three-part series on "the gender wars" hosted by antifeminist conservatives Fred Barnes, Laura Ingraham, and Larry Elder. The programs were underwritten by a consortium of conservative foundations—Olin, Bradley, Sarah Scaife, and others. Guests included Christina Hoff Sommers, author of *Who Stole Feminism?: How Women Have Betrayed Women,* Phyllis Schlafly, and David Horowitz, a former leftist who now monitored media on behalf of the far right.

Apparently seeing human rights as a zero-sum game, the series posed the question of "whether the advancement of women in virtually all areas of society can be achieved without a retreat, in some way, on the part of men." The first installment, "The War on the Boys," opened with the following quote: "If we don't start changing how we treat our boys, we are going to be heading toward a Gender Armageddon." The second part of the series was called "Politics and Warriors: Women in the Military," and the final installment was "Title IX and Women in Sports: What's Wrong with this Picture?" This episode attacked Title IX, singling out for special criticism a report by the American Association of University Women that summarizes evidence from thirteen hundred research studies indicating that girls receive inequitable treatment in education.

In reaction to the series, Jennifer Pozner, director of FAIR's Women's Desk, organized more than thirty feminist and gay rights leaders to sign a letter of complaint to PBS head Ervin Duggan. The group's letter was appended with a meticulous review of the final program's many factual errors. (For example, despite the fact that only sixty-five of twelve hundred football programs at NCAA institutions pay for themselves, men's athletic budgets still exceed those for women by a margin of three to one, and since the enactment of Title IX the number of male athletes has not decreased but has increased, from 170,000 to 200,000.) The letter also cited PBS for a "double standard" with respect to underwriting and for its discrimination against progressive voices. It called for a meeting between Duggan and a small group of the signers' representatives to discuss "programming solutions that will aid public television in becoming all it was truly meant to be—a voice for the voiceless in every community, helping Americans understand our culture 'in all its diversity.' "

Shanda Perry, of PBS Viewer Services, wrote a rebuttal to the group's letter, but it was addressed only to FAIR's Pozner. Duggan did not invite the group to meet. The feminist coalition constructed a series of specific requests of PBS: that it publish and follow a single set of program guidelines, that it air at least one weekly public affairs program with a "feminist/progressive host," that it support a series on gender issues hosted by feminists "equivalent in length and urgency" to those delivered on *National Desk,* and that it implement a plan to increase the use of women and people of color as sources on PBS programs.

National Desk executive producer Lionel Chetwynd, who has six more programs scheduled for PBS in 2000, characterized the coalition's concerns "as a petty, meaningless and barren debate" that is "almost Stalinist in its inflexibility." After comparing the women to the murderous Soviet dictator, Chetwynd reminded everyone that conservatives hold the power because the mandate of PBS and CPB "exist on a year-to-year basis."

It should be noted that Chetwynd is not a journalist or an educator. *Video Movie Guide 2000* lists him as writer/director of two commercial films. *The Hanoi Hilton* is rated "a turkey" that presents a fictionalized account of POW life in a North Vietnamese camp. *Color of Justice,* rated "fair," is described as "an insulting, moronic indictment of liberals, Christians, feminists, opportunistic politicians, and the media."

It took six months for the coalition's representatives to get their meeting with PBS officials. At the meeting, PBS officials rejected all requests except for checking the alleged factual errors in the series. Speaking to the *Boston Globe* on the subject, chief PBS spokesman Tom Epstein said, "We do not take orders from ideological special interests on what to air." Writing for *Current,* Karen Everhart Bedford pointed out that the *National Desk* series itself "might never have gotten CPB backing if conservatives had not exerted political pressure on the system to correct a perceived 'liberal bias.' "

At the meeting, the women objected that the foundations behind the series also subsidize a range of conservative publications, think tanks, and research and legislative initiatives, including several of the spokespersons in the *National Desk* series. According to FAIR's Janine Jackson, PBS officials replied that Scaife, Olin, and Bradley money was welcomed because these organizations support other public television programs as well. Perhaps Epstein meant that PBS "did not take orders from ideological special interests on what to air" unless they bring with them pressure from conservatives in Congress and lots of conservative foundation money.

In a similar vein, public television's recent coverage of environmental issues has also reflected the conservative establishment. *Frontline,* for example, has produced a number of documentaries arguing industry's or government's position on nuclear energy, the health impacts of electromagnetic fields, claims of chemical poisoning with regard to Gulf War syndrome, and claims of health problems from breast implants, all made by John Palfreman, former in-house *Frontline* senior producer. In 1994, Palfreman commented, "We're atoning" for the "liberal, environmental kind of stances" taken by PBS in the 1980s—stances that were "just basically wrong." He did not cite examples.

Palfreman couldn't have been referring to the broadcast of Don Widener's 1977 *Plutonium: Element of Risk.* Two days before its scheduled air date, Chloe Aaron, then PBS vice president for programming, sabotaged the documentary with a statement to the stations in the system that "this program does not conform to the PBS document of journalism standards." The program, finally, was seen on only twelve stations.

Neither could Palfreman have in mind Judy Irving and Chris Beaver's *Dark Circle.* In 1982, PBS accepted this film about radioactive contamination in the nuclear power industry for evening broadcast after it won the Motion Picture Academy's Certificate of Special Merit, among other awards. Then PBS officials imposed a series of extraordinary demands, from additional verification of factual claims to additional film footage to organizing a panel to debate the film's editorial content at the close of the program. The producers met all of these demands. Nevertheless, ten months later PBS withdrew its offer, claiming that *Dark Circle* was "advocacy film making" that lacked "balance" and "journalistic credibility." When PBS finally agreed to show *Dark Circle* seven years later—the film received a national Emmy Award for "outstanding individual achievement in news and documentary." Today PBS officials admit that the filmmakers were "right" and "ahead of their time with the story." Clearly, PBS, on the other hand, was behind.

Similar studies abound, like that of Mark Mori and Susan Robinson's *Building Bombs,* a film that focused on a whistle-blower's experience targeting the radioactive waste caused by nuclear weapons production at the U.S. Department of Energy's Savannah River Plant in South Carolina. In 1990 it was nominated for an Academy Award but rejected for PBS national broadcast with the charge that it did not "give adequate voice to those who are proponents of nuclear arms." Mori countered that the film includes interviews with five atomic weapons proponents and that five scientific experts on the subject of nuclear weapons production and waste disposal had found the film to be factually accurate.

Several experts in the media business, including Screen Actors Guild president Richard Masur, called the balance issue a "red herring." Columbia University's Erik Barnouw, the dean of America's television critics, called the film "brilliant" and charged PBS with being afraid of "offending the nuclear industry," including General Electric, a major underwriter of PBS programs.

Consistent with Barnouw's assessment, PBS then refused to broadcast *Deadly Deception: General Electric, Nuclear War, and Our Environment*, winner of a 1991 Academy Award as "best documentary short." The film presents dramatic stories from people whose lives were devastated by G. E.'s leading role in nuclear weapons production, including the cover-up of both "intentional" and "accidental" releases of cancer-causing radiation. PBS rejected *Deadly Deception* on the grounds that it was funded by an advocacy group that called for a G. E. boycott to discourage the company's participation in the nuclear weapons business.

The trend against advocacy filmmaking that challenged the interests of the powerful continued. In 1993, PBS rejected Robert Richter's award-winning film about the World Bank, *The Money Lenders*, with the statement "Even though the documentary may seem objective to some, there is a perception of bias in favor of poor people who claim to be adversely affected."

That same year, *The Panama Deception* won an Academy Award for "best documentary feature," but that wasn't recommendation enough for PBS. The film investigates the real purposes behind the Bush administration's 1989 invasion of Panama and reveals that between 2,500 and 4,000 people were killed in U.S. bombings and buried in mass graves far from President Manual Noriega's residence. All the major papers gave the film highly favorable reviews. The *Washington Post* called it "a meticulously researched investigation." However, PBS claimed, "its assertions about the intent of U.S. policy and the conduct of U.S. troops are not adequately substantiated." The film's director, Barbara Trent, cried "censorship," and a PBS inside source informed the *Los Angeles Times*, "There was a general nervousness [about the film]."

In 1997, PBS was scheduled to air *Out at Work*, an award-winning documentary about three gay workers' struggles for justice and dignity at the worksite. Director of news and information programming Sandra Heberer said PBS found *Out at Work* "to be compelling television responsibly done on a significant issue of our times," and it was scheduled to run on *P.O.V.*, the late-night summer series that had become the last place where one could see such work. But then the network reversed itself, claiming it had discovered that 23 percent of the film's $65,000 budget came from such "problematical" sources as a lesbian action foundation and several labor unions. One of the film's directors, Kelly Anderson, responded, "None of the funders in question gave more than $5,000 to the project, and most gave $1,000 or less."

Defending the network's decision as final, Heberer countered with a revealing statement: "PBS guidelines prohibit funding that might lead to an assumption that individual underwriters might have exercised editorial control over program content even if, as is clear in this case, those underwriters did not." In short, the mere possibility of someone making an erroneous assumption trumps PBS officials' knowledge of the truth. Thus, public ignorance is used to justify keeping the public ignorant—not a very good model for educational television.

Raising sufficient capital is the major barrier that independent producers confront in making documentary films. Some films take years to make as producers scramble for money wherever they can find it. Clearly, the primary organizations willing to spend money to educate the public about social problems would be public interest groups concerned with the issue in question. In this context, banning public interest underwriting amounts to a de facto censorship of content.

Underwriting Guidelines

The official justification for PBS discrimination regarding underwriting sources is contained in a 1990 document entitled *PBS National Program Funding Standards and Practices*, which asserts that "PBS must guard against the public perception that editorial control might have been exercised by program funders." The stated concern is that "should a significant number of reasonable viewers conclude that public television has sold its professionalism and independence to its program funders, whether or not their conclusions are justified, then the entire program service of public television will be suspect and the goal of serving the public will be unachievable."

This highly dubious proposition has never been systematically tested. Certainly none of these terms has ever been clearly defined. For example, how many would be a "significant" number of viewers, and how must their conclusions be manifested in order to be taken into account? Why would complaints about one program stigmatize the entire schedule? How can any organization be held responsible for conclusions about its practices that are not justified? Which public(s) are to be served, and why would a little controversy make that "unachievable"? The PBS document goes on to admit that there is no codification of standards available to guide such decision making. At best it can offer a few "examples to illustrate various applications of the perception test."

> A long-standing series of debates, accepted by the public as having an unassailable reputation, could be funded by a major corporation which might have a stake in one or more of the individual subjects debated. Here, the credibility of the series has been established and the debate format is less susceptible to manipulation than other formats.

Everyone knows that a debate format alone does not guard against bias in the choice of topics and the framing of positions. Neither does PBS indicate that it would ever suspend its prohibition against labor and public interest group funding—as opposed to corporate funding—even for a "longstanding series" with an "unassailable reputation." Finally, how do you measure "credibility" and "reputation" these days? Any public accusation can assail a reputation. Does the identity of the author of such charges make the difference?

PBS guidelines regarding "the commercialism principle" are just as bewildering:

> A manufacturer of photography equipment would be permitted to underwrite a general "how-to" series on photography composition and film developing, but could not fund a program which prominently featured the company's products or which compared products or services similar to those offered by the underwriter.

Wouldn't "reasonable" viewers conclude that it is in the financial interest of a manufacturer of photography equipment to promote an interest in photography? Of all the avocations that might be considered for a program series, why photography? Could it be the financial package put forward by the underwriter? Here's another example put forth in the guidelines:

> A major drug company could fund a 13-part series examining the working and functioning of the human body. The commercial tie between the funder's product and interests and the subject matter of the series is too tenuous to prohibit this funding arrangement, since the series deals with the human anatomy and not with health care.

I consider myself a reasonable person, and to me there is a rather intimate tie between my knowledge of the "working and functioning of the human body" and my attitudes toward health care. In fact, I'll bet there are a "significant number" of "reasonable" people who would agree with me on that. Moreover, in both of the cases above isn't it obvious that the companies are purchasing good will by associating their own commercial interest with that of public education?

Moreover, these examples are not purely hypothetical. In 1988, PBS presented *The Health Century,* funded by drug companies Eli Lilly, Pfizer, and Squibb, among others. As described by media observer Patricia Aufderheide, the program "charts the medical conquest of infectious disease, approaches to heart disease such as transplants, and the ways medicine is prolonging life." Obviously this focus promotes the benefits to the public of the underwriters' products. What other issues might a program on health care in America address? Aufderheide suggests a few: the "nursing crisis," the "commodification" of health services, "the skyrocketing cost of health insurance," and "whether heavy subsidies for organ-transplant research take money and research focus away from public-health programs."

Corporate Domination of Programming

Despite the Public Broadcasting System's officially stated concerns about avoiding any perception that programming has been unduly influenced by its funding sources, here are a dozen examples of programs shown on PBS in which corporate underwriters had a direct interest in content (all of these have been cited in the press):

| A show about Air Force One was partly funded by Boeing, the plane's manufacturer.
| The film *James Reston: The Man Millions Read,* about the *New York Times* columnist, was funded by the *New York Times* and produced by Susan Dryfoos, daughter of the late *Times* publisher Orvil Dryfoos and director of the *Times*'s Oral History Project.
| The eight-part PBS series *The Prize: The Epic Quest for Oil, Money, and Power,* was largely underwritten by Paine-Webber, at a cost of $6 million. Paine-Webber's subsidiary, Paine-Webber/Geodyne resources, based in Tulsa, Oklahoma, is engaged in oil exploration and production.
| A program about gems was funded by DeBeers and Tiffany's, and included plugs for both companies.
| *Heinz: The Story of an American Family* was produced by former press

secretaries for Senator John Heinz for WQED-TV Pittsburgh, with funding from the group People for John Heinz. The show included coverage on WQED board chair Elsie Hillman, a key figure in the senator's political career.

| *The Stuff of Dreams,* a three-hour series about the technology of materials, was underwritten by Dow Corning, a company that provides specialty materials, such as silicone, for various commercial products.

| *Jews of Boston,* produced by WGBH-TV Boston, featured New England businessman Steven Grossman and was underwritten by his firm.

| *New England Clambake,* also produced by WGBH-TV, was hosted by Roger Berkowitz, whose firm Legal Seafoods contributed up to $10,000 in food and staff time to the production.

| Northwest Airlines, which has Asian routes, backed the four-part series *Doing Business in Asia.*

| *Living Against the Odds,* a special on risk assessment, was funded by the petrochemical company Chevron. The program included the statement "We have to stop pointing the finger at industry for every environmental hazard."

| *The Machine That Changed the World,* a 1992 documentary about the computer, was partially funded by a $1.9 million grant from the Unisys computer company.

| *The Antiques Road Show,* one of the most popular new shows on PBS, is shot in a different location every week, and features experts appraising the value of stuff brought in by locals hoping to strike it rich. The expert provides details on an object's background and closes with an estimate of its value that is then flashed on the screen. This show is sponsored by Chubb Insurance, a company that insures antiques.

When confronted, PBS defended its decisions to broadcast these programs. For example, Mary Jane McKniven, PBS director of news and public affairs, said the Reston documentary was acceptable because it was "a co-production of WVIA/Scranton and the *New York Times,* but WVIA held editorial control." Also, "PBS determined the film was solid, not uncritical of Reston, and not a commercial on the *Times*' behalf."

Janine Jackson of Fairness and Accuracy In Reporting points out that this response shows that "at certain times, for some people, PBS allows considerations like tone or editorial control to mitigate worry about conflicts of interest."

The Impact of Corporate Funding

The practice of allowing corporate and conservative foundation underwriting while banning support from organized labor and public interest groups all but ensures programming that either is bland or conservatively biased. This, in effect, negates public broadcasting's founding mission to provide a forum for controversy and a voice for all members of the community, including those not normally heard.

Already by the mid-1970s, 74 percent of programming supported by corporate underwriters was classified as "culture." WGBH's Victoria Devlin advises, "Corporations are not big risk-takers when there's any perceived controversy." *TV Guide* critic John Weisman quoted one producer as saying, "Corporations fund me because I put them alongside Mom and apple pie and the American flag. And so I don't do controversial shows."

Detroit Free Press TV critic Marc Gunther elaborates: "Corporations like to support safe programming like the nature and science shows, British-made documentaries, how-to shows and historical documentaries that are staples of public television. . . . Fund-raisers for public TV stations say it's a constant struggle to get money for investigative journalism, children's programs, contemporary drama or controversy of any kind." After a while, many producers just stop struggling.

In his study of WGBH-TV Boston, sociologist William Hoynes writes, "ideas that are not fundable tend not to get proposed or, if proposed, to be tabled early in the development process." Producer Henry Hampton labored for six years before he was able to put together forty-four underwriters to raise the $2.5 million needed for the first six episodes of his wonderful series on the civil rights movement, *Eyes on the Prize*. Despite his success at PBS, in 1986 Bill Moyers complained, "The system leaves no room for independent journalists or a serious inquiry into our society." And in 1995, as he was anticipating his retirement, the *NewsHour*'s Robert MacNeil acknowledged, "We are not as provocative, innovative, creative or original as we should be. . . . Trying to ingratiate ourselves with the public by diluting what we do plays into the hands of the people who say we're either not good enough or not necessary."

In the summer of 1999, the *New York Times Magazine* ran a lengthy feature story on Ira Glass, the bright new star of public radio. The critical success of Glass's award-winning, cutting-edge show *This American Life* has been matched by its rising popularity. Despite starting outside the system, the show now receives CPB funding and is carried on 324 stations. Asked about doing television, Glass was quoted as saying that he needs a network that would give him real creative control. Glass's "one vow," according to *Times* writer Marshall Sella, "is to avoid PBS, which, he insists, 'is more beholden to corporate interests than commercial television and should be abolished.'"

Some have suggested that risk aversion has become so much a part of the PBS culture that it overrides all other considerations. After PBS declined a $5 million grant in 1992 to create unconventional election-year coverage, a senior public affairs producer who had just left PBS commented, "Anything apart from the norm won't be allowed. They aren't really interested in innovation."

As a consequence, while the CPB's Don Marbury asserts the "principle of diversity" in the name of conservative white males and "balance" in the name of big business and government, the list of award-winning documentaries rejected by PBS that are by, for, or about poor people, women, minorities, and citizen activists keeps growing. Worse, the programs regularly scheduled on PBS show the same imbalance. Over 1988–89, a group led by Stanley Aronowitz at City University of New York conducted a systematic study of who gets portrayed on public television. The researchers found that, for those two years, only 27 hours of programs were offered that "addressed the lives and concerns of workers as workers," as opposed to 253 hours that focused on the upper classes. Programming about workers represented less than one-half of 1 percent of all PBS programming hours. There was only a single one-hour program about union/management conflict.

In 1993, when I began my own research, the only three regularly scheduled public affairs programs on my public television station were hosted by John McLaughlin and William Buckley, associates of the right-wing *National Review* magazine, and the only program aimed at an African-American audience was hosted by Republican Tony Brown. When asked about this, former PBS official Barry Chase offered, "There happens to be an oversupply of entertaining, glib, right-wing commentators."

Today I get both nightly and weekly shows for big business and Wall Street investors on PBS television, but not one regular program for people interested in the workplace, the environment, human rights, or consumer affairs. Cultural affairs programs tend to be middlebrow or imported, only rarely presenting the most creative American talent in film or the performing arts.

A 1992 study by sociologists David Croteau, William Hoynes, and Kevin Carragee of who gets to speak on public television's public affairs shows found these programs to be dominated by the voices of government and corporate officials. Male sources outnumbered females four to one. Republican sources outnumbered Democrats 53 percent to 43 percent. People identified as "citizen activists" accounted for only 6 percent of all sources.

The *NewsHour* with Jim Lehrer is public broadcasting's flagship news broadcast. Originally the *MacNeil/Lehrer Report,* then the *MacNeil/Lehrer NewsHour,* the program has enjoyed generous corporate support from AT&T, Pepsico, and Archer Daniels Midland. In 1993, the *NewsHour* was watched by 4.6 million viewers each evening and 12.4 million at least once a week. A 1989 study by David Croteau and William Hoynes of guests on the *NewsHour* found that whites (90 percent) and males (87 percent) dominated. Scholars from conservative think tanks were featured frequently while those with opposing views, such as representatives of the Institute for Policy Studies, never appeared. Some 46 percent of sources consisted of current or former government officials. All public interest group representatives combined accounted for only 6 percent of the sources consulted on the program. The segments that focused on economic issues featured three times as many corporate representatives as labor representatives.

In 1991, Robert MacNeil defended these choices by saying, "The policy critics are not visible in our program because most of the time in our studio discussion . . . we are coming at the point when the debate has reached the question of policy and how that policy will be turned into action." In short, the program focuses on elite decision makers. Privately, Jim Lehrer has referred to spokespersons from peace and public interest groups as "moaners" and "whiners."

In December 1998, Hoynes replicated his earlier study, looking at 75 programs, including 276 stories and 651 on-camera sources over a two-week period. He found that PBS public affairs coverage had become even more provincial and elitist. Nearly 75 percent of the story topics dealt with domestic and economic news. Depending on the topic, from 75 percent to 90 percent of the sources that appeared on camera were "elite voices," that is, corporate representatives, government officials, and professional journalists and academics—the same voices one hears on commercial television.

Citizen activists accounted for only 4.5 percent of all sources, down from 5.9 percent in 1992. Members of the general public made up 5.7 percent of all sources, down from 12 percent in 1992. Only 21.5 percent of sources were women, down from 23.1 percent in 1992. Hoynes concluded, "This insider orientation makes it hard to define what, outside of the one-hour length of the evening news, defines public television as innovative, independent, or alternative."

Over the past few years the ratings have been falling for PBS public affairs staples like the *NewsHour* and *Washington Week in Review*. Writing in *Current*, former CPB official David Stewart referred to *NewsHour* discussions as "featuring predictable views held by an equally predictable set of lawmakers, military leaders, and professional pundits." Stewart wanted the program to be more "brisk" and "funny."

WETA caused a small scandal when it canned Ken Bode after five years as host of *Washington Week in Review (WWR)* in an effort to give the program more "edge," "attitude," and "opinion." Reacting to the fallout, WETA CEO Sharon Rockefeller recognized that her *WWR* audience was concerned about the possible "tabloidization of public TV." No one seemed to consider the possibility that more controversial topics and a wider range of perspectives might be just the cure for too-predictable news programming.

The Plight of Public Radio

As might be expected, public radio has traveled the same path as its television counterpart. When CPB funds were held up and slashed during the Reagan administration, NPR felt compelled to pursue "corporate underwriting" more aggressively. Corporations were attracted by NPR's relatively affluent audience, and corporate contributions soon quadrupled, from $2.7 million in 1983 to $10.6 million in 1988.

In time, more money and higher ratings affected the network's integrity. One NPR news staffer, who asked not to be identified, observed, "As we've gotten a larger audience, we've tended to be more mainstream. We used to be a lot more alternative and talk to different people."

Sociologist Charlotte Ryan's 1991 study of NPR included 2,296 stories, which featured 5,507 quoted sources over a four-month period. She found that 96 percent of NPR's regular commentators were white and 79 percent were male. Government officials were 26 percent of all sources; journalists, writers, and academics 22 percent; other professionals 15 percent; ordinary citizens 15 percent; and public interest advocates only 7 percent. News tended to be heavily reliant on government press releases, which were presented without comment. Ryan concluded that NPR news programming "tended to frame political debate as something that occurs within the government, not among the public." Worse yet, NPR entertainment programming also became staid and predictable. When Garrison Keillor offered the mild satire of his soon to be popular *Prairie Home Companion,* the head of NPR rejected it as "offensive to the middle class."

Between 1993 and 1996, when Congress rescinded $100 million in appropriated funds, public radio station managers were forced to start "entrepreneurial ventures," reach out for corporate underwriting dollars, and explore consolidation and other cost-sharing moves with other public stations.

In 1997, the CPB made federal funding for public radio contingent on a minimum audience size (as measured by Arbitron ratings) or level of fundraising. Some eighty stations were immediately put in jeopardy. By 1998, the list had shrunk to six, but "the casualty of change for many stations," according to *Current's* Jacqueline Conciatore, "has been the idiosyncratic or specialized shows typically heard only on public radio," including many ethnic music programs and informational talk shows. The ratings minimum doubles for fiscal years 1999 and 2000.

Marty Durlin, general manager of KGNU in Boulder, Colorado, points out that 43 percent of public radio stations are small, having budgets of $500,000 or less. In her view, "autonomy" and "localism" were the founding principles of public broadcasting and remain valid today. However, they are threatened by the withdrawal of public support and the growing domination of commercialism in public affairs. Under pressure from Congress, Durlin charges, the big stations have embraced focus groups, "all-professional staffs, subscribing to Arbitron, and running more national programming." Moreover, they have chastised the smaller stations for not following suit. To make matters worse, the CPB funding formula punishes the small stations for being efficient by using unpaid staff that allow them to "create unique programming for our local communities, and all on a shoestring budget."

The Myth of Liberal Bias

This critique of public broadcasting must seem strange to people who have been hearing for many years that the media, especially public broadcasting, are "too liberal" and in need of balance. This myth has been promulgated by conservative media watch groups like Reed Irvine's Accuracy in Media, L. Brent Bozell's Media Research Center, Robert and Linda Lichter's Center for Media and Public Affairs, and David Horowitz's Committee for Media Integrity. All these groups are generously supported by conservative foundations and have had their claims amplified by willing politicians like Bob Dole, Jesse Helms, and Orrin Hatch.

Considering the evidence we have examined, however, it is clear that this is no more than a strategy to intimidate the fourth estate into favorable coverage of conservative politicians, policies, and programs. A *Wall Street Journal* poll in 1996 found that only 22 percent of journalists considered themselves liberal. In 1981, Ruder and Finn, a major public relations firm, did a study for the American Manufacturers Association of CEOs of the one thousand largest American companies. Asked how they felt the media treated their companies, two-thirds said "excellent" or "good," with only 6 percent responding "poor."

Even some of the pit bulls of the conservative movement have conceded that the "liberal media" idea is a myth. Pat Buchanan has remarked, "The truth is, I've gotten fairer, more comprehensive coverage of my ideas than I ever imagined I would receive. . . . For heaven sakes, we kid about the liberal media, but every Republican on earth does that." William Kristol has confessed, "I admit it, the liberal media were never that powerful and the whole thing was often used as an excuse by conservatives for conservative failures."

Nevertheless, the pro-corporate right continues to promulgate this myth because it works to their advantage. Such chronic attacks make publishers and broadcasters very sensitive to conservative pressure, and the strategy has been especially successful with public broadcasters, who are dependent on federal appropriations. As Noam Chomsky has suggested, this "liberal" image gives what is actually a corporate media system credibility with the public: to be accused of being too hard on the rich and powerful and too soft on the poor and marginal enhances the perception of journalists as being defenders of the public interest—no matter how timid their actual work.

Those who complain most often about the lack of balance in the occasional documentary never propose any evaluation criteria that could be applied to all programs equally; they are simply "working the referees," as it were. And they have been most effective. As we have seen, the principle of balance is only applied to attack program content that is critical of established interests.

Certainly, no one would expect business programs to invite socialists to balance the views of capitalists, religious programs to invite atheists to balance the views of believers, programs on national security to invite pacifists to challenge the assumptions of military experts, or cooking shows to give equal time to vegetarians. Similarly, charges that one has failed to adequately balance the views of public interest groups with the views of government or corporate spokespersons are most often red herrings to distract attention from the media's ongoing censorship of those who challenge the system.

PBS spokespersons are fond of defending their service by pointing to criticism from both the left and the right as evidence that they must be doing something right. A more efficient conclusion is that all alternative points of view have typically been excluded in favor of programming dominated by establishment perspectives and sensibilities. Public broadcasting's unique mission requires that it include alternative voices rather than justify their exclusion.

In my view, this is not an issue that can be neatly reduced to political labels—liberal, conservative, left, right, or whatever. It comes down to a question of what stories get told and who gets to participate in the telling. If politics, economics and other social issues are covered only from the top down, interest groups and potential publics representing millions of citizens will be excluded from participation in public discussion and we all will be poorer for it. Surely the perspectives of government and corporate leaders are important. However, they must be balanced by coverage from the bottom up—with an understanding of what is happening to our workers, citizens, taxpayers, and environment.

Out of the Frying Pan and into the Fire

Raising the stakes on the conservative strategy to corporatize public broadcasting, House Speaker Newt Gingrich announced in February of 1995 that he now had the power to kill federal funding for public broadcasting all by himself and would do so: "They still don't realize that the appropriation is gone, that the game is over. The power of the Speaker is the power of recognition, and I will not recognize any proposal that will appropriate money for the CPB."

CPB board member Victor Gold, a White House operative during several Republican administrations, immediately tried to exploit the situation to promote more de facto censorship: "Hell, let the cultural things go on their own! ... Who needs Bill Moyers? Let him go to CBS or HBO. We've got to save what we believe is absolutely vital. If you're going to tell me that *Frontline* is going to bring down educational TV, let *Frontline* loose. The world has changed now."

PBS chief Ervin Duggan was defensive: "The implication that PBS's fare is somehow fraught on a daily basis with controversy and conflict is simply not consistent with the facts." Duggan had already acquiesced to the system's conservative critics by arguing that PBS must concern itself with balance *within* all programs, rather than just across the program schedule. The consequence of not doing so, he warned, would be the recurrence of the debate over fairness, "threatening the whole enterprise."

Also in February, CPB president Richard Carlson hired former GOP congressman and Gingrich ally Vin Weber to consult on how to work with Congress to achieve an "orderly transition" to a privatized future. Disclosure of Weber's hiring brought a stern reprimand from the CPB board, who refused to honor his contract. However, the board allowed Carlson to aggressively pursue the elimination of about one hundred "overlapped" PBS stations in the name of system efficiency.

In May 1995, the Christian Coalition issued its Contract with the American Family, which, among other things, called for the elimination of federal funding for the CPB. Despite PBS's typically modest fare, the coalition complained about profanity, nudity, and indecency in one or two documentaries.

Moderate Democrats, including Vice President Al Gore, were able to score easy points by defending the continuation of modest federal funding for "programs that enrich the lives of children." Appearing alongside Fred Rogers in a national press conference held at a Washington day care center, Gore asked rhetorically, "Can you say *children?* Can you say *education?*"

Attempting to appease its conservative critics, the CPB cited its 1994 poll findings that 88 percent of Americans agreed that public television is "something the whole family can enjoy" and 74 percent agreed that it "reflects traditional American values." According to a Roper poll, 57 percent of the public considered public television an "excellent" or "good" value. A poll by *USA Today*/CNN found that 76 percent of respondents favored federal support for public broadcasting. In fact, 49 percent wanted government to increase funding for public television.

Fearing that stations would become more commercial or fold, the American public rallied to the defense of public television. People for the American Way (PFAW) delivered hundreds of thousands of petitions to Congress in support of continued funding. PFAW spokesperson Leslie Harris boasted, "There's not an office [in Congress] that won't tell you the amount of mail they've gotten on public broadcasting is more than on any other subject, even health care." In July, the House Appropriations Committee defeated an amendment to "zero out" CPB funding for 1998 by a vote of forty to fourteen.

The Triumph of Commerce over Mission

By 1997, the debate over killing CPB federal funding was dead. The agency had an appropriation of $300 million for fiscal year 2000, less than for 1990 in real dollars but still $50 million over the amount appropriated for fiscal years 1998 and 1999. A bill to eliminate all funding was trounced by a vote of 345 to 78. Even a bill to cut the appropriation by $50 million was soundly defeated, 265 to 155. However, while funding has survived, the mission of public television has been seriously compromised. As syndicated columnist Norman Solomon observed, "There's more than one way to kill public broadcasting. It can be murdered outright . . . or gradually strangled by corporate embraces with the aid of government."

The encroachment of corporations into public broadcasting programming goes back to the early 1970s, when Mobil Oil's Herb Schmertz joined with Joan Wilson of WGBH-TV Boston to buy the U.S. distribution rights for British television dramas at the bargain-basement rate of about $1 million a year for some fifty hours. He offered them to PBS as *Masterpiece Theatre*.

It was a masterful strategy. According to writer Timothy Brennan, *Masterpiece Theatre* had powerful snob appeal as a kind of television "literature" that "can raise select groups above the thousands of others who simply aren't tuned to the right channel." In 1980, Schmertz opined that Mobil's use of public television as a promotional tool "has persuaded an important segment of our society to look at Mobil in a new light." Accepting an award from PBS for twenty years of *Masterpiece Theatre*, a Mobil spokesperson expressed his gratitude to the assembled: "You are building a constituency for Mobil." PBS now allows Mobil to attach its name to the title of the series. Given the recent merger, in 2000 it will become the *Mobil-Exxon Masterpiece Theatre*.

In addition to *Masterpiece Theatre*, Mobil sponsored *Classic Theatre* and *Mobil Showcase*. Exxon, Arco, and Gulf quickly followed suit. By 1981, the oil companies provided underwriting in full or in part for 72 percent of prime-time PBS programs, and critics dubbed PBS "the Petroleum Broadcasting Service." Business support in general for public TV increased sixfold between 1973 and 1980. In consequence, as Columbia University's Erik Barnouw observed, safe "cultural programming became the dominant feature of prime time." By 1974–75 corporate support had increased more than 200 percent and was also being used to fund and promote conservative public affairs talk shows and documentaries.

The payoff for the underwriters is access to public television's educated audience both as consumers and as opinion leaders on public policy concerns. The advertising director for General Motors, for instance, explained his company's support by saying, "The PBS audience is largely made up of thought leaders and peer group influencers," and Steve Bass, PBS director of corporate support, suggested in *Fortune* Magazine, "PBS is a different way for companies to get into the mind of the consumer." Patricia Aufderheide calls this "ambush advertising"—an approach designed to get "behind the defenses of a hard-to-reach, suspicious-of-advertising audience."

In 1984, during the Reagan assault on public broadcasting, the FCC further loosened its guidelines on public broadcast underwriting to allow for commercial-like announcements at the beginning and end of programs. Now permitted were "trade names," "logos or slogans," "product symbols," "product or service listings," "value neutral descriptions," and locations of stores or offices.

Other big business interests followed the lead of the oil companies. The financial industry underwrote a number of business shows: the brokerage firm A. G. Edwards & Sons, Inc., supported the *Nightly Business Report;* Prudential-Bache Securities, Travelers Corporation, and Massachusetts Financial Services underwrote *Wall $treet Week* with Louis Rukeyser; and Metropolitan Life Insurance Company supported *Adam Smith's Money World.* Large corporations and their foundations also sponsored cultural affairs and news programs on PBS: *American Playhouse* has been supported by Chubb; *National Geographic Specials* by Chevron; *Washington Week in Review* by the Ford Motor Company; *Technopolitics* by Pfizer, Inc., Anheuser-Busch, and Kraft General Foods; and the *NewsHour* with Jim Lehrer by Archer Daniels Midland Company, New York Life Insurance Company, and Pepsico.

Finally, corporations and their think tanks began funding conservative political talk shows: General Electric sponsored the *McLaughlin Group,* and the American Enterprise Institute underwrote *American Interests;* the John M. Olin Foundation and the Annenberg Foundation funded William F. Buckley's *Firing Line; Tony Brown's Journal* is sponsored by Pepsi-Cola. Despite modest ratings, these programs have been offered free to public television for years. *The McLaughlin Group* is carried by more than three hundred stations.

While individual supporters have always contributed more collectively than big business, their money is used for general station operations. Corporate money, on the other hand, is used almost exclusively to sponsor specific programs. In all, corporate and business underwriting in the 1990s accounted for about 30 percent of the funding for national PBS programming, and it was the largest single funding source, ahead of individual stations (28 percent), CPB (13 percent), producers of foreign cassettes (16 percent), and private foundations (6 percent). As the prestigious Twentieth Century Fund Task Force has pointed out, "This undercuts [public television's] non-commercial character."

In 1985, TV writer Les Brown observed, "Almost nothing can get on the Public Broadcasting Service without commercial underwriting, the euphemism for corporate sponsorship." In his view, this belies PBS's claim to be a "truly noncommercial service" making "its own decisions about what will be broadcast," as opposed to commercial television, which "answers to the wishes and needs of the advertising community."

Between 1982 and 1991, seventeen major corporations provided at least $5 million each to support public television programming. Then the tide turned. In the years between 1987 and 1992, PBS ratings dropped 22 percent, from 2.7 to 2.2. Faced with lower profits and harder advertising choices, corporations began to cut back on PBS underwriting. Corporate support dropped 3 percent in 1992 and 13.4 percent in 1993. The number of programs receiving exclusive support from major corporate underwriters declined from twenty in 1991, for a total of $17 million, to fourteen in 1993, for a total of $6.3 million. During this period, the overall decline in corporate support for PBS's National Program Service was from 28 percent to 23 percent of its total budget. This was still within the general range of corporate funding provided over the previous twenty years; nevertheless, the system was now so addicted to corporate money that the cutbacks produced a withdrawal panic among many in the industry. PBS senior vice president John Grant called it "a borderline crisis situation."

Rather than reevaluate their dependence on corporate revenue, leaders in the public broadcasting industry sought to bring the corporations back by advocating still more liberal guidelines for corporate identification. Al Vecchione, executive producer for MacNeil-Lehrer Productions, complained about competition from cable and then sold two-thirds of McNeil-Lehrer to Liberty Media, a subsidiary of the conservative TCI cable systems company. "A welcome infusion of capital into the *NewsHour*," said PBS president Ervin Duggan. TCI itself was then acquired by AT&T, one of the corporate giants that had crushed public service broadcasting in the 1920s in forming NBC as the first commercial radio network.

In 1997, Duggan presided over several lunches for advertising people in Los Angeles, Chicago, and New York, pitching advertisers to join PBS in "doing well by doing good," adding that supporting a PBS program "sends the distinctive and unmistakable message 'We care about quality.'" WNET president Bill Baker added, "Welcome to the new PBS. Corporate messages on PBS get more creative every year. You can show products. You can use slogans." Also, celebrity spokespersons, mascots, theme music, and underwriters' phone numbers and web addresses were to be allowed. Andrew Pappalardo of the advertising firm Young and Rubicam seemed pleased to observe, "What we have here is the commercialization of PBS." His client, Patrick Stasolla of International Home Foods, saw PBS as "more receptive to the use of a more commercial message," making it a "strong business decision" to have Chef Boyardee underwrite PBS children's shows.

Some PBS stations moved to longer commercial messages. The 1990 revised rules permitted fifteen seconds for one underwriter, twenty seconds for two and thirty for three. In 1996, PBS announced it would now accept as many as three fifteen-second messages for multiple underwriters of a national program. In 1997, many big-city community-based stations, like WQED, Pittsburgh, started selling local thirty-second underwriting credits on a cost-per-thousand basis. Indeed, leaders of the commercialization movement in public television have had to invent a new euphemism to cover what they are doing—they call it "super enhanced underwriting."

PBS Commercialism: From Creep to Full Gallop

▌ Former PBS president Larry Grossman proposed an experiment with weekend commercial programming on public television to raise money for a new production company that would seek production partners and investors to develop better programs. Top executives at public television stations in Chicago, Philadelphia, Detroit, Minneapolis, St. Paul, Miami, and Los Angeles expressed interest. Perhaps the most telling response came from Mike Hardgrove, CEO of KETC-TV St. Louis, in support of the plan: "Many of the harmful consequences associated with advertising already are taking place."

▌ The Community Station Resource Group, representing a large number of stations seeking to expand into thirty-second underwriting "spots," engaged top sales operations to assist them. One firm involved is headed by Bob Williams, former owner of National Cable Communications; the other is the newly formed PBS Sponsorship Group, which proposes to offer multimarket thirty-second spot sales wherever possible.

▌ In 1996, PBS entered into a deal with Devillier Donegan Enterprises, a unit of Disney/ABC Television International. Each party put up $15 million to produce nonfiction documentary films like *The Living Edens,* a twenty-part series on the world's most beautiful places. PBS controls the domestic broadcast rights and video sales while Devillier Donegan gets the international rights and sales. PBS then sold to Disney/Buena Vista the right to air the PBS-produced series *Bill Nye the Science Guy* on both commercial and public stations.

| PBS also announced a $20 million deal with Williams Companies, a communications and energy conglomerate, to expand the Business Channel, a PBS outfit that provides teleconferencing and information distribution to corporations that pay for the privilege.

This escalating commercialism has extended to the merchandising of videos and spin-off products. PBS created PBS Home Video and, in 1994, entered into a distribution agreement with Turner Home Entertainment, later absorbed by Warner Home Video. Gross sales of videos approached $27 million a year. During the period from 1996 to 1999, PBS also entered into various broadcast performance compact disc recording contracts with Warner Brothers, Time-Life Records, and Sony Classical.

In fact, PBS was dealing so fast and furious that its business practices came into dispute. In February 1999, a nine-member jury voted unanimously that PBS was guilty of breach of contract and fraud in dealing with former Monkees member Michael Nesmith over program video distribution through his Pacific Arts company. The jury awarded Nesmith $47 million in compensatory and punitive damages. When the case was settled for an undisclosed sum in July, Nesmith said he was happy; PBS's Duggan said the network would pay the settlement out of proceeds from its various revenue-generating businesses.

Despite public reassurances, the enhanced capacity of four-channel digital broadcasting does not ensure viewers more PBS community service programming. Instead, PBS has sought to exploit this opportunity for profit, asking the FCC for permission for public TV stations to do whatever they want with the additional channels that would become available. Options range from leasing to commercial broadcasters, home shopping networks, or infomercial producers to offering a subscription-fee channel featuring popular PBS programs. In the apparent hope of approval, public broadcasting entities WGBH, WNET, and PBS have paid for a feasibility study to develop a pay cable channel.

Given the enormous popularity of *Sesame Street* and *Barney* products, it should come as no surprise that children's shows in particular have been targeted by the pitchmen. Broadcasts for *Sesame Street* carry fifteen-second commercials for Discovery Zone, the operator of more than two hundred children's "entertainment" centers in the United States, Canada, and Puerto Rico. Chef Boyardee and the Chuck E. Cheese restaurant chain advertise on the kids' shows. The PBS children's show *Puzzle Place* has a joint marketing arrangement with Toys-R-Us, as does Microsoft, Ragdoll Productions, and Itsy Bitsy Entertainment Co., to develop interactive toys based on the PBS series *Teletubbies*. Communications scholar George Gerbner has remarked, "For most of human history our children learned their culture through stories by people with something to tell, not corporations with something to sell. It is a tragedy that a once safe public broadcasting environment has been invaded by these same commercial forces."

To address the question of how PBS program merchandising income would be shared, Ervin Duggan introduced the "station equity model" in 1995. PBS would drive harder bargains with producers on ancillary rights (for example, foreign sales, library rights, product royalties, etc.) and share the resulting revenues with the stations. In Duggan's words, this would make stations "investors rather than renters of programming." While this is fairer than the old system, it also compromises any principled opposition to merchandise-driven programming choices.

In the middle 1990s, two retail chains forged deals with PBS-affiliated stations to sell merchandise related to PBS productions. Both Learning-smith and Store of Knowledge offered a percentage of a store's net revenues in exchange for a station's willingness to license their name or call letters. By 1997 there were fifty or so stores operating in each chain. About two-thirds of the merchandise and half of the fifty top-selling items have no relation to public TV. Touring WETA's Store of Knowledge, a representative of *Current* observed "familiar public TV faces in every department; also videocassettes from cable networks and early television and lots of puzzles, craft kits, gyroscopes and rubber snakes."

Also in 1997, PBS announced its biggest deal yet—a five-year, $75 million production partnership with the Reader's Digest Association. According to the deal, PBS and Reader's Digest were to mutually select television programs to be syndicated worldwide and adapted to video and other products such as books, audio books, on-line content, and computer CDs. The emphasis would be on "family" entertainment.

Reader's Digest chairman James Schadt enthused that the deal would "heighten awareness of the Reader's Digest brand name, which will boost response rates from our other direct marketing efforts." Writing for *Current*, Rick Breitenfeld commented, "The decision to produce or not to produce apparently will depend upon the likelihood of a lucrative back-end for Readers Digest." He considered this "a new and troubling criterion" in the development of programming.

Meanwhile, Ervin Duggan crowed, "This is a powerful example of a new strategy of advancing our mission by doing business with companies that share our ideals while complementing our resources." Well, you may ask, what *are* those ideals? Some of you might recall *Reader's Digest* as a stalwart conservative publication. Over the years, it has cheered for an aggressive military policy in Vietnam and Latin America, denigrated the labor movement, and championed privately owned over publicly owned utilities. And in recent years, *Reader's Digest* has been a major contributor to the conservative Heritage Foundation, an aggressive opponent of federal funding for public television. In January 1998, *Reader's Digest* changed management and pulled out of the deal with PBS.

In 1999, Duggan boasted that PBS is "one of the most recognized brands in America." Addressing the problem of cable competition, PBS official Robert Ottenhoff proposed strengthening PBS "brand awareness," thus attracting "new partners" to generate "substantial new programming capital" so that the service can "earn significant new income from the use of these programs." This vision is quintessentially commercial.

Here's Steve Sherman, associate director of research at PBS, advising stations how to meet the cable challenge: "Public television has plenty of customers, but with the exception of our children's department, they're not buying a lot of merchandise. . . . We need to encourage a little more browsing. I fear some of our competitors may be doing a better job of moving inventory by attracting their customers to additional counters within their boutiques."

As we have seen, the commercial cable channels that Ottenhoff and Sherman envy suffer all the constraints of the marketplace—a preoccupation with market ratings, advertiser pressures, and profits. PBS, on the other hand, has a mandate to provide free, universal service that is noncommercial and local in orientation. Moreover, unlike its commercial competitors, PBS has a mandate to serve marginal members of society, explore the cutting edge of artistic performance, and provide a forum for controversy and debate. No commercial network can do that. Yet when PBS seeks to define itself competitively it chooses the language of the marketplace rather than asserting its unique public mission.

In 1995, former PBS program chief Kathy Quattrone observed, "Many program decisions are being based not on the program value they bring but what kind of a deal it can bring. The programming department needs to refocus toward the mission of creating distinctive programs and away from creative business deals." Bruce Christensen, president of PBS from 1984 to 1993, has warned that unless the funding problem can be solved, public broadcasting "will be a commercial medium in the next century."

In September 1999, Ervin Duggan resigned under pressure. Despite his success in raising $100 million in corporate underwriting, Duggan warned that "creeping commercialism undermines the arguments we use on Capitol Hill and elsewhere to justify public support." In particular, he cited thirty-second commercials, leasing DTV transmission capacity to ad-supported programmers, pledge programming that resembles the fare offered on home shopping networks, and corporate names in program titles.

Again, I believe that PBS continues to deliver some quality programs not found on commercial channels. Nevertheless, this chronic pandering to conservative politicians, corporate underwriters, and wealthy subscribers has been enormously costly to the service's editorial independence. The biggest losers have been the taxpayers, the local viewers, and the general public, especially the unserved and underserved publics for whom public television was created and in whose name it is often defended.

Chapter 4

The Battle to Reform WQED

In 1993, Pittsburgh was served by one major daily, the *Post-Gazette*, owned by the Block family's Blade Communications, based in Toledo, Ohio. After a lengthy Teamsters strike, this paper had recently acquired its rival, the *Pittsburgh Press*, and by 1998 it enjoyed a daily circulation of 245,000 and a Sunday circulation of 437,000.

The *Post-Gazette*'s new competition came from the *Greensberg*—now *Pittsburgh*—*Tribune-Review*, owned by Richard Mellon Scaife, heir to banking, oil, and steelmaking fortunes. *Forbes* estimates Scaife's fortune at about $1 billion, making him one of the four hundred richest people in the United States. He is also perhaps America's biggest supporter of right-wing causes; his contributions have been estimated at more than $340 million to well over forty groups since the 1970s. Scaife has given more than $23 million to the Heritage Foundation, for instance, where he sits as vice chairman of the board of trustees.

Scaife used the *Tribune-Review*, along with his *American Spectator* magazine, to promote right-wing conspiracy theories in order to attack President Clinton and other Democratic leaders, including accusations of murder. In 1997, *Time* named Scaife one of the country's twenty-five most influential people. The *Tribune-Review*'s circulation was expanded through subsequent acquisitions; at the end of 1998, the corporation's total regional circulation was 178,000 daily and 195,000 on Sundays.

In 1994, Pittsburgh had two alternative weeklies. *In Pittsburgh News-weekly* had a circulation of about 70,000 and an estimated readership of about 150,000. The *City Paper*, which had a smaller base, was newer, more corporate oriented, and not as well written. For example, a May 1996 *City Paper* feature which purported to be an overview of WQED's problems and possible solutions ran about thirty-five hundred words but was based almost entirely on an interview with WQED CEO George Miles.

In Pittsburgh was edited by Andy Newman, a progressive who had come to Pittsburgh after editing an Idaho paper recognized for its investigative journalism. Newman, reporter Chris Potter, and others at *In Pittsburgh* insisted on traditional journalistic standards of documentation but took on subjects that the mainstream media wouldn't touch and expressed opinions rarely heard elsewhere. They had an impact. For example, when Beverly Enterprises' Murray Manor nursing home began curtailing visiting hours for patients whose family members had complained about understaffing, *In Pittsburgh* ran a story exposing the practice. The restrictions were lifted.

Making the News

In the first few years, the QED Accountability Project got plenty of press coverage, for several reasons. First, the one exception to the domination of news by elites occurs in the wake of major accidents or scandals. Such events are unusual and dramatic. They also raise the question of responsibility and reveal some of the behind-the-scenes operations of those in charge, which in turn allows grassroots groups to gain access to the newsmaking process.

It also helped that the U.S. news media are more likely to pursue stories that portray problems in the public, tax-supported sector than problems in the private corporate sector. It is difficult to get people to talk about corporate abuses, and when they do, corporations wield a censorship power through their advertising dollars and their willingness to sue. In addition, criticism of public institutions appeals to conservatives ideologically opposed to government programs as well as to average citizens concerned with good government.

Another reason that our campaign got newspaper and broadcast coverage has to do with journalism as a profession. Despite a known pecking order based on the size of each organization's circulation, reporters do compete with each other for sources and recognition. Finally, all the developments that make the press so accessible to public relations specialists also make them accessible to media activists who are knowledgeable about public relations. Indeed, there are many groups now consulting with public interest organizations on how to "frame" or "spin" stories with the right "hooks," "angles," and "news pegs," and how to "pitch" them to journalists.

Since the media watch each other and pander to news fads, if you can break into one paper or station you have a much better chance of pitching the story successfully to another. One challenge is to keep the story "fresh" by bringing in the necessary dramatic elements—new and interesting characters, conflict, and the possibility of resolution.

Early on, the QED Accountability Project was helped considerably by the alternative weekly *In Pittsburgh*. The paper ran long in-depth features and editorials that we used to solicit new members, and it also provided free ad space by cosponsoring events like the Project's "Banned by PBS" film premiere and talks by FAIR's Jeff Cohen. I also persuaded editor Andy Newman to institute a local "Media Watch" column and frequently fed ideas and information to the assigned columnist.

Of course, once you have the media's attention, the struggle is then waged over how the event will be framed in the reporting. As Charlotte Ryan explains, those in charge are privileged to employ the culture's "dominant frames," which "build on assumptions so taken for granted that the mainstream media perceive them as the only logical approach to a situation." In the case of WQED, such assumptions included "The bad leaders are gone and the new leaders deserve a chance"; "We are a city in decline and can't afford current services"; "National forces dictate our situation"; and various business truisms concerning the wisdom of laying off workers and liquidating assets to pay down debts and make profits.

We, on the other hand, often found ourselves challenging prevailing political assumptions. For example, years of conservative propaganda have promoted a pervasive cynicism toward political participation and the possibility of good government. In addition, years of anticommunist free market ideology have eclipsed a more traditional cultural appreciation for community property and public services.

Another "dominant frame" we had to confront was the prevailing notion that the media—and especially public broadcasting—are "too liberal." To criticize public broadcasting as "too conservative" challenges the conventional wisdom. We realized that this position could be presented as an interesting spin on what everybody thinks they know—we agree that public broadcasting *is* ideologically biased *but* in a conservative, not liberal, direction—and enhanced by appealing to people's distrust of corporate monopolies. However, this strategy opens you up to being counterframed by the dominant group as too liberal (once again) and/or naive, as when WQED corporate governance committee chair Hugh Nevin was quoted by a reporter as calling me a "child of the '60s" who was "not ready" for the 1990s. This kind of labeling was used frequently by WQED officials in discrediting my claims in particular.

Our challenge, then, was to frame our story in ways that would make it newsworthy to media gatekeepers while at the same time trying to do justice to the complexity of the issues, which required some time and space to develop. Consequently, we ignored television news in our campaign and concentrated on newspapers and talk radio, using the major dailies for news releases, reaction quotes, op-ed pieces, and letters to the editor. The *Tribune-Review* had a much smaller Pittsburgh circulation than the *Post-Gazette;* however, radio news sometimes picked up its stories, and people connected with WQED also read and talked about the *Tribune-Review* if the story was about them.

In addition to *In Pittsburgh,* we used community and campus newsletters to announce events and solicit members. For example, the Merton Center's *New People* went out to about five thousand activists every month. Coverage in these smaller publications helped expand the movement, which, in turn, gave us greater credibility with the larger media. The *Pittsburgh Catholic, Pittsburgh Business Times,* and others also occasionally picked up on us. In addition, I made myself available on a regular basis to WDUQ, the Duquesne University–based National Public Radio station, and KQV, "all news" radio, home of many news and talk shows. Finally, I guested on talk shows on WTAE (ABC) and other radio stations.

We must keep things in perspective here. We did not make the story. We worked to reframe a breaking story and to promote our own agenda in the process. If WQED's financial problems had not already been news, we might have been able to promote the story of the station's undemocratic operations and programming as news, but the coverage would have been different.

If WQED had declined to respond, the whole story would have lacked conflict and reporters would have lost interest. On the other hand, if we had chosen to promote conflict in order to attract attention, our tactics would have obscured our message. In this situation, WQED's need to regain credibility with funding sources, including subscribers, motivated it to keep the story of its reform in the news while we served as a counter voice.

Some candor about the coverage we received seems in order here. Reportage on the QED Accountability Project was generally deeper in the alternative weeklies than the dailies and in the smaller-circulation *Tribune-*

Review than in the main daily, the *Post-Gazette*. The one exception to this was when the *Post-Gazette* reporter assigned was Sally Kalson, because she had the combination of curiosity, skepticism, and persistence to do good investigative journalism. A very lively writer, Kalson also wrote a weekly humor column with an edge. In fact, Kalson was one of the reporters involved in the original exposé of WQED. As far as I was concerned, she was the only reporter at the *Post-Gazette* who "got it" when it came to ethical issues like fairness and justice. Unfortunately, in 1996 Kalson was dropped from the media beat and reassigned to cover family and workplace issues.

The three other *Post-Gazette* reporters who covered our story were TV and/or film reviewers rather than investigative reporters. All were competent scribes, but none were interested in ethical or background questions and they usually merely reported what the various parties said. As communications scholar Dan Hallin observes, it is characteristic of American news media "to frame and analyze events in terms of strategies and tactics, success and failure," removing ethical judgements in favor of handicapping contests of power. In contrast, Todd Gutnick, the reporter at the conservative *Tribune-Review*, seemed to have a nose for controversy and some insight into the contradictions within the statements of those in power. Unfortunately, when he left in 1997 his position was allowed to remain vacant, and subsequent coverage at the paper became scant and superficial.

When I would challenge the major *Post-Gazette* reporter about printing a WQED claim without documentation (for instance, the estimated value of a station, the reason for an FCC decision, the causes cited for a corporate action), she would usually complain that she had too much to do and too little time to do independent research; it would be up to me to investigate and make the counterclaims, whether that involved calling the FCC, Congress, the Mellon Bank, or whatever. Later, when I became persistent about following up on some of these questions, she got annoyed with me and stopped calling my partner or me for comment.

The failure to cover in depth the issues raised by the WQED story was more than a matter of workload, however. I learned firsthand that journalists today frequently settle for just getting the opinions rather than the facts. Even in the national press, fear of alienating powerful sources will all too often stop reporters from telling the public what they know if it contradicts an official statement; instead they will seek to have an opposition spokesperson make such charges and let the public sort it out. Lacking the knowledge or resources to investigate on their own, most readers remain confused.

The major difference between the two mainstream papers in their coverage of the WQED story was that the *Tribune-Review* considered it a regional-page or (sometimes) front-page story. On the other hand, the *Post-Gazette* quickly assigned it to the magazine page under TV, often just above or below the daily schedule; several times the story was written into reviewer Barbara Vancheri's weekly column, along with other media items. Except on the occasion of two FCC decisions, in six-and-a-half years, the WQED story only once made the front page in the *Post-Gazette*, despite the fact that it concerned a failing $34 million business that had laid off about 130 employees and was involved in scandalous disclosures, government challenges, and legal actions. When I tried gently to provoke Vancheri into fighting for better placement, she replied laconically, "I guess the thrill is gone."

After 1997, we were virtually ignored by the Pittsburgh press. The publishers and editors of both dailies actively supported WQED and criticized our opposition. Although many of our letters got published on the editorial page, we were not usually called for comment on WQED stories and had little success in getting our own announcements or disclosures covered. At that point, however, the terrain of the struggle had shifted to Washington, and we were able to generate our own evidence of public concern. Nevertheless, we never stopped pitching.

Talk Radio: Staying on Message

When talk radio calls, the challenge is to stay "on message." Don't get distracted by questions or comments from the host or callers that put you on the defensive or lead you down a blind alley. Of course, this is fairly easy to do if your group organizes to call in when you are on, with questions that set you up to deliver your message. We did this and it worked like a charm.

Many times, however, the opportunity comes unexpectedly and leaves no time for such preparation. In October 1993, for instance, Sally Kalson of the *Post-Gazette* revealed that WQED planned to broadcast a tribute to the H. J. Heinz family, founders of the Pittsburgh-based Fortune 500 corporation that makes "57 varieties" of condiments. In researching the project Kalson had uncovered many violations of the conflict-of-interest provisions of WQED's underwriting guidelines.

Two of the tribute's key producers were former press secretaries to the late Senator John Heinz. Worse, one of them was a recent WQED director of corporate communications now employed as a media consultant to the Heinz family. Moreover, the Heinz Endowment had recently contributed $2 million to WQED's capital campaign. Finally, at the time, Theresa Heinz,

John's widow, was considering a challenge to Representative Rick Santorum for the Republican Party's nomination for the vacant Senate seat. This latter concern raised a question of equal access in some people's minds.

When Sally Kalson called me for comment, I noted that WQED had declined to air the documentaries *Deadly Deception* and *The Panama Deception* on the grounds of alleged conflict of interest and violation of the station's standards of fairness and objectivity. In my view, the fact that the station would then turn around and use Heinz money to produce a laudatory film on the Heinz family proved that "WQED clearly has a double standard with respect to what they show and don't show and the reasons they give for their decisions." In Kalson's subsequent story, PBS spokesperson Karen Doyne was quoted as saying, "Every case is a judgment call. The guidelines are a framework, but the bottom line is human judgment."

The next day I got a call from a WTAE producer asking me if I would be a guest on local host Ann Devlin's radio talk show to discuss this matter. I agreed, assuming that the producer knew of my interest in the subject and would so inform Devlin. I was introduced on the air and Devlin then asked me to comment on whether broadcasting the Heinz program would be unfair to Republican senatorial candidate Rick Santorum. When I responded that the important issue for me was fairness and diversity in public television programming, this shift of topic baffled Devlin, who protested that she didn't understand what I was talking about. Neither did she ask me a question to resolve her confusion.

At one point, a caller made the usual claim of liberal bias on public broadcasting, citing as evidence that he had often heard this complaint when he fund-raised over the phone for WQED. Devlin said that since I claimed one thing and the caller claimed the opposite, there was no making sense of the issue of bias on the station. Devlin then tried to move me back to where she wanted me, but I responded that not all opinions are equal and proceeded to cite the evidence of several FAIR studies on the issue. Her exasperation was audible. I was treated rudely, but I knew that this was part of the game. I had a chance to get our message out and I took it by piggybacking on an issue that had been framed by the dominant political assumptions and expanding it.

Recruiting Members

To recruit activists, we also publicized our campaign at forums sponsored by other movements. In addition, we planned a major event for September

1993—a "Banned by PBS" film premiere featuring two films that had won Academy Awards for "best documentary" but been denied a showing on PBS and WQED: *Deadly Deception: General Electric, Nuclear War, and Our Environment* (1991) and *The Panama Deception* (1993).

As the theme of our recruitment drive, I borrowed a slogan from the film *Network:* "We're mad as hell [about corporate control of PBS and QED] and we're not going to take it anymore." I identified us as a "grassroots watchdog" group seeking to "put the public interest back into public broadcasting." I cited our accomplishments and listed our issues—board election by subscribers; board meetings publicly announced, with minutes and financial records open for review; more representative programming; and a truly representative community advisory board. The film event increased our mailing list to three hundred names, and more than a hundred people signed our petitions calling on WQED and PBS to stop censoring controversial programs. We netted eleven hundred dollars and recruited twenty new participants to our regular meetings. Slowly through such actions are movements built.

WQED'S Story: Bad Guys Gone, Good Guys in Charge

Over the next few months, the elites in control of QED moved to frame their financial scandal as partly an accident caused by market forces beyond their control, partly bad judgment and miscommunication by the former CEO of QED Communications, Lloyd Kaiser. Their complicity, they alleged, was only in not acting quickly enough to limit the damage. No one, especially not QED board chair Elsie Hillman, offered to explain why the problems were allowed to fester for eighteen months after the station's basic problems were first exposed in the three-part *Post-Gazette* series of 1991.

In response to that initial exposé, Hillman had acknowledged the need to "balance the budget," expressed confidence that the community would support the station, and stated, "We are very committed to the current administration and the course they've laid out." In June 1993, shortly after the second wave of scandal had broken, Hillman allowed that the board was "not happy" when informed of the large cash-in insurance payments made to top QED executives because they had "to be concerned about [WQED's] image." A bit later, in August 1993, Hillman said, "I just think there weren't proper procedures for oversight"; however, she protested, it was not the board's role "to get into hands-on day-to-day operations." Later still, at a September 1993 QED board meeting, Hillman conceded, "I'm partly responsible. We should have been more vigilant." But, she claimed, "we were late coming to the problem. Boards and auditors only know what is told to them by management." Hillman also revealed a rather casual operation in which Lloyd Kaiser "was only charged with breaking even on operations. . . . If we needed new equipment, the board of directors would have a capital fund drive."

In January 1994, Hillman told the *Post-Gazette*, "I feel I was more trusting [with the station's financial office]; maybe I should have been more vigilant." To the *Wall Street Journal* a month later she said, "It wasn't that the wool was pulled over our eyes, but that I wasn't looking at the right things." Despite her disclaimers, Hillman left no doubt about who was in charge. It was at this point that she asked for Kaiser's resignation and, at the June 15, 1993, board meeting, unilaterally disbanded all board committees (acknowledging casually that it was "undemocratic") and announced that she would be proposing a sweeping restructuring.

As part of this effort, the strategy of QED's acting CEO, Don Korb, was to control all information about the organization, despite complaints from the press and the public. In apparent defiance of FCC regulations, he advised me that even board members were entitled only to materials relevant to a motion that they are called on to approve. At the same time, he sought to present himself as a reformer whom people could trust with their money. In a May 21 press interview, Korb claimed, "We did our first meaningful strategic planning ever. We really looked at our strengths and weaknesses."

At the September 1993 board meeting—under increasing scrutiny from us and the press—members were clearly distressed. Thrift Drug CEO Robert Hannan said to Korb, "I hope in the future your organization keeps us informed." Gerald Voros of Ketchum Advertising asked, "Why not give us the monthly report the finance committee gets?" Long-time board member and Hillman friend Diana Janetta echoed, "We're entitled to know." Voros added, "Mellon Bank is not very happy and they're very strong." The *Tribune-Review* reported that Janetta had asked Hillman and Korb to draft a statement "promising truthfulness in further management dealings," but apparently she was already willing to go on record with the statement that "communication is going to be better in the future." The *Post-Gazette* made no note of board dissatisfaction at all, although this was the only known occurrence of QED board members criticizing management at an open meeting.

Heavy personal lobbying and a "them against us" damage control strategy worked to keep the board in line. As usual, the media were a convenient target. At the QED board meeting of December 6, 1993, Don Korb complained that membership contributions were down because "the media tends to print negatives. . . . They continue to talk about the past and not about what we're doing now." "We're beginning to tell our story," he went on. "We control a magazine, radio station and two TV stations. . . . We will tell what's happening." One of the board members piped in, "We should put out a factual communication with a positive spin" to the media.

In January 1994, the *Wall Street Journal* ran a long feature on the station detailing its woes. The story quoted Lloyd Kaiser to the effect that WQED's problems simply reflected "the precarious position of public TV nationally." In the main, however, the story suggested that the station's problems were due primarily to the national ambitions, fiscal misjudgments, and lifestyle excesses of Kaiser and his top aide, Tom Skinner (for example, world travels to scope out sights for *National Geographic* shoots, working retreats at a nearby ski lodge, fancy Christmas parties, and the like).

In November 1994, the *Tribune-Review* ran a large series on QED's problems in which Don Korb charged that "Kaiser didn't see the problems until it was too late. Better financial briefings [might] have allowed the board to detect the problems sooner." He also blamed Kaiser for "telling the board he was optimistic that other big funding could be found," and asserted that if he had been "running the ship," he "would have cut expenses sooner." Kaiser countered that if anyone had deceived the board, it was Korb: "The board knew precisely the station's financial position all the time and I kept the board fully informed. Mr. Korb decided what would be reported to his committee and the form in which it was presented. Anything Korb wanted, he got. The board was supreme under his direction." Everyone else contacted for the story refused to comment.

Korb claimed that the board's finance committee did not receive reports directly from the finance officer, but from the CEO, implying that such reports were doctored to mislead the board. I do not know where the truth might lie here, but given Korb's ten years as chair of QED's finance committee, his claims of ignorance are no more excusable than those of board chair Elsie Hillman. The problem was clearly structural. The board had failed to protect the public interest by exercising proper oversight over management practices.

At the time, one former board member advised the *Wall Street Journal*, "I'm not sure how much any board member—even the officers—was aware of the nuts and bolts of what was going on over there. It was a big operation with a big board, and authority gets a little bit fragmented." A member of the finance committee told me that he and his colleagues didn't have the expertise to challenge management's reassurances about future revenues. In response to my follow-up question, he acknowledged that they could have sought outside professional consultation, but he shrugged this off as too much time and trouble. An African-American member of the board confided to me, "With so many big shots in the room I felt sure they knew what they were doing." Besides, another board member added, "they are many and we are few and we have no real power. They will decide who is the next CEO and that person will decide on staff."

Embezzlement Cover-up

In October 1993, reporters Valerie Reitman from the *Wall Street Journal* and Roger Stuart from the *Post-Gazette* met with me to research stories on WQED. Both showed particular interest in the anonymous letters the Accountability Project had received alleging embezzlement at the station. I had finally found an informant who was willing to talk for the record, but it was unclear how close she was to some of the alleged crimes. She gave me another source, but I had yet to contact that person, and other people I spoke to expressed concern about reprisals from the corporate leaders who controlled WQED.

Just two days after my meetings with the reporters, Don Korb called a press conference to announce that WQED had hired a Pittsburgh law firm to investigate "rumors" of "inappropriate" and "improper" business practices, like "personal work" being done "for certain executives of QED by QED employees on company time." My informant had identified one staff member who had done such work. He was one of those victimized by the mass firings, she said, but he had advised her that he would soon be back on the payroll because he had done personal work for one of the executives and he had that over them. Sure enough, he was quickly rehired.

Earlier that same month, on October 1, 1993, the station announced the end of the twenty-two-year tradition of the "Great TV Auction." Korb and Hillman claimed that this traditional fund-raising project consumed too much staff time and had become less profitable. Instead, the station was preparing a direct-mail sweepstakes featuring on-air promotions that would include as prizes items like a new Saab, and it would also put more effort into its annual "Priceless Playthings" live auction of luxury items for wealthy patrons.

Meanwhile, eager to dispel the "cloud hanging over WQED," Don Korb promised that the board would take all appropriate action and make the report of the investigation public. "Our intent is to cause the public to realize there was no wrongdoing or, if there was, that appropriate action has been taken," he announced. "There is no possibility that it [the report] will hide something. We've lost some of the trust and we have to earn it back. You can't earn it back if you try to cover things up." The attorney chosen to conduct the investigation, J. Alan Johnson, was a personal associate of Elsie Hillman. I was informed that WQED paid Johnson $30,000 for the job.

In January the *Wall Street Journal* article was published. There was no mention of any wrongdoing. I called Valerie Reitman, who told me she had followed up on my leads and confirmed some of the charges; however, she explained, her editor had deleted all such references because he wanted the piece to "conform" to an article run the previous day on PBS station problems generally. I asked Reitman if she would share with me what she had discovered. She refused. I then called the *Post-Gazette*'s Roger Stuart, who said that his editor had asked him to drop the story within a couple days of the assignment. In response to my questions, he told me he had not called anyone whose name I had given him.

A year passed. In October 1994, there was word that the law firm's report was completed but that the new QED CEO, George Miles, was sitting on it. Finally, on June 23, 1995, some twenty months after the original press conference, new WQED board chair Jim Roddey gave the press an official release and asked them to leave the room. He then summarized the report's findings for his board.

The report concluded that all charges were "baseless" except for a discrepancy of $10,000 related to executive expense, taxes, and severance pay. Hillman's personal lawyer and friend Wendell Freeland had deposed all those involved in the investigation. No copies of the report were given to the board. Board member Allen Kukovich told me he had requested one at the meeting, but that Roddey had dismissed the report as "old news" and said, "We don't want to get into this." Kukovich asked what he should tell his constituents if questioned about the matter. Roddey told him to refer them to Elsie Hillman or to him. Hillman told the press, "It was really a matter of bookkeeping adjustments."

I later spoke to the reporter who covered the meeting and wrote up WQED's press release for her paper. She was not going to pursue the matter further; she assumed that no one would be willing to talk and that hard evidence about the alleged "improper business practices" would be difficult to come by. Over the next two or three years I referred to the buried report several times with reporters. Not only did the report stay buried, but so did all of my references to it.

As for fund-raising, WQED's 1996 "Priceless Playthings" auction featured a tropical theme and offered an "expedition through exotic food stations, open bars, and live music" in addition to the auction itself. Also in 1996, WQED hosted an event at the Carnegie Museum that it called the "For the Love of Elsie Celebration," featuring "fun, food, music, and dancing" for $150 per person. That same year, WQED named its main meeting room the Elsie Hilliard Hillman Room. In 1997, "Priceless Playthings" was themed "Black Tie and Denim" and, according to the society page report, was set with "wooden fences, rustic barrel-and-plank bars complete with an Absolut Vodka Luge, road kill and bales of hay with the 'black tie' room of soft lighting, Oriental rugs and chandeliers." There was a "festive mix of gourmet food stations," cool jazz in the black-tie room and a dance band in the denim room—all for $150 per person. The auction of playthings included "a Leer jet trip to New York City for a fashion consultation with designer Mary McFadden, a 1997 Saab 900SE convertible, a calla lily diamond brooch, [and] a 14-carat yellow gold cigar cutter."

The direct mail went out under the theme "The QED Sweepstakes: Dreams Come True." It solicited contributions to the station with the lure "You could win a new, 1994 Saab 900 SE, FREE shopping sprees worth $5,000, FREE VIP trips to Europe, or even FREE FOOD FOR A YEAR from Giant Eagle."

After a two-year hiatus, the "Great TV Auction" again became a fixture on WQED. No reporters asked how the station solved the previously alleged problems of too much staff time or declining profits. Certainly no one questioned the elitist and materialistic values that permeated station fundraising for noncommercial public broadcasting.

Mano a Mano with the General Manager

At a December 1993 meeting of the Pittsburgh Society of Professional Journalists, labor historian Russ Gibbons set up a debate between WQED-TV general manager Mark Smuckler and me on the topic "Is There a Future for Public Television?" Smuckler and I each spoke and then responded to questions from moderator Bob Mayo of WTAE-AM and the audience. The event was covered by *In Pittsburgh* and the *Tribune-Review*.

Smuckler and I differed sharply on issues of program diversity and gov-

ernance reform. He defended the station's four hours a week of business programs, like *Wall $treet Week*, as "not just for business people, but for anyone
who wants to invest." In response, I pointed out that at the time only about
6 percent of the American public bought or sold stock through a broker every
year. I emphasized that we at the Accountability Project were not calling for
cancellation of *Wall $treet Week*, but for balancing it with shows of interest
to workers, like *We Do the Work*. Smuckler argued that the market was weak
for public affairs shows. As evidence, he said that *Tongues Untied*, a documentary about gay black men, had got about a hundred calls, half negative
and half positive. In contrast, switching one of the station's children's programs had generated three hundred calls. Moreover, he claimed that coverage of controversial issues on *The Editors* and other locally produced public
affairs shows "get only a weak public response."

In the course of the debate, Smuckler conceded that there was "probably
not . . . enough diversity" on WQED but stated flatly, "We are not going to
cede control over programming decisions to outside special interest groups."
I asked him whether he was calling working people a special interest group.
He did not respond.

As for subscriber election of the WQED board, Smuckler called it a "stu-
pid idea," warning that it would result in the kind of personal quarreling for
which the Pittsburgh City Council was notorious. I criticized the present
board for being "very provincial" and called for more "diversity."

After the debate, the news manager at KQV-Radio approached me,
scoffed at WQED's wastefulness (for instance, sending copies of their videocassettes to radio stations), and invited me to appear on his station anytime.

Reforming the Station's Bylaws

As part of the promised restructuring of QED, in June 1993 board chair Elsie
Hillman designated a corporate governance committee to review and revise
the station's bylaws. While this might have been just a strategy to control
the damage of the scandals and restore public confidence, I still saw it as an
opportunity to learn—and perhaps to have an impact. I accepted Hugh Nevin's invitation to participate.

The committee consisted of fourteen members: three from QED's
board of directors (from law, banking, and academia), including committee
chair Nevin; another bank executive and his invited friend, a vice president
and general manager of the ABC affiliate in town; four heads of nonprofit
foundations; a lawyer; a private school headmaster; the executive director of

the YWCA; and me. Katherine Blue, WQED's general counsel, also participated, handling communications and reporting back to Elsie Hillman.

The committee met six times over six months. Attendance averaged
about nine or ten of the fourteen each time. The firm of Cohen and Grigsby,
where Hugh Nevin practiced, provided the site. Only four members attended all the meetings—Nevin, his colleague David Kalson, Katherine
Blue, and me.

We also broke down into four subcommittees: one to outline the func-
tions and responsibilities of the board; one to outline the size, committee
structure, and selection process of the board; one to gather information
about other public television stations (specifically Boston and San Francisco); and one to decide the role of a new community advisory board. I
served on the last three subcommittees, which met a total of five times and
communicated by mail, fax, or phone in between.

Three members submitted materials and/or memos for the corporate
governance committee's consideration. I did this twice. I also responded to
all drafts of the bylaws in development. In short, I was an active member,
and my persistence was rewarded on some key issues even if I lost on our
main goal of getting a subscriber-elected board.

WQED's Missing Mission

A 1986 memo from Ceci Sommers, then WQED-FM station manager, to
CEO Lloyd Kaiser reveals lack of mission to have been an issue at WQED
for some time: "We defend ourselves with lofty statements about 'mission'
even though we go where the money is like everyone else. . . . As recently as
last year's retreat, there was no mission statement for Channel 13."

Five years later, the minutes of a 1991 corporate board retreat included
such strategy and action plans as "creating opportunities for underwriters
as we study their special needs," "start marketing SWAT teams to major
companies," "better research . . . to help target underwriter needs," "try to
give underwriters more," "attempt anew to add underwriter's name to
promo," and "add commercial statement to post-production cassettes."
There was even a proposal to "explore" underwriting specifically from "Toy-
ota, Nissan and Rangos."

By 1993, WQED's mission statement still included only one simple reference to providing "suitable educational and cultural television programs."
There were no specifications for values, goals, standards, or constituencies

to be served, and consequently there could be no basis for strategic planning or performance evaluation for these.

In its 1994 final report, the corporate governance committee (CGC) "strongly" recommended that "the Board define the mission of QED and provide a clear statement of purpose and strategic direction for QED." Further on, the board is proposed to be accountable for "ensuring [the mission's] implementation, measuring success against the mission, and regularly reviewing and adjusting the mission."

The CGC was provided with the bylaws for eight other nonprofit corporations, including public broadcasting stations in Boston, Florida, New York, Philadelphia, and San Francisco. The differences between these and that of WQED were dramatic and easily explained how so many miscommunications, bad decisions, and abuses had been permitted.

The QED board was enormous—fifty-seven members on paper; it was so huge, in fact, that no one could feel any personal responsibility for participating. Members nominated their own successors without soliciting public input, so the board was effectively insulated from the broader community. There were no directives in the bylaws for diversity of membership. Of the fifty-seven members, there were only twelve women and four African Americans. There were no representatives of organized labor. And while directors were required to leave after two consecutive three-year terms, there were so many exceptions to these limits that several key figures had been around for many years. These long-standing board and committee members socialized the new members to business as usual.

The National Charities Information Bureau sets ethical standards for nonprofit corporations and recommends that the CEO be the only paid staff member on the board of such an organization. However, WQED's bylaws did not prohibit board membership for management. WQED's CEO and four vice presidents served on the board, and fifteen different staff people sat on the board's eighteen committees. This presented a situation rife with obvious conflicts of interest. According to Brian Foss, vice president of the Independent Sector, a national lobby for tax-exempt corporations, "You can't have arms-length transactions [i.e., no personal gain] when there are vested interests." He concluded, "No one would defend having another staff member on the board." Wendell Freeland, Hillman's friend and personal attorney, disagreed; in his view, it was all right to have a few staff members if the board was big enough.

There were only four regularly scheduled WQED board meetings per year, and they typically lasted only an hour and a half over lunch. This compared with six to twelve meetings per year for the other boards studied. Despite the infrequency of the meetings at WQED, typically fewer than half the board members attended, and there was no penalty for missing meetings. At other stations, directors were removed if they failed to attend a majority of meetings. Katharine Blue even admitted that some people had been invited to sit on the board with the assurance they would not have to attend *any* meetings.

Attendance really didn't matter, because only one-fifth of all "directors" were required for a quorum. In addition, only five days' notice was required to call a meeting. Hypothetically, the chair and the CEO could call a meeting at the beginning of the week and sit down at the end of the week with only nine other directors, four of whom could be staff, and make any official decision they wanted.

Such manipulation never was necessary, though, because the general meetings were only a formality. The real power rested with an executive committee "composed of the officers of the corporation and other board members" that in between board meetings "shall possess and may exercise all the powers" of the board in directing and managing the corporation. This committee was composed of sixteen people, four of whom were staff; it included only four women and no minorities.

The executive committee discussed and prepared recommendations on almost all the important matters that came before the board. Only one-third of this committee (six members) was required for a quorum. The board rarely discussed its recommendations; at that stage voting was a mere formality. I even saw voice votes in which there was no call for nays or abstentions. Given the strong alliance between board chair Hillman and CEO Kaiser, manipulation of the board appeared to be all too easy.

This undemocratic board structure and undue influence by management made certain outcomes rather predictable. *In Pittsburgh* reported, for instance, that there were more officers and managers at WQED than there were office and clerical workers; yet when the station laid off seventy-four employees over 1992–93, only one of the forty officer or management positions was cut.

What We Got, What We Didn't

While the QED Accountability Project lost within the CGC on the issue of subscriber election, the proposed changes in the corporation's bylaws were substantial. The thrust of these changes would ultimately increase the diversity of the board and the accountability of management to its members.

The new bylaws called for "diversity of occupation, race, gender, age and geographic community of residence." Further, to "ensure such diversity, nominations are to be actively solicited by the [Nominations] Committee through *Pittsburgh Magazine* and other media." (The new twenty-five-member board announced in May 1994 was proportionately more diverse. There were eight women, three African-Americans, and one representative of organized labor.)

According to the new proposals, members could still serve two consecutive three-year terms, but would have to be off the board for at least two years before becoming eligible for membership again. The CEO of the corporation was to be the only member of management permitted to sit on the board. Employees would still be permitted on committees, but so would non–board members from the community. These provisions were designed to dilute the potential for conflict of interest.

The number of board meetings was to be increased to six, fewer than the nine recommended but more than the previous four. Fifteen days' notice was required to call a meeting. A member would have to attend a majority of meetings (four) or be asked to resign. Also, a majority would be required to constitute a quorum.

The number of committees was to be reduced from eighteen to six, and they were to be made more functional. The executive committee was to include the four board officers, chairs of the six committees, and up to four other members subject to approval by the full board. Its powers would still be great, but more circumscribed by the full board. (In practice, the new executive committee was composed of ten members, including three women and one African American.)

In fall 1993, acting CEO Don Korb announced that a weekend retreat was planned for the new year, to consider the "strategic direction of the corporation" and vote on the proposed new bylaws. After eight months of work, I very much wanted to be there to observe the final discussion and decision, but Korb told me the retreat would be closed to the public. There was still one more barrier to overcome.

FCC regulations require that all public broadcasters advertise meetings of a station's governing board, community advisory board, and any committees on the air, in the radio, in the television schedules of local newspapers, and in the station's program guide. All meetings must be open to the public except under certain circumstances recognized by law. In such cases, there must be a written statement of explanation for closing the meeting. At our request, attorney William Wekselman wrote a letter to Korb (November 4, 1993) citing FCC law and asking for "notices of such meetings or, where appropriate, explanations of closed meetings." We also asked that announcements of future "meetings and retreats" be sent to the Accountability Project.

Less than a week later our attorney got a response from Korb. He refused to send future meeting notices and asserted that the board retreat was not a "'meeting' as that term is defined by Section 397(5) of the Communications Act and as such will not be open to the public." He instructed us further to "watch the Pittsburgh *Post-Gazette* and our stations" for notice of future board and committee meetings. In response to my follow-up question, Katharine Blue told me that such notices would be found in the legal notices section of the *Post-Gazette*.

On November 29, Wekselman replied, quoting from the Federal Communications Commission Act that indeed "deliberations" of "a governing body" to "take action" on "matters relating to public broadcasting" constituted a meeting. He explained, "It would not be permissible to hold all substantive discussions behind closed doors and then hold an open meeting merely for the formality of voting." He warned that if necessary we would be considering legal action. Korb then called to invite me to meet with him personally after the board meeting of December 6. We talked for ninety minutes or more. We agreed to a compromise whereby representatives of the Accountability Project would be allowed to observe just that segment of the board retreat dealing with discussion and approval of the proposed new by-laws. (One reason I agreed to this compromise is that we had brought in another attorney, Jay Hornack, to research what legal action might be available to us. Hornack had advised us that there is no precedent for a private legal action against a public broadcasting station for noncompliance with federal law. That is the province of the FCC.)

I perused the legal notices section of the *Post-Gazette* for weeks, until the date of the retreat; there was no mention of any meeting whatsoever. I called Don Korb, who advised me to come to the retreat at noon. Retired Presbyterian minister Dick Sigler and Citizen Action staff member Brian Rieck accompanied me.

General counsel Katharine Blue barred the door. She advised me that they were running very late. I was angry for not being called about the delay and having to wait for what turned out to be two and a half hours. I complained that I had read the paper every day and not seen any notice of the meeting. She said the meeting had been mentioned several times on WQED-FM and posted in the *Tribune-Review*. I pointed out that the *Tribune-Review* had a very small circulation in metropolitan Pittsburgh and asked her whether she really felt this constituted sufficient notice to the public. She said she did.

The Board Votes on the Bylaws

The February board retreat was attended by only twenty-two of the board's fifty-seven members. Hugh Nevin moderated the discussion of the new by-laws recommendations. Apparently, board members had been sent copies of the governance committee's report and some had called him for comment. Complaints that nine meetings a year were too many quickly led to the proposal to change this to six. I and another governance committee member who also served on the board protested, but the leadership had their arguments already prepared. Nevin announced that he was "flip-flopping" on the issue and the change passed by voice vote unanimously.

The report our committee had submitted stated that the committee had rejected public election of the QED board but suggested that "solicitation of nominations through *Pittsburgh Magazine* and other media . . . would open up the election process . . . and generate broader public interest in QED and its Board [which] should broadly represent the various communities . . . served by QED." Unfortunately, in the final bylaws document this language was reduced to a brief reference to solicitation "through *Pittsburgh Magazine* and otherwise," and in subsequent years not even the magazine was used to solicit nominations.

During the February meeting I raised the issue of insufficient public notice of meetings. Moderator Hugh Nevin joked that if I didn't listen to (classical station) WQED-FM, I shouldn't be considered interested in WQED's reform, and Korb claimed with a straight face that they had posted notice in the *Tribune-Review* rather than the *Post-Gazette* because the station had money problems and it was cheaper—"I am sensitive concerning costs."

I pressed the issue, stating that the corporate governance committee had recommended promotion of board meetings in a broad diversity of media, including African-American radio stations. A member of the board asked whether notices weren't routinely posted in *Pittsburgh Magazine*. Elsie Hillman responded that such notices appear "only when the timing of the meeting and publication are right." She then turned to me and asked whether I ever had the experience of calling the station to ask for the date of a board meeting and not being told. I paused a long time and answered, "No, but I'm already interested. The problem is how to make members of the general public aware and interested." At this point, board member Gerald Voros, bringing the discussion to a close, stated, "We should make every effort to publish meeting dates widely and, if that isn't done, the board will express its concern."

In 1998, WQED's public relations director, George Hazimanolis, acknowledged that board meeting dates are posted, without agenda, only in the *Pittsburgh Magazine,* with perhaps three mentions on WQED-FM a week in advance of the meeting. He also said that committee meetings are never posted. In a March interview with *Current* editor Steve Behrens, WQED's Washington attorney, Lawrence Miller, made the station's position very clear: while CPB itself has open meeting requirements, the FCC doesn't enforce them. Obviously, WQED felt it could violate these regulations with impunity. In point of fact, however, the CPB issues millions of dollars of community service grants to all member stations and could make them conditional on compliance with its regulations. CPB, however, is complicit with the FCC in not enforcing the law.

The governance committee's final "specific recommendation" to the QED board called for "a Transition Committee, consisting of a diverse group of directors, non-directors, and staff which might work with an outside consultant . . . to ensure that the changes adopted are actually implemented and to help QED cope with the sweep of these complex and far-reaching changes." We even recommended two firms that specialized in consulting to nonprofit boards.

At the close of the meeting, Elsie Hillman announced she would establish "an implementation committee to decide how soon, fast, well and orderly we can make this transition." I asked if that meant the board approved the recommendation for the outside consultant and the independent transition committee. Don Korb objected that the station couldn't afford such expense. I replied that it would cost far less than the $30,000 being spent on a law firm to investigate rumors of fiscal impropriety and be far more important to the future of QED.

When Hillman made it personal, stating that she hoped we had "confidence in the board to make these changes," I persisted, asserting that good intentions were not enough. Even organizations willing to change need help in unlearning old behaviors and learning new behaviors appropriate to changing relationships. In the final analysis, the goal was to make management more accountable to the station's board of directors, community advisory board, and subscribers. Simply choosing a new board would not get that done.

Hillman sought to close the discussion by stating, "I'm comfortable that the board has the commitment to discharge its responsibility." She then announced that "an implementation committee will examine the bylaws and make the final recommendations for the June board meeting. I'll be calling you. We have a lot of work to do."

I replied that the job was a lot more complicated than apparently anyone realized and volunteered my services to the implementation committee. Don Korb nodded assent, but Hillman brushed me off: "I'll have to decide later. There are a lot of people who want to serve on the committee." Not willing to let it go, I replied, "I have a lot of relevant experience and I don't see a long line of people who want to serve."

This last exchange was reported by the press, along with my prescient reservation: "There's a lot of ambiguity in these provisions. If they simply leave the same people who've been running things in the past in charge of these reforms, I'll be very concerned about real change occurring, especially in making the board more open and responsive to broad community participation."

Chapter 5

Old Wine in New Bottles:
Reproducing the Station Culture

Many people congratulated me on my role in promoting the bylaws changes at WQED. What we had accomplished was to bring WQED into closer conformity with standard practice in the nonprofit world. However, all of these changes were on paper.

Having managed the bylaws revision and controlled the transition process, Elsie Hillman and her colleagues continued on their path of repairing the station's reputation without really changing its structure. When she introduced the new board, on May 26, 1994, a majority of its members, thirteen of twenty-five, were holdovers from the old board. The executive committee also had a majority, six of eleven, who were holdovers from the old board. Proponents of accountability and reform had only two potential allies on the new board, United Steelworkers of America internal communications director Gary Hubbard and state representative Allen Kukovich, both of whom called themselves "token liberals" and asked me to consult to them on how to be effective in their new roles.

WQED chose Gary Hubbard to take their board's long-vacant "labor seat," finally filled in response to our campaign's pressure. Hubbard was from the "labor business" school; he admired President Clinton and was wary of labor activists. His pitch on organized labor was that people should respect it because it was good for business—it disciplined the labor force and facilitated management. Better yet, Hubbard added, organized labor was a big business. The Steelworkers serviced 600,000 members across a great diversity of job categories, with a large professional staff housed in its own modern high-rise overlooking the confluence of Pittsburgh's three rivers. Hubbard felt that if more people understood organized labor in that way, it would get more respect.

A graduate of Kent State University and Duquesne University Law School, Allen Kukovich had recently been elected to his ninth term in the Pennsylvania House of Representatives. He was majority policy chairman from 1989 through 1992, and had received more than seventy-five awards and citations for his legislative work. Some of his major bills aimed to save homes from mortgage foreclosure, prevent elder abuse, stop medical overcharges, provide health care for uninsured children, fund community legal services, and establish government ethics standards.

The public interest community had helped Kukovich early in his career, and he stayed true to those ideals. (Later, in 1996, he won a seat in the state senate.) Kukovich considered his appointment to the board a fluke: he had met Elsie Hillman at a Planned Parenthood event and she had personally invited him. Kukovich proved to be the one independent thinker in the bunch and an invaluable asset to our struggle.

WQED's CEO Search

Meanwhile, Elsie Hillman appointed James C. Roddey, a QED board member since 1987 and chair of the strategic direction committee, to chair the search committee for a new CEO. The sixty-one-year-old Roddey had grown up in North Carolina, graduated from Texas Christian University, served in the Marine Corps, and worked for Ted Turner. He had moved to Pittsburgh in 1978 to get rich in the billboard business. By 1994, Roddey was managing general partner of Allegheny Media, an equity and management firm specializing in communications; president of Star Cable Associates; chairman of International Sports Marketing; president of the Bantry Group, a health services provider; president of Wexford Health Services, Inc.; president of Business Records Management; and chairman of Production Masters, Inc. He also chaired or served on the boards of numerous organizations.

In a front-page *Post-Gazette* profile in 1998, Roddey was quoted as saying that he liked to be the boss and acknowledged that his wife called him an "obsessed" "control freak," a characterization he disputed. (When he led the committee to select the University of Pittsburgh chancellor, I am told, faculty and student input was not solicited and largely ignored. And after a strong editorial boost from the *Post-Gazette*, Roddey was named to the board of the Allegheny County Sanitation Authority, whereupon he immediately contested the chair.)

Roddey tightly controlled the process of choosing the next CEO of WQED. The original search committee had seventeen members, including four staff representatives and Bob Norman of the QED Accountability Project. (I had lobbied Hillman for Norman's inclusion, both personally and in the press.) A professor at the Graduate School of Public and International Affairs of the University of Pittsburgh, Norman was certainly qualified. However, as some other members of the board made clear to him, he was not one of them.

The committee decided to enlist an executive search firm. Open postings of the position, of course, would have been more democratic, since they invite the widest possible range of applicants, including women and minorities not in the "old boys" network. A search firm solicits through private networks and screens applications before the board can see them; it seemed to me that the $75,000 or more cost should have been a deterrent to an organization whose acting CEO said he was reluctant to spend an extra few dollars to post notice of a board meeting in the main daily. However, as Bob Norman advised me, Roddey had offered to raise the money personally and so it was done.

Early on, the Accountability Project had sent a memo arguing that the search for a new CEO should wait until the corporate governance committee had determined the new governing bylaws and the board had defined the station's mission. As Richard Ingram, an expert on nonprofit corporations, advises, prior to a search process the board should "review the organization's statement of mission and purposes and ensure its adequacy" so as to "establish priorities for the next period of executive leadership." The search committee did not respond to this memo. In addition, at one point I discovered that several vice presidents and managers had been conducting meetings to draft their own version(s) of a "corporate strategic plan" for WQED. Apparently, the board of directors was not involved in this process. I wrote to Hugh Nevin to express my concern. He did not respond.

Interviewed almost a year later, near the end of 1994, new CEO George Miles replied to a reporter's question about WQED's mission with "There's probably a mission statement that exists somewhere and one of the things we're going to do is develop a whole strategic plan." Mission obviously played no role in the search committee's work. Instead, they started by developing the job description and choosing the search firm.

Bob Norman's assessment of the search committee was that they were a bunch of fat cats "out of touch with ordinary Pittsburgh." They drove luxury automobiles (Jaguars, Mercedes), took island vacations, and ridiculed the $45,000 salary accepted by the new head of the Salivation Army and his wife. Only one member of the committee routinely asked whether the search firms employed African Americans and at what level, a question Norman said made many firms nervous. According to Norman, there was "no talk of unions ever." To the press, Norman said, "I don't hear much talk about change, except to get things back on the rails—presumably the same old rails."

Indeed, the establishment had a corporate agenda. Jim Roddey stressed getting an executive with "turn-around experience" who could "restore an enterprise to profitability" especially by "producing something that can be sold." Don Korb was looking for a candidate "with experience in for-profit business somewhere in his career, and not 30 or 40 years ago." In contrast, in consultation with me, Norman argued for a candidate "with extensive background in effective public broadcast administration" capable of working with a "strengthened" community advisory board in making sure that programming was of "service to the community."

The list of search firms was narrowed down to four. One specialized in affirmative action choices and not-for-profit corporations, another specialized in public broadcasting, and a third was described by Norman as "young and aggressive and involved in all aspects of media." These were all rejected in favor of Hedrick and Struggles, Inc., a Chicago-based firm that specialized in corporate business, thought they could find someone with "turn-around" experience, and pushed the committee to think in terms of a higher, "more realistic" compensation package. Their fee was one-third of the CEO's first year cash compensation, plus out-of-pocket expenses. (In 1998, Hedrick and Struggles acquired Fenwick Partners to become the largest executive search firm in the nation.)

Elsie Hillman then advised that there would be a "paper cut" that would narrow candidates down to between fifteen and eighteen finalists. After some hedging, it was agreed that all members of the search committee would have access to the relevant paperwork. In April, however, Roddey announced that seventeen evaluators were too many and only a small subcommittee would be permitted to meet with candidates for their interviews. Hillman, Korb, Roddey, and executives from Heinz and Alcoa were in; Norman and all other community people were out.

Bob Norman later commented to the press, "We've been involved by virtue of the fact that we pushed from the outside and I think we've been treated accordingly." In fact, at the end of the process, Norman was kept in the dark until called on July 13, 1994, to attend the news conference scheduled that very day to announce the station's choice for CEO.

When Jim Roddey's work was done, Hillman appointed him to succeed her as chair of the board, a position he assumed without discussion.

Introducing George Miles

The board's choice, an African American named George C. Miles Jr., at first appeared to be a good compromise—but then they knew him and we didn't. He had degrees in accounting from Seton Hall and Farleigh Dickinson. During the civil rights and Vietnam era, from 1963 to 1969, he had spent six years with the Department of Defense Contract Audit Agency. This was followed by nine years with Touche Ross and Company (the accounting firm employed by WQED) and six years with Westinghouse Broadcasting operations, including two years at KDKA in Pittsburgh, where he had been business manager and comptroller.

Miles had moved to public broadcasting in 1984, when he became executive vice president and chief operating officer at WNET New York. WQED had offered Miles a salary of $180,000 plus $63,000 in benefits, only $15,000 less than the compensation package for Lloyd Kaiser that had once created such a stir, and well in excess of that of Frederick Breitenfeld, the CEO of WHYY Philadelphia, in the nation's fourth largest market.

An aggressive politician, the six-four, 250-pound Miles is a sight to behold as he works a large room, smiling broadly, shouting loudly, and pressing the flesh. The highest-ranking African American in public television, by 1998 he would become one of the most visible figures in the business: former board chair and a member of the Association of America's Public Television Stations (APTS) core working group developing a future governance proposal for public TV, member of the PBS board, and member of the CPB's issues and policies task force.

In short, Miles was and is a leader in the field. Throughout his reign at WQED he has been able to command support for his initiatives from the highest officials in public broadcasting—and so his policies and practices at WQED provide a good measure of the direction of the whole public broadcasting system.

Certainly, if the WQED search committee had examined Miles's record at WNET more critically, there would have been reason for them to be cautious about hiring him. WQED was a station that had gambled on remaining a national production center despite corporate cutbacks. Consequently, it had very little local programming, was deeply in debt, and had a bad public image for being wasteful. Since WQED board members were blaming management for hiding the corporation's fiscal problems from them, there was language in the job description such as "consistent with prudent budgetary considerations," "foster an open and participative style of management which promotes teamwork, individual empowerment and the sharing of ideas at all levels," and "rebuild the credibility of QED in the community and in banking circles."

WNET, where Miles had served for ten years, was one of the three top PBS national production centers. However, according to a 1992 survey of fifteen stations in ten major cities, it had absolutely no evening local programming. *New York Newsday* TV critic Marvin Kitman disparaged the station for spending millions to rehabilitate an "old flophouse" in Manhattan (marble walls and all) despite its New Jersey corporate address, while at the same time crying poverty and cutting local programs.

WNET was indeed in financial trouble. Between 1991 and 1993 the station laid off 129 of 279 employees. In 1994, it faced a deficit of $4 million to $8 million on a budget of $107 million. In March 1994, a concerned group of independent PBS producers wrote a letter to *Harper's* magazine claiming WNET was the worst of all stations for top-heavy staff and dearth of local programming produced.

Among the ideas to address WNET's debt, Miles had made at least two recommendations. One was to shut down WNET's production studio, home of the *MacNeil/Lehrer NewsHour* and *The Charlie Rose Show,* among others. His board rejected that. The other was to introduce a home shopping service on WNET after midnight, when the station was not broadcasting its own or PBS programs. Miles admits that the "FCC didn't think it was a good idea, and also, I think, members of the board didn't like it." In Kitman's assessment, "I think the record speaks for itself. WNET was in financial trouble before George Miles came, and it was still in financial trouble when he left. They're not building any statues to him here."

At Ceci Sommers's invitation, I attended the July 30 WQED picnic on Don Korb's horse-country estate, hoping to get a chance to meet Miles. I was sure that my reputation would precede me but naively hoped that I could open his mind with sincerity and a cooperative attitude. I talked with him about the Project's concern to improve local programming to address community issues. I offered him my support. He replied, "We can't please everybody." I would hear this comment from him more than a few times over the years.

Interviewed by the press just after this first encounter, I reflected, "I went away not knowing fully what [Miles] meant, but hoping he didn't mean he wouldn't try to please anybody. WNET [has] practically no local programming addressing community issues. We're hoping he recognizes that Pittsburgh has its own needs and the mission of QED must be different."

This quote provoked a call from Miles. We played telephone tag for several days, and I began to entertain the hope that he wanted to establish a dialogue with our group. When we finally connected, however, he criticized me for my comment about lack of local programming on WNET. He claimed otherwise, said I was not in a position to know and that my statement was "a disservice" to them and to him. He admonished me never to speak with the press about him again unless I called him first and got it from the horse's mouth. Then he whinnied like a horse.

Hired in July, Miles moved into his office in September and immediately began shaking things up with new commercial ventures and an employee gag order. He contracted with Fox and Scripps-Howard to produce for-profit programs like Fox's *Clubhouse*, the House and Garden Channel's *Jane Nugent's Garden Party*, and *Lucille's Car Care Clinic*. In an interview with the *Tribune-Review*'s Todd Gutnick, Miles said that such commercial partnerships were WQED's future. He also emphasized the importance of "multimedia enterprises, including transfer of its programs onto CD-ROM" and reestablishing WQED "as a national production center with a 'Web of Life' ecology program . . . and a documentary, 'Health in America'" to be aired nationally on PBS.

At about the same time, Miles issued a memo forbidding all employees from speaking with the press on penalty of "discipline up to and including dismissal," and when B. J. Leber was hired as QED communications director all communications had to go through her. A couple of years later, Greg Andorfer claimed he was fired for speaking to a reporter from the *Wall Street Journal* on behalf of a TV program he produced called *Frank's Garage*. Questioned by the press, Leber "did not respond" as to whether Andorfer's dismissal was "linked to violation of a company gag order."

Miles actively courted all board members in small meetings of one, two, and three at a time. He met privately with Gary Hubbard and Allen Kukovich. When Hubbard requested assignment to the strategic direction committee (as I had suggested), Miles replied, "Done." Hubbard was pleased, but I found it disturbing that Miles was already assuming that he controlled board assignments. Apparently trying to drive a wedge between us, he complained to Hubbard and Kukovich that I had given him a hard time at Korb's picnic.

In June 1995, under Miles's direction, WQED finally did issue a "Vision/ Mission Statement." The core mission statement read,

> Our Mission: To provide vital services to our community, audiences, supporters, customers and colleagues by:
> ▌ Listening and responding to their needs
> ▌ Producing and distributing high quality products
> ▌ Educating, enlightening and entertaining
> ▌ Being an integral part of the community
> ▌ Valuing diversity and demonstrating our respect for all.

This was pretty vague, but certainly a start. The next step would have been to develop a strategic action plan with operational criteria and timetables for evaluating performance relative to these general goals. This never happened. Neither was there any perceptible willingness on the part of the board to solicit community input on what their needs might be. Was the community being educated? Did WQED produce programs that responded to their needs? After a token first step toward meeting this recommendation from the corporate governance committee, the process of defining and implementing QED's mission stopped.

In March 1995, WQED management polled the board regarding its involvement, then summarized the responses of nineteen of its members. Nine wanted more presentations at board meetings, but only three had any topics to suggest for discussion. Only two felt the need for more "board dialogue," and even then it was only to "enforce commitment."

Of course, private mail surveys of individuals do not serve to provoke collective reflection on board members' mutual needs, perceptions, and responsibilities. The implicit message is that management is not really interested in members' voices. It would have been far better to raise these issues for general discussion at a special meeting. Even given this constraint, however, one can't help but be struck with the lack of imagination these responses betray. Like the musicians aboard the *Titanic,* this board seemed determined to play the same songs over and over while the station sank.

Community Advisory Board: Black Hole of Volunteer Energy

The Telecommunications Act of 1978 amended the original FCC Act of 1934 to require that all public broadcasters establish community advisory boards.

Congress believed that these boards could assist the stations in developing programs and policies that address the specialized educational and cultural needs of the communities that they serve. Corporation for Public Broadcasting regulations further state that the purpose of the community advisory board (CAB) is to provide for "effective public participation in planning and decision making."

The federal law requires stations to make "good-faith" efforts to ensure that community advisors fairly represent the ethnic and cultural makeup of the community and attend meetings regularly; CPB regulations require that the CAB be a body "distinct from the governing board"; and the CPB is prohibited from distributing funds to stations that do not comply with the community advisory board requirement.

WQED had conducted two CAB meetings in 1992, one in 1993. For the 1993 meeting, only thirteen of twenty-three members showed, and all but ten minutes of the hour-long session were taken up with staff presentations. As quoted in the *Tribune-Review* near the end of 1994, one 1993 participant said, "I don't know of any change in station policy that was a result of that meeting. I don't think [QED officials] were taking public opinion very seriously." Another said, "I wrote a memo afterward with my thoughts, but I never heard anything back. I don't think they were really interested."

In 1993, Hugh Nevin appointed a CGC subcommittee to meet with WQED staff to "brainstorm" structure for a new CAB. I consulted with Pat Rudebusch of the CPB, who sent me information about community advisory boards at stations in Boston, Chicago, New York, Los Angeles, San Francisco and Washington, D.C., and in the end I was given the opportunity to write the final draft of the recommended bylaws. The CGC's general recommendations emphasized that the CAB is "mandated by federal law," "is vital to the success of WQED," and should "be strengthened." The bylaws specifically called for a CAB of fifteen to twenty members appointed by the board for two-year terms, and stipulated that this group be diverse by "race, gender, age, and community of residence." Furthermore, "Leaders of public interest organizations, including organized labor and those involved in community service, should have substantial representation. Representatives of business and government also should be included." In order to achieve this diversity, nominations were to be "actively solicited by the Board through *Pittsburgh Magazine* and other communications media."

The CAB was to meet "at least four times per year." Its charge was to "advise the Board with respect to whether the programming and services of the Corporation are meeting the needs of the communities served by the

Corporation and . . . make such recommendations as it considers appropriate to meet such needs" to the board, which "shall consider such recommendations and, if approved, pass them on to the staff to develop and report back to the Board."

To concretize the connection to the board of directors while respecting the autonomy of the community advisory board, the corporate governance committee recommended that the chair of the CAB be elected by that body and not appointed by the QED board. This individual would then take a seat on the board of directors.

Still determined to work for change within the system, I moved the QED Accountability Project to survey, recruit, and select potential CAB candidates.

We asked each potential candidate to provide a detailed biographical statement and attend at least one Project meeting to discuss their candidacy. We wanted people who would stimulate community interest, represent new programming and service ideas to the station, and then generate community support for station initiatives. In short, if the system was going to be allowed to work, we wanted people who were willing and able to work within it.

We put forward seven candidates who met these criteria—three women and four men, two of whom were African-American. I wrote to Ceci Sommers in her new capacity as vice president of public relations that this was "not a slate" but rather seven "distinct individuals each of whom works and lives in a different community with potential for different outreach." In fact, this was true. Only two of us were acquainted with any of the others before coming to the Project. We included capsule resumés with our recommendations, which went forward in mid-June 1994—just as the new bylaws were being formally ratified and the new board of directors was being confirmed.

Immediately violating both CPB regulations and their own new bylaws, QED management appointed the future chair of the new CAB—Gwen Elliott, a middle-aged African-American female police commander—and gave her a seat on the board of directors. I asked around and was told she was a busy person, sat on many boards, and could not be counted on to challenge station authority even if the situation demanded it. She was, after all, a police commander.

I met Gwen Elliott at the same Korb estate barbecue where I met George Miles. Since she speculated that the committee could use all of our nominees, we expected a quick response to our submissions. However, months passed and we heard nothing. In November, the *Tribune-Review* ran a series of articles critical of the station, one of which focused on the CAB. (I had helped the reporters with their research and they repaid me by calling for my inclusion on the advisory board. Kukovich told me that Hubbard and he had lobbied for inclusion of our nominees.) I learned from the *Tribune-Review* reporters that the CAB was actually being chosen by a group that included Elsie Hillman, Don Korb, George Miles, Gwen Elliott, and Ceci Sommers. I called Sommers, who told me that Miles (who had taken office only two months earlier) would be the last one to sign off on the nominees. This, of course, also violated the new reforms. There was no active solicitation of candidates through the media and no formal input from the board, and the CEO was given final authority to choose who would represent the community.

The CAB selection process took seven months, and only three of our seven nominees were chosen, two of whom accepted—Billy Jackson, an African-American filmmaker, and I. There were no CAB meetings throughout 1994. Just before the end of the year, management got approval from the board of directors to amend the bylaws to expand the CAB from twenty to thirty, although the corporate governance committee had deliberately limited the CAB's size to maximize participation. B. J. Leber, who had just inherited Sommers's position, told me the station wanted "greater inclusiveness."

Eventually twenty-four people were appointed to the CAB, including Gwen Elliott as chair. In contrast to the male-dominated board of directors, the advisory board included eighteen women and six men. There were five African Americans. The first meeting was called for a Tuesday morning, one of only two days a week I had told WQED I could not attend during the academic year. I was free the other three weekdays, all evenings, and on weekends. I wrote to Leber and Elliott reminding them of this and advising them that I would have to send another Project representative. They were tentative about approving this, but as it turned out, Elliott's schedule required a change to Wednesday, so I was able to attend.

The first meeting of WQED's new community advisory board was held at the station on February 13, 1995, a full year after the board retreat to consider the new bylaws. By my count, only thirteen of twenty-four of those invited actually attended. We sat around a huge table that distanced us considerably from each other. As at many meetings to follow, presentations by station leaders took up most of the time, with occasional comment from committee members.

George Miles spoke excitedly about the station becoming "a real resource in the community." He said that "only one of ten listeners and viewers is a member of WQED, but if we can bring that up to two or three of ten, a lot of our problems will be over." Miles acknowledged that the station was also "dealing with some of our past sins." B. J. Leber joined in to acknowledge that "quite frankly, this organization has not connected enough with the community. And when it has connected, it has not always listened. Those days are over." This kind of populist rhetoric gave me hope that my plan for a more active CAB might have a chance.

Gwen Elliott said the CAB could become the "voice of the community." To the press and to us she asserted, "We're not just going to hold a few meetings and act like a rubber stamp. We're going to have some real input." She then promptly sabotaged the structural arrangement that would have allowed the CAB to have that input, by saying that she didn't want it "all on her" to be liaison with the board of directors. When I cited the bylaws she asserted cavalierly, "It's up to us to write our own bylaws."

Elliott also suggested joint get-togethers with the board of directors, holding events in various communities, and inviting the public into the station to "refute charges of elitism." But whatever her intentions, rejecting her role as specified by the station's bylaws meant severing the linkage between the CAB and the governing board called for by FCC regulation. A reporter covering the meeting whispered to me that if anything was going to get done, it would have to come from the group, not the chair.

When we were allowed to speak, some members mentioned the kind of programming they would like to see. One wanted to "network with the religious community," another to be "an advocate for the arts," still another wanted programs that would orient newcomers to local neighborhoods. Others requested information from the station so they could evaluate the situation properly; one asked for a mission statement and annual report.

Billy Jackson wanted to know what kinds of programming were being submitted to the station and what kind of funding was available for local programming. He also said he hoped the CAB would examine the station's definition of "acceptable" production values as they apply to community-based programming. Jackson was still burning over cuts WQED had made on his film on youth violence. The young people themselves had been involved in its production, and the result of this forward-looking experiment apparently looked rough in places; WQED had decided that was not acceptable.

Eager to get started, one member suggested we break into committees

around particular interests to begin thinking and networking. Howard Selikman, a schoolteacher from a wealthy suburb, cautioned against breaking
into committees until we got to know each other better as a group. Several
people felt that four ninety-minute meetings a year would not be enough to
get any work done. Wendy Lomicka of Shadyside Hospital, also eager to get
started, proposed we take a half-day or full-day retreat. Others concurred,
and we agreed to plan one for April.

To the press, Elliott said, "I think that we're moving in the right direction and I think that this is an all-inclusive plan." I said it was "a positive
step forward," but that I would wait and see: "I still don't have a very clear
sense of how the board and the station will be able to work together to mobilize community input and support."

Three months passed before the retreat was held, on Friday, May 12. It
was facilitated by a consultant under contract to WQED. As we discussed
our goals I was taken aback when Miles and Leber referred to viewers and
subscribers as "customers." I urged that we think of the station as a cultural
resource—like a library or museum—that had citizen members to be
served, not customers to be sold. I proposed the term "customers" suggests
a business model, where profit is a primary consideration. Another member
of the CAB agreed with me that although community service might not always pay for itself in monetary terms, it was our primary goal. Miles and
Leber said they thought "customer" was a positive term because it implied
a corporate obligation to please. No one else joined the discussion.

The group was somehow steered into establishing three overarching
goals: (1) identify external customers, (2) plan to share new missions and
goals and have an ongoing dialogue, and (3) plan to increase funding from
our customers. We were then moved to two new tasks. One was to decide
what two constituencies the CAB would identify for service.

The facilitator proposed that the constituencies we identified at the retreat would serve as a principal measure of whether we had accomplished
our mission, and that we should assess our specific accomplishments against
the agreed-upon plan at the end of twelve months. The two groups finally
singled out were "youth/teens" and "concerned citizens."

The other task was to focus on process and come up with a plan for how
the CAB would communicate with the community externally and with the
board of directors internally in order to have "real input" into programming. This had become a problem only because Gwen Elliott had refused to
play the role called for in the corporate bylaws. The facilitator proposed that
over the next six months the CAB create a "feedback loop" with the board

of directors and staff to communicate regularly with the entire community. No one appeared to have any idea what this would look like.

At lunch the facilitator confided to Jackson and me that he once had served on the previous WQED CAB and been alienated by the lack of participation allowed. He said he had left feeling "turned off." However, during the afternoon session, when I expressed concern about staff follow-through on CAB recommendations in the absence of board of directors oversight, he asked rhetorically, "Didn't George Miles say this was a new day?"

The most revealing directive came from B. J. Leber at the close of the retreat. She instructed everyone to send all communications directly to her rather than to Elliott or each other because "we need to speak with one voice" and "don't want to raise any false expectations."

At the next meeting of the directors, Leber reported that the CAB reception and retreat "were successful in making CAB members feel a part of the QED team." George Miles said that Gwen Elliott would be reporting back to him and he would "be in constant contact with the group." Jim Roddey recommended an annual joint meeting between the two boards and Miles supported the idea. Another recommendation was adopted to publish profiles of CAB members in *Pittsburgh Magazine*. The profiles started appearing in the magazine, but the first joint meeting featured speakers, with no discussion, and was over in twenty-five minutes. CAB member Ann Sutherland Harris commented, "I really don't think the board listened to the community board or vice versa. In other words, another empty event." The goals established at the retreat were never referred to again.

The CAB met again on June 23. The entire meeting was taken up by Miles and Leber presenting the station's newly fashioned strategic plan, during which they, once again, acknowledged such problems as "poor image," "lack of vision, mission, and direction," "need for focus," and "community feels detached." Miles also stated, "Just asking for money is not a relationship." I noted that in the organizational chart the community advisory board was listed just below the board of directors and on the same level as executive management; however, it was the only entity not connected to anything else in any way.

I got Miles's attention to point out that although there were six items on the day's agenda, his and Leber's presentations had covered only the first two and there were only five minutes left for the meeting. Miles replied that he had thought we might be interested in the information. I said the information was fine, but perhaps we had an unrealistic agenda for the time allowed. Privately I felt that the information about the strategic plan should have been sent by mail in advance of the meeting, and meeting time should have been devoted to questions and comments by CAB members insofar as the plan affected our mission.

Since we still had no minutes from the retreat six weeks earlier, the facilitator tried to summarize the entire list of recommendations in five minutes, without handouts. He spoke so fast that his summary was incomprehensible. After the meeting, Sutherland Harris complained to me that she thought the meeting was a waste of time and sensed that I did too, and asked whether we might talk about what might be done. She also complained to Elliott, who defended Miles: "He just wanted us to know what they had done."

That weekend, my wife, a friend, and I attended a fund-raiser for WQED at a downtown hotel. Miles was there, glad-handing the crowd. As he breezed by us he greeted me as "the QED Accountability Project" and did not stop to be introduced to my wife and friend. WQED station manager Michael Fields and he often used this salutation, but in this context it felt like a taunt.

Inside, I ran into Wendy Lomicka, who asked me what I thought of the last meeting. She thought it was an inappropriate use of our time. I told her about Ann Sutherland Harris's comment and suggested we get together to compare notes. Subsequently the three of us met to talk about the station over tea and cookies. I shared my experience at trying to reform the station and my doubts about management's commitment to the process. Lomicka revealed that she was liaison between the station and Shadyside Hospital, which provided $145,000 a year to WQED to underwrite *Health Talk* on its UHF station, WQEX. She said she had once called Michael Fields to express some concerns about the first program and he had exploded, asking her rhetorically how "dare" she challenge him—he was the "station manager" and he "makes the decisions about programs."

Lomicka saw her membership on the community advisory board as an opportunity to learn more about programming and production. She was frustrated by the slow pace. Before the evening was out, she was worked up enough to propose that she call a meeting of CAB members to reflect on our lack of progress and how to get us going.

A few days later I got a memo from Lomicka advising me that she had "chosen not to risk polarizing our relations with the management team." Instead she was going to discuss her concerns with B. J. Leber. I wished her well, but pointed out that if she called only Leber she would be complicit in compromising the CAB's autonomy from management. She later advised me that Leber and Elliott were upset that we had met privately. They soon announced their intention to establish an executive committee to plan future CAB meetings and activities.

Sutherland Harris, on the other hand, fired off a letter to Leber in August to complain that neither of the meetings she had attended "seemed worth the price of the bagels" provided. She called the June 23 meeting "a waste of our time" and criticized the language of the strategic plan for sounding like "something lifted from Dale Carnegie." She eschewed any desire to micromanage, but charged that "what is happening now seems to be purely a token presence that fulfills some legal requirement." Her letter closed with four concrete suggestions: "(1) Supply specific information just to board members with relevant knowledge and ask them to respond in writing or in small focus meetings; (2) Send reading materials in advance and call full meetings only on topics we all need to discuss; (3) Vary the day and time of meetings. Tuesday is not good for me during the teaching semester. Why not meet at the end of the working day [or] Saturdays at 10 AM? (4) Have Board members consult their own communities and report back ideas and responses to you for discussion by all or some of the board." She signed the letter "Yours sincerely but impatiently" and sent a copy to Gwen Elliott.

On August 17 I was dismayed to read in the *Post-Gazette* a lengthy presentation of WQED's and WQEX's complete new fall program schedules. The CAB had not even been informed of, let alone consulted, on any of these choices. I was reminded of a comment from board of directors member Gary Hubbard regarding publication of the WQED "President's Financial Statement" in the *Post-Gazette* earlier that summer: "It would have been nice of them to wait a day for approval by the board of directors." As management expert Peter Drucker says, "There is nothing more embarrassing than for board members to learn about their business first in the newspaper."

Throughout the summer I wrote, faxed, and called Gwen Elliott and B. J. Leber to volunteer my services for the executive committee, remind them that no minutes had been provided for the first three CAB meetings, and propose that the CAB adopt a scheduling strategy that would maximize attendance. I reminded them both that two other teachers and I could not meet on Tuesday and Thursday mornings. Leber never responded, and it took weeks for Elliott to get back to me. My attempt to have a "heart-to-heart" about my concerns was rebuffed. Nevertheless, I was invited to serve on the executive committee.

WQED Rejects Election Programs

The first real opportunity to test management's responsiveness to the recommendations of the community advisory board occurred at an August 17 meeting to solicit CAB input on "Ballot 95," a WQED project to promote voter education for the coming November elections. We were encouraged to think creatively. Like most people, I have been distressed by the increasing role of big money, campaign consultants, and television "attack ads" in American politics. I feel strongly that public television should do more in terms of voter education, including providing free time for political candidates to discuss their views. For additional input and support, I invited Kenny Steinberg—an attorney active in state and local politics—to the meeting. I informed B. J. Leber of his attendance.

Present for the meeting, in addition to Steinberg and I, were Leber; station manager Michael Fields; CFO Mel Ming; Ricki Wertz, assigned to WQED from the Public Television Outreach Alliance; Gwen Elliott; and one other member of the CAB. When we convened, Fields announced that he had decided to improve on the practice of candidates running thirty- or sixty-second "sound bites" on commercial stations by providing them with free two-minute spots on WQED; however, he was concerned that "with anything longer we'd lose our audience." Fields wanted us to advise him on which races were "worthy of tying up two regional television stations." I said that this seemed like a rather limited agenda given the many possibilities for public education and asked whether the matter was closed. Leber assured us that management was open to a much fuller discussion.

We explored various options over the next two hours and came to consensus on a plan. The two-minute spots would be reduced to ninety seconds, preceded by a thirty-second description of the office. Candidates would be taped in WQED studios and would not be able to submit any of their own footage. These spots would be offered to all candidates and would run about two hundred times before election day.

In addition, there would be two one-hour programs, one featuring all candidates for superior court seats in Pennsylvania, the other all candidates for the state supreme court. There would be a general solicitation from the public for questions to pose to these candidates under the theme "The People Want to Know." These questions would be screened and organized for presentation by a professional program host, and the candidates would be given an allotted time for reply. These live shows would provide viewers with the opportunity to hear the candidates' spontaneous answers to questions of general concern relevant to the offices they were seeking. We also agreed that there would be extensive school outreach on these programs, with educational kits for teachers who wished to assign viewing for their students. Finally, there would be cross-promotion with Pittsburgh-area public radio station WDUQ, but, curiously, not with WYEP or their own WQED-FM. (Fields said "our [classical music format] FM radio station doesn't lend itself to this, but DUQ's does.")

During the meeting, Fields was negative toward almost all of those proposals. He said that candidates would not accept this free exposure and he doubted people would write, call in, or even watch. He said that the only ones interested would be "senior citizens" and even *MacNeil/Lehrer* only gets a local rating of less than 1 (about 11,000 households). Everyone else seemed to be enjoying the brainstorming, however, and after a while they started to tease Fields for being such a naysayer.

Most of us certainly thought the candidates would come. We also talked about the importance of public service rather than ratings as a measure of public television performance, and about how such initiatives must be given time to build an audience. Despite his misgivings, Fields softened and personally summarized the above plan to close the meeting. We all left feeling we had accomplished something.

Of course there was nothing ground-breaking in these proposals. In 1994, public radio stations in California, Kansas, Massachusetts, Minnesota, New Hampshire, Ohio, Texas, and Washington had devoted substantial time to innovative voter education programs with strong community involvement. In some cases, the partnerships had included local television stations. The various broadcasters had conducted citizen polls, organized citizen forums where folks could deliberate with each other and with candidates, co-sponsored town meetings or debates, incorporated citizens' issues and insights into election coverage, done voter registration, promoted school essay contests, and given candidates short spots to state their positions. I was glad that Pittsburgh was going to make a contribution to this kind of citizen movement.

Having heard nothing for several weeks, I called Public Television Outreach liaison Ricki Wertz for an update on Ballot 95, only to be informed that the two one-hour programs and the school outreach had been dropped. She said Fields's only explanation was that the candidates wouldn't come and in any event it would have made for "bad programming." In effect, we were back to his original proposal with the one minor addition of the thirty-second job descriptions.

I later informed Kenny Steinberg, who wrote a letter to CFO Mel Ming expressing his disappointment. The NBC affiliate WPXI and the Pennsylvania Cable Network proceeded to do just the kind of program we had envisioned, featuring candidates for the state supreme court. It was underwritten by the League of Women Voters, Blue Cross, ARCO, and the Steelworkers. All four candidates participated. It was informative.

Head to Head at the Executive Committee

The meeting of the new CAB executive committee was scheduled for September 13. On September 6, after some indecision, I sent a six-page memo to Elliott, Leber, and all members of the committee. Having exhausted my attempts to influence Gwen Elliott privately and having no confidence that another meeting would address the various stalemates, I would appeal to the executive committee for intervention.

The memo was intended to provoke discussion. It pointed out that, in violation of the station's own bylaws, "there [had been] no public solicitation of nominees, very few directors had any input into the selection, and the Chair was chosen for the CAB before it even met." I continued, "The issue for me here is not the quality of the people now chairing and serving on the [community advisory board] but the degree to which management is in control of a process that is supposed to represent the public interest and to which management is supposed to be accountable." I pointed out that CAB attendance had been spotty and suggested that this might be due to the fact that "meetings are scheduled on weekday mornings, which may be convenient for staff, but is not for many members. Evening meetings have never been offered as an option despite requests." I called attention to the lack of minutes for the first two meetings and failure of management to provide CAB members with all the information they requested.

I then criticized WQED's paucity of local programming, citing two national studies and two press articles as documentation. I quoted George Miles's conflicting statements about whether he was committed to more local programming and asked, "Is WQED willing to do any serious local programming *about* Pittsburgh?" I asked what funds might be available for such efforts.

I also spoke about station services that should be part of our CAB evaluation, citing projects at other stations like workforce retraining, employment bulletin boards, literacy training, and foreign language instruction. I then described CABs in other major cities that we might consider as models for our own work.

I closed with a series of recommendations: (1) CAB members should be setting the agenda and facilitating the meetings; (2) our requests for information should be respected and responded to as soon as possible; (3) we should have more than four meetings a year if there was real business to discuss; and (4) we should support Gwen Elliott in making our recommendations directly to the board of directors and management. I voiced optimism and a willingness to serve, but also a concern not "to be used for mere public relations." I closed with "What's it going to be?"

Advisory board member Howard Selikman called me immediately. He was furious. Referring to my introductory statement, he sputtered, "We don't need any watchdog group." He considered my action an offense to the chair and wasn't interested in my motivation. Apparently not concerned with the lack of movement in the past eight months, he instructed me that we needed "time" for the CAB to produce "quality." I stayed cool. At one point he became so agitated he began shouting at his children without covering the mouthpiece of the phone. He was the only one to call me in response to the memo.

Dressed Down by the Police Commander

The CAB executive committee meeting was held at Gwen Elliott's offices at the City/County Building. Those waiting chatted amiably among themselves until led into the large inner office. Elliott sat us down and instructed us that despite B. J. Leber's presence, her own secretary at the back of the room was there to observe and record the meeting for Elliott's "protection."

We were informed that WQED had installed a hotline to take calls from viewers regarding programming. The committee had not requested such a thing; in fact, it seemed to me a potential ploy to counter claims by CAB members regarding public concerns. And that, in fact, is how it later functioned—barely promoted and hardly used. Nonetheless, Leber would later cite few or no hotline calls as evidence of lack of public concern about station deficiencies.

The next item was the scheduling of meetings. After some discussion, the committee was polled; five preferred evening meetings and two were indifferent, so we proposed that at least every other meeting be scheduled for evening hours. We also proposed that some meetings be held at a site other than WQED.

None of the other issues raised in my memo were on the agenda. I had a dinner date and so excused myself to leave early. Elliott called me to the table and, while I was standing there with my coat on, proceeded to dress me down in full police commander style. She complained that everyone had been sent a copy of my memo but her. I protested that I had sent hers first and asked what sense it would have made for me to exclude her when she would be chairing the meeting where I hoped these matters would be discussed. Elliott counterd that she was "not dumb" and accused me of plotting to take over the committee, including (in apparent reference to the tea) conducting "secret meetings." I asked plaintively whether we weren't allowed to meet with each other without Leber or her being present. At some point Lomicka intervened to say that she believed I had sent a copy of the memo to Elliott and that no ill will was intended. Elliott then conceded that members should be able to meet on their own if necessary, but Selikman wanted to make sure I understood that the chair should be consulted if such actions were considered in the future.

Because it was on a Tuesday morning, I was unable to attend the next general advisory board meeting of October 3, 1995. I was later informed that when the question about meeting times was raised, one woman said she wouldn't come to evening meetings and the matter was then dropped. As reported by Todd Gutnick in the *Tribune-Review,* those assembled talked about what their role might be, but no plan emerged; Elliott "deferred formation of committees"; and one CAB member "predicted it could take as long as a year before the board is ready to assume its role."

George Miles, on the other hand, already knew what he wanted from members: "I need for you to be ambassadors for us." While urging members to learn more about the station on their own, he asked people to be patient because he wanted "everyone to have the same song sheet."

Persistence by Lomicka, Jackson, and others finally paid off, and program and education subcommittees were established. Throughout the fall and into the winter I participated in communications and meetings with these two committees. Whenever there was a session I could not attend, I called colleagues to learn of developments. Typically, I was told such things as "We're not sure of programming policy" "It's not useful to listen to what's being planned after decisions already have been made" (Lomicka), or "It [the meeting] didn't add anything to my knowledge" (Jackson).

I Get to Produce a Show

Throughout this period, I continued to do research and communicate with other media activists. In summer 1994, Cambridge Documentary Films, Inc., solicited me to write letters of protest to PBS and CPB over their refusal to air its film *Defending Our Lives*. Winner of several awards, including the 1994 Oscar for "best documentary short," the film is based on the testimony of battered women who finally killed their mates in self-defense and were sent to prison. Having spent two years organizing conferences on this issue, I was most interested.

PBS had rejected the film on the grounds that one of the producers was a member of a human rights group concerned with the issue and thus had a "direct self-interest in the content of the program." The producers protested that the organization in question was only a nine-member prison support group and the individual neither funded, profited from, nor controlled the final product. PBS replied that the policy and its decision were not subject to review, that the "perception" that shows are being "created to advance the aims of [a] group" is "as important as the fact."

At a press conference in July 1994, PBS head Ervin Duggan mistakenly claimed that the film was rejected because it was funded by "women's groups," which was a form of "financial self-interest that violates PBS standards." He was challenged by reporters who asked him how such funding differed from brokerage firms funding *Wall $treet Week,* and dodged the contradiction with the disingenuous disclaimer that he wasn't familiar enough with *Wall $treet Week* to make a comparison.

I requested the film from the producer, previewed it, and was profoundly impressed. I decided that a Pittsburgh broadcast of *Defending Our Lives* would be good for both the battered women's movement and WQED. On July 15, I wrote to Mark Smuckler, then the station manager, to describe the film, protest the PBS rejection, and suggest putting it on WQED-TV.

Smuckler liked the film and was willing to show it along with a half-hour discussion. However, he felt the distributor wanted too high a licensing fee. He said a representative told him she would settle for $1,500, but Smuckler said, "We normally pay in the range of $500–600 for a single half hour." I told him I might be able to get it for $750. He suggested we look for "a little bit of local funding." I wrote back with some suggestions.

The next thing I knew, Smuckler was out. Only weeks in office, George Miles had begun to shake up the staff, promoting people with whom he had had a past relationship at KDKA (CBS) in the early 1980s. In early October,

Ceci Sommers was replaced by B. J. Leber and Michael Fields was moved up from station manager of UHF second station WQEX to be vice president and station manager for both WQED and WQEX television. (By 1999, WQED was being referred to in Pittsburgh broadcasting circles as "KDKA East.")

The labor people in our coalition fingered Fields as the one who had killed funding for *Labor's Corner* a few years earlier. Meanwhile, Mark Smuckler was made vice president in charge of television production, engineering, and special projects for both TV stations. He explained that he would stay on as support for Miles, who had additional responsibilities in national and regional organizations like APTS. "I didn't expect things to happen the way they did," Smuckler cracked, "[but] we're learning very quickly to keep our feet planted in mid-air."

WQEX Programming: Air in the Scoop

George Miles and Michael Fields expressed parallel attitudes toward WQEX. Miles called it "a smart local station that people can have a lot of fun with." Fields called it "lovely, wonderful, quirky," "cheeky," "a little nutty," and "a toy." These characterizations hardly suggest a forum for public discussion or a vehicle for public education.

At lunch one day, Fields told me about his earlier career as owner of an ice cream parlor. The secret to profit in the ice cream business, he advised me, is to make sure you get enough air into the scoop. One of his major contributions to programming on WQEX was to schedule two or three hours a week of reruns of commercial network programs from the 1950s. The station carried *Perry Mason, Gunsmoke, The Honeymooners, Lawrence Welk,* and other such oldies under the oxymoronic banner "Classic Television." Miles said he liked "classic television." Fields was getting plenty of air into the programming scoop.

Defending Our Lives

Allowing a decent interval for him to move into his new job, I called Fields on December 9, 1994, about *Defending Our Lives.* For several minutes he tried to brush me off, starting with "I don't think follow-up is appropriate." He dismissed the Academy Award recognition: "Anyone can win. Look at Liz Taylor in *Butterfield 8.*" I referred to the O. J. Simpson headlines and my own conference-organizing experience with regard to the issue of domestic abuse, and reassured him that there was a big audience for a show on this topic. I reminded him of his mission. Fields acknowledged that the film was "a valuable piece of work" and "everyone here [at WQED] is very impressed."

The problem, Fields said, was that the $1,500 license fee was "not a reasonable price." He said that "$300 to $400 is the usual amount we spend for a program." I told him that his predecessor and I had talked about $750 as a potentially acceptable fee. Fields replied, "I'm better at doing this than Mark. That's why he is where he is." I asked Fields how much he was spending for *The Honeymooners*. "Quite a bit," he snapped back, "but without it we wouldn't have a Channel 16." This assertion contradicted the conventional wisdom that people watch programs, not stations. He claimed that he had spoken to Kweilin Nassar in their marketing department and she had complained, "It takes as much time to raise $1,500 as a million and a half."

Then suddenly Fields began to think creatively about how it could be done. He said, "Maybe we ought to be thinking bigger," and suggested a regular prime-time program that would be like a "recurring local *Frontline* thing." There would be a film followed by a "town hall meeting." It would be "gritty" and "cutting edge." Moreover, I could "help in formatting."

Of course I was intrigued. However, I was also cautious. I could see myself investing tremendous amounts of time, energy, and resources into outlining programs that would never get off the drawing board. I said I would like to pursue that concept but wanted to start with this program as a pilot. He suggested that it would be a lot cheaper to do if we folded it into an already scheduled program. He thought it would be perfect for *Cullen-Devlin*.

Developed by Fields himself, this one-hour weekly show was hosted by a Jewish liberal (Lynn Cullen) and an Irish Catholic moderate (Ann Devlin). Both had radio followings and contrasting styles as well as politics. Each show brought in guests to debate different issues. Fields suggested that we could expand the usual program into a two-hour special, probably for March. I supported his proposal enthusiastically. We also agreed that the deal depended on my being able to deliver *Defending Our Lives* for $750. We set an appointment for December 28 to discuss the larger program concept further.

I persuaded the distributor to lower the fee to $750 and met with Fields as scheduled. We discussed his larger program proposal and what my responsibilities would be: suggesting topics, selecting the films, identifying effective guests, and organizing community outreach. We did not talk money, however, I did tell him that for that kind of work I thought I deserved credit as "associate producer." He was thinking "program consultant." I persisted. He said he would discuss it with Miles for the purpose of drawing up a contract for my approval.

I wrote to Fields the very next day to confirm our understanding in writing. I summarized my responsibilities, argued for the credit, described my office and university resources, and made it clear that he was getting "my expertise pro bono and with minimal expense." On January 9, 1995, I came home to a message on my answering machine from Fields's secretary, Suzanne Pearson, who informed me that he had lost my letter. At her request, I faxed another copy. I also spoke with a couple of public television producers who assured me that the credit I was requesting was reasonable for the work proposed.

A month after our initial meeting, I still had not received the contract. I called Fields. He was hostile and accusatory. He claimed that I had asked for "compensation"—to be "a paid producer"—and that this "changed our understanding so fundamentally" that he had had to express his concerns to Miles. He stated that they agreed that it was "inappropriate" for a "critic" of WQED to be offered a job with the station.

When I protested that I had never requested any money, he insisted that I had, and threatened to hang up on me if I persisted with such a line. He conceded that we had never discussed a figure, but refused to acknowledge that he might be in error. I saved the conversation by several times conceding that we had obviously had a misunderstanding but the important thing was that I was now telling him that I was not seeking compensation, so the only real questions were whether or not he wanted to do the show and whether or not there were any other obstacles. He closed by saying he was glad that money was no longer an obstacle.

The series idea was never referred to again, but the original one-shot *Defending Our Lives* program proposal was on. New WQEX station manager Jim Wiener, *Cullen-Devlin* producer Jaci Clark, and I met at WQED in January 1995 to discuss it. I provided lists of potential guests I knew to be articulate on the issues—therapists, attorneys, and advocates. I also provided several relevant topic questions and background reading for the hosts. I promised lists of outreach contacts for free newsletter listings as well as flier distributions and postings. Finally, I suggested that the station use pledge phones lines for call-in questions and local shelter referrals, a kind of "domestic abuse hotline."

For my part, I was looking forward to learning whatever I could about the particulars of producing a program for television. Jaci Clark indicated that she would consult with me and, at the least, keep me informed about the progress of the program. I called for Clark and left messages on several occasions in February. I looked for her when I was at the station for a community advisory board meeting. At the suggestion of Ricki Wertz, I even left a message for Clark with B. J. Leber. I also sent Leber all outreach contacts on computer disk, as she had requested.

The press release for the March 9 show went out on February 24. Only days before the show itself, I finally heard from Clark, who was excited to inform me that she had just booked Cheryl Curtician for the lead interview after the film. About a year earlier, Curtician's story had been in the papers after her husband had sexually assaulted her and beat her almost to death before kidnapping her to his trailer and later to his mother's vacant home in Illinois. Curtician was to be followed by a therapist who works with male abusers, two women from local crisis centers, and an attorney specializing in domestic abuse cases. Two of the four were from my guest list.

In response to my question, Clark said she had talked with George Miles and he had decided that credit as "program consultant" was appropriate—if I wasn't satisfied, I could call him. I accepted this offer and did so. Miles several times repeated the decision and challenged me, "You got a problem with that?" I responded calmly, "Yes, I do," and told him why. He finally conceded. It cost him so little (there was no mention of money); in the end, the credits rolled by so fast you could easily have missed my name.

On April 24, 1995, I wrote to Miles concerning various matters and closed with my account of the whole affair. I asked him for "some explanation" for "the abrupt dropping of the [series] proposal" and to "please find some time in your schedule over the month of May or, at least, June for us to sit down and sort this out." Neither Miles nor his office ever replied.

At a City Council meeting the following year, Miles accused me of trying to promote myself into a paid position at WQED. I shouted back, "That is a lie and you know it!" The *Tribune-Review* printed the exchange. Months later, a reporter at the *Post-Gazette* told me that Fields had told *her* that Miles had a letter in his desk drawer from me in which I tried to extort a job, but he was "too nice" to use it. These accusations make it hard not to believe that the whole thing was a clumsy attempt at entrapment to begin with—which is a shame because it was a great series idea.

Certainly the *Defending Our Lives* show was a huge success, albeit largely despite rather than because of WQED. B. J. Leber never did any outreach mailing with the list I provided. *Post-Gazette* reporter Barbara Vancheri did run a long favorable preview the day of the show; however, the article failed to note that the film had won an Academy Award. I called her and she assured me that had she known she would have been certain to note it. As for what was behind the production, Vancheri's article closed, "Producer Clark says when Michael Fields, vice president and station manager at WQED and WQEX saw the film, he decided it was so powerful that QEX would run it and do a live follow-up. Tonight may not be the only time 'Cullen/Devlin' departs from its usual format. 'If we can tackle topics like this one and do it well, offer advice and outreach to people, I would like to do it as often as possible,' Clark said."

On the night of the broadcast I met my friend Dave Russell for dinner. He was slated to be one of the guests. After dinner we drove to the station and found the appropriate room. Cheryl Curtician was there with her attorney; her case was coming up for trial, and consequently she was not permitted to talk specifically about her own experience. All the other guests were assembled and advised me that they had been contacted only days before. They were given only a brief orientation just minutes before going on.

Jaci Clark, the producer, came and went without even speaking to me. Lynn Cullen came in and was polite. She later acknowledged that Clark was angry because I had insisted on an associate producer credit and gotten it. Ann Devlin came in, greeted everyone else, and without looking at me extended a limp hand in my direction. I stared at it for a moment, then touched it and said my name. She looked away and walked out.

The show opened with the film—powerful testimony from seven abused women then in prison for killing their abusive partners to defend themselves and their children. The moment the film ended, the station switched to a raucous laugh-track promotion for a sitcom, a decision that Jim Wiener later commented completely broke the mood. Curtician came on and was redundant as another victim; having been instructed not to discuss any of the specifics of the case, she spoke very softly in generalities. The hosts spoke to her in quiet slow tones, making for deadly television. Clearly this was an effort at tabloid journalism gone awry.

The three other guests followed, and the show picked up with a discussion of legal, therapeutic, and political solutions to the problem. However, Dave Russell, who works with male batterers, complained to them and to me later that the questions directed at him were hostile. Indeed, they had made him symbolic of all male abusers and took his somber evaluation that therapy has limited success with long-time batterers as almost tantamount to a confession that he was taking money under false pretenses. In addition, technicians kept forgetting to flash the relevant numbers on the screen and then got the hotline referral and call-in numbers mixed up.

Still, according to reports, the ten hotline operators got an average of ten calls each during the ninety minutes of discussion. Some one hundred people were referred for help. Connie Hughes, a community education specialist from Crisis Center North, told me that every call she got was from a child about a domestic violence situation. Hughes wrote a two-page letter to Jaci Clark the next day, commending everyone on doing the program and proposing another on the effects of violence on children. She noted Clark's comment in the paper about doing more shows and talked about what her organization had learned from its high school outreach programs. Since public television was doing several programs on violence by and among youth, a program like this would have added depth to the public's understanding of the problem. Hughes suggested possible guests. She sent copies of the letter to Cullen, Devlin, and me. She later told me I was the only one to respond.

About a month later, Ann Devlin did her own show on the subject on WTAE-TV, the ABC affiliate. She asked Dave Russell to be on. He said he accepted with her assurance that "this show is not going to be contentious." More solution oriented, it was a better program. Although Clark gave Fields credit for the program in her press interview, Fields often cited *Defending Our Lives* in conversations with members of the community advisory board as an example of the station's willingness to work with CAB members. This remained the only such example, however. Frankly, I couldn't imagine anyone else putting up with what I had endured.

Still, I was proud of the fact that two programs on this important but typically ignored issue were done for a responsive public. At the least, it showed me that it is possible for a representative of the public to get a local public television station to compensate for PBS timidity and show an Academy Award–winning film on a serious social problem.

Not in Our Town

In December 1995 there was another incident that showed both the potential of public television and WQED's alienation from the community. An organization called the California Working Group produced a show called *Not in Our Town,* describing what had happened in Billings, Montana, when people stood up for neighbors who'd been under attack by white supremacist hate groups. The precipitating incident was a rock thrown through the bedroom window of a child—a window that displayed a paper cutout of the eight-candle Chanukah menorah. Among other actions they took in response, people all over town had pasted paper menorahs in their windows.

The program was being promoted to public television stations for "Not in Our Town Week," December 10–17. There were many activities recommended, with national coordination of information.

Over the previous five years, police had recorded five hundred hate crimes in western Pennsylvania, one of the highest rates in the nation, and the Pittsburgh community would soon be assaulted by a Klan rally. I called the station to find out whether and when *Not in Our Town* was scheduled. I discovered that WQED board member Allen Kukovich and CAB member Margaret Tyndall had also been calling; for Tyndall, head of the local YWCA, it was to be part of a national antiracism campaign being sponsored by her organization.

We were surprised to learn that the film wasn't scheduled during the designated holiday week, but not until January. While this seemed strange, I felt the additional four or five weeks would allow us more time to organize. I called Jan Neffke, coordinator of the Pittsburgh Coalition to Counter Hate Groups, to inform her about this opportunity. She called the station to find out whether her group could help in promotion and whether they could produce a companion program with WQED on the situation locally.

Neffke called to tell me that Fields told had her it would cost $5,000 to $6,000 to produce a half-hour program on WQED on the subject. She raised the money quickly and called Fields back; he then informed her that the half-hour following the broadcast of the film had already been scheduled.

With WQED not willing to provide a forum for discussion of this critical issue, the coalition joined with *In Pittsburgh* and the group Pittsburgh Filmmakers to show the film and hold its own meeting. January 4, 1996, was a cold, dark winter's night, but 150 people attended the event and joined in the discussion. Later, Neffke prevailed on her friend Lynn Cullen to do an edition of *Cullen-Devlin* on the issue. In the early spring a march against the Klan drew 4,000 participants under the banner "Not in Our Town"—this clearly was another opportunity rejected by WQED to serve the public interest.

The CAB Challenges Management

Near the end of 1995, with support from Margaret Tyndall, Billy Jackson, and me, Wendy Lomicka assembled a series of informational requests and shared them with Public Television Outreach liaison Ricki Wertz. They included such queries as, What shows are carried by other public television stations but not shown on WQED/WQEX? What is the industry standard for local programming and how does WQED compare? Are there any plans to go beyond "popular nostalgia" shows in order to reflect "what is happening in the city today"? Is WQED "open to public requests for programming"? and, Beyond programming, what other services are being evaluated?

Lomicka was also interested in process questions, like how programming decisions were made, how audience input was gained, how WQED measured its success, what its current programming goals were, and what prevented improvement and change. She obviously thought WQED would have such information and should share it with its community advisory board.

After no response to these informal inquiries, in January 1996 Tyndall composed a formal letter of request on behalf of the program subcommittee. She stated that the CAB had "an important responsibility" to represent " 'the ownership,' namely the taxpayers and community that support public television." However, she went on, the advisory board had "been hampered in carrying out our responsibility by the lack of substantive information. Despite previous requests . . . we still lack answers to some basic questions." Focusing on just "a few," Tyndall asked for answers in writing within the next ten days.

To paraphrase her questions: (1) What is the process for deciding on nationally available programs for Pittsburgh and how far in advance are these decisions made? (2) How does QED local programming compare to that of other public stations? (Please share CPB studies on this question.) (3) What is the budget for community outreach and how does this compare to the past and to those of other stations? (4) Is there a written record of calls to the hotline we could have? How many have there been and what have they been about? (5) We have heard of several cases of resistance to community groups' attempts to cooperate with the station—what is the policy or strategy for dealing with special interests?

Two weeks later, Tyndall sent me a note on WQED's response: Miles said he thought that these questions had already been answered in the education session and suggested that "committees should not meet without staff"; Gwen Elliott spoke to Tyndall briefly at the joint meeting, saying she was surprised Tyndall hadn't called her; Tyndall had lunch with B. J. Leber, who said that "people were working on pulling together the information we requested."

I spoke with Tyndall ten days later. I asked about her lunch with Leber and she said, "I told B. J. there was no structure [to the CAB], really. We come to the meeting—the agenda comes from who knows where. There is no continuity in the focus of the discussion and work." She told Leber that the program committee should have an annual calendar with all meetings listed in advance and that the CAB committees should be "made functional" and, through their work, create the agendas for general meetings.

Since these recommendations seemed standard operating procedure, I asked Tyndall why she felt Leber and Elliott were not doing this already. She said that Elliott was simply "not willing or able" and that Leber lacked "experience" and was "concerned about stepping over the line."

B. J. Leber wrote to Tyndall a month after receiving her letter. To paraphrase Leber's point-by-point responses: (1) PBS is the main source of programming for both stations. The "scheduling begins two months in advance for both stations," but many decisions are "long term; we are buying programs for next fall's schedule now." Moreover, "beginning this spring, we will be holding sessions for CAB members to discuss upcoming programming, to have input into programming." (2) "We know of no CPB studies that compare local programming from market to market." WQED is researching that and will report back. (3) There are "virtually no moneys for community outreach and no full-time local outreach staff person." (4) There "have been 26 calls to the CAB Hotline since its inception, and they were forwarded to the proper people for response." The stations keep "viewer call logs" which "can certainly be shared" with the CAB. (5) "We are puzzled by comments that community groups have met with resistance. I am looking into one specific incident we discussed regarding *Not in Our Town*. If there are others, please advise."

The reference to program sources was sorely incomplete. First, there was no acknowledgment that the station chooses from among many PBS national program service offerings. Second, programs also come from as many as three hundred sources other than PBS, with the American Program Service being the largest. As for local programming, since I had cited two CPB studies in my September memo to the CAB executive committee, their claim of ignorance was disingenuous.

Nor was there any acknowledgement that Ricki Wertz's salary was being subsidized so that she could provide outreach services for WQED; Ricki had complained to me more than once about management's failure to utilize her. The call log was never provided to the CAB. As for incidents of resistence to community groups, there was the lack of follow-up to *Defending Our Lives,* and the rebuff to the Allegheny County Labor Council, which had been reported in both newspapers over the previous December and January. (I will take up this episode shortly.)

As for the spring CAB meetings to "discuss and have input into upcoming programming," the best was yet to come. On March 27, 1996, the CAB programming subcommittee meeting finally took place. Already forewarned that station representatives would try to sidestep the hard questions, I came armed with information. Present for the meeting were general manager Michael Fields, program directors Jim Wiener and Chris Fennimore, B. J. Leber, Gwen Elliott, and seven members of the CAB—Margaret Tyndall, Wendy Lomicka, Billy Jackson, Howard Selikman, Bill Watercotte, Ray Reeves, and me.

Once again, a great deal of time was taken up by staff presentations. Fields made the point that 54 percent of WQED's schedule was taken up with children's programs seven days a week. He talked about the five locally produced programs (one of which only included a local wrap), three of which aired on WQEX. He said that WQED was "locked in," but that second station WQEX "gives us a tremendous amount of flexibility and latitude to do the things we can't do on Channel 13." Fennimore also commented that two stations gave us "the best of all possible worlds."

Fennimore spent at least thirty minutes discussing the concept of "common carriage." As he explained it, in order to take advantage of promotion by underwriters of national programs, member stations are supposed to run around 350 hours of the same nightly programs a year. Local programs are run in places not committed to common carriage, like Saturday evenings. When asked why *Not in our Town* was not run December 10–17, as all the other PBS station broadcasts of the program were, Fields replied that he didn't consider it to be a holiday story.

Billy Jackson expressed concern over the paucity of local programming on WQED. Leber again claimed to have no evidence of this, and other staff praised their local programming. At this point I pulled out and quoted from the relevant news clippings describing studies of local programming. As had become her strategy of late, Leber interrupted me with the taunt that this was "old news" and I needed to "look forward."

Referring to several cooking shows that ran all St. Patrick's Day, Fennimore pouted, "Maybe you don't count these as local shows, but people came up afterward and said how proud they were of us"; Fennimore, host of *WQED Cooks,* evidently took my remarks personally. I said that I was only making the point that there have been studies, that they found local programming here wanting, and that until we acknowledged there was a problem we would not be able to "look forward" to a solution. After some more staff huffing and puffing, I was told I was wasting valuable time and we had to move on.

Fennimore said scheduling was done at least two months in advance of air time. We asked him about the sources from which he chose the programs he scheduled and the timetable for this. He described some of the catalogs available. I asked whether members of the CAB might see some. Fennimore said, "No, it will only confuse you." Leber advised us, "You don't want to get bogged down reading menus." Fennimore said, "There are almost six thousand programs in inventory." Leber said she had looked at some of the catalogues and her "eyes glazed over." Bottom line—request denied for our own good.

When Michael Fields spoke enthusiastically about the wonderful local programming he had "in the pipeline," I asked whether the committee could have a report on them for the next meeting. He said, "Yes, sure, I don't see why not." Then he did see. Down the table, B. J. Leber was shaking her head no and saying it would be "premature." Fields stopped talking.

Howard Selikman noted that PBS had several programs on the Holocaust scheduled for April. He said he had been approached by many local survivors who were eager for the opportunity to tell their stories and discuss the issues. He asked what it would take to produce a local program on the subject to supplement the upcoming national ones.

Fields said that a one-hour special once planned on the legacies of different ethnic groups was projected to cost $150,000; the Italian community had said they would raise the money, but couldn't. He estimated that it would cost about $35,000 to do a show like the one that had been suggested. I interjected that I had learned that $5,000 to $6,000 was sufficient for a half-hour studio talk show, which, I gathered, was all Selikman was proposing. Fields acknowledged that on Tuesday, Wednesday, or Thursday you could do a show like that for $5,000 or $10,000. He suggested that Selikman call Leber to get an appointment to work out programming. Nothing was done.

Jim Wiener then demonstrated the kind of input station leaders would entertain from CAB members. He said that several episodes of *P.O.V.* were scheduled for the coming summer; in the past this show had run at 10 P.M., but because of "the language" he now felt it was better to move it to 11 P.M. and wanted to know what we thought. I told him it was my favorite PBS program and I go to bed early—please keep it at 10. It later was moved to 11.

In the CAB meeting promotional handout distributed at the May meeting there was a boxed message: "Alert: Be aware of lobbying effort by producer for NETWORK Q 'Out Across America' weekly gay/lesbian half-hour feed early in May." Wiener also warned us about a possible protest of a decision he had made not to air a new gay- and lesbian-oriented program on WQEX. The show, Network Q's *Out Across America*, offers ten episodes shot on location in ten different cities, including Pittsburgh. Each program features gay and lesbian news, travel tips, profiles, and entertainment.

Wiener objected to the show's "plugging" of certain business establishments that are congenial to gay and lesbian clients. He said this was a violation of PBS guidelines. I thought this a peculiar criticism coming from a station that had its own series on "Pennsylvania Diners," or the best places to get hot dogs or ice cream, or the best amusement parks, not to mention PBS national shows on best companies in which to invest. However, I said nothing. Wiener also criticized the series' lack of "production quality."

In an article Wiener provided, the show's producer said he believed the reason for its rejection at WQEX and many other PBS stations was that the show was "considerably more alternative than they were prepared to deal with." He also said he was revamping the show completely to meet objections. Wiener was quoted as saying that he thought there was a need for gay and lesbian programming and hoped that more and better shows would be offered. Two years later, gay and lesbian programming was still negligible on Pittsburgh public television.

As the meeting drew to a close, I tried to summarize what we had learned and to inquire about next steps. I said that we had been told we might not look at national programming offered to the station nor even at programs in development; consequently, we could only learn of these programs when they were scheduled, two months in advance, at which point there would be no opportunity to produce and schedule a local follow-up program involving community input even if money were available.

I asked what could be done. Fields suggested we call Fennimore or Wiener. Looking down the table, he quickly corrected himself, "No, call B. J." As I walked to my car in the parking lot, Howard Selikman came up to me and said, "These [local] folks are really interested in doing a show on their Holocaust experiences." I told him that given what we had been told, I had no idea how such a thing could be done. That was to be the last meeting of the community advisory board I would attend.

As a consequence of such unresponsive management, CAB attendance suffered. WQED's own figures claim that of twenty-five members invited, eighteen attended the first quarterly meeting. Subsequent general meetings through the two-year terms of the first CAB members drew an average of eleven; attendance after the meeting described above was down to six.

Labor Lockout at WQED

From 1987 to 1990, Steffi Domike, Russ Gibbons, and Lou Pappalardo produced a thirty-minute show on WQEX called *Labor's Corner*. The program went out over seven cable systems to thirteen communities in the greater Pittsburgh area. Over three years, the producers raised about $60,000 in donations and underwriting from unions, largely in contributions of under $1,000.

According to the producers, Ken Tiven, then WQEX station manager, also subsidized the program with anywhere from $5,000 to $25,000 annually. In its newsletter, the producers of *Labor's Corner* said Tiven saw the program as one "that would attract a new constituency to the station and which would begin to address the lack of programming about workers and unions." Early in 1990, as QED Communications' debt crisis became severe, Tiven resigned from WQEX and was replaced by Michael Fields, who saw Tiven's subsidy as "irresponsible." Fields introduced an austerity program, laying off two producers and a graphic artist, and canceling four programs, including *Labor's Corner*.

Amidst considerable tension, Fields and the *Labor's Corner* producers continued to meet. They came up with a new program concept, *Labor Live!* to originate at the QEX Channel 16 studios "with a professional host well versed in issues facing working people." The guests would "vary week to week, chosen for their expertise in the weekly topic." Fields informally pursued funding from the state AFL-CIO, but no agreement was ever reached.

The frustrations of my first several months on the CAB had given me profound doubts about the possible success of an inside-the-system approach. I decided to pursue a complementary strategy at the same time. While working on the CAB, I would try to help mobilize public interest groups to approach the station directly with program requests.

In September 1995, I proposed to the media action committee of the Allegheny County Labor Council (ACLC) that they approach WQED about labor participation in the station. The ACLC is a coordinating group for 157 member unions representing 80,000 members; if members' families were included, the outreach potential ranged up to 250,000 or so. ACLC director Paul Stackhouse had worked for thirty-five years for the Steelworkers, followed by another twenty-five at the Service Employees International Union (SEIU), all of which overlapped with thirty-five years on the ACLC.

We held an organizing meeting at the headquarters of SEIU 585. President Rosemary Trump had taken over the local in 1973, at the age of thirty, and multiplied its membership from a few hundred to 10,000. Well-tailored and polite, Trump was nonetheless a fiery speechmaker and a tough negotiator. She is credited by many with paving the way for women in the labor movement.

The nucleus of the task force that carried forward the campaign consisted of Paul Stackhouse; Rosemary Trump; Russ Gibbons; Mark Wirick, executive director of the Pittsburgh chapter of the American Federation of Television and Radio Artists (AFTRA); Glenn Plummer, public affairs director, UFCW local 23; and me. I facilitated the meeting and coordinated the subsequent campaign.

I recommended we make *We Do the Work* (*WDTW*) the centerpiece of the proposed partnership. *WDTW* was the only nationally distributed television series devoted exclusively to chronicling the issues, changes, and problems facing American workers. By this time the half-hour program was being carried by a hundred public stations, including three in Pennsylvania. On September 27, 1995, Paul Stackhouse sent a letter to Michael Fields (now a QED vice president and station manager for both WQED and WQEX), offering "an opportunity to enhance the public service performance of your stations while broadening your base of viewers and subscribers in the community." He proposed *WDTW* for WQED's Friday evening public affairs block to "balance" the station's many business programs.

In exchange, the ACLC offered to help WQED "promote the program to our hundreds of thousands of members and to remind them in the process that programs like this are available only on public broadcasting which, now more than ever, is in need of public support." The letter closed with a request for a meeting "in the near future to discuss this proposed collaboration."

Three weeks passed before Stackhouse got a reply, from WQED program director Chris Fennimore. He defended the business programs as "popular," "useful," and not requiring balance since they did "not put forth any particular political or economic philosophy." Fennimore listed about a dozen labor-related programs over the past two years as evidence that the station had already addressed the issues.

Fennimore also suggested that *WDTW* did not have much of an audience and that there were problems with repeats and limitations on rights in running the available series of programs. He advised that WQED was in contact with the show's producers, expected "eight or ten half-hours for consideration" for spring 1996, and would "be happy to screen these programs when they are available and evaluate them for broadcast on WQED or WQEX."

Plummer and I evaluated Fennimore's letter, called *WDTW* communications director Valerie Lapin, and discovered that they were offering twenty-three shows that had never before been broadcast on WQED, available as of Thanksgiving 1995, and would not run out of these until March 1996, when new episodes would be ready.

Because the series was underwritten by corporations, free to the station, and an award-winning production, the ACLC decided that the demand for *We Do the Work* was nonnegotiable. At their next meeting, they also moved to expand their outreach to the eight other labor councils in the greater Pittsburgh area, come up with nominations for WQED's board of directors and its community advisory board, and repeat the request for a meeting with station leaders. In addition, the ACLC decided to introduce discussion of a half-hour show to follow *WDTW* that would "localize the issues in the program." Finally, they agreed that in the unlikely event that WQED refused to meet, they would call a press conference and announce an escrow fund to which people could contribute for labor programming on public television.

This time Stackhouse's letter went to CEO George Miles. He wrote to complain that Fennimore had "essentially made light of our concerns and advised us to wait several months when WQED will decide whether future episodes of *We Do the Work* are worthy of broadcast." The letter went on to refute claims that business programs did not advocate a point of view or that a dozen PBS shows on workplace issues over a two-year period were sufficient. Stackhouse also reported to Miles what his group had learned from the program's producers about available programming. He advised that they would be coordinating outreach with eight other labor councils in southwestern Pennsylvania, accounting for more than forty newsletters with a total circulation of greater than 150,000 members: "It is our intention to make *We Do the Work* WQED's most popular show." Stackhouse also put forward concerns regarding "the underrepresentation of organized labor and working people" on WQED's board of directors and community advisory board. In view of the two months already lost, he called for "a meeting before mid-December."

December came and went with no answer to the letter. Russ Gibbons arranged with Rosemary Trump to house the Public Television for Working Americans Escrow Fund at SEIU 585, and a press conference was scheduled. The press releases went out prematurely and the next morning's paper announced, "Labor Council Criticizes Television Station." Regarding *We Do the Work,* Mark Wirick was quoted as saying, "They are bending over backward to find excuses not to run the program." The paper also reported his description of the escrow fund's purpose as "to provide local programming ourselves on alternative outlets (or) public access cable stations."

As soon as Miles saw the story, he called Gary Hubbard, who then faxed a copy of the article and a memo to all of us describing that conversation. According to Hubbard, Miles now advised he would meet "anytime and anyplace." The big meeting was scheduled for the morning of January 29, 1996. Plummer, Wirick, Gibbons, and Stackhouse were there on behalf of the labor council. Stackhouse was the ceremonial leader, but Plummer did most of the talking. Hubbard was there as both a labor member and a WQED board member and he had arranged for Allen Kukovich to participate by speakerphone. I was there as a witness from the community advisory board.

Miles brought with him Fields, Fennimore, and Leber. Dressed in a three-piece suit, Stackhouse tried to set a cordial but businesslike tone. He opened the meeting by reminding everyone of the three items on the agenda and indicating that Plummer would be the point person for the labor group. Miles talked fast and was all bluff and bluster—posturing, interrupting, and challenging. Plummer was physically unimposing, with a high smoky voice and a mild manner; he was, however, an experienced negotiator, cool and focused on the issues at hand.

The discussion of *We Do the Work* was intermittently stormy and agreeable. On the one hand, WQED officials revealed that they had already decided they would run some episodes in the spring on the bigger VHF channel. They suggested that prime time during the week would not be good (too much competition) but acknowledged that the public affairs block on Friday night was scheduled locally. On the other hand, George Miles continued to assert that he was "the final arbiter" on programming and Michael Fields criticized some *WDTW* episodes as "technically terrible." At one point Miles and Russ Gibbons shouted at each other. Concerned about potential censorship, Glenn Plummer asked that his group be consulted on any programs WQED decided not to show. Fields agreed: "We will bring you in on that decision."

On the subject of *Labor Live,* Miles again became angry and said, "I give my guys a lot of credit. I see what my guys have done—developing a concept, clearing a whole slate." Fields, in turn, said he was "incensed." The reason the show never came together was "not our fault," he claimed. "Bill George and the labor movement didn't even return our calls."

Gary Hubbard tried to smooth things over, expressing his conviction that both parties had a "mutual need" to get the program done. He was "very excited," he said, and had "a lot of correspondence with Pennsylvania AFL-CIO leader Bill George," but, "we need a producer, we need to create a working model. . . . You have to meet us halfway."

When Fields reiterated how "frustrating" this all was, Miles cut in and asked Hubbard to spell out what he needed. Hubbard replied, "We need an operating budget, a pilot, and a song-and-dance act to go at it again with the state [labor] federation board." Miles summarized the request: "Let me be clear, you need a producer assigned, a budget, a program concept, and a dog-and-pony show, but you know the program will not be on the air without funding."

Hubbard exclaimed that Miles's response was music to his ears, and Miles rejoiced: "You're preaching to the converted. That is good news!" Miles said he didn't think money would be such a problem "if we get follow-through," and Fields joined in, "I'm not too busy for this." With such support, Hubbard then offered, he could just "pick up the phone and call [AFL-CIO president] John Sweeney."

The funding question led to discussion of the escrow fund. Calling the escrow account a deal-breaker, Miles insisted he would never stand for separate accounts. "We have to work together jointly to raise the money." Tension grew over this issue. Plummer said he was hopeful about their cooperation but added, "We are holding the option of the escrow fund just as you hold out the decision on *WDTW.*" After several more exchanges, Mark Wirick said the dispensation of the escrow fund would be up to Miles: "We could set it up one way if we reach agreement and cooperation and another way if we don't." Miles expressed the aspiration that *Labor Live!* could debut on Labor Day 1996. He also said he would get in touch with the people at *WDTW.*

Plummer expressed surprise about the recent appointment of a WQED labor representative to the CAB and advised Miles he wanted him to work through the ACLC regarding future appointments. Miles said he had deferred to Gary Hubbard on that nomination. Allen Kukovich suggested that there would be an opportunity to present names to the nominations committee at the next board meeting.

In his letter of commemoration, Paul Stackhouse specifically referred to Miles's agreement regarding *Labor Live!* "to immediately put together a program concept, statement, set a budget, assign a producer and put on a 'dog and pony show' to sell the idea and raise funds." Stackhouse suggested Peter Argentine as "our preference" for the *Labor Live!* producer. As both the son of a labor leader and a former staff producer for WQED and WGBH, Argentine looked like a good bridge between the groups. Finally, Stackhouse said he also expected to be asked to submit nominations to QED's board of directors and to its CAB "when openings occur."

Bad Faith

By March 1, we still had not heard from George Miles, so at my suggestion we scheduled a meeting with Peter Argentine to help develop the concept for the program. Argentine prepared some briefing materials to facilitate the meeting. The meeting was set for March 29. Just before we met, Stackhouse got a letter from Miles (dated March 26) that boded ill for our collaboration.

In the letter, Miles claimed that WQED had received "four sample programs from the upcoming season of *We Do the Work*" and all were "episodes from previous seasons that will be incorporated into this season." Since the "new programs won't be available to screen until April," Miles announced, the series would run on Fridays at 11 P.M., beginning on May 3, 1996, and WQED would "screen all the episodes as they become available and if any are inappropriate, we will hold them."

As for *Labor Live!*, Miles said his staff would be "developing this project over the next few months and we look forward to a joint marketing campaign to secure adequate funding to move ahead." He promised an "update" on "a program concept statement and budget by early Summer." Finally, Miles requested nominations for an expected opening on the CAB.

When the ACLC met on March 29, they discussed the letter. They noted that Miles had referred to openings on the CAB, but not on the board of directors. They also felt that the time scheduled for *WDTW*, opposite the local news, was not good. They preferred something no later than 10 P.M., even Sunday morning if necessary. They were also puzzled as to why Miles would proceed with the program concept and budget without input from the people he expected to underwrite it. They decided to work on the concept and budget themselves so that they could comment intelligently if and when WQED presented their proposal. Over the next few weeks, members shared numerous constructive suggestions by fax and in general meeting.

Stackhouse sent a letter to Miles on April 3, commending Miles for launching the series but expressing disappointment with the 11 P.M. scheduling. He suggested 7 to 10 P.M., or even Sunday morning between 9 A.M. and noon. "We had expected to be afforded an opportunity to comment before any decision was made," Stackhouse noted. He also informed Miles that our task force was "in the process of gathering ideas" for *Labor Live!* which would be "edited into a proposal" to "present for your consideration." However, we needed to know whether Miles agreed with the choice of Peter Argentine as producer "as we move forward on this show concept." Finally, Stackhouse advised, names would soon be submitted for consideration for places on both boards. He closed with hopes that "we would have an opportunity to address items of concern before final decisions are made and announced."

The Final Break

The next day, Glenn Plummer called Miles on the phone to follow up on Stackhouse's letter regarding the scheduling of *WDTW*. Plummer told me that B. J. Leber was in the room and Miles put the call on speakerphone. Plummer described Miles as "out of control," "screaming at me" like a "madman." According to Plummer, Miles said he was "pissed off" and had "called Gary [Hubbard] about this." When Plummer tried to reconstruct the communications, Miles interrupted, called it "a bunch of bullshit" and hung up.

On April 8, Plummer wrote to Miles asking him to apologize for his "irrational and rude behavior." He closed, "Neither Paul nor I would tolerate screaming and profanity from anyone on our committee and we expected to engage in a civil discourse with you. I, quite frankly, am disappointed." Miles did not respond.

On April 26, still keeping the faith, Stackhouse sent a letter to Miles recommending four candidates for openings on the two boards. Two of them were Mark Wirick and Glenn Plummer. Miles did not respond to Stackhouse's letter for more than ten weeks. However, *WDTW* did debut in May and ran as a summer replacement for twelve weeks, until mid-July. No representative of WQED made any contact with anyone at the ACLC regarding any of the matters supposedly under discussion. Given what had happened, none of the council committee members felt moved to promote the program.

On June 19, Miles sent an "update" on the three issues. He pretended as if the names submitted were for the community advisory board only and said the nominees would be notified by the committee of their status. Plummer was subsequently invited to serve on the CAB. Miles ignored the *Labor Live!* program planning altogether and made a vague reference to "local labor programming" being on WQED's "broad agenda" for "quality local programming" once their "financial situation is resolved."

In the end, George Miles banished *WDTW* forever. After some minor quibbles about repeated excerpts and advertising videos in the middle of the program, he concluded, "Overall, the past season of *We Do the Work* is not up to the standards of WQED 13. We would air the program again only with major improvements in the quality of production and better editing."

On July 3, Plummer wrote to Stackhouse, "Paul, it's pretty obvious to me and others on the media committee that there has been a lack of good faith on the part of WQED management in dealing with you and our representatives. They need to be reminded of our earlier agreement." From this point forward, labor concerns were off the agenda for WQED programming.

Looking back, I still believe that an active partnership would have been good for the station and for organized labor. How much this sorry ending had to do with the national bias in PBS against labor, which provided cover for George Miles, and how much it had to do with his own unwillingness to work with a community group around common objectives, I do not know.

In an interview with me, Corporation for Public Broadcasting staff member Pat Rudebusch said that CABs need "community leaders who can bring together different factions of the community." However, she advised, some CABs don't work because you have the "old way of thinking . . . usually among management, that any kind of outside involvement is bad because they will want to control programming."

As the second year of my service on the community advisory board was drawing to a close, WQED announced that CAB members were invited to extend their terms beyond the limits set by the bylaws. Management would decide which applications were accepted. This, of course, was a replication of the successful strategy that had been used to control the board of directors: retain a number of loyal followers, put them in positions of leadership, and have them socialize new members into their version of the committee's history and way of doing business.

By this time, the situation had changed dramatically. WQED had introduced a plan to commercialize and sell its second station, WQEX, that would effectively preempt any future requests for alternative programming. Having determined that the community advisory board was a black hole of volunteer energy, I resigned to concentrate on opposition to the sale of WQEX.

Chapter 6

What Am I Bid?
Stripping Assets at WQED

On April 25, 1996, the whole terrain of the battle to reform public broadcasting in Pittsburgh changed dramatically. That evening I got a call from the *Post-Gazette*'s Ron Weiskind, asking my opinion of legislation that would expedite FCC approval for WQED to convert WQEX's license to permit the station's use for commercial broadcasting, an act he said would "certainly" lead to its sale.

According to Weiskind's subsequent *Post-Gazette* story, George Miles denied that the station was in imminent danger of going dark: "Times are very difficult for all of us. But I don't think the bank would have shut us down at all. The bank would have worked with us. I have no doubt about it." Nevertheless, Miles looked forward to reviewing his options and retiring WQED's "debt of more than $10 million" with enough left over "to allow the station to invest in new technologies that would ensure its future health." He admitted that he had "spent most of [his] time over the past year dealing with this issue." Actually, such considerations might have started with WQED CEO search chair Jim Roddey's hiring discussions with Miles almost two years earlier, in May 1994.

Roddey—now chair of QED's board of directors—was active in the state and national Republican parties and an advisor to Republican county commissioner Bob Cranmer through the Richard Scaife–subsidized Allegheny Institute for Public Policy. He was also an outspoken advocate of privatizing government services, either by selling them outright to commercial providers or contracting them out while laying off government employees. Through the Allegheny Institute, Roddey had proposed contracting out potentially profitable Allegheny County Port Authority lines to private carriers, as well as the privatization of one of the four county-run Kane Regional Health Centers.

Several of Roddey's companies do business with the government. His Wexford Company had been awarded a $100 million state contract to provide medical services to nine prisons in central Pennsylvania. In 1999, activists revealed that Wexford had been found guilty by the U.S. Justice Department of several violations, a report that led to the termination of Wexford's services to the Wyoming state prison health care system. Upon questioning, a spokesperson for Wexford claimed that the corporation was the target of 212 lawsuits in several states. Of these, 7 were settled out of court, 80 were dismissed, and 125 were still pending.

Selling the Sell-off

At the June 30, 1995, joint meeting of QED's finance and strategic planning committees, the debt question took center stage. Only eleven members of the board were present. Money was still coming in: $7 million of $10 million in pledges for the capital campaign and $2 million in corporate and foundation grants had been received. CFO Mel Ming proposed that "operating relief of $3.5 million could . . . reduce the debt to a reasonable level."

Initially, Roddey suggested going to the bank "with a debt reduction plan." Don Korb asserted that the approach to the budget should be to "*aim for a high level of profitability, even if it meant selling assets to do so*" (italics mine). Roddey and Miles rejected selling the magazine and closing down television program production, even though the latter, in Ming's view, would allow the station to "probably do very well."

Roddey and Miles then unveiled what was to become "the plan." Roddey asked whether "most of [WQED's] operations could be covered with one television station." In his view, the "fair market value just for [WQEX's] license alone could be anywhere from $20 to $30 million." Cautioning that it could take "five to ten years to change the noncommercial license," Miles said they would have to go "to legislators to attach a change to a bill to . . . convert the signal to a commercial license." Roddey suggested getting "support from the Pittsburgh business community and their lobbying sources." Jane Johnston wondered whether "there would be any objections by any of the constituents of Channel 16 [WQEX]" and Miles agreed that they would have to "be sensitive to the negatives of a sale." The following September, Miles hired Washington lobbyist Don Dutko of Dutko Associates to promote his privatization proposal to legislators.

From 1990 to 1994 WQEX had grown to be the third most watched "second station" in the nation. Former WQEX station manager Michael Fields later reflected that his predecessors had invented a different style for WQEX because they believed that "Pittsburgh needed an alternative public voice, not a mere copy of WQED." Once the deal was on the table, however, no one at WQED, excepting Allen Kukovich, ever questioned the planned conversion and sale on behalf of WQEX's viewers in the community.

At the December 7, 1995, board meeting, Roddey asked the press and public to leave because the board was going into "executive session." Before complying *Post-Gazette* reporter Sally Kalson asked that "an objection be recorded to show cause why the meeting be closed." After the room was cleared, the minutes record a discussion of the settlement of a lawsuit by Sullivan Entertainment, Inc., of Toronto, against WQED for nonpayment of fees related to the production of two *Wonderworks* films. It was also recorded that the station was "awaiting word on the amendment which would allow [WQED] to take one of our licenses and convert it to commercial and sell [it] on the market." According to FCC and CPB regulations, neither of these topics constituted cause for excluding the public from the meeting.

Finally, on January 19, 1996, a short article by the *Post-Gazette*'s Barbara Vancheri breached the secrecy surrounding WQED's planned sell-off of Channel 16. While Miles was vague about the station's intentions and Vancheri was cautious about the project's possibilities, both acknowledged that WQED was seeking special new legislation—as part of the 1996 telecommunications bill—that would permit WQED to convert Channel 16 to a commercial frequency. Vancheri called it a "historic switch," but you wouldn't have known it from the story's placement and brevity.

Members of the community advisory board had never been informed, let alone consulted, on the plan to commercialize WQEX, and they chose not to talk about it. In my view, however, it would mean the end of community-oriented programming at WQED. At the same time, I naively assumed that an "act of Congress" to set "an historic" precedent surely would require a very public debate and formal decision. That, at least, is what I was taught in my high school civics class. The call from Weiskind began a new lesson.

WQED did not succeed in getting the legislation it was seeking included in the telecommunications bill, but the matter didn't end there. Pennsylvania Republican senator Arlen Specter and Democratic Congressman John Murtha had been assigned to negotiate the compromise between the House and Senate versions of the 1996 Omnibus Budget Bill. Taking advantage of their position, they surreptitiously buried language in the expense authorizations for the FCC and the Federal Maritime Commission which would permit WQED to petition the FCC to delete WQEX's designation as noncommercial and sell the channel to whomever it wanted. Furthermore, once WQED petitioned, the FCC would have only thirty days to reply, and although the FCC could "solicit such comments as it deems necessary," the determination would be made "without conducting a rule-making or other proceeding."

Prior to this budget bill maneuver, under existing regulations, a licensee was required to petition the FCC for a change in the character of the channel assignment. This process usually takes several months, sometimes years, and is done with extensive public comment. Moreover, once the licensee's petition is granted, application must be opened to competition from all parties who might wish to operate the new commercial station. In such a manner, the FCC protects the public interest in channel assignments from media profiteering. The proposed legislation would have permitted WQED to claim its second channel as its own property and sell it for profit with almost no opportunity for the public to express its interest in the matter.

I called the FCC, asked for the legal division, and finally found a staff member named Bob Hayne who was witness to the deal's origins. He said that sometime around the beginning of April, certain FCC officials had been called into the office of allocations division bureau chief Roy Stewart. Claiming "pressure from the Hill," Stewart reportedly asked them what it would take to have an asterisk (designating noncommercial status) removed. Hayne told him that this was forbidden by a provision, standard to every budget bill, that specifically forbids the FCC from doing anything to decrease the number of noncommercial channels available to the public.

"What if the provision were missing from the upcoming appropriations bill?" Stewart asked. Hayne told him that regulations would require a rule-making procedure, followed by extensive public comment, to remove the reservation. He added that in such a case "there would be strong opposition, perhaps a fight to the death." A week later, Hayne told me, he noticed something in the trade press about Pittsburgh and "knew something was up." He also estimated the value of a commercial UHF frequency in Pittsburgh's $185 million advertising market as a "windfall" worth between $20 and $40 million.

Without fully realizing what it would take, I committed myself to stopping this deal. Pittsburgh needed this alternative station, I believed, and it was unconscionable that it be looted to cover debts incurred by management waste and—perhaps, embezzlement. Moreover, this wasn't just a local matter. As Steve Behrens reported in the trade paper *Current* on May 13, "If WQED persuades the FCC to give its okay, the station sale may become the model for similar revenue-generating moves in other cities." Bob Hayne and others projected that a precedent like this could jeopardize almost seventy stations nationwide in markets with at least some degree of "overlap." One could easily imagine the many stations in the several state-owned networks being eyeballed by governors and legislators looking for a quick fix to their revenue shortfalls. A reporter told me he had overheard Miles boasting to a roomful of executives that other public broadcasting officials were calling the budget bill's language the "Miles amendment."

Mounting a Challenge

To stop the deal I needed to recruit a communications lawyer with FCC experience. Since we at the Accounting Project had no money, it would have to be someone willing to work pro bono. I also knew that success would depend on the extent to which we were able to turn an inside deal into a public controversy with national implications. That meant broadening the movement locally and writing and placing stories in the local and national press. The basic idea was to put public pressure on decision makers at all levels to do the right thing, from the WQED board to the FCC commissioners. I also knew I couldn't possibly do all those things without considerable help.

Since I had the necessary knowledge of the issues and national media connections, I looked for someone to take over local organizing. I approached Linda Wambaugh, of the Alliance for Progressive Action (APA). Wambaugh, then forty-three years old, had served as vice president of the APA until 1996. Seeking to get involved with bigger issues like racism and human rights, she resigned as full-time union organizer for Service Employees International Union 585 after thirteen years and in the spring of 1996, became full-time coordinator of the APA. This meant choosing projects to work on in the name of the organization and trying to raise funds to support her own salary in the process.

When I approached Wambaugh at the end of April 1996, the timing was perfect. She was impressed with the level of community support for the QED

Accountability Project and saw this new campaign as an opportunity to expand APA's coalition work, especially around the issue of opposing privatization. Looking back, she reports that the main excitement was in representing the anger of station donors who felt disenfranchised from the decision-making process.

Wambaugh agreed to become cochair of the campaign, concentrating on local organizing while I attended to legal representation, writing position pieces, and generating national press coverage. I turned over to her the Project's three-hundred-member computerized mailing list and other useful materials. We agreed that the immediate focus would be to call for public hearings on the question, starting with a membership mailing and a press conference. Wambaugh also proposed a demonstration at the next board meeting. To symbolize the new partnership we decided to call ourselves the Save Pittsburgh Public Television Campaign.

Finding an attorney was another matter. I definitely had a sense of urgency. WQED continually referred to June 1 as the intended filing date for their petition to commercialize WQEX—and already it was May. I knew I would soon be out of town for three weeks, on a long-planned trip to Italy with my wife and friends. Who knows how many months WQED had spent putting together its case and marshalling the support of "the Pittsburgh business community and their lobbying sources"?

WQED's public relations campaign was already in high gear. Miles and Roddey booked themselves on WQEX's *Cullen/Devlin* show to boost WQEX's commercialization, without opposition (I was later told the call-ins to the show were mostly critical). Miles also promoted a puff piece in the *City Paper*, and he and Roddey had a meeting with the editorial board of the *Post-Gazette*. Based on the reactions of supporters and focus groups, they had developed a whole new sell, now claiming that WQED was in danger of insolvency: "If you look at our balance sheet, if we were a commercial outlet, I think they would turn the lights out tomorrow." A month later, Miles warned, "Every day that goes by here, we get closer and closer to the edge."

Miles and Roddey also claimed that they had not decided what they would do once the "dereservation" was granted by the FCC. They described their options as selling WQEX outright, leasing it, or operating it as a for-profit venture in a kind of partnership the media industry calls a "local management agreement." Therefore, they insisted, there was no need yet for board approval of the FCC petition.

To downplay their ambitions, Miles and Roddey dropped talk of national productions and promised more local programming on WQED. Finally, station leaders offered pie in the sky: WQED would go to a twenty-four-hour schedule so that it could carry all programs currently scheduled on both of the two stations. Moreover, they claimed, the new digital technology that the money from the sale of WQEX would afford would enable WQED to broadcast "four separate, programmable signals," easily enough to provide programming for everyone.

As the campaign went forward, Miles and Roddy offered any arguments they thought the public would buy. One argument lamented the decline in the region's overall market and concluded that Pittsburgh could no longer afford two public television stations. They also claimed that similar legislation was being drafted in Congress for all the "duopolies" in the country. Miles, who chaired the APTS board, never acknowledged his central role in these national policy discussions.

Although we had answers to all these claims, it wouldn't matter unless we had legal counsel to oppose WQED's FCC petition. The first attorney to come to my attention as a possibility was Fred Polner, of the Pittsburgh firm of Rothman Gordon. An article by Barbara Vancheri on May 2 quoted him as saying, "It's a shame that WQED has used backroom politics to sell off a community asset which has been entrusted to them to be held in the public interest, not for their own self-aggrandizement."

When I called Polner to see if he would take the case, I learned that he was a graduate of the Georgetown University Law Center, after which he had worked for many years for the FCC. Polner said a campaign like this would consume a lot of time, work, and money, but invited me to send him a written solicitation. Although when we next spoke Polner turned me down, he continued to watch developments in the press and began calling to give me advice. And eventually he would become even more involved.

A May 6 Associated Press piece quoted Andrew Jay Schwartzman, executive director of the Washington, D.C., Media Access Project, as saying, "It sets a terrible precedent. . . . Just because WQED has botched things financially doesn't mean it should eat Pittsburgh's seed corn for public discourse." I called him. Schwartzman was sympathetic but had too many things on his plate just then. He referred me to the Institute for Public Representation of the Georgetown University Law Center, where I spoke with director Angela Campbell. She too sympathized, but the timing of my request was bad for her; it was the end of the semester, no student interns were available, and her staff was already committed to other cases. She promised to keep me in mind.

Within the next couple of weeks I pitched our campaign to ten nationally known communications attorneys, including Nick Miller, former FCC commissioner Nicholas Johnson, and David Rice, who had battled KQED for twelve years on behalf of the Committee to Save KQED (in San Francisco). These last three offered advice and limited support, but none of them could take the case, and they had cautionary words about a citizen's group challenging a broadcaster at the FCC.

Making the Issue Public

Meanwhile, I wrote a twelve-hundred-word feature for *In Pittsburgh* under the headline "Plan to Sell Public Channel Angers Activists." In the article, I exposed the background for the sale and contrasted the WQED establishment's interest in "a windfall of $20 to $40 million" with their obligation to preserve a public trust for community service programming. In the piece I rejected the threat of creditor Mellon Bank's shutting down the station only to inherit its meager disposable assets and a whirlwind of bad publicity. (In fact, WQED's total net worth in 1991 was reported as only $4.0 million). I highlighted the fact that, according to Allen Kukovich, despite past scandals "the WQED board had never even discussed what would be done with all that money" from the proposed sale of WQEX. And Kukovich and I raised the specter of a national precedent.

In conclusion, I called WQEX "a community resource for public information"—like our libraries and museums. "Given the drive toward privatization," I asked rhetorically, would there soon be nothing left that was guided by public service rather than profit-making—"nothing left that is owned by the people?" Finally, I called on people to "stop this fire sale" by contacting the FCC and the APA and attending our June 4 press conference and rally.

I got a shorter version of this article into the *Tribune-Review* and wrote an op-ed piece for the *Post-Gazette* in which I accused WQED of proposing "to destroy public television in order to save it." I reviewed the parent corporation's shortcomings, pointing out that it was controlled by a small local elite that manipulated a "rubber-stamp" board of directors, and that its community advisory board was "a black hole of volunteer energy." Since 80 percent of WQEX's station's support had come from taxpayers and subscribers, I proposed that "if WQED no longer wants to operate it as a public station, then the FCC and the community should find someone who does." I called upon the WQED board "to stop the mad rush toward dumping . . .

a valuable community resource" and closed with an invitation to the rally and instructions on how to contact the FCC and the APA.

Around this time I got a call from Larry Rogow, president of Venture Technologies, Inc., in Los Angeles, who advised me that he had called Michael Fields about buying WQEX. He reported that Fields boasted that the station consumed only about $1 million of WQED's budget and made a profit of $200,000 or more each year. In the end, Fields told Rogow that WQED wanted a lot more than Rogow was willing to pay for WQEX and they expected to get it.

Responding to my *Post-Gazette* letter with one of his own, Jim Roddey put me down as "a self-proclaimed expert on public broadcasting" and characterized my opposition as "strident, inflammatory and uninformed." He said that, contrary to my objections, hiring a consultant to guide the station's transition would have been a waste of money, and that keeping many of the old members on the new board had been necessary for "continuity." Roddey went on to call the FCC petition "the moment WQED has been waiting for almost two years" and "a blessing." He promised that the corporation's debt would be paid off and the public rewarded with "a 24-hour a day WQED 13 with a nightly local presence." My challenge, on the other hand, was threatening "the destruction (through financial collapse) of public broadcasting in Pittsburgh."

Three days later, Miles and Roddey announced layoffs that they claimed would save the station $1.8 million per year in salaries. A month later it was revealed that Mellon Bank had been paid $2.3 million out of WQED's "restricted" capital campaign fund at the end of April. Lest anyone think that its creditor would be satisfied with such progress, WQED continued to maintain that the bank would settle for nothing less than the cashing in of WQEX. The press did not question this nor challenge the bank to comment.

In response, Linda Wambaugh organized a demonstration outside WQED for their upcoming May 24 board meeting. In a departure from its usual placement, the *Post-Gazette* ran the story on page one with a large picture of Roddey and Miles with sad faces and their hands folded in a praying position. The headline read, " 'Tight Money Crunch' Claims 14% of Jobs at WQED." Actually, twelve positions were cut and another fourteen converted to freelance in what Miles described as a plan to adopt a "studio model," in which the station would expand and contract according to production needs. He claimed the move would enable the station to hold its debt at $12 million.

At the meeting, Allen Kukovich questioned the speed with which the process was moving and what the loss of WQEX programming would do to the viewer base for public broadcasting in Pittsburgh. He also suggested that WQED might address public concerns about the sale of its second station through a series of public hearings. Finally, Kukovich asked whether the board of directors should vote on the decision to petition the FCC for dereservation. Roddey told him it wasn't necessary. Miles responded only, "The longer we wait this out, August or later, we will just continue to bleed." Kukovich was the only board member to question the impending deal.

The next day, the *Tribune-Review* led with our protest. The story was headlined "WQED Board Snubs Protest Group, Slashes 12 positions." It featured a photo of one of our pickets ("WQEX Is a Community Asset"), but Wambaugh was quoted only briefly: "They run this place more and more like commercial TV all the time. This isn't a business, it's a public trust."

A longer story in the *Post-Gazette* quoted some of the protestors' signs: "WQEX Is Not Yours to Sell," "Keep Public TV in Mr. Rogers' Neighborhood," and "We Question Secret Decisions." Wambaugh, who had been denied permission to address the board, focused her statement to the *Post-Gazette* on the exclusion of subscribers and contributors from "input into the sale" of a "public trust" and accused WQED management of arrogance. Roddey was reported as saying that Wambaugh had not been allowed to speak only because our group had not notified the board in advance; he complained about the picketing and asserted, "They really haven't asked to sit down and discuss the facts of the issue." He was losing his absolute control of the situation. Clearly we were getting to him.

Both the board meeting and the protest were covered on public radio station WDUQ and the "all news" station KQV. Chris Potter's *In Pittsburgh* "Media Watch" column protested the shutting off of "community dialogue," the secret legislation, the manipulation of the board, and the increasing influence of corporations on the station. One of our members, Mark Ginsberg of the University of Pittsburgh, wrote to the *Post-Gazette* to protest the "unneighborlyness at WQED" and to urge Miles and Roddey to use their "political capital" to increase funding for public broadcasting rather than sell off WQEX.

As the public debate widened, Duquesne University communications professor Robert Bellamy wrote an op-ed piece against the sale, suggesting that the gain "would be temporary and no guarantee against future money problems." He called public television "the last outlet for accessible programming not solely dependent on the audience as commodity," pointed out that the need for such "noncommercial service" was greater than ever, and urged WQED to "explore any and all alternatives—including alliances with educational institutions, foundations and community organizations—to support the maintenance of WQEX."

I called Bellamy to ask him to approach his own university's administration about taking over WQEX. As previously noted, Duquesne already operated National Public Radio's WDUQ, and it had a large broadcast communications program. Bellamy approached the WDUQ-FM station manager and the university's provost, both of whom he considered friends. Within two days a memo from the university's president, John Murray, was on the desk of Bellamy's department chair, instructing him to order Bellamy to "cease and desist" all such inquiries. It turned out that Roddey had already seen Murray in order to preempt just such an option. (Two years later Murray would join WQED's board.)

On June 2, two days before the Save Pittsburgh Public Television press conference, the *Tribune-Review* editorialized on behalf of the sale of WQEX. The editorial raised the specter of a Mellon Bank shutdown and repeated "one estimate" of the station's value as $60 million. It went on to say, "Miles wants to recapture WQED's lost status as a primary supplier of quality programming to national and regional audiences." Despite the lessons of the past, the *Tribune-Review* considered this a "bold agenda," an "embrace of realism," and a "sound business plan." Our objection that the station was a public trust was dismissed as "rhetoric."

As of the day of the press conference and rally we still had no legal representation and WQED was saying they would file their petition in three days. In a desperate holding tactic, I prevailed upon Jon Pushinsky to write to the FCC as our counsel and to announce our intention to oppose WQED's petition to dereserve WQEX. While a student at the University of Pennsylvania in the mid-1970s, Pushinsky had taken a seminar with me. He had gone on to obtain a law degree, move to Pittsburgh, and become active on behalf of public interest causes. On June 5, he wrote to the FCC on our behalf, requesting that it "refrain from considering the petition" until it received our response.

On June 6, my plea was answered. Angela Campbell of Georgetown's Institute for Public Representation had persuaded an attorney named David Honig to take our case. Honig called me and described himself as "the last resort" for those in need. He expected strong political and technical support and only required funds to cover his travel and lodging in Pittsburgh should these prove to be necessary. At his request, I sent him a large file that included the text of the budget bill legislation, Pushinsky's FCC notification, a summary of our campaign and legal advice received thus far, and a large packet of our press clippings. I was elated and called Wambaugh to share the good news. The fight to save WQEX was going to the FCC!

The Federal Communications Commission

The campaign to save Pittsburgh public television had entered a new arena, so some introduction is in order. Congress established the Federal Communications Commission (FCC) in 1934 for the purpose of regulating the broadcasting industry for the "public interest, convenience and necessity."

In 1946, the FCC established that stations had an obligation to broadcast: (1) noncommercial programs (because they served minorities and allowed for program experimentation), (2) live local programs, and (3) programs devoted to public discussion, and to eliminate commercial advertising excesses.

In subsequent years various FCC and court decisions reaffirmed the First Amendment rights of people to receive information from greatly divergent sources, to hear competing sides of an issue, and to reply to biased statements. Another series of rulings from 1969 to 1979 curtailed advertising excesses, especially for children. Since 1952, the FCC has reserved approximately 25 percent of television channels for noncommercial use.

Unfortunately, the FCC is heavily influenced by the industry it is supposed to regulate. Commissioners' personal contacts are much more likely to be with representatives of the industry than with ordinary citizens. Most commissioners take positions in the communications industry after their terms of service. In such an environment, broadcasters' appeals on behalf of their ability to make a profit tend to become persuasive.

Worse yet, commissioners are subject to constant lobbying, often by political officials who control the FCC's budget and appointments. In the history of FCC regulation, to the best of my knowledge, no local license transfers and only three license renewals have ever been denied.

In the 1980s, Reagan-led deregulation reversed almost all the public interest gains in favor of the property interests of broadcasters. Petitions to deny became very infrequent because the FCC seldom ruled on behalf of citizens' groups. The constraints on negotiated settlements were tightened to the point where citizen's agreements had no teeth anymore.

Reagan's FCC commissioner Mark Fowler, pledged "to take deregulation to the limits of existing law." In 1984 the FCC abolished the guidelines for local, news and public affairs and non-entertainment programming. By 1989, one of three network affiliates offered no public affairs programs and one of six no news. The limit on prime-time advertising was rescinded and commercial time doubled. By the end of the 1980s, a new format, program-length infomercials, consumed 3 percent of broadcast time. Restrictions on children's program advertising were abandoned, albeit later restored.

The most significant step backward was to repeal the Fairness Doctrine requiring that broadcasters address controversial issues of public interest and provide a fair representation of opposing views. After that, free speech belonged only to those with the big bucks to own a station. The rest of us, in columnist Norman Solomon's phrase, had "the right to speak, but not to be heard."

These vested interests and legal precedents obviously constrained the arguments and evidence we could use to save, let alone improve, our local public broadcasting station. At the same time, each case raises new issues, and this one had no precedent. Moreover, each case presents opportunities for new rulings that might serve others struggling for greater media democracy.

Our Legal Campaign Begins

David Honig sent me a copy of his resumé and some quotes for the press. A 1983 graduate of the Georgetown University Law Center, Honig is a communications lawyer with offices in both Washington, D.C., and his home in Miami Beach, Florida. At the time, he had litigated seventeen federal appeals in four courts and participated in over eighty FCC rule-making proceedings and hundreds of adjudicatory cases.

He and I talked regularly on the phone as he advised me on the campaign, requested documents (WQED and WQEX program schedules, for example), and suggested actions. As we came closer to the filing deadline his many other commitments caught up with him, but fortunately he was able to recruit the additional support needed to complete the filing.

We had heard that *Post-Gazette* editor John Craig had given Miles and Roddey a forum to advocate their case without opposition on his WQED program *The Editors*. On June 10, as expected, the *Post-Gazette* ran a five-hundred-word boxed editorial urging the FCC to grant WQED's petition to convert WQEX's license to commercial.

The editorial invoked WQED's "storied" past as a "nationally renowned" producer, praising the very policies that had brought the station to its financial crisis. The editors wrote off WQED's "past mistakes and lax management" as irrelevant because cutbacks in corporate underwriting were a "national phenomenon." They concluded that Pittsburgh couldn't afford two public television stations and should settle for "one strong one rather than two weak ones," a phrase that echoed WQED's rhetoric.

I quickly knocked out a reply of similar length and sent it to Wambaugh for her to submit in order to preempt its rejection on the grounds that my opinions had recently been published. I characterized the editorial as "a re-hash of WQED press releases," lamented that we had lost a competing editorial voice when the *Post-Gazette* took over the *Pittsburgh Press* in 1992, and expanded this into a discussion of the "trend toward media monopolization" and its consequences. I criticized WQED for its "self-serving management," "rubber-stamp board," conservative programming, and national producer "ambitions," and called for "no sale" of this "public trust."

Now the issue was hot. People were calling the Alliance for Progressive Action to volunteer, and petitions and letters were pouring in. Two letters from folks we didn't know were published in the *Post-Gazette*; each praised WQEX, protested the dereservation, and threatened the loss of contributions to WQED if they dumped their second station.

Fortunately, WQED was behind schedule in assembling its petition, so we still had time to get our own case together. On June 24, Honig wrote to the FCC commissioners to announce his representation of our organization, alert them to the likely national ramifications of the case, and request adequate time to respond to WQED's filing. We were granted ten days from the day of WQED's petition to submit our paperwork in opposition. The FCC would then have fifteen days to make a decision.

Under Honig's guidance, we started assembling our materials right away. Wambaugh accelerated the solicitation of letters and the circulation of citizen petitions opposing the dereservation. I organized my notes and wrote lengthy statements about the WQED violations of FCC regulations that I had personally witnessed.

Taking the Fight to City Hall

In the days before the press conference/rally, I had come up with the idea of using the Pittsburgh City Council as a forum. While it had no legal claim on WQED, that body did have a responsibility to consider whether the public interest would be served by the sale of WQEX. I figured that since the council itself was newsworthy, the action would generate more media attention, and this in turn might add to the pressure on WQED board members. I looked for help from City Council president Jim Ferlo, a radical community organizer in his youth. I spoke with Ferlo's chief aide, Paul Gerdany, and soon got the go-ahead to prepare a resolution for Ferlo to introduce.

In consultation with Gerdany, I drafted the resolution that councilmen Ferlo and Gene Ricciardi cosponsored; which called for the City Council to communicate to the FCC its opposition to the commercialization of WQEX. Since Ferlo advised me that success depended on a strong showing to persuade the council of the public's concern, campaign staff person Benita Campbell called around to rally support. The week before the council's next meeting, I sent a cover letter and packet of clippings as background to all council members, following up with phone calls. Only Councilman Dan Cohen was available to talk, and he claimed to be ignorant of the issues; I gave him some background and urged him to read the clippings.

On May 16, the day of the council meeting, the *Post-Gazette* ran a note quoting Ferlo as trying to stop a "rush to judgment" that would "sever an important public trust." He said WQED executives should be held account-able for past mismanagement and that he found it "offensive that we're allowing WQED, whose existence is owed to public support . . . to engage in this downsizing, profiteering move."

Mayor Tom Murphy was invited to the hearing but did not attend—he later wrote a letter supporting the sale. Ferlo presided over the hearing, which he described as preliminary. George Miles, Jim Roddey, and Gwen Elliott spoke for WQED. Seven core members represented us: Russ Gib-bons, Mark Ginsberg, Molly Rush, Linda Wambaugh, Benita Campbell, Bo-nita Johnson, and me. Attorney Jonathan Robison also spoke. Of the nine counsel members, only councilmen Ferlo, Cohen, and Dan Onorato stayed throughout. Four others either left early or came late, and two never even showed.

It soon became clear that the council members were ignorant of the is-sues and that WQED had lobbied some of them personally. Councilman Mark Hertzberg admitted that he and Councilman Sala Udin had spent "two hours at WQED getting a presentation on their debt situation" and that he had "no solution." Cohen seemed stuck on the assumption that I had a re-sponsibility to either offer WQED a solution to its debt problem that it was willing to accept or step aside for the sale.

Councilwoman Valerie McDonald, while critical of "WQED's failure to inform the public" for such "downsizing," nevertheless said she wouldn't "tie WQED's hands as long as there is no solution to the debt," whereupon Jim

Ferlo pointed out to her that we were requesting public hearings precisely so that such alternatives might be explored. Onerato stated that he "strongly support[ed] the sale," but he betrayed a fundamental misunderstanding of its ramifications. He thought that WQED could simply commercialize WQEX and continue to run the same programs as before. He considered this "a golden opportunity. . . . We can have WQED and, at the same time, we can have WQEX which can make a profit. . . . In fact, the money from a commercial WQEX could be used to subsidize WQED."

Later, under questioning, Roddey admitted that under present law WQED could not operate WQEX as a commercial station. I don't know if Onerato understood the relevance of this concession, but by this time he had said what he had planned to say and was done; when Roddey rose to leave, both Onerato and Cohen leaped to their feet and followed him outside to shake his hand.

Gene Ricciardi, cosponsor of the resolution, whispered encouragement to me but never spoke and also left early. Ferlo later complained to me that unless we were able to do a better job at educating his colleagues this would be the last council hearing on the issue. We had no time to follow up, and it was.

Still, the hearing was successful in a number of ways.

First, we used the occasion to announce David Honig as our counsel and this got a sidebar in the *Tribune-Review* coverage. Second, Ferlo's pithy quotes ("Basically, WQED operates like a benevolent clique. WQEX is going to become the next Home Shopping Network. I think there's no question about that") ran unopposed, with Councilman Onerato noted as "WQED's only vocal supporter" and other council members listed as undecided.

Third, I had more time than usual to lay out our case while all the media were there. In response to Miles's apocalyptic prediction that failure to solve the debt problem could cause the community to "lose both of our public television stations," I was quoted as saying, "It's our television frequency. If this corporation should fail, people should know, it would not mean the end of public television in Pittsburgh. . . . It would just mean the end of the WQED corporation, a corporation that perhaps should face the consequences of its own mistakes, rather than pass them on to the public. Other institutions in this community would then be invited by the Federal Communications Commission to step forward and make application."

And public radio's WDUQ aired the following excerpt from my testimony continuously for two days: "If I saw someone stealing a book out of the public library, I would yell, 'Stop, thief!' It would not matter to me if such person complained that he'd gambled his money away and needed to sell the book to cover his debts. This proposed conversion and sale is equivalent to selling off half the public libraries in the greater Pittsburgh area."

Fourth, the issue of the lack of an effective decision-making process at WQED got a lot of attention, and this forced those in charge to go through the motions at their next board meeting. In addition, the WQEX sale had been brought into a new political arena and its salience raised for the public.

Finally, Miles and Roddey out and out lied to council members about their plans. Paul Gerdany later told me that this happened all the time at council hearings. Since the hearing was tape-recorded, however, we were able to transcribe the testimony and document their lies in our FCC petition.

In an apparent attempt to downplay the importance of both the dereservation petition and the fact that the board had not voted to approve the action, Roddey told the City Council: "We keep hearing this referred to as the sale of [WQEX] and that in fact is not yet determined. Once the . . . station is designated as . . . commercial, we would then begin . . . looking at several options. One option would be the sale of the station. Another option would be leasing the station to someone that would operate it as a commercial property and we would still hold title. Another option would be to petition the FCC to allow us to operate the station as a commercial license or a portion of it as commercial." At the time, however, WQED had already signed a binding agreement with Cornerstone TeleVision, Inc., operator of WPCB Channel 40, regarding how to share the revenue from the sale of Channel 16. (I was never able to persuade the main dailies to print this evidence, even later, while Roddey was running for county executive. Needless to add, both papers endorsed him.)

Railroad Job: The Decision to Commercialize WQEX

In anticipation of the WQED board meeting on June 21st Wambaugh had requested by registered mail that I be granted fifteen minutes to address the board, and I had written a speech for the occasion. As planned, on June 21st, in advance of the meeting, a diverse gathering of about twenty-five of our supporters picketed against the sale outside of WQED.

Only sixteen of the twenty-four board members were in attendance for the meeting that proposed to change the corporation forever. Also present were eleven WQED staff and several media people. When the board had been seated, our supporters were allowed to crowd in around the table and against the wall. The room was full and heavy with drama. After approval of the minutes, Roddey started to ask the board for approval to file the FCC petition. I interrupted, asking if I could address the board. Roddey told me that I would be allowed to speak at the end of the meeting. I replied that my purpose in speaking was only to influence the outcome of the vote. He then granted me ten minutes to make my case.

The first part of my speech reviewed the scandals surrounding the station's financial problems and the failed attempts to empower the board to think and act independently. Roddey turned around, tapped his finger, and instructed me to "get to the point." "These are my ten minutes," I shot back. "Yeah," said Wambaugh from the side of the room. Roddey swiveled back around to face his board.

I looked out over the board. In thirty years of teaching and public speaking, I had never seen such implacable faces; absolutely no expression. I motioned toward the citizens crammed against the wall and implored the members of the board to postpone their vote until they had a chance to hear from "these good people." Not one even turned a head. "You need to give the community a chance to help you save this station," I pleaded. "It belongs to them." I closed by challenging the board to show us this was not "a railroad job" by voting to withhold submission of the petition until the people had been heard.

Reacting to this challenge, Roddey asked executive committee member William Rackoff to chair a subcommittee to meet with us. Rackoff agreed and Roddey appointed five others to join him. There was no explanation offered or requested as to the purpose and parameters of this new subcommittee. Roddey then called for a vote to file the petition with the FCC. There was no discussion and the vote was unanimous. Allen Kukovich was not present and Gary Hubbard voted his approval. Roddey said he expected that the subcommittee would meet, and in another gesture for the press he got a WQED attorney to confirm his assertion that WQED could always withdraw its petition later if it chose to do so.

I motioned for Wambaugh and Mark Ginsberg to join me outside to discuss this action. I argued that this was a cynical maneuver designed to give WQED the appearance of openness and they agreed: meanwhile the petition was going forward and the clock would be ticking on our mere ten days for response. We decided to accept the invitation only if the subcommittee's meetings had potential consequences. We put forth two conditions that I sent in writing to Rackoff: (1) that "the filing be postponed until we have had a chance to meet and you to report back to the board", and (2) that our meeting be broadcast live or on tape on one of the stations.

Wambaugh advised the press that Roddey's "compromise" was "a cynical way of setting us up and circumventing real public input." "There's no rush in filing the petition," she explained. "But once it's filed, there is a rush because the legislation calls for it to be expedited. It's just not possible to get a full public hearing and serious consideration of all the issues and alternatives in thirty days." Rackoff wrote back that they were not empowered to comply with our two requests.

WQED Filing Contains Bombshell

Attorneys Steven Lerman and Barbara Gardner filed WQED's "Petition to Delete Noncommercial Reservation" on June 24, 1996. The *Post-Gazette's* Sally Kalson got a copy ahead of time and called to advise me that the petition contained "a bombshell": there, buried under Point 9 on page 7 of Exhibit 4, was a "Contingent Obligation."

This was the confirmation that earlier, on May 23, 1996, WQED had signed an agreement with Cornerstone TeleVision, Inc., licensee of WPCB Channel 40. Should the FCC decline WQED's petition, the agreement required Cornerstone "to exchange Channel 40 for Channel 16 to permit WQED to assign the license for Channel 40 to a commercial buyer" subject to FCC approval. In such event, "Cornerstone, a non-profit corporation," would operate Channel 16 "as a noncommercial station." The agreement provided that "the net proceeds of this sale will be evenly divided between Cornerstone and WQED, except that Cornerstone [shall] be entitled to 60 percent of any proceeds in excess of $45 million."

There was more. Should WQED's original petition succeed, it would still pay Cornerstone $7.5 million just for making this contingency plan available. When we were finally able to get a copy of the "asset exchange agreement," about a year later, it also revealed a $1 million payment to Cornerstone to relocate the Channel 16 antenna to Cornerstone's studio.

Within a week of the board meeting, WQED sent letters and a summary of the FCC petition to all board members. The vote was described as "unanimous." The only reference to Cornerstone stated that "Cornerstone TeleVision will receive a monetary benefit for its willingness to exchange a valuable commercial license for a substantially less valuable noncommercial license for the benefit of WQED Pittsburgh." The amount of the benefit was unspecified. Many board members learned the facts first from the press, including information about Cornerstone itself.

Cornerstone: Televangelism, Commercialism, and Right-wing Politics

Evangelist Russell Bixler launched Cornerstone TeleVision in 1979. Bixler has said that he grew up in a "nonbelieving" family in Boston, went to high school in Maryland, and attended a Church of the Brethren–affiliated college because they offered him a scholarship. There he met his wife Norma. Together they have four children. Bixler claims that at age twenty-seven God told him to become a minister. A few years later he enrolled at Bethany Theological Seminary in Chicago; eventually he was ordained and posted to the Pittsburgh Church of the Brethren. After thirteen years as pastor there, Bixler spent six years evangelizing across North America and Europe.

Bixler also claims that God then told him and Norma to found a television station. Cornerstone's stated mission is "to educate people in the United States and abroad and to spread the Word of God." Its articles of incorporation state that all of the organization's purposes "shall bring glory to Almighty God, and . . . promulgate the Gospel of Jesus Christ and the truths of the Holy Bible by whatever means possible." In 1996 Bixler stated, "[We] entertain in order to evangelize and edify." President Oleen Eagle added, "[We] educate as far as Biblical terms, Biblical teaching."

The station was officially founded in 1969, but it took ten years and $2 million to actually get it on the air. Jim and Tammy Faye Bakker helped in the early days, by using their show to raise $50,000 in one-dollar-bills to buy the land on which the station sits. By 1996 that small transmitter building had grown into a modern communications complex through two building expansions that housed three sets, two tape libraries, four production studios, and various offices. Cornerstone's total holdings included WPCB-TV Greensberg-Pittsburgh, PA Channel 40, WKBS-TV Altoona-Johnstown, PA Channel 47, three low-power stations in Pennsylvania, and other properties.

Cornerstone programming was carried on eighty-six cable systems and on a five-story satellite dish that covered all of North America. The station claimed an operating budget of $6 million a year, a workforce of seventy-four full-time employees, twenty-plus part-timers and two hundred volun-

teers. It operated thirty-two phone lines staffed by volunteer "prayer partners" seven days a week; in 1996 the station claimed to have received 1.25 million calls over the previous year.

Investigating Cornerstone

We at the Save Pittsburgh Public Television Campaign organized ourselves
to research Cornerstone intensively. Several members taped programs and
wrote them up. We engaged a firm to conduct background investigations
into the officers and directors; Sam Husseini at FAIR did Lexix/Nexis
searches on the on-screen personalities, and I interviewed two former program hosts who were reported to be disgruntled.

In time, we learned that those in control of Cornerstone represent only a
narrow fragment of the greater Pittsburgh community. Cornerstone officers,
directors, and advisers are all related to one another, hold similar religious
positions, and/or share the same narrow sectarian views. Cornerstone's vice
president of programming, David Skeba, is the nephew of president and director Oleen Eagle; corporate secretary Dolores Richert is married to vice
president Blake Richert; and other relatives of Cornerstone's officers and directors, including Norma Bixler, Paul Bixler, and Mary Ann Skeba, are employed by Cornerstone as on-air personalities or production staff. None of
the station's officers had broadcast experience before coming to Cornerstone: Russell Bixler was a minister, Eagle a fashion coordinator, and Skeba
a truck driver and bible school dropout.

Cornerstone's seven board members were all employed full-time in
Protestant ministries with strong ties to evangelical Christianity. Cornerstone also has an advisory board that meets twice a year "so that Cornerstone
can understand and respond to the needs of the community." All but four
of the thirty-two members of the advisory board are Protestant ministers,
and two of the others have clerical offices.

As of 1995, Cornerstone produced three daily and seven weekly programs that aired on its station and were carried throughout the country.
Members of the board of directors provided much of this local programming. Founder Russell Bixler taught on television at least five times per
month. One of his programs, *Origins,* was dedicated to uncovering the
"myths of evolution." Station president Oleen Eagle oversaw the production
of ten programs broadcast on Cornerstone.

Although a nonprofit organization, Cornerstone occupied a commercial frequency and made good use of it. Station officials frequently solicited money from viewers, promising miracles from God in return. Many shows promoted products, in some cases even when unrelated to the broadcast. For example, in between one program's interviews, its host, Bob Larson, advertised a video, entitled *In the Name of Satan,* a cassette on occultism, and an encyclopedia of cults; another Cornerstone host, Bob Enyart, used his show to promote a variety of products, such as a vitamin pack, gold and silver merchandise, a telephone service, books and videos, and a computer screensaver portraying such messages as "Born Homophobic" and "Somewhere a homo teacher is molesting a child."

Cornerstone's accountability was so loose that in 1997 Russell Bixler devoted half a dozen programs to Dennis Lee, a man who claimed divine revelation for a perpetual motion machine that would provide free heat and electricity to any house; he offered the machine to viewers in return for payment of half the amount that a user would earn by selling electrical power back to the utilities. A Professor Lee Schaefer advised us that, when he called the phone number provided, he was told that the CIA had stolen the plans but he could buy a local dealership for $10,000 while the machine was being reengineered.

Indeed, some shows were just "infomercials" for products. For example, one episode of Bixler's "Getting Together" was dedicated to promoting Lifeline, a for-profit long distance company. Representatives argued that their service was preferable to others, particularly AT&T because AT&T promotes "the homosexual lifestyle." Cornerstone urged viewers to change to Lifeline because the station would receive 10 percent of the company's earnings.

Cornerstone's *Optimum Health* was a program-length infomercial for its own company of the same name. Produced by Eagle and directed by one of Bixler's sons, the program promoted Optimum Health vitamin and mineral products, the Optimum Health store, and the chiropractic services of its hosts. The company did $1.6 million in sales in 1994, showing a profit of $165,000. It gave Cornerstone $60,000, its largest single contribution in 1995.

In addition, there were children's shows that even on a commercial license were in violation of existing regulations regarding product advertising. In fact, some were little more than program-length commercials for kids. For example, the show *Kids Café* featured children demonstrating how to make various recipes, all featuring sponsors' products. In one episode, the kids wore T-shirts featuring logos and slogans for commercial food products. The recipes demonstrated included (1) Kellogg's Crispix Mix Savory

BBQ Style, (2) Jell-O Pudding in A Cloud, (3) Totally Tasty Tacos with Lawry's Taco Seasoning, (4) Chip Dip (using ChiChi's Salsa), and (5) Chocolate Marble Cake (using Bosco chocolate syrup). The brand name products were listed, described as essential ingredients, and praised by the children as they went about their business.

In his office, Russell Bixler displays a framed photograph of himself and Pat Robertson with their arms around each other. Robertson's Christian Broadcasting Network is a media empire that earns $140 million a year. Robertson's *700 Club*, which has 7 million weekly viewers, airs twice each weekday on Cornerstone.

In August 1996, Tom Green, producer and host of the very popular Christian music video program *Lightmusic*, announced that he was quitting Cornerstone. Green explained, "Christian television's formula continues to be: find a bunch of old people who will give you their life savings and program not to offend them. I have seen the simple desire to serve God transformed into endless flow charts and the cynical pandering to people's worst instincts."

When I spoke to him, Green said that Cornerstone officials Eagle and Skeba were true believers in Pat Robertson's "new world order" thesis—promulgated in a book by that name—that most wars and other horrors have been caused by Jewish international bankers and a secret religious society called the Illuminati. Robertson has said that American presidents unwittingly serve "a tightly knit cabal whose goal is nothing less than a new order for the human race under the domination of Lucifer." Cornerstone frequently aired programs under the series theme of *The Money Masters* (how international financiers are dominating free peoples) and *Global Bondage* (how the United Nations is enslaving free peoples).

The Anti-Defamation League has denounced Robertson's book as anti-Semitic "kookery" that should be "a national issue." At dinners for the "President's Club" of large Cornerstone donors, Skeba lists alerting the public to this danger as one of the station's three main goals. Robertson's solution to this alleged threat is to make the United States into a Christian theocracy. He refers to others faiths—like Episcopalians, Presbyterians and Methodists—as having "the spirit of the anti-Christ." He calls Buddhism and Shintoism "satanically inspired."

Robertson's former co-host, Danuta Soderman Pfeiffer, recently listed some of Robertson's other "policy statements": Christians and Jews should be the only people able to hold office in the United States; AIDS is a punishment from God for homosexuality; separation of church and state is a leftist lie; Planned Parenthood teaches kids to fornicate and masturbate; and fires and floods in California are signs of God's displeasure with godless people.

Another regular Cornerstone host is the Reverend John Hagee of Cornerstone Church in San Antonio, who calls attention to the "number of crimes [that] warranted the death penalty in the Bible: murder, adultery, incest, sodomy, rape, kidnapping, witchcraft, blasphemy and disobedience to parents." (Hagee made the news in 1994 when he publicized a school fundraising event as a "slave auction" of students who would be expected to work at the home or business of the highest bidder. "Slavery in America is returning to Cornerstone," Hagee announced. "Make plans to come and go home with a slave." Hagee expressed surprise when black leaders in the community took offense.) When our campaign began monitoring Cornerstone, Hagee was recorded making the following political solicitation: "A moral sewer is taking the nation under. We need righteous men to go to government or the godless, the immoral, the tree hugging neo-pagans, the radical lesbian homosexuals will still rule Washington, D.C." His view on welfare reform was that "it is time for this nation to live by the principle, if you do not work, you should not eat, period."

On James Kennedy's *Coral Ridge Ministries Hour* we are taught that AIDS education covers an activist agenda to promote the homosexual lifestyle. "The federal government promotes homosexuality at the taxpayer's expense," says Paul Merlo, former chief of staff to Congressman Bob Dornan. "That's about $1.2 billion a year. That's money that goes straight to the homosexual organizations." Ominous music plays as the screen goes pink, overlaying footage of money rolling off a printing press. In 1998, Coral Ridge Ministries sponsored a $500,000 nationwide advertising campaign promoting the idea that gays and lesbians "can change."

Kennedy's other targets include the major teachers' unions, which he accuses of wanting to "destroy this nation" Its teachers are said to be "deliberately deceitful" in stripping children "of any sense of moral or ethical absolutes." In 1999 Kennedy called for the impeachment of a federal judge who had ordered an Alabama public school to stop sponsoring school prayer and other religious activities. Kennedy declares, "God has called us to engage the enemy in this culture war."

In *Crisis in the Classroom,* produced by the Eagle Forum and narrated by Phyllis Schlafly, discipline breakdown and lower test scores are blamed on a concerted plan by ideologically minded educators to inculcate "socialism."

New curriculum innovations are claimed to lead children away from their parents.

In the program *Behind the Green Curtain,* viewers are warned that environmentalism is a conspiracy of rich elites to curtail property rights, acquire public land, and exert control over the people. The real agenda of the environmentalists, the narrator advises, is "transferring power to the U.N. to bring about one-world government." On the subject of inequality, Bixler advises viewers to reject the teachings of "the secularists and humanists" and to "thank God for your paycheck. I never did that before. When I started to do that my life changed." In this new theology, God is on the side of the bosses and the "secularists" and "humanists" have replaced the communists as the new evil.

In Bob Anderson's *Exposing the Lie,* we are told that unless you're born again, you aren't really Christian. "It doesn't matter what the name is on the door of the church because there's only one body of Christ. That's the born-again believers. And it doesn't matter what the door says—whether it's Methodist, Baptist, or Episcopalian or Lutheran or Congregational . . . that doesn't make a person a Christian." Later in the program Anderson refers to the Unitarian-Universalist faith as a "cult."

Almost all of Cornerstone's programs are driven by a sectarian evangelical mission. Most also contain ultra-conservative political messages. Even ostensibly secular discussions of public policy are biased by this agenda. For example, the host of *Focus on the Issues,* Jerry Bowyer, is head of the conservative libertarian think tank the Allegheny Institute for Public Policy, funded by Richard Scaife. Bowyer also sits on the board of directors of the Pennsylvania branch of the Christian Coalition along with its head, Rick Schenker, the original host of the show. And Bowyer is a former leader of the National Reform Association, where he advocated making the United Nations into a theocracy with Jesus Christ written into its constitution.

The religious right has learned to make television and radio broadcasting its most important tool. The tax-exempt status of many of its organizations gives it an enormous advantage over competing voices—a situation brought suddenly into being when the Reagan administration leaned on the FCC to lower its standards for approving license applications from religious organizations. This represented the coming together of free-market conservatives and religious/social conservatives into an effective electoral coalition.

Under further Reagan administration "deregulation," the FCC dropped the requirement for applicants to demonstrate educational credentials for reserved "educational" frequency broadcasting: all one had to do was to state educational *intent*; moreover, bible teaching, while not sufficient for the entire program schedule, now qualified as educational instruction. In sum, political pressure on a weak bureaucracy had brought about a revolutionary redefinition of indoctrination as education.

At the 1986 National Religious Broadcasters convention, attorney Colby May announced the "official death" of the Fairness Doctrine at the hands of Reagan's FCC. Reagan federal court appointees Robert Bork and Antonin Scalia had done the deed: broadcasters were no longer constrained by the obligation to provide "equal time" for "opposing views." White House communications director Patrick Buchanan called on religious broadcasters "to make the Reagan Revolution prevail" and declared that the Republican Party needed to "draw . . . more recruits" from America's "religious revival . . . [to] tap into this new patriotism and [convert] it into a new nationalism."

In a six-minute videotaped speech, President Reagan referred to such issues as "right to life," voluntary school prayer, and the balanced budget amendment, and praised religious broadcasters for "helping to change the world for the better." Reagan's FCC majority permitted religious broadcasters using satellites to feed huge networks of radio stations and translators broadcasting on reserved frequencies. Most of this programming was canned and syndicated for play across the country. As media critic Ron Kramer noted recently, "The FCC took no action to preserve any portion of these frequencies for local radio purposes" as called for by FCC regulations.

From 1984 to 1994, the number of Christian radio stations in this country doubled, to a total of 1,648, and that of Christian television stations tripled, to 274. Religious programming, with an audience of 20 million, had become the third largest radio format in the nation. Christian radio stations accounted for 8 percent of the total in 1981, 10 percent in 1990, and 13 percent in 1997.

Many of the religious organizations behind these stations have abused existing regulations regarding commercialism, localism, community representation, fairness, and partisan politicking. Worse yet, Ron Kramer claims, there are corporations claiming to be religious in purpose whose primary business is speculating in frequencies and/or peddling merchandise. Because most politicians fear their power, however, they are rarely challenged. (When they are, they typically mount the high horse of the First Amendment and claim that their opponents are guilty of religious discrimination—as if the Constitution guarantees any entity with enough money exclusive control of one of the public's scarce broadcasting frequencies.)

In March of 1995 I had had my own encounter with Cornerstone, as a two-time guest on *Focus on the Issues,* with Bowyer and Schenker as cohosts. Bowyer, who was interested in me as a critic of WQED, objected to government subsidies on principle but had no interest in the issue of corporate welfare. He described all taxes as "coercive" and supported the move to cut all federal funding for public broadcasting. I argued for an independently funded public broadcasting service and Bowyer challenged, "Where is it written that every interest group has a right to hundreds of millions of dollars of broadcast communications equipment?" He stated matter-of-factly, "In a free society those who can afford access to the public airwaves are the people who get access to the public airwaves. The only way to change that is to make it a less free society and I don't think that's the way to go."

"What you've described," I responded, "is a society that's free for rich people and not free for people who don't have money." After the show, Bowyer's black cameraman suggested to him that he have me on the program more often.

Now, a year later, Bowyer and Cornerstone stood to be major beneficiaries of WQED's mismanagement. At the same time, those of us who had contributed to WQED all these years were expected to suffer the death of WQEX without complaint. Not in my backyard!

WQED Files for Dereservation

WQED's 1996 FCC appeal was organized around two main points. First, the station was "one of the nation's leading public broadcasters"; second, WQED was "technically insolvent" and "on the verge of bankruptcy," a condition that "imminently" threatened the "loss or impairment of local public broadcast service to Pittsburgh." These conclusions were based primarily on a study performed by a team from Duquesne University.

WQED blamed the debt on "former management's failure to scale back" national production when funding for such had dried up. WQED also blamed its problems on the decline in Pittsburgh's population and "potential viewer base," the loss of "many" of the community's major corporations, and "new competition from cable."

Of course, these arguments conveniently omitted the fact that almost a dozen cities with smaller populations and fewer large corporations continued to support two public television stations and stay in the black, including Dayton, Ohio; Falls Church, Virginia; Knoxville, Tennessee; Oklahoma City, Oklahoma; Tucson, Arizona; and Wartown, New York. Here again the press failed to examine critically WQED's justifications.

In explicating its debt, now claimed to be $14.5 million (up from $10 million when Miles took over), WQED revealed that less than half ($7.1 million) was owed to the Mellon Bank. In fact, almost a third of the debt was owed by WQED to itself. The station dramatized its financial condition by claiming it could not even replace a leaking roof or fix heating and cooling system problems. WQED told the FCC that "only the conversion of WQEX" could "insure its survival."

Since expected revenue from the sale of WQEX would certainly exceed the debt, WQED proposed that the balance be put into "a permanently restricted endowment," the income from which would "fund programming initiatives and major fixed asset acquisitions," like the equipment required for the "transition to advanced [digital] television broadcasting." The argument that individual stations would be solely responsible for generating significant capital for an imminent transition to digital broadcasting went unquestioned in the press.

WQED further argued that the sale of WQEX would "add a new commercial voice to the market," thus enhancing the "local diversity of voices." Moreover, WQED stated, it would increase its broadcast hours from seventeen to twenty-four a day, resulting in a likely net increase in program hours. WQED also claimed that WQEX was no longer needed for classroom instruction, "the purpose for which it was reserved."

Invoking its powerful sponsors, WQED asserted that its request was consistent with congressional legislation "pending" for all public television duopolies because two or more educational stations in the same market are viewed as "economically unrealistic" and "an inefficient use of spectrum." Moreover, WQED claimed, "the requested course of action enjoys broad local and national support."

The most revealing statement in the petition is that "the primary businesses that give [WQED] its identity and purpose" are "the production of high-quality local and national broadcast and non-broadcast products, and the distribution of those products to the regional, national and international markets awaiting them." This appeared to be the real mission driving the station: producing "products," including "non-broadcast products" for other "markets."

The reader will recognize this as Elsie Hillman and Lloyd Kaiser's strategy for overcoming the city's image as "a dirty little steel town." When that brought the station to financial crisis, you'll recall, Don Korb stepped in. At one meeting during his tenure as CEO, he had listed a number of cooking and health programs in development and commented, "If we're smart, we can make money at them." When one board member asked, "At what point do we discuss program philosophy?" she was ignored.

After George Miles replaced Korb, this remained the plan for the station's new "future." This is the ambition that the conservative *Tribune-Review* applauded as a "sound business plan." This is the final triumph of big-business thinking over any semblance of public interest. This is the threat that public broadcasting faces in this new age.

WQED's petition included about well over a hundred letters urging FCC approval. There was one from Texas Republican Congressman Jack Fields, chair of the House Telecommunications Subcommittee. There were eight letters from local and state-level politicians. There were almost thirty letters from business leaders, including the CEO of Bayer, the CEO of Pittsburgh Plate Glass Industries, the CEO of Blue Cross, the CEO of PNC Bank, and William Block, publisher of the Pittsburgh *Post-Gazette*.

There were letters from about fifteen educational leaders, including the presidents of four universities and half a dozen public school superintendents or principals. There were letters from about 15 public television station heads, including William F. Baker of WNET New York, Mary Bitterman of KQED San Francisco, Frederick Breitenfeld Jr. of WHYY Philadelphia, William McCarter of WTTW Chicago, and Sharon Rockefeller of WETA Washington, D.C. And there were letters from APTS president David J. Brugger and CPB president Richard Carlson.

All senders followed fairly closely a sample letter WQED had provided for their convenience; the reasons they offered mirrored the language of WQED's petition, sometimes exactly. Interestingly, although all the letters were dated one to four weeks after WQED signed its contingency agreement with Cornerstone TeleVision, not one supporter referred to the Cornerstone payoff.

As with the investigator's report on "improper business practices," the QED Accountability Project had learned that members of the board of directors had never seen a copy of the Mellon Bank loan agreement. Nor had they requested any other relevant documents, like inquiries from potential buyers, information on the cost and possibilities of digital technology, or membership surveys regarding the likely impact of dumping WQEX on future contributions. When board member Allen Kukovich wrote to Roddey before the filing of the petition, asking for the above information, Roddey referred him to Miles, who declined to provide the documents requested. It was several months later that the board voted to enter into an "asset exchange" agreement with Cornerstone TeleVision even though members admitted privately they had never seen the exchange document itself. This passivity gives a whole new dimension to the phrase "rubber stamp."

For ten days running, Linda Wambaugh and I worked on our opposing petition, collecting and copying, phoning and faxing, and consulting on the arguments. It was submitted on July 5, 1996. We countered all of WQED's arguments and made some of our own. Working from David Honig's outline, another firm handled the actual FCC submission.

We attacked WQED's "fiscal irresponsibility" and its overemphasis on national program production at the expense of local programming. We complained that WQED had provided no information about the board "that it claims would oversee the trust" that would control the funds left over after payment of its debt. This was especially critical, we pointed out, given that the "WQED Board of Directors and Community Advisory Board have been powerless entities that WQED management has consistently failed to consult or inform." Given all of the above, we surmised, "it is crystal clear that WQED will use the available funds to subsidize its other business activities."

We charged the corporation with "scare tactics" and recommended that it explore less radical options for addressing the debt, like selling some of its non-broadcast assets, such as *Pittsburgh Magazine* or the *Wonder Works* library, or seeking the protection of Chapter 11. At the worst, we suggested, if its petition were denied WQED might be forced to sell WQEX "to an entity that would then provide a more local and economical public television service to the community." As it now stood, we suggested, the primary beneficiary of WQED's proposal would be WQED, not the people of Pittsburgh.

Certainly, we argued, WQED had "provided no evidence that there is a need in Pittsburgh for a seventh commercial station greater than the need for the continued operation of noncommercial station WQEX-TV." Moreover, twenty-four-hour broadcasting on WQED would in no way compensate for the lack of alternative programming during normal, especially prime-time, viewing hours. We pointed out that despite the recent loss of general population, the community now included even more people who were racial minorities, lower income, and/or elderly—precisely the people public television is mandated to serve.

Most importantly, we emphasized, "The decision the Commission reaches will establish precedent and have policy implications for non-commercial broadcasting in every community with more than one non-commercial station."

In the relatively short period available to us we were also able to produce enough evidence of community support to neutralize that claimed by WQED. We provided about 35 letters and more than a thousand petition signatures. Our national supporters included well-known media scholars like George Gerbner, Robert McChesney, and Jerry Landay, producers Danny Schechter and Rory O'Conner, and FAIR executive director Jeff Cohen. McChesney wrote a special supplement to our main submission, on the importance of second stations to mission-driven programming.

Our petition in opposition to the dereservation of WQEX was submitted jointly by the QED Accountability Project and the Alliance for Progressive Action. The latter claimed to represent 41 public interest groups, about a quarter of whom wrote separate letters. The Allegheny County Labor Council also presented an opposition petition on behalf of its 157 labor union locals, representing 80,000 members.

There were seven other filings. Four consisted only of short letters of protest from small stations in New York whose cable broadcasts would have to compete with a commercial Channel 16. There were more substantial filings from the Association of Local Television Stations (ALTV) and Channel 29 Associates, a local Warner Brothers (WB) affiliate. (ALTV's members include traditional independent stations as well as three emerging networks, Fox, UPN, and WB.) Both of these petitioners stood to lose by the addition of another commercial station in the market.

Another Tactic in the Battle

The final filing in opposition to WQED's plan came from the newly formed Pittsburgh Educational Television (PET) and will require some background by way of explanation.

Fred Polner, one of the lawyers I had approached in May, had been tracking the case and calling me with friendly advice. At one point I responded, "That sounds like a good idea Fred. I guess if you were my attorney I would listen to it." And so he finally came on board.

Convinced that the FCC would most likely overlook all of WQED's transgressions, Polner had developed a different approach to the case, something he called "a viable option strategy." In his view, we needed to propose another organization to operate WQEX in the public interest; thus FCC approval of the petition to dereserve WQEX specifically would deprive an entity willing and able to serve the community. Having given up on the possibility of any local educational institution stepping up, Polner recommended that we incorporate our own.

There were two dimensions to this strategy. We would file a petition to revoke WQED's license to operate WQEX on the grounds that WQED's financial condition rendered it unqualified. We would also oppose the petition to dereserve Channel 16 on the grounds that it would deprive a viable alternative entity of the opportunity to serve the public interest.

A young family man, Fred Polner had a strong social conscience and agreed to take our case pro bono. His formal business attire and measured speech contrasted with his red hair and obvious relish in taking on the corporate establishment. Following Polner's lead, I recruited a board of directors and he incorporated PET. I was listed as president and the rest of the board consisted of labor leader Rosemary Trump (vice-president), Pennsylvania state representative Allen Kukovich (secretary), Pittsburgh City Council president Jim Ferlo (treasurer), and "labor priest" Monsignor Charles Owen Rice, still fighting the good fight in his eighties.

Polner filed both an "opposition" to the dereservation and a "petition to revoke license" in PET's name. The longer "opposition" argued that WQED's financial problems were not grounds for "amending television's Table of Allotments" or depriving the community of a valued educational resource. It stated, "If WQED is no longer interested in running an educational station, it has a duty to turn in its license and to allow another interested party to serve the public interest by operating on Channel 16." Although "still in its formative stages," if invited, PET would make such application.

The "petition to revoke license" was sheer judo. We would take WQED's claims that it was "technically insolvent" at face value and argue that according to FCC guidelines, this disqualified them as a suitable broadcaster. Therefore, "the public interest will be best served by revoking its license for Channel 16, requiring it to vacate that channel, and letting others apply to operate a public television station on that frequency."

Polner's strategy forced WQED into backing down from earlier claims. They also argued that they were not required to show WQEX's financial resources; instead they asserted, "The de facto financial qualifications standard for retention of a broadcast license is to remain on the air—which WQEX has done for nearly four decades and will continue to do."

There it was. Despite all the hyperbolic rhetoric about being "close to

the edge," "technically insolvent," having the "lights turned out," "on the verge of bankruptcy," and "imminently threatened," when actually confronted on these claims, WQED was now saying that WQEX would continue to broadcast. On the other hand, WQED complained, it would be forced to retreat from its "laudable mission" of producing programs for commercial entities and national and local audiences. They weren't content with providing broadcast service to the local community. They wanted to to be a national producer again.

WQED appended additional letters of support to its reply, including a letter from the Republican governor, Thomas Ridge, and a letter signed jointly by Republican senators Arlen Specter and Rick Santorum and Democratic congressmen Bill Clinger, Mike Doyle, Phil English, Ron Klink, Frank Mascara, and Jack Murtha. In an apparent contradiction, the latter still argued the case on behalf of WQED's "financial survival."

Town Meeting: Political Theater at WQED

On the day WQED submitted its dereservation petition to the FCC, CEO George Miles announced that WQED would hold two community meetings at the station to discuss the matter, on the morning and evening of July 18. Since this would be only a week before the FCC decision was required, the hearings were obviously intended as a public relations gesture. Still, evidently Miles was confident that he would win over public opinion. On July 2, he advised the *Post-Gazette*, "Once we start to sit down and talk to folks about our case and what we need to do, I see it across the board, one by one [they say], 'Oh yeah, I got it. I see what you need to do.'" Despite the fact that we knew WQED's management wouldn't really be listening, we felt obligated to show up in force and speak our minds.

WQED instructed people to call in if they intended to attend and to sign up to speak once they arrived. The meeting was held in the large open WQED studio. Miles sat high up on a dais, flanked by board members Keith Kappmeyer and Gwen Elliott. Kappmeyer, the CEO of Blue Cross, was sitting in for board chair Jim Roddey, who reportedly had a bad back.

Miles had asked Linda Dickerson to moderate the meeting. Dickerson had been a Republican candidate for county commissioner and was owner and publisher of the magazine *Executive Report*. (When she finally gave up the magazine at the end of 1997, the *Post-Gazette* described it as "a mouthpiece for the region's corporate elite and self-anointed economic development gurus." Nevertheless, she went on to write a weekly column for the

Post-Gazette. Executive Report, renamed *Pittsburgh Prospects,* became a part of WQED's *Pittsburgh Magazine* in June 1998.)

The castle and other props from *Mister Rogers' Neighborhood* stood on either side of those presiding. About a hundred bridge chairs were arranged in rows and two microphones were available for members of the audience. *Post-Gazette* reporter Barbara Vancheri estimated attendance at about seventy in the morning and forty in the evening. I'm sure there were more, but I didn't count. Todd Gutnick, who did not cover the evening meeting, said there were twenty-four speakers in the morning session in addition to the many watching.

Dickerson set the ground rules—only five minutes per speaker in the order in which they had signed up. She asked her audience to engage in "only polite and professional dialogue," adding, "Hopefully that goes without saying." "Everything here goes without saying," said someone in the audience.

One thing that certainly went without saying was that Miles and his aides would have as much time as they wanted to lay out their case. Miles took good advantage of that with a rambling introduction that restated all of his arguments in no particular order. He boasted about board support for his "downsizing" of the corporation, credited Mellon Bank for its patience, and pleaded for money to invest in digital technology, which he touted as the solution to all programming problems. He rejected a normal FCC application as too time-consuming and filing bankruptcy because it would be "irresponsible to forget about people we owe money to."

Many of our people spoke, including those who had come to the campaign in recent weeks. Keith Powell picked up on the theme of responsibility and asked Miles, "Who keeps hiring incompetents?" La Roche College professor Ken Boas complained that Miles and his crew saw the problem as "them against us. You are not moving into the community and hearing the voices of the community and letting them become a part of the solution."

Miles and Gwen Elliott claimed that both the board of directors and the community advisory board had held many discussions over the past two years trying to solve "this problem" and could not. Elliott said, "We're looking for input all the time." Miles said, "If there is another solution, I would like to know what it is." I sat in the back, chilled by the overworked air-conditioning and frustrated by the lies coming from the dais. I realized that I was probably the only one in the room who knew the truth about all these claims. To maintain my sanity, I began to make a list of Miles and Elliott's false statements.

More speakers stepped up. University of Pittsburgh professor Carol Stabile warned that the demise of WQEX would mean a loss of local and alternative programming. One speaker charged that public involvement was needed at an earlier stage and a quick fix wouldn't solve the station's underlying management problems. Another said that all the other cities he had lived in had had more public affairs and cultural programming on their public stations than did WQED. University of Pittsburgh professor Joe White criticized the "rudeness and arrogance" of Roddey's response to me in the *Post-Gazette*. Rosemary Trump announced that despite being shut out at WQED, organized labor represented "every group" in the community and Pittsburgh Educational Television was "prepared to take responsibility" for operating Channel 16.

Several speakers criticized the Cornerstone contingency plan, but Miles insisted that his choice of Cornerstone was based on practical criteria and therefore he would not comment on its programming. Attorney Jon Robison attacked Miles' claims about Congress's "legislative intent" as "malarkey." Linda Wambaugh quoted Miles's statement that the plan was "in the works for years" and asked him why he hadn't held public meetings "in a timely fashion."

Duquesne University professor Rob Bellamy pointed out that WQED was "not technically the owner of the station," and if WQED was no longer willing or able to operate WQEX, it should turn it in. On the other hand, if WQED were to be successful with its petition, Bellamy warned, "it will be open season on public broadcasting stations across the nation." A woman named Mary Blooming said she preferred WQEX to WQED and that privatizing the station fit the pattern of government abdication and corporate monopolization that was threatening free speech nationwide.

Schoolteacher Martha King, who described herself as "a life-long subscriber," considered the action "a great betrayal." Had she known of the station's financial distress, she said, she would have "cancelled cable for a year and given [WQED] the bucks." Computer programmer Gordon Marshall also struck this theme: "I've been a viewer and sponsor for many years . . . but to be quite honest with you [my co-workers and I] feel that the support for public TV will not be there anymore because of this betrayal."

Nat Melamed, a retired research scientist, lamented, "Throughout all the appeals and fund-raising requests, I never received a letter saying 'We're in deep trouble.' It really, really hurts that never did I get a sense you're in trouble." Miles replied that focus groups had indicated that the perception of WQED's financial problems discouraged contributions. I wondered how the focus groups were chosen. Did they include subscribers? Were they presented with the scenario of losing the station? Could such strategy have missed those really committed to WQEX? On the other hand, why would subscribers be motivated to contribute to WQED in the future, after it got millions for cashing in WQEX?

To be sure, there were some that spoke in favor of the sale, almost all of whom were board members or employees. Corporate CEO and board member William Rackoff blamed the station's financial problem on "a numerically declining and aging population" and called the dereservation plan "brilliant." Diana Janetta, another WQED board member, warned that if something wasn't done about the problem, "we will become a wimpy feeder for national programming." Celeste Nowasky implored Miles not to be thwarted by the "hostility in the room" and to "make us solvent." And community advisory board member Michelle Jones said, "Let's move on [with the sale]."

The longer Miles argued with those in the audience, the longer my list grew. When the meeting ended I drove straight to my office and worked through the afternoon researching his statements and preparing a five-minute response. I came up with a list of about fifteen misstatements and put them in an order that started with objective questions of fact like who produced *We Do the Work,* how long a normal FCC rule-making procedure takes, whether Pittsburgh was too small to afford two stations, and what the timetable was for converting to digital technology.

I then moved on to challenge some of Miles's more egregious claims: that both boards were fully involved in shaping the deal, that there had been widespread press coverage of station plans from the beginning, that WQED had an "outstanding record" of local programming, and that corporate contributions accounted for most of the station's money.

By the time I finished it was almost time for the evening meeting to start. I had missed dinner, I was tired and hungry, and it was raining. I jumped in the car, passed through a drive-in, and scarfed down a hamburger on my way to the station. By the time I checked in I was way down on the list of speakers. I didn't know if I could hold on. I spotted my friend Mike Vargo, who said he was third on the list; when I showed him what I had prepared, he generously offered me his spot. When they called his name, I stepped up to the microphone in the front of the room, advised that I had been given his place, and started speaking.

Barely a minute into my speech, someone behind me said, "At last. Some truth for a change." I went on and the crowd began to buzz. Someone proposed that my time be extended. Several people agreed. I declined the privilege and went on. Miles interrupted to challenge me as to how *I* would solve the station's debt. I was prepared. I asked him to give us access to WQED's books, its deal with Cornerstone, its loan agreement with the Mellon Bank, and its investigation into improper business practices. "You give us those, George, and we'll sit down with you and try to figure this out." He didn't respond.

I concluded with two questions: How much money has WQED spent on lawyers and lobbyists this past year? and, How will the new endowment fund be administered? I elaborated on this last question: "How will people be chosen? Will they be elected by subscribers? How can we possibly be guaranteed accountability for the money?" When it became clear that Miles wasn't going to respond to these questions either, I went back to my seat and shortly thereafter left the building.

The next day's *Post-Gazette* headline read, "TV Turnoff," and Barbara Vancheri, who wrote the report, stated, "Sentiment among those who asked to speak ran largely against the sale." We had left the meeting feeling reassured that we spoke for most of the community and WQED did not, but with nothing to do but wait, the week passed slowly. The last word from David Honig was that a source at the FCC had told him they thought our pleading was "an exceptional piece of work." They now seemed to be leaning toward a license transfer option as a less "drastic approach" to the problem. Apparently, Honig dared, "we're not in as bad a shape as I thought."

The FCC Decides in the Public Interest

On July 24, while sitting in my office, I got a call from the *Post-Gazette*'s Ron Weiskind. WQED had gotten the word from the FCC and called the *Post-Gazette* themselves to put their "spin" on the story. Weiskind said we had won and he wanted to know if I had a comment. My heart started racing and my voice trembled slightly. "We won? The FCC decided in our favor?" Weiskind confirmed that they turned down the request for dereservation.

I asked him for time while I called Linda Wambaugh and David Honig. They were as excited as I was. Honig giggled and Wambaugh let out a hoot. Fighting the good fight is one thing, but winning? That's really sweet. I called Weiskind back and kept it short: "We're extremely proud that the campaign to save public broadcasting in Pittsburgh was able to secure a victory for the public interest." Gracious in victory, Honig suggested, "The best thing anyone in Pittsburgh can do is write a check to WQED with a note that says, 'Keep both stations.'"

As it turned out, the victory was somewhat qualified. PET's petition to revoke WQED's license for WQEX was also denied. Polner was so convinced that the FCC was wrong that he quickly appealed the decision to the Circuit Court of the District of Columbia. Polner stated to the *Pittsburgh Business Times:* "WQED is not qualified to transfer anything. WQED is clogging the airwaves by holding on to a license for a TV station which it admits it can no longer afford to run."

On October 24 the FCC filed a motion to dismiss the appeal and WQED responded in support. A week later, Polner responded in opposition to the motion to dismiss. He argued that the issue of a broadcaster's financial qualifications is "core to the FCC's statutory mission," that it has a "continual oversight responsibility," that the FCC had "abused its discretion," and that its action was "reviewable"; in order to demonstrate these points we would have to have our day in court.

Seven months later, on May 22, 1997, the court finally granted the motion to dismiss. Nevertheless, Polner's challenge had served an important purpose by forcing WQED to acknowledge that it would not "go dark if . . . unable to sell Channel 16." The FCC noted this and stated, "We are not persuaded that there exists a clear and present 'threat to the public of losing or impairing local public broadcasting service' that would warrant the dereservation of Channel 16." Noting that the "combined viewing share" for the two stations was "double the national average for noncommercial station viewing in a market," the commission stated further that it could "not conclude that there is no need for a second noncommercial channel" in Pittsburgh.

While WQED had demonstrated severe financial distress, it had "failed to make the compelling showing necessary to support an exception to the Commission's strongly held policy disfavoring dereservation of noncommercial educational channels." Further, such dereservation was not necessary to relieve WQED's financial distress because its agreement with Cornerstone "would apparently afford WQED significant financial relief," albeit less than would be gained from dereservation. The FCC promised a prompt consideration of the Cornerstone asset exchange agreement but was "not prejudging any applications that might be filed based on that agreement."

The *Post-Gazette* headline read, "WQEX Cannot Be Sold Outright," and the lead was "Hold the 'For Sale' Sign." Reporters described the decision as "surprising." The *Tribune-Review* headline read, "WQED Dealt Setback by FCC" and the lead called it "a heavy blow" to WQED's "preferred option." I would have preferred something more like "Community Group Saves

WQEX." I also would have liked for one of us to be quoted, but a win is a win. Both papers quoted Miles as being "disappointed" and went on to speculate about next steps, with emphasis on the Cornerstone deal.

Story Behind the Story

Finally, both papers, without comment, offered Miles's explanation that his "strong petition" had been rejected because of partisan politics. Miles claimed that "going into the last week [WQED] had the votes," but then, on July 23, Democratic congressmen John D. Dingell of Michigan and Edward J. Markey of Massachusetts had drafted a letter that urged the commission to deny WQED's petition on the grounds that it would "establish a corrosive precedent for policy affecting the public broadcasting community and its viewership." Dingell is the ranking member of the House Commerce Committee and Markey of the House Telecommunications Subcommittee. "This Dingell is a very powerful man in Washington," Miles said. "This letter, quite frankly, turned [the tide]."

"Is that how it really works?" I wondered. After all, WQED had argued congressional intent and produced letters of support from the governor and the entire Pennsylvania delegation, plus Congressman Jack Fields (who chaired Markey's committee) and the presidents of CPB and APTS. Four days later, the *Post-Gazette's* Robert Bianco published an interview with PBS president Ervin Duggan, who admitted that he had also "had some conversations at the FCC" about the WQED petition and was "a little surprised about the negative judgment." Duggan also noted that as chair of the APTS board, George Miles had managed to mute criticism of the sale from several stations in that system. This looked like a lot of political clout on their side to me.

Maybe the reporters were not interested in the story behind the story, but I was. I called Dingell's office and spoke with his aide, David Leach. I identified myself, quoted Miles's statement and asked Leach whether my gratitude was appropriate. He laughed and said Dingell could take "only half the credit."

Normally five seats, the FCC was down to four and deadlocked with commisioners Reed Hundt and Susan Ness opposed to the WQED petition, and James Quello and Rachel Chong in favor. I was informed that Dingell and Markey were opposed to the deal from the beginning, but had been willing to hold back comment out of deference to their colleague Pennsylvania congressman Ron Klink, who was writing in support. When Klink changed his mind, they sent the letter. Although a conservative Democrat for Nixon, Quello had been helped to gain his FCC seat by his protégé, Michigan Democrat Dingell. The speculation was that Dingell moved Quello and then Chong followed to make it unanimous. They had agreed to promote the Cornerstone deal as a compromise solution. Leach suggested that I call Congressman Klink to get the full story. In his view, Klink would be "key" to any future opposition.

Ron Klink knew who I was and called me back. In one long conversation he gave me still another education in federal broadcasting politics. According to Klink, Congressman Jack Murtha had proposed a solution to WQED's debt problem to Miles in March of 1996, offering to insert certain language into a continuing resolution that funded the government after the 1995 shutdown, language which would have given WQED unprecedented authorization to sell WQEX to a commercial operator without even having to seek the consent of the FCC. Klink was in on the deal and later told the press, "Jack Murtha had the ability to get it done. . . . And then it would have been, 'Oh, by the way, as part of this bill, the sale is made legal.'" According to Klink, "These things happen all the time. Depending on where you are on an issue, it's either the greatest thing about our legislative process or the worst."

There was a catch, however. While WQED would be able to pay off all of its creditors, any money left over would have to be returned to the CPB to be used for public broadcasting. WQED could then apply to the CPB for additional funds. Klink agreed with these terms on the grounds that he "didn't think WQED should be allowed to profit from past mismanagement"; he was "willing to save it, but not reward it."

To Klink's surprise, George Miles rejected the offer. "I was befuddled," Klink later said to the press. "If you're in the severe financial straits that were portrayed to me, and someone shows you the way out, I would not turn it down." Obviously, Miles was after a whole lot more than just a debt-free station. Upon further reflection, Klink allowed that "from a strictly business perspective, [Miles] may have been right. He thought he had a stronger option, and he wanted to exercise it." The stronger option, of course, was the special continuing resolution legislation that would give Miles a shot at "$30–60 million" minus the Cornerstone payoff.

Only four days separated the letter of support Klink signed and the letter of opposition Markey and Dingell sent. Apparently in those four days Klink changed his mind. He told me he had called his colleagues and said, "I'm not asking you to lay off." But, Klink explained, "at some point during the process, my antenna went up and I realized something was amiss."

For one thing, there was Elsie Hillman. Despite her resignation from WQED's board of directors, she was very active in politicking on behalf of the newest legislation and she called to lobby Klink, who still harbored some resentment over her changing the concept of a TV series that he and Michael Fields had planned. And then there was Klink's former aide Dennis Casey, who had found a new home at Cornerstone, where he ranted regularly against the character and politics of his former boss. Casey and Klink had worked together at KDKA-TV from 1988 to 1992 and Casey managed Klink's successful 1992 congressional campaign. According to the *Tribune-Review*, after the election, Klink went on the payroll of the Dennis M. Casey Company and was paid $60,000 for campaign expenses. However, Casey later sued Klink for fees he alleged Klink had refused to pay, whereupon an Allegheny County arbitration panel ordered Klink to pay Casey $10,000. Klink hated Casey and couldn't abide the thought of Cornerstone profiting from WQED's mismanagement.

While all of this was instructive, I was not so cynical as to dismiss the FCC decision as just "partisan politics." There were matters of great substance at issue and our reasoned opposition and community support were necessary, if not sufficient, in any accounting. We had fought the good fight and, best of all, had won. However, WQED was not done yet. Their fallback plan threatened to be even more of a disaster for our community than their original one.

Chapter 7

Round Two, the Battle over WQEX

In August of 1996, WQED pushed its Plan B into action. It would swap reserved Channel 16 with Cornerstone for commercial Channel 40, Cornerstone would start broadcasting on reserved Channel 16, and WQED would sell commercial Channel 40 to an outside bidder and split the proceeds with Cornerstone. Barely a week had passed since the FCC's rejection of its petition to dereserve WQEX, and WQED claimed to be still considering its options, but the *Post-Gazette* rushed into print to endorse the Cornerstone swap and sale.

Shortly thereafter our campaign held an organizing meeting of core supporters in the back room of a popular restaurant. About twenty people showed up to toast our victory and plan for the next round. Recruiting legal representation remained my responsibility. I lobbied my original benefactor, Angela Campbell at Georgetown University. To the relief of all of us, she came through. Attorney Karen Edwards was assigned to direct the case, with Campbell as supervisor and associate. Several students were enlisted as assistants, including Charles Blackburn, Sana Coleman, Alan Marzilli, and Anandashankar Mazumdar.

In September I got permission from Ron Klink to break the story about the offer from Congress that Miles had rejected. We were still trying to provoke members of WQED's board into taking more active responsibility for the station's decision making; if we could create internal dissent, so much the better. I assembled all the supporting materials for *Post-Gazette* reporter Sally Kalson. She did additional research, and her story was published on September 19, the morning of the next WQED board meeting.

In the press report, Miles acknowledged that he had decided to reject Congress's offer without consulting the full board. "I only had a few hours to decide," he claimed. "I couldn't stop and call a board meeting." Jim Roddey recalled that there had been about a week between the offer and the decision, plenty of time to call everyone; nevertheless, the only board members consulted were Roddey himself and three other members of the executive committee, including Mellon Bank's David Lovejoy. According to Miles, Mellon supported his decision to decline Murtha's offer. No paper commented on the obvious contradiction between Mellon's earlier approval of Miles's decision to turn down an offer that would have meant full repayment of its Mellon loan and the current alleged pressure from Mellon on WQED to sell WQEX to pay back the loan.

Kalson also noted that community members had not been informed about the Cornerstone contingency plan when they were solicited to write letters in support of the dereservation. State representative Greg Fajt said, "If I had known about that, I definitely would have reconsidered the letter. I thought I was helping WQED survive. I had no idea who else was going to profit."

That day, questioning from some board members was uncharacteristically sharp. Miles said the idea of sending money from the sale to Washington made him "sick to [his] stomach. Any money from the sale of WQEX has to stay here in Pittsburgh." No one spoke for public broadcasting nationally, which, if Miles had taken the offer, would have realized between $35 million and $50 million for programming and now would get nothing.

Alternatives to the Sale of WQEX

Curious about what the board members saw that I didn't, I sent copies of the budget statements given to board members to Mitch McKenney, a top nonprofit corporation accountant in the city. I asked him what he would do if he were on the board. McKenney said, "I'd want a whole lot more detail in writing before I made a final decision about anything. I'd say, show me what your options are and then come back to me with some justification." McKenney added that, as in other cases with which he is familiar, this board should bring in another auditor to look at management's claims and report back to them. Their failure to do so, he reflected, defied explanation.

At the community meeting back in July, Miles had rejected Chapter 11, saying it would be "irresponsible to forget people we owe money to." Is that what Chapter 11 means? I asked Kenneth Steinberg, an attorney who specializes in bankruptcy and other forms of corporate reorganization, to consult to us on this question. Steinberg said that if the debt was felt to be burdensome and Mellon was willing to work with the station, then the repayment terms could be adjusted. If Mellon was not willing to adjust the terms, the station's next alternative would be to sell some of its non-broadcast assets, like the magazine or its tape library.

As a last resort, Steinberg explained, "reorganization becomes a viable alternative." The debt payments could be lowered, the term could be extended, or the collection could be delayed until assets could be sold to pay down the debt. In fact, the courts might even approve such a plan over the objections of creditors. Typically, however, a Chapter 11 plan is mutually acceptable. In his written advisory to us, Steinberg said, "Most of the Chapter Eleven cases handled by [his] firm have resulted in confirmed Chapter Eleven plans in less than one year." Creditors get paid and the corporation continues to operate. "It's done all the time."

KQED San Francisco offers a recent example of such an approach. In 1996, due primarily to a bad building investment, KQED faced a long-term debt of greater than $13 million and a short-term debt of almost $5 million. In the spring it sold its magazine for about $3.1 million and its books and tapes division for $1.2 million, wiping out its short-term debt and restoring its credit.

According to the Mellon Bank loan agreement, WQED's non-broadcast assets were valued at twice that of KQED's. As for the long-term debt, KQED sold $13.4 million in twenty-five-year tax-exempt bonds issued by the California Economic Development Financing Authority. The bonds are guaranteed by the Wells Fargo Bank, the Lucille Packard Foundation, and the Bernard Osher family. Pittsburgh has the Mellon Bank, the Heinz Family Foundation, and the Henry Hillman family. I am certain there would have been enough WQEX supporters to buy the bonds.

On December 18, 1997, the *Post-Gazette* reported that WQED was selling its Wonderworks Family Movie Library (fifty-four shows) to Bonnieville International Corp., of Salt lake City, Utah. WQED got about $4.5 million, 75 percent of which went to the Mellon Bank. Overall station debt was now down to $6.3 million (not counting money WQED owed to itself). Nevertheless, the WQEX swap and sale was still going forward.

The Digital Con

After the FCC decision, it was harder to maintain the fiction of WQED's demise should it not be permitted to sell Channel 16. Explaining the rejection of the Murtha offer, Miles and Roddey had said they needed money to fund new digital technology in order to protect "this organization's health in the long term." The argument for digital technology holds that it will enable a higher definition picture or up to four different concurrent program streams, thus solving all program diversity problems.

I interviewed David Liroff, vice president of technology and planning at WGBH Boston, the nation's leading public television producer. He indicated that a limited low-power on-air capability transmitter could be purchased for as little as $1 million to $1.5 million. A major producer seeking to replace all of its equipment at once might spend as much as $5 million to $10 million. This cost is expected to drop considerably in the future.

Even today, the cost of digital equipment is comparable to that of the old analog equipment. Stations are already replacing worn-out analog equipment with digital as needed. Liroff advised me that until all questions about standards and costs were resolved, WGBH planned to lease all the digital equipment it needed for the next five or six years.

Indeed, in October 1999 nearly three hundred of the nation's sixteen hundred television stations would file petitions with the FCC formally requesting a revision in the previously approved digital television standard, claiming that the system was too unreliable. At least one FCC commissioner urged an open mind on the matter despite the predictable delay this would cause in achieving the transition.

Since all stations faced the same transition issues, a collective plan was already in the making. In October 1997, public broadcasters, under the direction of David Liroff, submitted a proposal to the federal government for $771 million to fund 45 percent of the projected transition costs of $1.7 billion (about $5 million per station), to be spread over three years. (Since the vast majority of stations do not produce programs, many observers considered this estimate excessive.) By summer 1999, the White House and Congress had agreed to the plan, but the donor list scandal seemed to upset the timetable. By the end of 1999, less than $30 million had been allocated. Nevertheless, all that seemed to be at issue was whether FCC conversion deadlines would be met.

In addition, PBS announced a plan to raise $1 billion in transition funds from foundations, state governments, and viewers, and many stations are developing their own public financing plans. Some have gone to their state legislatures for funding—$35 million in California, $20 million in Florida, $17 million in Georgia, $12 million in Ohio, and $6 million in Utah. By the end of 1999, the total raised through these channels had reached $300 million.

Public broadcasting has until 2006 to become fully digital and return the old analog spectrum to the government. Experts have advised that even this deadline could be extended if digital TV doesn't get widespread public acceptance. The enhanced resolution of digital broadcasting is apparent only in sets with screens forty-two inches or larger. Such sets are expected to start selling at $7,000 or more and would require separate remote controls for analog and digital. Set-top decoders for those with cable or satellite dishes will allow only a "modified" digital signal and should cost between $300 and $600.

All of this, of course, leaves out the one-third of the population without either cable or satellite dishes or considerable discretionary income. This group consists largely of the poor, racial minorities, and those in rural areas—precisely the people for whom public television is intended. Liroff's committee advises that "even the most optimistic projections predict that it will be 10 years before DTV receivers can be found in 30 percent of households." In 1996, the *New York Times* reported that "the full transition from analog to digital broadcasting is expected to last 15–50 years."

Finally, even with the eventual arrival of digital a near certainty, there is as yet no restriction on how stations are to use the additional spectrum. As mentioned, they can produce a superior-resolution picture for larger screens by concentrating all four signals, they can transmit four separate program streams at once, or they can do anything in between.

What public broadcast officials don't tell you is that in the absence of public pressure, most of the expanded capability probably will not be used for additional public programming but rather for income-producing activities. In August 1997, PBS asked the FCC to allow public TV stations to do whatever they wanted with the additional channels, from leasing them to commercial broadcasters, home shopping networks, or infomercial producers to offering PBS programming for a monthly subscription fee.

A board member at a leading PBS station reported to me that a private consulting group advised his colleagues that focus-group research found subsidizing digital conversion to be the most persuasive appeal for getting donors to give money to the station. A national reporter confirmed that all the big stations as a subgroup had agreed on this solicitation strategy. I gave reporters fact sheets on the digital issue, but they continued to repeat WQED's arguments without comment.

Lobbying the FCC and Congress

In mid-December 1996, Linda Wambaugh and I traveled to Washington, D.C., where we met with our counsel face-to-face for the first time. The primary purpose of the visit was to lobby public officials concerning the case. John Podesta, more recently White House chief of staff, was at the time a visiting fellow at Georgetown's Institute for Public Representation and working on our case. He had set up a number of key appointments with congressmen and the FCC's mass media bureau.

It was a hectic, tightly scheduled day, made more difficult by a steady rain. We took taxis back and forth between the FCC and the congressional office building, dining in the House cafeteria at midday. On December 16 our whole crew met with Clay Pendarvis of the mass media bureau and FCC attorney Joyce Bernstein, who had been involved in the first-round dereservation decision.

Pendarvis said he'd had an hour meeting with WQED's counsel and had explained to them that Cornerstone would have "a lot of restructuring to do to qualify as a public television station." Furthermore, if the FCC qualified the station as educational, it would then be eligible for community service grants and carriage of PBS programs. Wambaugh and I looked at each other in disbelief.

But before that happened, Pendarvis advised, Cornerstone would have to "diversify their board of directors and meet the educational station requirements." For example, he suggested, they would have to "reach out and find people like Jerry [me] to sit on the board." In fact, Pendarvis wanted to see a "large, really diverse board that might include representatives from the AFL-CIO and the Urban League."

The other point at issue was the licensee's mission. Although religious broadcasters can hold educational licenses, their primary purpose must be education, not religion. Citing the *Way of the Cross* decision, Pendarvis said that if we wanted to block the transfer of WQEX to Cornerstone, we would have to argue that the "primary purpose" of its programming was not educational but religious. One measure of this is whether the applicant seeks to "advance one particular point of view." After hearing a description of Russell Bixler's creation science program *Origins*, Pendarvis said that the program could be considered educational if Cornerstone offered another viewpoint in the same or another show.

Pendarvis referred to a couple of cases in which religious broadcasters had qualified to operate on reserved channels. In one case the board of the station in question consisted of just a few Korean Protestant ministers, and the programming schedule was sparse and only religious. Pendarvis said that in this case the licensee had diversified its board by bringing in minority and white representatives and restructured its programming. With these changes it "just slipped over the line."

Pendarvis said that FCC staff under delegated authority would make the decision. He anticipated a thirty-day petition cycle with a decision following in a couple of months. Staff members would examine sample schedules to determine whether they reflected educational or religious content. Based on the record, the staff would either approve the application or designate it for a hearing to determine who was telling the truth.

After the meeting with Pendarvis, we met with aides for four congressmen. All were young white males who were also smart, liked the game, and knew how to protect their bosses by hiding behind speculation and not making specific promises.

We met jointly with Matt Dinkle from Congressman Bill Coyne's office and Peter Madaus from Ron Klink's office. Dinkle was somewhat noncommittal, but Madaus offered that Klink was critical of WQED's mismanagement and had asked George Miles to pursue "other avenues." They both urged us to seek support from other politicians in the region. Madaus added that "regardless of the Pennsylvania delegation's concerns" we would "need emphasis by Markey and Dingell. Their role in the last setting was influential."

After lunch we met with Markey aide Colin Crowell, who was upbeat and very supportive. He asserted that "Pittsburgh should not lose another public asset due to the mismanagement of the station and failure to seek other debt-remedying alternatives." Crowell thought that the license should be turned in to the FCC, where there would be "a clamor of people willing to bid on the station." He indicated that Markey would focus on "the public policy arguments" because this was "an allocation decision that will set the precedent for how CPB is organized."

David Leach of John Dingell's office encouraged us to work with Klink and also to "pitch" the CPB about "protecting its own interests" in this matter. Like Klink and Crowell, he felt there were educational institutions in the Pittsburgh area that could take over the license.

Home Shopping It Is

On April 24, 1997, WQED's board of directors approved the deal to swap Channel 16 for Channel 40 and then sell it and split the proceeds with Cornerstone. The man who made it possible was Lowell "Bud" Paxson, co-founder of the Home Shopping Network. Councilman Jim Ferlo was prescient—we would be offered some version of home shopping instead of public broadcasting.

After selling his interest in the Home Shopping Network for $70 million in 1992 to Barry Diller, Paxson went on to found the Infomall TV Network, featuring "infomercials" produced by others who pay for them to be aired. Sales in 1996 totaled $145 million, up 67 percent over the previous year. The recent Supreme Court ruling that cable systems "must carry" the signals of all TV broadcasters in their area guaranteed Paxson a slot on cable boxes reaching two-thirds of the households in America. Paxson reports that when he heard the decision he drank champagne until he was hungover.

Paxson Communications offered $35 million for Channel 40. It also made a deal with WQED for studio space and up to five hours of programming a week, compensation to be paid later. It is important to note that this deal threatening to cost Pittsburgh its public television station and benefiting a conservative religious station was not the only option that was available to Paxson at the time. The Supreme Court's "must carry" decision also made Channel 19, a Warner Brothers and later UPN affiliate, a much simpler choice. The owners, Venture Technologies of Los Angeles, were looking to sell this high-power station. In fact, one of the owners offered it to Paxson when the latter's WQED-Cornerstone deal got bogged down at the FCC. Venture Technologies finally sold Channel 19 (WNPA) to Paramount for $39 million in fall 1999.

Given this scenario, why did Paxson push the envelope here? First, Paxson apparently sees public broadcasting licenses as resources to be plundered rather than public trusts. In 1995, he bought New York public station WNYC-TV for $207 million, despite tremendous community opposition (see chapter 10). Second, Paxson is a self-described "born again" Christian who already was familiar with Bixler, having purchased WOCD-TV Amsterdam, New York from Cornerstone for $2.5 million in 1996. In fact, despite the apparent conflict of interest, the same law firm—Dow, Lohnes & Albertson—represented both Paxson and Cornerstone in the WQED deal.

Another peculiar thing about the contract for the three-way deal was that it had a backdoor. If, after the closing, later FCC or court action were to find that Cornerstone must return Channel 16 to WQED, then Paxson would use its best efforts to return Channel 40 to Cornerstone (in exchange for return of its share of the money) and WQED would transfer a debt-free WQEX with assets to Paxson and try to help Paxson qualify to operate Channel 16.

For us, this had two meanings. One, once the deal was signed we never would get back Channel 16 again. Two, Cornerstone already was worried that its programming might be found to be not in compliance with FCC educational standards and it did not want to risk losing its Pittsburgh TV ministry for $18 million.

After he had explored a number of more modest propositions, Paxson says, God told him to launch his own network, Pax TV. At his November 20, 1997, New York City news conference, he announced an August 30, 1998, network debut, featuring a mix of "family values" syndicated programming, overnight simulcasts with a Christian cable network, infomercials during weekend days, and three original shows.

Pittsburgh already had three religious channels, three shopping channels, and infomercials and reruns on several of its other channels. Paxson's deal would reduce us to one public channel. The *Post-Gazette* printed the AP news wire release under a headline whose irony should have been apparent to many: "TV Viewers About to Get Another Choice."

Throughout 1996 and 1997, the debate over WQEX's future raged. The papers ran several letters from Miles and Roddey favoring the deal and from members of our campaign in opposition. Keith Powell, Doug Miller, and Mike Schneider criticized "the corporate bigwigs" deciding "what is best for the community," proposed selling other assets or Chapter 11 as options for WQED, and hammered the *Post-Gazette* for its failure "to investigate claims and alternatives." Rosemary Trump accused Miles and Roddey of following "a privatization path that involves the unashamed sell-off of a public trust for the enrichment of the station" and of having "contempt for community and labor groups."

Roddey repeated the line that western Pennsylvania simply could not support two public stations, and praised the diversity and prestige of the station's board of directors and community advisory board and the openness of the decision-making process. I responded that WQEX cost only about 5 percent of WQED's budget and had made a small profit in the past. Moreover, I reminded readers, the FCC had said there was still "a compelling need" for a second public television station in Pittsburgh. I also contended that the claim that the boards and the public had been fully consulted and had participated in the decision was hogwash.

Miles and Roddey produced a half-hour WQED-TV special, "A Brand New Original WQED," to promote their new plan without the inconvenience of dissenting voices. We resumed our pickets in front of the station for scheduled board meetings.

WQED Files with the FCC

On June 3, 1997, WQED Pittsburgh, Cornerstone TeleVision, and Paxson Communications submitted their license transfer applications to the FCC. Miles said that WQED was "optimistic [that] by the first quarter [of 1998] this all will be done" and warned that if this FCC decision was negative "public broadcasting as you know it today will not exist. All you will get —possibly get—is the national feed into Pittsburgh, no local presence at all."

All former promises to the contrary, WQED management then confirmed plans to suspend all locally produced programs, saying it would use the rest of the summer to evaluate them. Ann Devlin of *Cullen/Devlin* speculated that this could be a strategy to take her show off the air with the least amount of backlash: "I can clearly say there's reason to be concerned." Lynn Cullen had advised me months earlier that, lacking sponsorship, the program would certainly be cut, but that she wasn't allowed to comment publicly. Producer Tom Waseleski of *The Editors* also seemed to know that it was curtains. He talked about the show's nine-year run: "We're eager to continue providing this kind of information to the region's viewers—if not at WQED, then certainly somewhere else." Neither of these shows returned in the fall. The *Post-Gazette*'s Barbara Vancheri commented, "It's a shame we are without [them] at a time when we desperately need serious discussion about the proposed regional sales tax, along with any number of other topics."

In its petition to take over the license of WQEX, Cornerstone described itself as a "noncommercial educational station that values education of children, teens and adults on moral, ethical and community issues through lifelong learning and through the teaching of matters related to religion and practical Christian living." It provided an annotated list of its programs and resumés for members of its board of directors, presented its new thirty-two-member community advisory board, and talked about plans for future "for-credit Bible study courses."

WQED Offers Meeting

From May 21 to mid-June of 1997, WQED's attorneys prodded us to meet directly with Miles to negotiate a settlement in exchange for withdrawing our opposition to the WQEX deal. According to his attorneys, Miles was willing to explore "any options short of not selling the station." When we pressed them to be more specific, Miles's representatives mentioned "input on programming, input on evaluating programming, coverage of particular issues, and keeping the station relevant in covering Pittsburgh issues."

We held a meeting of our core group and after considerable debate decided to go ahead with the meeting. At least it would prevent WQED from arguing that we refused to talk with them. At best, since the FCC might grant the transfer, our attorneys suggested it would be worthwhile to consider what actions by WQED "would serve the Pittsburgh community and blunt the loss of WQEX."

We agreed that APA president Rick Adams, Linda Wambaugh, and I would represent the campaign. Our attorneys offered WQED three meeting dates in late June and faxed the following "proposed agenda" of "issues" for discussion:

1. Subscriber election of the WQED board of directors and community advisory board through a nomination and balloting procedure designed to ensure fairness and diversity.
2. Compliance with FCC and CPB guidelines with respect to open and accountable public broadcasting, including:
   a. Public notice of board and committee meetings with time, location, and agenda posted at least a week in advance in newspapers of general circulation;
   b. Procedure for placing concerns of members of the Pittsburgh community on the agenda of the board of directors' meetings;
   c. Public and timely disclosure of minutes of all board of directors and committee meetings and of financial statements;
   d. An expanded role for the community advisory board in programming decisions.
3. Weekly broadcast of public affairs programs, including *We Do the Work, Rights and Wrongs, America's Defense Monitor,* and *In the Life* at times when a substantial amount of the audience would be able to watch.
4. Written commitment to work with the Allegheny County Labor Coun-

cil to develop and fund a locally produced, weekly, half-hour program
on labor issues.

5. Representation on the committee that [would] manage the program
   endowment fund to be created after the transfer of WQEX.

6. An effective mechanism for enforcing any agreement that we [might]
   reach.

7. Program on WQED and WQEX to present any agreement to viewers.

One of WQED's attorneys, Barbara Gardner, replied, "Although WQED is
not necessarily in agreement with every component of each Alliance proposal, our client is prepared to discuss each one in detail and is hopeful that
a mutually satisfactory overall result can be achieved." They offered a meeting on June 30 or July 1 and we accepted July 1 and agreed on no press until
the FCC ruled on the case or the parties withdrew from the deal.

I looked forward to the meeting. Despite a long string of disappointments, I thought that economic rationality would dictate a cooperative attitude from WQED. We had already stopped a $52 million deal. Now we stood
in the way of WQED's last chance at a $17 million deal. Every month they
had to wait cost them about $60,000 in debt service and interest. They
seemed to think the wait would be at least six months, but could be longer
and they could lose. Finally, our demands were modest, in many cases simply
compliance with existing FCC regulations.

Klink Takes a Pass

While this was going on, I got a call from Congressman Klink's office asking
me for whatever information I had about the parties to the deal. I spent three
hours with Klink's top aide, Joe Brimmeier, and sent him away with a large
packet of notes and clips very damaging to WQED and Cornerstone. I was
assured of a strong statement of opposition, perhaps made publicly, hopefully coordinated with one from Congressman Bill Coyne.

On June 26, 1997, I was stunned to see a story by Barbara Vancheri in
the *Post-Gazette* headlined "Klink Takes to Sidelines in WQEX Swap with
Cornerstone." To be sure, Klink's comments on the deal were unequivocally
critical. Nevertheless, he said, he didn't have "a real suggestion . . . as to another direction," so, "for the time being," he had agreed to "remain neutral."

Two months later, Todd Gutnick reported in the *Tribune-Review* that
pressure from Klink got his former aide Dennis Casey banned from Corner-

stone, where he had been making regular appearances on *His Place* and Jerry Bowyer's *Focus on the Issues*. According to Bowyer, Cornerstone went so far as to edit Casey out of an already taped edition of his program, dubbing in his own voice instead. A letter to Bowyer written by director of programming David Skeba confirmed that the ban would be in place until the FCC approved the deal.

We Finally Sit Down with WQED

WQED hosted the meeting in their corporate law firm's skyscraper downtown. We were given a long meeting room with a walnut conference table that sat as many as twenty in comfortable chairs. We were represented by attorney Karen Edwards, Rick Adams, Linda Wambaugh and me. Representing WQED were attorneys Steve Lerman and Barbara Gardner, George Miles, B. J. Leber, head of stations and production Carolyn Wean, and new CFO Neil Mahrer.

Mahrer had replaced Mel Ming in January 1997. A former CFO at WETA-TV, he had replaced CEO Sharon Rockefeller there for six months while she recuperated from automobile injuries. Mahrer had reportedly stepped on a lot of toes, including Rockefeller's. He acknowledged to the Washington *Post* that he was a "little bit confrontational." That was confirmed quickly enough. Throughout the meeting he glared at me, rolled his eyes, and/or threw up his hands almost every time I spoke. Rick Adams later asked me about our "history" and was astonished to learn we had just met.

Lerman established "the ground rules of the conversation": (1) no press unless and until we reached agreement or the FCC reached a final order; (2) their goal was to reach an agreement that would not require the FCC to review it. This was our first warning that WQED did not intend to make any meaningful concrete concessions. Lerman also warned us against using the meeting to fish for information. This effectively put a clamp on any frank discussion of current policy and procedure, a definite handicap in negotiating a compromise.

Karen Edwards countered that we had a need for agreements that reflected "specificity and enforceability," which was a lot to accomplish in the "very short time" remaining before the filing deadline for petitions. She asked them whether they would be open to continuing talks even after we filed. Lerman said he wasn't interested because the FCC would still have to consider the allegations made in the filing. Since we did not want to forfeit our right to file, we seemed to be at an impasse.

At this point Miles proposed that he start responding to our list to see where we were. We agreed and he began reading from some handwritten notes. I asked him whether he had a handout that we could refer to and he said no. Moreover, he cautioned, any agreement would have to be approved by his full board: "If I send a memo of understanding to the board and they blow us out of the water, I've got other kinds of problems."

Starting from the top of our list, Miles rejected subscriber election as too expensive. I countered that the cost would be very reasonable since WQED could use its own media for nominations and elections, either mailing ballots with solicitations or providing them as tear-outs in the magazine. (Some months later, WQED mail surveyed its members to see which WQEX programs they thought should be moved to WQED. A mail ballot would not have cost any more.)

Miles then objected that subscriber election wouldn't ensure diversity. Rick Adams proposed that we reserve seats for different constituencies and conduct elections within those categories. Miles didn't respond. He already had his counterproposal in mind: three "at large" seats each for the board of directors and the community advisory board. He said he would leave it to the lawyers as to how to set up the nominating process.

Edwards asked Miles how he had decided on three as the appropriate number. Miles said there were thirty-one members on his board, so he simply applied the 10 percent quota that had been in effect at WETA. I pointed out that Mahrer had said ten *seats*, not 10 percent, and moreover, that those were elected not appointed seats.

Sticking to his reframing of the issue, Miles indicated he would be willing to increase the number of at-large seats to five, to be nominated by a special committee that itself would include at-large members. Because it was clear that Miles was unwilling to discuss how subscriber election might be possible, we agreed to let him go through the whole list before we tried to negotiate any items individually.

Miles complained that our requests under point two constituted an "expansion" of FCC guidelines. I couldn't see it but held my peace. Taking a page from Don Korb's book, he rejected publishing notice of meetings in newspapers of general circulation as "too expensive." I made no comment about the full-page *Post-Gazette* ad WQED had taken out just weeks before, advising readers to "watch this space" for future program announcements. He suggested maybe using their "hotline" to provide the meeting agenda for anyone who called.

Miles then asked Linda Wambaugh what she had in mind regarding procedures for placing the concerns of the public on the agenda. Wambaugh replied that the process should be "accessible" and "not too intimidating." In an echo of Elsie Hillman's comment about "Kooks with gripes," Miles said he did not want just anybody to "show up and start filibustering." He suggested members of the public could be allowed to speak to the board, but not during a meeting. Miles and his people discussed this briefly and suggested such exchanges should take place after rather than before meetings. He quickly added that there would have to be a time limit or board members would leave before hearing the speakers.

Miles then went on to propose other public forums he would be willing to conduct. He said he would host a "shareholders" meeting every November and also a show on WQED every quarter. Miles enjoyed being on camera, so I knew we would probably get these shows whether or not we wanted them. Miles also proposed that the community advisory board host four community forums a year. As for an "expanded role for the CAB in programming decisions," however, Miles declared, "The ultimate responsibility for programming is mine as management."

Looking at the alternative public affairs shows we had asked for, Miles noted, "Some of these programs we have aired," however he made no indication that he would put any of these programs on again. As for labor programming, Miles said he would continue to try to work with the ACLC but was "not sure anything is ever going to happen because of the funding issues." Apparently he did not consider any of the proposed program endowment fund supported by revenues from the sale of WQEX to be available for such purposes. Miles added that he and Carolyn Wean were planning a local public affairs show for independent producers for an hour each week and maybe one of those could be about labor.

As for the endowment fund committee, Miles said there was a selection process to be worked out by board chair Roddey. Wambaugh and I looked at each other knowingly. We were thinking of Frank Cappelli, who had hosted a WQED pilot at first praised and later dropped by Miles. Cappelli had filed a complaint with the WQED board and the FCC against WQED for refusing to give him back the rights to his show, the master and submaster tapes, and $16,000 in unspent production moneys.

Cappelli claimed that Roddey's Hawthorne Group had been permitted to invest $300,000 in the pilot. When Miles dropped the show, Cappelli told us that Roddey had informed him that Miles had agreed to reimburse Hawthorne Group in full out of the proceeds from the WQEX station sale. Roddey told Cappelli that he would be made "whole again" and that Cappelli should try and make his own deal. Cappelli named three witnesses to this conversation, which indicated apparent conflict of interest and potential abuse of funds. Cappelli had attached supporting memoranda to a letter to the FCC opposing WQED's license transfer application. In 1999 neither the two dailies nor the *City Paper* would touch this story, despite—or perhaps because of—the fact that Roddey was then running for county executive.

Miles said the committee would involve members of the board of directors, the community board, and outside members. I asked him whether there wasn't any more detailed proposal now available. Miles complained that they were waiting for approval to get the money and were too busy trying to keep the station going. It had been more than a year since the board first voted to dereserve and sell WQEX. I asked Miles, with a tone of incredulity, if he was saying that the reason they had no clear plan for monitoring the money was that they "didn't have enough time."

At this point Mahrer leaned forward, jutted out his jaw and challenged me, "Have you ever run anything?" Having had enough, I replied, "I've never run anything into the ground."

Miles and Mahrer reared up on their haunches. "We haven't either," Miles protested. Mahrer snapped at me, "When do you want the plan?" I suggested, "How about thirty-six hours?" adding that if they were serious about getting an approved proposal before the filing deadline, why not start now? As the meeting neared an end, Miles began to think out loud: "How about one-third BOD, one-third CAB, and one-third outside members?" Finally, Miles rejected the joint program on WQED announcing our agreement, saying we would "just have a joint press conference after the board."

Late in the meeting, I proposed a hypothetical situation in which there would be blocks of time reserved for public affairs programming—maybe an hour a week, maybe two or three—and a WQED contract with an independent producer mutually agreeable to both sides. This seemed to me an acceptable compromise that the FCC would approve, but Miles didn't even want to consider it, returning to his refrain that programming authority was "non-delegable."

In an effort to communicate the substance of our concerns, I explained that it was not just a case of program topics, but of whose perspectives were represented. They seemed puzzled, so I offered a concrete example. About three years before WQED had done a program on the national health care proposal debate, after which an APA member group, Health Care for All, had called me to complain that there was no one on the panel to represent the Canadian single-payer model. They had called the station and offered one of their physicians as a spokesperson for that position. They were told the panel was too large already and the host would have someone representing another position also refer to the single-payer option. At this point in my illustration, B. J. Leber, as was her wont, interrupted to chide me that I was stuck in the past and they wanted to move forward. I protested that if we couldn't agree on the problem, we could never agree on a solution. Carolyn Wean quietly acknowledged that single-payer "probably" should have been included, but there was no acknowledgement of the larger concern I was raising.

As suggested by Gigi Sohn of the Media Access Project, Wambaugh asked about reserving some of WQED's anticipated digital frequency for public access programming. Suddenly the four-channel future disappeared. Wean said that they would "need all the frequencies for high definition telecast." When we questioned them about how much programming would actually be done in high definition, Miles allowed that there might be some time where public access could be possible, but he would be no more specific than that. It was clear to me that WQED would be able to play a shell game with the digital frequencies that no directors or community board would ever question.

As for our concerns about Cornerstone, Miles said he would try to facilitate a meeting but couldn't promise anything. He added, his voice trailing off, "We have been talking to those people for two years . . ." Steve Lerman then distributed a memorandum of understanding that called upon us, should we reach agreement, to join WQED in petitioning the FCC to approve its application and to drop our motion to compel evidence of the Mellon Bank loan agreement.

At this point we requested a break to reflect on Miles's offer. We called Angela Campbell, who found much of it laughable. I was angry. Not only had they not kept the promise to seriously address our issues, they had been insulting in the process. On a couple of occasions, Lerman and Miles had made self-righteous statements about how none of this would be necessary if the first FCC petition had been approved, implying that somehow we were at fault for their predicament.

At the same time, they made no acknowledgement of our power in this situation. At one point, Miles had complained that all kinds of community groups might complain that WQED is not serving them, but you can't please everybody. Perhaps not, but they did not request a meeting with "everybody" because "everybody" did not stand in the way of their cashing in a public trust. In addition, Miles blamed the *We Do the Work* fiasco on organized labor. I explained to Miles that those people are our constituency, this is what they have told us and it does not help matters for him to say they are wrong. He defended himself by saying he was always willing to go anywhere and talk to any group. I replied that this might be the problem—he was willing to talk but not to listen.

A whole day had passed and we had to drive Karen Edwards back to the airport. Miles proposed and Wambaugh agreed that his people would stay late and put the whole agreement, such as it was, into writing. I said nothing. We huddled in the lobby outside and agreed to continue working on our petition.

The next day Edwards got a faxed copy of the "agreement." It ran four pages and spelled out everything that Miles had offered, but not one thing that we had requested—no subscriber election, no nominations solicited in the newspapers, no alternative public affairs programs, no labor show, no public presentations to the board, no effective community advisory board, no representation on the program endowment committee.

There were a couple "at-large" members among eleven on the nominations committee and three among nine on the endowment fund committee, but WQED—and no one else—would choose them. In this context, "at-large" had no meaning to me. Oh yes, and WQED would meet with the Alliance for Progressive Action twice yearly to discuss "programming and other matters."

We chose not to respond to the proposed agreement. Compounding the insult, Steve Lerman sent letters accusing us of "deceptive conduct" and Karen Edwards of "disingenuous posturing." All of this bluster served no purpose except to give us a good laugh and harden our resolve. We had defied all pundit predictions in the first round of the battle over public broadcasting in Pittsburgh, and our movement had grown. Despite the odds, we could not be counted out.

Our Campaign Files Opposition with FCC

Our July 1997 opposition was filed by Karen Edwards and Randi Albert, again under Angela Campbell's supervision. From the first petition to "Plan B" our support clearly grew and WQED's diminished. This time our seventy-page opposition filing was supported by seventy-two letters and fourteen hundred petition signers, along with thirty-five declarations. Eventually the number of petition signers would reach four thousand. The declarations were necessary since the FCC does not accept newspaper reports as evidence.

One of them was from Allen Kukovich concerning his frustration as a board member at being denied key documents. We also provided two videocassettes, totaling three and a half hours, of Cornerstone programs, along with annotated descriptions.

Congressmen Markey and Dingell sent a letter that was appended to the filing later. They dismissed WQED's justification as not "compelling," emphasized that the license "was issued to serve the community," and suggested again that "if WQED no longer believes that WQEX is able to fulfill its public service mission," there would be others in Pittsburgh who would be "grateful" to do so.

We proposed that WQED's deal was no more than an "indirect means to achieve the same result" as the earlier petition to dereserve would have produced. Pittsburgh would still lose the unique programming on WQEX; two educational channels and one religious channel would be replaced by a single educational channel, one religious channel, and another outlet for infomercials and network reruns.

Traditionally, public interest messages and profit-seeking commercial messages have been regarded as distinct, even antithetical. Accordingly, we contended that the assignment of Channel 40 to Paxson would violate the public interest because its programming "would consist almost entirely of sales presentations."

Paxson's and WQED's reading of the recent Supreme Court "must carry" decision was that since sales presentations are now considered to be "of public interest," they also must be "in the public interest" and to judge otherwise is an elitist justification for unwarranted government intervention. This assault on the English language threatened to undermine a distinction fundamental to preserving public service broadcasting.

We challenged WQED's qualifications to transfer its license under the Jefferson Radio case policy that "a licensee may not assign its license when its basic qualifications are at issue." We focused on WQED's "character qualifications," citing the FCC's long-standing concerns with "acts of willful misrepresentation." We knew that the FCC never held stations accountable for deception in their public relations. However, we proposed, WQED had obtained board and public support for their plan under false pretenses, and this amounted to lying to the commission, the one offense for which broadcasters have been penalized.

In addition, we charged WQED with repeated violations of the Communications Act requirements to maintain an effective community advisory board, give reasonable public notice of meetings, hold open meetings, provide access to the station's public file, and file specified documents with the FCC. None of these charges made it into local press reports.

In its opposition, WQED pointed out that no reserved channels would be lost, reiterated its claims about "crushing debt" and "digital television challenges," and insisted that the Cornerstone deal was "simply implementing the very alternative" the commission "encouraged WQED to pursue, in denying relief that would have provided more significant financial support for WQED." Furthermore, WQED called on the FCC to dismiss our "frivolous, trumped-up and reckless charges" concerning WQED's character. They claimed that "no matter what their nature, statements made to a third party are not representations to the FCC."

WQED appended declarations from nineteen of the twenty-five members of the board to their filing, "attesting to the fact that they disagree with Kukovich, and have been so apprised of relevant considerations as to be able to discharge their fiduciary obligations to WQED." These particular declarations are in standard format. The signers claim to have read Kukovich's declaration and they all refute his charge that "management did not provide sufficient information for Board members to evaluate solutions that the management was recommending." Significantly, none of them claimed to have seen any of the documents denied to Kukovich and cited in his declaration, although through private conversations, we knew of some who definitely had not. Nor did any of them claim to have been consulted on the rejected Murtha offer. Taken literally, these declarations indicate only that these board members have very low standards for discharging their fiduciary responsibilities. Apparently, six board members declined to sign even this modest declaration.

WQED also attacked my credibility. They claimed that I had stopped attending CAB meetings after 1994, even though I wasn't appointed to that body until 1995. In response, we cited eight or so meetings I had attended over 1995–96 in addition to many letters and phone calls that demonstrated my involvement. They also produced letters from seven members of the twenty-five-member advisory board that they claimed contradicted my contention that its members were "kept in an information vacuum by WQED management, or that recommendations and concerns were ignored."

In my response, I pointed out that one letter came from someone who had joined the CAB in 1997 and could have no personal experience of the matters at hand. Four others merely advocated the swap and sale plan with no reference at all as to how well or poorly CAB members were informed or treated. A fifth writer was content to attack my character for being "an enemy of progress" who engaged in "radical-style maneuvers." Another claimed that "the facts [concerning the CAB] are quite the opposite of the manner in which they were presented by Mr. Starr" but did not refute any of the numerous specific allegations I made, even though (or perhaps because) he was in a position to know.

The final letter, from chair Gwen Elliott, was riddled with false and contradictory statements. For example, she claimed that "CAB meetings had been announced in the local newspapers," in contradiction to a declaration from the WQED director of corporate communications that such notification was not done because he believed it was not required by the Corporation for Public Broadcasting. Elliott also claimed that she had "personally tried to accommodate Mr. Starr's schedule for meeting attendance as well as other members"; however, she also stated that she "scheduled all CAB meetings the day after the WQED Board meetings to report all pertinent WQED matters." As examples of the station's "responsiveness" to the CAB she cited the institution of the "hotline" and the "Ballot '95" two-minute candidate statements.

We provided a declaration from Ann Sutherland Harris, who urged the Commission to understand that members of the CAB "were never provided with any financial data about WQED's situation . . . nor was the plan to sell QEX . . . ever mentioned . . . until after the plans were made public in the local press." In the final analysis, she said, "our role [as CAB members] was to answer phones for a telethon during the John Tesh broadcast and to applaud and approve what was in the programming works once it was settled." Sutherland Harris concluded, "I had no impact on any aspect of the station's programming as a CAB member."

In my view, the most revealing argument made by WQED was its recommendation that the FCC rely on "market forces to achieve programming diversity in local markets" rather than try to "regulate program formats." We responded, "In view of the fundamental purpose of noncommercial educational stations to serve audiences that are underserved by commercial broadcasting . . . it would make no sense to rely on market forces to ensure that community programming needs are met." This very important discussion was not reported in the local press.

WQED's petition was appended by fifty-six letters of support, only twenty-five of which were from members of the community not already serving on one of their boards. This time there were only five letters from politicians, including two from county commissioners, one from Mayor Tom Murphy, and one signed jointly by Pennsylvania Republican senators

Arlen Specter and Rick Santorum. Most writers were businessmen, including *Post-Gazette* owner William Block, who called us a "strident minority" who "offer no viable alternative."

In addition, there were fifteen letters from people in the public broadcasting industry, including PBS president Ervin Duggan, CPB executive vice president Robert Coonrod, and APTS president David Brugger. Duggan asked that WQED be regarded as a "special, urgent case," Coonrod warned of the threat to "the continued viability of both stations," and Brugger argued that a twenty-four-hour schedule would make up for losing WQEX and money was needed for the digital conversion. Notably, all three letters were mistaken about the actual mechanics of the proposed deal.

The heart of our petition challenged Cornerstone's qualifications to furnish a nonprofit and noncommercial educational broadcast service. We contended that Cornerstone intended to operate Channel 16 "as it currently operates Channel 40, to promote the beliefs, politics, products and services associated with its brand of evangelical Christianity." In fact, thanks to project staff member Benita Campbell, we even had a direct quote from Russell Bixler reassuring viewers that after the transfer "the only difference [will be] instead of watching on Channel 40, you'll watch on Channel 16." Oleen Eagle then adds, "Nothing changes for you as the viewer. You're going to see the same programs, you're going to see Russ [Bixler] and Norma [Bixler], you'll see us, we're going to be here. . . . Nothing changes. The only thing that changes is that we move to another parking lot."

Taken at face value, we proposed, this indicated that Cornerstone planned to continue programming that not only was commercial but violated FCC rules regarding commercials on children's programs. Commercialism aside, we proposed that Cornerstone was not qualified because it had failed to "present a clear statement of educational purpose," to select officers and directors broadly representative of the community, and to provide educational programming that served the diverse needs of greater Pittsburgh. In fact, we pointed out, Cornerstone had added "educational" to its mission statement only a month before filing for a noncommercial license. We detailed the exceedingly narrow and marginal base of Cornerstone's officers, directors, and community advisory board members in the community. And we detailed the station's pervasive commercialism.

In addition, we produced numerous declarations from academics and clergy critical of Cornerstone programs. For example, Dr. Carol Stabile, of the University of Pittsburgh, had watched Cornerstone's children's program *The Sunshine Factory* and concluded that it "had no clear educational content or substance." Science writer Michael Schneider noted that Bixler's "creation science" program *Origins* "makes no effort to balance its narrow perspective"; likewise, Carnegie Mellon University physics professor Lincoln Wolfenstein cited "misinformation" and found that *Origins* had "no educational value and in fact [is] harmful to the public understanding of science."

We also charged that Cornerstone's programming violated the Commission's "fair break" doctrine, which refers to "the repeated making of irresponsible charges against any group or viewpoint without regard for the truth of such charges and without determining in advance of their publication whether they can be corroborated or proven."

University of Pittsburgh public health professor Anthony Silvestre found the "portrayals of homosexual men and lesbians" on the *Coral Ridge Ministries Hour* to be full of "misinformation and cruel stereotyping." In his view, this creates "a hostile environment for young people and others who need counseling and education, and misleads non-homosexuals who may need accurate information." The program *Exposing the Lie* condemns other branches of Christianity, including Unitarianism and the Church of Jesus Christ of Latter-Day Saints (Mormonism), calling the former a "cult" and claiming that the latter promotes divorce, teenage pregnancy, and venereal disease. Cornerstone's "flagship" program, *Getting Together,* refers to Hinduism as "the Kingdom of the enemy." In an area in which eighty-three percent of church-goers are Catholic, Monsignor Charles Owen Rice found at least one of the two programs identified by Cornerstone as "for Catholics" to be "not your normal Catholic fare." In fact, he noted, ads for other Cornerstone programs were "hostile to Catholics." University of Pittsburgh professor Mark Ginsberg found Cornerstone's programming "extremely offensive to someone like myself who was raised a Jew."

Cornerstone's response was most revealing. Rather than promise programs that professionals would recognize as educational, it sought to justify its religious instruction as having larger educational importance. It rejected the declarations of our academics as "irrelevant" and provided declarations from Russell Bixler, Mary Ann Skeba, and two officers of the National Religious Broadcasters trade association that asserted their opinion that the majority of programming on Cornerstone was educational.

The main thrust of Cornerstone's pleading aimed at capitalizing on the FCC's laxity in enforcing public interest standards over the years. Cornerstone cited cases of FCC-approved noncommercial applications where the board members or officers were related, where all directors were members of one ethnic group, and where there were no more than seven directors in all or no more than five who were local. Cornerstone also claimed that its "educational showing is far more detailed and complete than other showings approved by the Commission."

Cornerstone also tried to justify its commercial violations, claiming it received no direct compensation or that the products were promoted by a nonprofit entity. In any case, it claimed, it would change its practices if necessary. And, confusing the "fair break" doctrine with the Fairness Doctrine, Cornerstone claimed that the former was unconstitutional. In its closing arguments, Cornerstone charged the FCC with threatening the First Amendment by "discriminating against a religious broadcaster [in favor of] a persistent and vocal conglomeration of splinter groups in the community."

Cornerstone's Oleen Eagle said to the *Post-Gazette*'s Barbara Vancheri, "Our educational emphasis is going to be biblical and Christian, and we're not hiding that fact. That is definitely who we are. I believe most people feel 'QED will be able to handle the educational services to the general public, and I think we're serving two completely different segments of the population, and they're both important and both should be served." In another article, Linda Wambaugh replied, "We support their right to operate on a commercial channel, but they don't meet the qualifications to operate on a noncommercial channel."

Chapter 8

The Killing of WQEX
and the Final Showdown

The summer of 1997 was just coming to an end when WQED's board next met. At that September 19 meeting they approved the decision to bring WQEX to an end as well. George Miles announced that as of November 2, WQEX would simply "simulcast" the programs shown on WQED. In his report to the board, Miles said airing the same programs on both channels at the same time would save money and prepare for the transition once the sale of Channel 16 was complete.

At the same meeting, the board approved expanding underwriting credits from ten to thirty seconds. "They are not commercials," Miles hastened to add. These "enhanced underwriting" credits would run only during breaks between programs, and there would be limits on content: they could not involve comparisons to other companies and products, mention prices, or call viewers to take action. One board member noted that both the *Boston Globe* and the *Christian Science Monitor* had written editorials critical of these kinds of spots. Jim Roddey replied that "lots of stations are doing this" and WQED "cannot afford not to." Miles said the spots would be sold on a cost-per-thousand basis at rates comparable to those charged by other stations. Roddey estimated the new spots could bring in as much as $1 million more a year than the current ten-second messages.

In my press comment I said, "These are commercials pure and simple, and dozens of other stations have pledged publicly not to carry them. They have no place on a noncommercial medium supported largely by taxpayer and viewer contributions." Having seen several of these "enhanced under-writing spots," I had concluded that they most certainly were commercials, although stylistically they were appropriately understated to appeal to af-fluent consumers of upscale products like luxury automobiles, home enter-tainment systems, and travel.

I condemned the killing of WQEX as "arbitrary" and "an outrage to the citizens of Pittsburgh." Informing readers that Miles was a major figure in a national movement to commercialize public broadcasting, I challenged him rhetorically: "He could be spearheading the movement for a public trust to provide permanent independent funding for public television in-stead of leading the pack to sell out its birthright for easy money."

At the *City Paper*, Andy Newman and Chris Potter put their heads to-gether and came up with one thought—in order to be "cost-effective," they would start simulcasting their columns. They proceeded to lampoon the de-cisions to simulcast on WQEX and run thirty-second commercials in identi-cal columns run side by side under separate bylines.

Campaign Complains to FCC and CPB

On September 30, attorneys Randi Albert and Angela Campbell sent a letter to Lillian Fernandez, general counsel of the CPB, advising them of WQED's intentions. We pointed out that WQED was receiving about $1.5 million in community service grants for the period from 1996 to 1998 on condition, among other things, that "each station . . . provide a separate and distinct program service for the community of license."

We also advised Fernandez that "as of November 2, WQED will no longer be in compliance with CPB rules" and encouraged her "to take strong action to address WQED's waste of grant funding." Linda Wambaugh ad-vised the press, "We think there's a certain public accountability and respon-sibility that comes when you receive large amounts of taxpayer money." In response, Miles stated that he had gotten tentative approval from the CPB months before.

On October 10, associate general counsel Steven J. Altman wrote back to say that WQED management had requested that CPB waive the separate programming requirement in June of 1997. Because of the station's "severe financial distress," Altman asserted, adjusting WQED's community service grant "would have . . . compromised the station's ability to maintain its pri-mary program service." His agency did not consider WQED's behavior a "waste of grant funding" but rather "an effective and appropriate use of community service funds." In effect, the CPB was choosing to ignore FCC rulings and CPB regulations and permitting Miles to violate the rules without consulting the community as to whether they were being served by such inaction.

On October 7, our attorneys petitioned the FCC "to investigate the qualifications of WQED Pittsburgh" and "to request immediate submission of applications for license renewal" for both WQED and WQEX. We noted that WQED justified its simulcasting as a " 'transition' in preparation for the Commission's approval of its application for transfer of Channel 16." Since that decision still was pending, we argued, WQED's action "undermines the Commission's authority and denies Petitioners the opportunity to seek meaningful relief."

We cited the FCC decision in the dereservation proceeding, which stated that the commission could "not conclude that there is no need for a second noncommercial channel at Pittsburgh" and that "this programming cannot be fully replaced simply by extending the hours of operation of WQED." We noted that the commission "has found that non-commercial public television stations which go dark for a significant period of time may lose their license to broadcast because they are not adequately serving the public"; in fact, the decision becomes automatic after "any consecutive 12-month period."

We cited a case in which the FCC had conducted an early review and held that a station had misled the agency because it had revised its promised programming on the grounds of fiscal exigency. We charged further that WQED had violated FCC rules by failing to notify the commission of its plans to simulcast and were already past such a deadline. We also cited WQED's plans for enhanced underwriting to generate $1 million annually and noted that WQED had not demonstrated why this new money could not cover the lesser cost of continued operation of WQEX.

Barbara Vancheri gave WQED's Steve Lerman three long paragraphs of reaction in the *Post-Gazette,* in which he characterized our pleading as "a bogus piece of garbage" and attacked us personally. Vancheri, who had not called us for comment, closed her piece with "They, of course, argue otherwise."

On October 21, WQED's attorneys asserted that there were no rules against simulcasting and branded our petition "a classic frivolous pleading" filed "for the primary purpose of delay." WQED urged the FCC to "impose appropriate sanctions on Petitioners and, if deemed appropriate, on their

counsel for their repeated and blatant abuses of the Commission's processes." Attorney Campbell called the response "a transparent attempt to intimidate us by challenging our alleged motives," and I told the *Post-Gazette:*
"We are trying our very best to save WQEX from people who would rather
strip our assets for easy money than devise a sensible long-term plan to save
a precious educational frequency. We are for program choice that serves the
diversity of our community."

In our FCC response, we countered that there was no specific rule
against simulcasting because neither Congress nor the FCC ever envisioned
"such an obvious waste of scarce spectrum." Furthermore, since the FCC
relies on the public to monitor the conduct of licensees, we were only doing
our duty, whereas instead of offering any justifications for its decision to
simulcast, WQED offered only "baseless charges" and "false accusations regarding Petitioners' conduct."

This latest flurry of activity provoked more letters to the newspaper opposing the sale. A teacher who had been blind since birth lamented the loss
of educational programs on WQEX, some of which she taped and used in
class. Another woman catalogued WQED's "deceptive arguments" and proposed that the deep pockets step up and save WQEX. Keith Powell urged the
Post-Gazette to "examine the roots of this disaster" and hold "accountable"
those responsible. And a poem by Christine Doreian Michaels praised Mister
Rogers and English plays and lamented raising the axe over WQEX while
mouthing "platitudes that only dredge up dread of Right-wing station." She
finished, "Oh QED your drives made me a giver. Through waters clean,
you've sold me down the river."

Commercialism versus Community

The chasm between the station and the community was increasing. Viewer
contributions were now down about a half-million dollars. WQED looked
more to advertising, merchandising, and corporate services for its support.
In October 1997, it announced the opening of the WQED Store of Knowledge in the South Hills Village shopping mall, a venture in which it was an
equity partner.

Later in the month, Patricia Lowry reported in the *Post-Gazette,* "With
individual memberships down, WQED is courting the business community
with an innovative perk designed to increase its leadership role in the community—and fatten the station's coffers along the way." The story described

WQED's business partners program, sponsored by Sprint PCS, which had been running since 1991. In the last two years corporate memberships had gone up 50 percent to 180.

Business partners members attend "breakfast briefings," a series of quarterly panel discussions on topics affecting the local economy. Members are also invited to private screenings, station tours, and "a private cocktail reception featuring a national PBS personality." WQED's station manager of corporate giving, Terre Tumminello, described the breakfasts as "a prospecting tool." In 1997, general admission tickets were sold for $15. (By April 1998, WQED had moved up to three-hour "business forums" with tickets set at $25 per person.)

At the same time, the station formally rejected its public service obligations in arguments made to the FCC. In its October 22 motion to "strike" our petition, WQED argued that our petition was "frivolous" because "the Commission does not require noncommercial stations to address" what we had termed "'the needs of the unserved and underserved audiences.'"

We countered that the FCC is on record as stating that "diverse programming with sensitivity to [those] underserved by commercial broadcasting remains central to the unique service provided by Public Broadcasting." Moreover, it is also a policy of the Corporation for Public Broadcasting to "encourage" programming that "addresses the needs of unserved and underserved audiences, particularly children and minorities." WQED accused us of dictating programs and shot back, "like all noncommercial licenses, WQED is under no obligation to tailor its programming to suit the taste of a select group of listeners."

By the end of the year, WQED had cut all lesbian/gay and HIV-related programming from their schedule. Jay Michael Curlovich, a writer for a gay monthly, interviewed WQED's B. J. Leber and George Hazimanolis about this development. As published in *In Pittsburgh*, Leber told him this was only "an interim schedule." Curlovich charged that "WQED apparently decided that thirty-year-old reruns of *Lawrence Welk* are more important to the Pittsburgh community than programs that address gay/lesbian issues." Leber replied, "You can't look at it that way" and promised that the station would be able to do "more" when "the "QEX sale goes through." Curlovich cited a "Britcom" gay character who he said was "offensive" to the gay community and complained, "You're axing all the positive gay programming and keeping the ugly caricatures." Leber told him again, "You can't look at it that way," and claimed that the community advisory board had a hand in programming decisions. Upon questioning, she conceded that there were no gays on the advisory board. Hazimanolis said, "This doesn't mean there won't ever be gay programming on WQED again. . . . We've always done something in June for Gay Pride Month, for instance."

In March 1998, WQED-TV announced the debut of *UPMC Health News*, sponsored by the University of Pittsburgh Medical Center, a huge and rapidly expanding health care delivery complex in the area. The *Post-Gazette*'s Vancheri reported without comment, "In keeping with the show's sponsorship, most of the guests will be from UPMC, although WQED isn't ruling out newsmakers from other hospitals." The *Tribune-Review* editors, on the other hand, criticized WQED for allowing itself to become "a marketing tool for the UPMC Health System," including "'convenient' telephone numbers to call for UPMC 'physician referral.'" In their view this amounted to "an infomercial on what's supposed to be *non*-commercial television" (italics in original).

In defense of the new program, WQED producer Deb Acklin claimed that it merely filled a void left by *Health Talk*, a recently canceled WQEX show underwritten by Shadyside Hospital and featuring its own physicians. The media, of course, had never questioned the propriety of the Shadyside arrangement or of the Allegheny Financial Group putting up $13,000 a year to underwrite *Wall $treet Week*. Would the vested interest in such "underwriting" be clearer if Harrah's were to sponsor a WQED program on "How to Win at Casino Gambling"? Hungry for money and unconstrained by mission, WQED's appetite for commercialism had become gluttonous.

Public Television as Corporate Billboard

The worst was yet to come. However, this next story requires some background.

As one of the oldest cities in the country, Pittsburgh has been the home of the baseball Pirates and the football Steelers for decades. The Pirates were established in 1886, the Steelers during the Depression. In 1997, both teams played in Three Rivers Stadium, built in 1970 for $35 million. Due to various improvements, plus city money provided to the Pirates during hard times in the mid-1980s, the debt on Three Rivers had actually grown to $41.4 million. Nevertheless, over the course of the year, the owners of the Pirates and Steelers decided that they each needed their own new stadium.

The Pirates had recently been sold to a consortium headed by a thirty-five-year-old media entrepreneur from Sacramento named Kevin McClatchy. The McClatchy Company publishes eleven daily and thirteen community newspapers in six states. McClatchy promised to keep the team in Pittsburgh if he could make it pay, and the Stadium Authority granted the Pirates lease enhancements worth $5 to $7 million a year. At this point, the front office dropped all of the team's stars, reducing the payroll to $9 million, the lowest in the major leagues. In 1997, the franchise was valued at $71 million, a little more than half the average of $134 million for all other teams. Among the new owners was *Post-Gazette* owner William Block, who anted up $2 million. For months the paper ran a "Pirates Memories" box on the front page and vigorously boosted an "overachieving" team that lost more games than it won but finished second in a weak division.

The Pirates had an option clause with the city which, when triggered, would give the city nine months to find another buyer or face the transfer of the franchise. There were two conditions for exercising the option: financing for a new stadium not being in place by February 1998 and the team's losses under McClatchy's ownership exceeding $15 million. The Pirates had about $7 million in operating losses for 1996, but did much better with its dramatically reduced payroll in 1997.

The Steelers' motivation for a new stadium was based in the NFL's 1993 collective bargaining agreement which guaranteed revenue-sharing with players under a system known as the salary cap, a minimum and maximum limit set on the total of all players' salaries for each team. The system was supposed to level the playing field between big market and small market teams with respect to the talent they could buy.

The salary cap is based on a percentage of total league revenues and has risen rapidly. The primary source of such revenues is television contracts. As they have increased so has the cap, from a minimum of $33.5 million in 1997 to $41.5 million in 1998. The 1998 maximum was $51.5 million. Teams that don't make enough money to cover the mandate of the agreement stand to lose money. Since stadium revenues were left out of the league sharing agreement, however, owners have contrived to increase their profits and gain a competitive advantage by making more money from their stadiums for themselves. Such revenue includes private luxury boxes, club seats, concessions, parking, and advertising signage. According to NFL commissioner Paul Tagliabue, differences in stadium revenues account for some teams being able to spend less than half of their revenues on players while others are forced to spend up to three-quarters.

In the past, many sports teams were owned by families who were rooted in the community. The exploding value of the teams, primarily due to television, has led to the current era of more corporate ownership with fewer local ties. Such organizations have felt free to promote competition among American, Canadian, and one day perhaps Mexican cities for their franchises. The price is a big fancy new stadium on the most generous terms.

Many other public projects are subsidized primarily by their private beneficiaries. For example, the Pittsburgh International Airport received two-thirds of the $800 million needed to construct it from the airlines that do business there. Like all other cities, however, Pittsburgh was under pressure to subsidize professional sports franchises with public money.

Pittsburgh's Rooney family, owners of the Steelers, did not threaten to leave town, but they complained that the Steelers also needed a new stadium in order to remain competitive, and the team's contract included an option to move the team with two years notice. Interestingly, the Steelers were already more than a year behind in their rent to Three Rivers Stadium, a total of $1.5 million.

Corporate "Partners" Propose a Plan

In the first few months of 1997, the corporate establishment in Pittsburgh organized what they called the Regional Renaissance Partnership, comprised of six organizations with a total of two hundred board members. This alliance was formed under the leadership of the Allegheny Conference on Community Development and headed by Tom Usher, a major figure in the Pennsylvania Republican Party and the head of the USX Corporation, formerly US Steel.

The partnership proceeded to come up with a plan to increase county sales taxes in the region by half a percent over the next seven years. (The tax had already been raised from six to seven percent in 1994.) They anticipated $700 million in additional revenue from the new tax. In Allegheny County the money was to be used to build the two new sports stadiums, triple the size of the convention center, and pay for new projects in the city's cultural district. In the ten outlying counties, 25 percent of the money was to be put into a pool to help fund the Pittsburgh projects and the remaining 75 percent would be used for local economic development. Public funding would amount to 80 percent of the cost of all projects. The actual cost to individual residents would range from $11 to $124 per year, depending on income, with a median of about $50.

For their parts, the Pirates offered to contribute $35 million toward the cost of their stadium, the Steelers $50 million toward theirs. None of this money would be up front, however. In fact, both teams were vague about when and how their shares would be paid, but both were willing to sign leases that they said would keep them in Pittsburgh for the next twenty-five years.

Renaissance Partnership organizers brought in Les Francis, a former White House aide and political consultant from Washington, D.C., to design the campaign. The L. A. firm of Winner, Wagner, and Mandabach received more than $3 million to purchase air time for commercials. Much of the design and printing of pamphlets was done in Baltimore, Los Angeles, and Sacramento, with clip art from California and Colorado photographers. The editor of the alternative weekly *City Paper,* Andy Newman, considered this contracting inconsistent with an initiative that stressed local development.

The whole plan was to be put to voters in all eleven counties. It included provision for an authority based on political appointments to administer the revenue. The number of board members, anywhere from eight to eighteen, would depend on how many of the eleven counties passed the tax increase. One member was to be chosen by the mayor of Pittsburgh, two by the governor of Pennsylvania and four by the leaders of the state legislature.

Opponents branded the initiative a "stadium tax." While this label is not entirely accurate, it is fair to say that the stadium demands provided the impetus for the measure and constituted by far the largest items in the proposed budget. As compared to the other ten counties, Allegheny would realize a major share of the money.

None of the outlying county commissioners were involved in the planning, and in fact only three of the twenty-seven who expressed an opinion planned to vote "yes" on the initiative. Two days after the election, one of them remarked, "We felt a group of elites in Allegheny County came up with a way to tell us how we could help ourselves, but we were really helping them."

Money, the Media, and the Vote

In advance of the vote, the Renaissance Partnership spent about $5.5 million on a blitzkrieg media campaign that included radio and TV spots, newspaper ads, expensive direct mail brochures, public events, signs, buttons, etc. Funding included about $700,000 each from the Pirates and the Steelers; most of the rest came from some of the city's biggest banks and corporations. It is worth noting that although representatives of several of these corporations sat on the WQED board, none of the $700 million expected from an increase in county sales taxes was to be directed toward debt relief to save WQEX-TV.

During the week of the election there were four commercial TV public affairs shows devoted to the tax debate. Proponents consisted of members of the largely Republican corporate establishment and the Democratic political machine. Despite the existence of other organized opposition, the media designated Gerald Bowyer and Jake Haulk of the libertarian Scaife-funded Allegheny Institute for Public Policy to represent the opposition. As *City Paper* reporter Chris Potter observed, "This set up a false dichotomy—between the political mainstream and right wing extremists—when the real divide was not between left and right, but between those on the economic top and those on the bottom."

In Pittsburgh, recently taken over by a Philadelphia chain, supported the tax; the *City Paper*, now under Andy Newman's editorship, opposed it. The *Tribune-Review* editorialized against the tax; the *Post-Gazette* led the cheers.

The *Post-Gazette* featured interviews with NFL commissioner Paul Tagliabue and the proprietor of Dick's Sporting Goods (whose spokesperson was former Steelers quarterback Terry Bradshaw), reports on Steelers quarterback Kordell Stewart's pro-tax appearance at a local tavern, a letter in the sports page from Pirates owner Kevin McClatchy, and, as if that weren't enough, a story in the news section reporting that McClatchy had written the letter. When Republican county commissioner Bob Cranmer backed the tax hike, it was reported on the paper's front page. Conservative Republican Senator Rick Santorum was given a thousand words to editorialize in favor of the tax (Santorum justified his uncharacteristic support for a new tax with an equally uncharacteristic appeal to community spirit). The *Post-Gazette* even reported as news the fact that its publisher, John Robinson Block, challenged *Tribune-Review* publisher Richard Mellon Scaife to a public debate on the initiative. Elsie Hillman led a throng of her wealthy cronies at a lunchtime demonstration in the middle of Mellon Square downtown.

On the night before the election most Pittsburghers were glued to the tube to watch *Monday Night Football*, featuring the Steelers and the Kansas City Chiefs in a game with important playoff implications. Al Michaels did the play-by-play, Frank Gifford and Dan Dierdorf provided the color, and Lynn Swann, a former Steeler, did the sideline interviews. During the game, the guys in the booth made the county sales tax question a national issue. While the camera focused on Steelers owner Dan Rooney, they praised his family as a "class act" and editorialized on behalf of the tax. Gifford dismissed criticism of the initiative as "lots of rhetoric" and argued that the Steelers needed to build a new stadium to increase revenues to make the team competitive in the years ahead. Dierdorf asserted that all the other teams were building new stadiums. Gifford assured everyone that in any event it was not just a stadium tax, as opponents charged, but money for many other projects as well.

This turned out to be just a warm-up for Lynn Swann's halftime interview with Rooney, who repeated all of the above. Reflecting back, the *City Paper*'s Chris Potter commented, "It was the dumbest thing Rooney could have done. He not only confirmed our suspicions about the real reasons for the tax, but he highlighted the way in which tax supporters had most of the media at their disposal."

The next day, despite windy, dark weather, turnout was unusually heavy at the polls. At some polling stations, the wait was up to thirty minutes. Thirteen communities had a turnout of 60 percent or more. Three-fourths of them voted against the tax. When all the votes were counted, there were 509,852 "no" votes (64 percent) as opposed to 285,291 "yes" votes (36 percent). Even in Allegheny County the measure went down 58 percent to 42 percent. (By my calculation, the Renaissance Partnership had paid more than $20 per "yes" vote.) The fifteen "strongest Republican" communities supported the tax by a slight margin while the fifteen "strongest Democrat" communities went nearly two-to-one against; residents of the fifteen "highest income" communities supported the tax by a small margin while those in the fifteen "lowest income" communities went three-to-two against.

The Partnership's Plan B

There were various post-election spins on the tax defeat: supporters starting too late, people being against higher taxes generally, people not trusting city leaders, people being against new stadiums, the lack of inclusiveness in planning the initiative, etc. Political leaders who criticized the elitism of the planning process called for wider collaboration on developing a "Plan B" to address the issues.

In the aftermath, Pittsburgh mayor Tom Murphy formed an alliance with county commissioners Bob Cranmer and Mike Dawida that excluded Commissioner Larry Dunn, City Council president Jim Ferlo, and other critics of the tax. Their new Plan B proposed $803 million to triple the size of the convention center ($267 million) and build a new baseball park ($228 million) and football stadium ($233 million). It also included money to raze Three Rivers Stadium, pay off its existing debt, and develop a tourist center on the North Shore. Funds to pay for these projects would come out of the additional 1 percent sales tax instituted in 1994 and dedicated to supporting cultural institutions in the community.

This plan would not be submitted to the voters. Instead, the board of the Regional Asset District Fund (RAD) would vote on it. In May 1998, the Pennsylvania Poll found that voters were opposed to Plan B by a margin of 55 percent to 32 percent, with 13 percent undecided. Not willing to risk the fallout, the Renaissance Partnership put more pressure on the sports teams to increase their contribution.

On June 21, the *Post-Gazette* assumed the role of press agent for the new plan's architects. "Plan B Scores a TD," the front-page headline roared. "We have accomplished what nobody thought was possible," Commissioner Dawida crowed. Stadium construction costs were lowered from $495 million to about $417 million. The Steelers' Rooney had increased his contribution from $50 million to $76.5 million, agreed to cover all construction overruns, and committed to "stay at home" through 2031. The Pirates' McClatchey had increased his contribution from $35 million to $40 million and agreed to the same two conditions.

Neither owner was specific about when and how their money would come. It was reported, however, that the Steelers' additional $26.5 million would come from increased ticket prices. Even if the private commitments were honored, however, the money involved would amount to just 28 percent of the projected stadium costs and 15 percent of the total package. All the rest would be the public's money, including a $150 million contribution from the state. Public opinion was still opposed, but, as mentioned, the voters would no longer be trusted with this decision.

One week before the May primary election, the *Post-Gazette* refused to endorse Pennsylvania state representative Ivan Itkin for the Democratic nomination for governor on the grounds that he opposed the tax initiative, a new expressway, and a controversial county governance reform proposal. The paper also charged him with expressing such "reckless views" in an editorial board meeting as his opinion that "the trend toward corporate mergers will result in 'a few large businesses that dominate the country, the government and the press.'"

According to the charter of the Regional Asset District Fund, two negative votes are sufficient to defeat a proposal. Just weeks before the RAD vote, Commissioner Cranmer forced one member off the board who had said he was philosophically opposed to using public money for sports stadiums and in July the RAD board voted six to one in favor of Plan B: the fund would put up $13.4 million a year for the next thirty years to secure loans for the new construction. One citizens group filed suit, claiming that the law creating the RAD didn't justify the use of tax moneys for building new facilities, only for improving existing ones.

Calling WQED to Account

It is clear that a controversy such as this would make a perfect subject for public television. Covering such complex important local issues is, in fact, its mandate. This was all the more the case since the balance of resources to ensure coverage in the commercial media was so one-sided. Public television could have been a "place for controversy and debate" while being "a voice for groups in the community who might otherwise be unheard." But what role, in fact, did WQED play in this situation?

In mid-October 1997, I received a call from *Tribune-Review* reporter Todd Gutnick, who advised me that, at least since the beginning of the month, WQED had run six spots advocating the tax increase. He had ascertained that these political advertisements were paid for out of a $15,000 contract with the Community Alliance for Economic Development and Jobs, the political action committee of the Regional Renaissance Partnership.

Gutnick also noted that WQED CEO George Miles had been quoted in the *New York Times* as advocating the increase: "There is no longer an industrialist climate here of Big Daddy or Big Momma taking care of you— those days are over. If the tax doesn't go through the region could start to go adrift." Upon further inquiry, Gutnick had been informed by WQED that they would provide time for tax opponents to respond only if they came up with the money to pay for it. Gutnick wanted to know if this was legal and what I thought about it.

I called Angela Campbell and Randi Albert at Georgetown, who quoted from rule 399B of the Communications Act of 1934. Strictly forbidden to public broadcasters was "any message which is broadcast in exchange for remuneration and which is intended to express the views of any person with respect to matters of public importance."

Just as soon as Gutnick called WQED back for more details for his story, he was informed that they had suddenly changed their mind. The station was going to refund the $6,800 already received and provide equal time for tax opponents in thirty- and sixty-second spots. They would also schedule a public forum on the issue for the evening of October 28. As spokespersons they chose former KDKA news anchor Patti Burns and Gerald Bowyer, a corporate establishmentarian versus a libertarian critic.

Although Miles had personally approved the ads for airplay, he claimed that the station had been misled into believing the alliance was a not-for-profit organization and that this was the only offense that WQED had committed. WQED never acknowledged that running paid political advertising was an FCC violation regardless of the status of the sponsoring organization or that attempting to influence legislation was a violation of their own corporate bylaws regardless of whether or not the ads were paid.

B. J. Leber claimed, "This is a very gray area." Board chair Jim Roddey absolved the board: "Normally, the staff doesn't get into that much detail with the board." WQED attorney Steve Lerman claimed, "It's not running the ads that's bad, it's being compensated for the ads that's bad." Later, picking up on the new spin, Leber said, "We found out it was a mistake. . . . So what you do when you make a mistake is you say, 'Gee, we're not going to make that mistake anymore.' . . . We will not take a penny for the spots."

I asserted to the press that public television had "an *ethical* obligation to provide equal time for all points of view" and that this, in fact, was its reason for being: "The Pittsburgh community already is drowning in commercial messages from the wealthy establishment backing the tax. Instead of performing public television's congressionally mandated mission to provide space for the community to respond to the powerful, George Miles sells noncommercial time to the establishment to echo their position."

State representative Don Walko was incensed and called upon the attorney general of Pennsylvania to investigate potential violations of state law by WQED. Walko claimed a "serious breach of public trust" and noted that WQED's own articles of incorporation "provide that no part of its activity shall be the carrying on of propaganda, or otherwise attempting in any manner, to influence legislation."

The attorney general, a local Republican, told Walko that this was a matter for the FCC. Our Georgetown attorneys prepared a letter of complaint for Walko to FCC chair William Kennard citing the violation and also the simulcasting as a "blatant waste of scarce spectrum which denies the Pittsburgh community the popular programming currently aired on WQEX." In addition, Walko urged the commissioner "to investigate WQED to assess whether it is qualified to serve as a noncommercial educational licensee."

Our attorneys then decided to add this complaint to our emergency petition asking the FCC to make WQED and WQEX file for immediate license renewal. They argued that by "airing advertisements offering only a one-sided presentation of the facts on a controversial ballot initiative," WQED showed "incredible disregard" for the "objectivity and balance" responsibilities of public broadcasters and "a complete lack of understanding of the law." Steve Lerman retorted that the problem was already solved and this was "an irresponsible, reckless pleading" intended only to "clog up the process and delay the commission action as long as possible, because [we] had no case." He called upon the FCC to censure us.

On the day of WQED's hastily scheduled public forum, the *Post-Gazette* reported that more than seventy people had signed up to speak at the WQED special, entitled "The Community Speaks on the Regional Tax." The show was scheduled for 9 P.M. Renaissance Partnership spokesperson Jerry Bowyer and Patti Burns would both open and close the show with comments. In between, participants registered to speak would get one minute each to express their views.

The debate was moderated by Chris Moore of *Black Horizons,* who announced the format and said that speakers would alternate from each side. This went on for about ninety minutes until Moore determined that the last opposition speaker had spoken. He then announced that the show would then continue until the last proponents of the tax had had their say. Tax opponents protested. They asked if some of their members could have another turn. Moore said no.

Moore rejected complaints that this was unfair by claiming that this was "not a matter of sides" but of individuals who had a right to speak. He blamed the tax opponents for not "mobilizing" their "own people" and warned them that if they failed to do so on election day, they would lose. As tax proponents paraded one-by-one to the microphone shouts of "unfair" could be heard from the back, especially from attorney Jon Robison.

As the shouting persisted, Moore began to reprimand those in the back to shut up. Voices got louder and more strident and Moore became flushed. Tax opponent Dan Sullivan rushed forward and claimed that Moore had instructions on his monitor to stop the debate when either side had exhausted its speakers. Sullivan later told me that he could not verify the station's claim

that the problem was that some of "his people" failed to show up, since there was no signup for the debate.

On February 15, 1998 (the day after Valentine's Day), some three months after the election, all the usual suspects gathered together for a black-tie affair called the Elsie Awards. The hosts, billionaire Henry Hillman and WQED's former board chair Elsie Hillman, claim the awards "honor love" in the areas of communication, community, and compassion.

On this occasion, the recipients were the late Bill Burns and his daughter, Patti Burns, for communication; Dan and Pat Rooney, for community; and Frieda Shapira (of Giant Eagle supermarkets and a WQED board member), for compassion. WQED board chair Jim Roddey acted as master of ceremonies. Of the three hundred or so guests, some thirty-five (and their spouses) were cited by the society reporter on the spot. They included Pirates owner Kevin McClatchy, George Miles, and several WQED board members, including the Mellon Bank's David Lovejoy.

According to the next day's society-page reports, for the affair at the Carnegie the Hillmans had "imported a greenhouse of exotic palms, rare plants, tangerine trees and lavish sprays of forsythia, pear blossoms, heather and magnolia to line the marble halls leading to the Music Hall foyer. Inside it was pure romance. Red roses in silver cupid vases graced each candle-lit table and made the cavernous hall look intimate and inviting. A buffet of soups, pasta, baby lamb chops, beef and seafoods prepared by the Duquesne Club chefs was followed after the ceremony with an assortment of divine pastries."

Like all stories, this one probably has different lessons for different people. Certainly in this case, regardless of the merits of the tax proposal, the gut instincts of ordinary citizens prevailed over the propaganda of well-funded tax increase proponents. However, pulling a lever is the simplest of political acts and opposing something is always easier than organizing something. The latter really does require a well-developed political culture nourished by publicly available information and analysis.

Looking back on the legislation that authorized public broadcasting, it is clear that "high society" is not the public, certainly not the *only* public, for whom it was intended. There is frequent reference to racial minorities, children, the aged, and the underserved generally. At a time when only public broadcasting is free to inform citizens without the subtle but ubiquitous censorship of corporate sponsors, the usurpation of this precious public resource by self-serving elites is not just a scandal but a threat to our democratic way of life.

Our Reform Campaign Gets National Support

As WQED's collaboration with the religious right and capitulation to commercialism accelerated, our movement's importance became more widely recognized. In the fall of 1997, the AFL-CIO held its national meeting in Pittsburgh. One night I hosted labor filmmaker and activist Steve Zeltzer in my home. A short, stocky bundle of fast-talking energy, he had been active in the struggle for democratic media for many years and never seemed to get discouraged.

Zeltzer was running for the board of KQED-TV San Francisco. Long aware of our struggle, he was surprised to learn that KQED CEO Mary Bitterman had written two letters in support of the WQEX sale. He gave a copy of the letter to a reporter at the *San Francisco Bay Guardian,* who interviewed me and ran the story "Spreading the Gospel: KQED Prez Advocating Privatization."

A board member at Working Assets, the public interest–minded long distance telephone service, read the article. He recommended us to the company's citizen action director, Janet Nudelman, to be their cause of the month. Every month, with their billing statement, Working Assets invites their 300,000 customers to "make their voices heard" on two issues. Subscribers can check one box to have a form letter sent to the appropriate official in their name and another box to be given a free telephone call to the same individual to argue their position. If they choose the latter, Working Assets provides them with a page of talking points they can follow.

By this time the *ex parte* rules were in force with regard to our latest FCC filing. We could not solicit letters to be sent to the commission without having them also served on all parties to the proceeding. In this context, the telephone calls, in particular, were problematic. The solution was to craft the statement of support in more general terms. Our statement was titled "Keep the Public in Public Television." It alerted people to the danger that commercial broadcasters were taking advantage of financial pressures to buy up public stations. We asked Working Assets subscribers to call FCC chair William Kennard and "urge him to oppose the continuing commercialization and loss of public television stations." The text referred to WNYC New York, recently purchased by Paxson, and to the WQEX three-way deal, also involving Paxson.

The solicitation went out with Working Asset's November billing statement. On December 4, 1997, Todd Gutnick reported in the *Tribune-Review* that "in the last two weeks thousands of 'concerned citizens' have lodged complaints" with the FCC. Working Assets president Michael Kieschnick was quoted as saying, "We're a telephone company and our customers all over the country are politically active people. All of these customers are people who are making choices." According to Nudelman, the final tally was 33,537 letters and calls to Kennard, a good response for a Working Assets cause.

One FCC official said that almost none of the complaints had originated in Pittsburgh and that "people reading from a script" and sending "form letters" didn't have as much weight as individual calls and letters from Pittsburgh. It was the kind of statement expected from a bureaucrat trying to minimize public pressure. I wondered how many unique calls and letters from Pittsburgh would have added up to the 33,537 we laid on them through the Working Assets campaign. In the end, given the enormous influence the Christian right and others have achieved using this same technique, I found his disclaimer disingenuous. At least now the FCC definitely knew that people all over the country were watching this decision.

In the midst of all this, PBS's Ervin Duggan breezed into town to "celebrate" WQED's "turnaround." Duggan applauded the "hard decisions" Miles had made since taking over WQED, said that Pittsburghers had to look at the sale of WQEX in terms of the digital future of four channels on WQED, and stated that he was impressed that local programming had not been abandoned in the middle of all this. Duggan was particularly impressed with producer Rick Sebak's pop culture documentaries, noting that Sebak's ice cream special had been picked up by a PBS service that provides entertainment for airplane passengers. The following month, Duggan co-signed a letter with the CPB's Coonrod and APTS's Brugger urging the FCC to act on WQED's application "without delay."

Former PBS president Bruce Christensen wrote a contribution solicitation letter on behalf of WQED. He praised Miles effusively and warned of the consequences that would follow the "loss of WQED." By this time, WQED had admitted to the FCC that losing WQED-TV itself was not a possibility. Nevertheless, it was still trying to scare a naive public out of its money. Moreover, Miles was able to get PBS officials to front this claim. In another solicitation, Miles attacked his critics as "naysayers" who "appear to have brought everything but a financially sound solution to their prescription for WQED's fiscal ills."

The way the public broadcasting bigwigs circled their wagons on this one disturbed me. I understood that these people had been solicited by a colleague whom they perceived to be in trouble. However, WQED had rejected an offer that, at least according to hearsay, would have wiped out its claimed $14 million debt and delivered $38 million to the Corporation for Public Broadcasting. Imagine the programming such funds would have subsidized.

Instead, as one congressman put it to me, George Miles chose to gamble for the whole bundle for himself. In justifying this decision, Miles had denigrated the CPB as "Washington," disavowing any common interest in public broadcasting as a whole. He had then agreed in advance to hand over at least $7.5 million to a right-wing evangelical station that regularly fulminates against the arts, education, and public broadcasting. When that gamble failed, he had entered into an agreement to hand over slightly more than half of the $35 million WQEX sale price to the same station. The Corporation for Public Broadcasting would get nothing—and yet here were Coonrod and Duggan praising Miles and lobbying Washington to approve his deal.

The FCC Questions Cornerstone's Qualifications

On March 27, 1998, the FCC sent Cornerstone president Oleen Eagle an eight-page letter giving Cornerstone thirty days to "amend its application or provide supplementary information" to satisfy FCC concerns. The letter was signed by Barbara A. Kreisman, Chief, Video Services Division of the FCC's Mass Media Bureau. One problem, Kreisman advised, was that Cornerstone's board was "self-perpetuating" and did "not appear to be 'broadly representative' of the Pittsburgh community." Kreisman listed a great many institutions, professions, and constituencies not represented.

Another problem was programming. Kreisman acknowledged that "programs that involve the teaching of matters relating to religion" qualify as educational; however, FCC regulations require that the proposed station be "used *primarily* to serve the educational needs of the community" (italics in the original). Kreisman noted that Cornerstone's "goal still appears to be primarily religious" and "it is not clear to what extent" Cornerstone would pursue its claimed educational purposes. Kreisman cited a previously approved application in which less than a fourth of adult programming was religious and the program schedule was organized into "appropriate" categories, like general educational, public affairs, and cultural.

Still another problem was commercialism. Indicating that many programs currently aired on Cornerstone would not comply with restrictions on advertising or an educational channel, Kreisman requested information on what steps the station "will take to comply with the Commission's rules regarding advertising and fund-raising on noncommercial educational stations."

Angela Campbell and Randi Albert discussed the Cornerstone letter with public interest attorney Andy Schwartzman and John Podesta in Washington, D.C. Campbell reported to me that they considered it "highly unusual" and felt "the letter sends a strong signal to WQED, Cornerstone and Paxson that the FCC may not approve the transfer." Fred Polner, in contrast, thought that the letter just might be setting us up. If the FCC's concerns were that substantial, Polner reasoned, the application should now be designated for a public hearing. Also, the letter was addressed only to Cornerstone, so the commission had apparently passed on all of WQED's transgressions regarding openness and accountability. Still, if we could stop the deal, we had a chance of reclaiming WQEX.

Soon afterward, Barbara Vancheri quoted me in the *Post-Gazette* as arguing, "This confirms everything we have been saying. . . . We hope this energizes those who have given up to phone, fax, email or write to the FCC to tell it to stop the swap and give the people a chance to save public television in this community." WQED's B. J. Leber noted that the commission was moving ahead and that only one of the three applicants was being questioned. She added, "We're sure Cornerstone has good responses to the questions and will provide those responses so it can keep moving forward."

Cornerstone filed two pleadings in response to the FCC's letter. One provided additional information on its qualifications. Acknowledging that "programs involving religious teaching" were included, Cornerstone followed the FCC's guidance and listed all of its programs under the "appropriate" categories, including "instruction" from Oral Roberts's University of Life-Long Education. Cornerstone also appended a videocassette, approximately an hour and a half in length, "so that the Commission can appreciate the full flavor of Cornerstone's educational programming."

Cornerstone also provided various assurances that in the future it would comply with FCC regulations concerning noncommercial programming. Finally, it insisted that its current seven-member board and three-member management team meet the "representativeness" requirement. In support, Cornerstone listed all of directors' affiliations and accomplishments in bullets under various "appropriate" categories. This alone took up seven pages.

In its supplementary pleading, Cornerstone took the offensive, arguing that "FCC staff is imposing an inappropriately rigorous standard to the review of this application simply because of Cornerstone's religious orientation." They cited several cases of approved applications that they claimed were no better than theirs.

Seeking to exploit the erosion of standards, Cornerstone also challenged the FCC's definition of what is meant by "educational." It proposed that "if a program parsing the language and meaning of the literature of Shakespeare is 'educational,' then a program parsing the language and meaning of the Bible must be 'educational.'" Thus, in Cornerstone's view, deconstructing Shakespeare's text in order to particularize its meaning in relation to its context, and thus relativizing it, is the same thing as citing passages of the Bible as absolute and eternal truths to be applied directly to current affairs.

Here was another assault on conventional wisdom that was deliberately designed to obliterate meaningful standards in educational broadcasting. Our view, of course, is that the transmission of one-sided opinions and invalid information does not constitute education. If it did, indoctrination, propaganda, and proselytizing would be indistinguishable from the pursuit of truth—not a good prospect for the future of civilization.

Cornerstone's concluding statement charged the FCC with threatening to violate Cornerstone's First Amendment rights. It accused the commission of being "biased against Cornerstone because of its religious, Christian viewpoint" and warned that "the Commission needs to pull back from this abyss." We in turn indicated that we had no objection to "Cornerstone serving its sectarian audience on a commercial frequency" but we objected "vigorously to Cornerstone taking over one of Pittsburgh's only two reserved educational frequencies for this purpose."

To the *Post-Gazette*'s Vancheri, Oleen Eagle stated, "Quite frankly, this may not be politically correct to say, but I think it's turned into a political issue. . . . There are some congressmen who feel this is not what they want to happen. When it gets into that arena, it loses its reasoning power." To the *Tribune-Review*, WQED attorney Steve Lerman commented, "I thought [the pleading] was fully responsive to the commission's questions. It clearly establishes that the programming is educational . . . and that their board members have substantial ties to the community in multiple disciplines." WQED's B. J. Leber said, " "We're very glad it's moving forward." Our reform alliance was not called for comment.

Under the circumstances, we were delighted with Cornerstone's pleadings. They declined to present any supplementary information to satisfy FCC concerns about educational programming, commercialism, or the representativeness of its board, and some shows noted by the commission as being clearly "unsuitable" because commercials were integral to their content were still included on the list of programs Cornerstone proposed for broadcast. In fact, Cornerstone had submitted the exact same program list that it had provided in its original application, except that the programs were grouped in various categories. Some programs were listed in more than one category, giving the false impression of greater diversity. I reviewed their video and took notes on each segment. Despite the new labels, virtually every program communicated an evangelical religious message.

In describing its directors and officials, Cornerstone simply reformatted the same biographical information from the original application into several categories, again listing many items more than once. Moreover, some of the entries were very questionable. For example, one board member was cited for past involvement with local government because he had once received a citation from the Pennsylvania House of Representatives. Another claimed to represent the Pittsburgh business community because he had once owned a garage. In sum, we proposed, Cornerstone's self-perpetuating officers and directors still failed to represent broad segments of the Pittsburgh community, including those central to the mission of public broadcasting.

We also argued that Cornerstone's allegations of religious bias against it were not credible in view of the fact that about 20 noncommercial television stations and 400 noncommercial radio stations are affiliated with the National Religious Broadcasters. Most of the cases they cited as relevant precedent were concerned with FM radio rather than television licenses, where standards are necessarily higher because of the much greater spectrum use. Others were cases in which the license had not been contested, whereas this application was being opposed by a substantial "grassroots expression of concern." We also listed several cases similar to that of Cornerstone in which petitioners had indeed been questioned about the adequacy of their educational showing.

We emphasized to the commission that we were concerned about the wide diversity of viewpoints that Cornerstone was not proposing to air. We wanted programming that complied with the "fair break" doctrine and other rules. We wanted programming that served everyone in the community, including members of other faiths and those who hold no religious beliefs at all.

In sum, we felt that Cornerstone had refused the opportunity to "expand its Board and program offerings" to meet the FCC's standards. Instead it had "dug in its heels and refused to do so," indicating that "it does not intend to make any real changes in its application." This being the case, we concluded, the commission could not approve this application and should designate it for hearing.

In a statement to the *Post-Gazette* I said, "Cornerstone clearly is not qualified to operate one of Pittsburgh's only two noncommercial educational frequencies. It is controlled by a small circle of officers and directors committed only to communicating their sectarian, evangelical message. Rather than make the reforms necessary to serve the broader community, they have tried to intimidate the FCC with bogus charges of religious bias."

WQED attorney Steve Lerman saw the whole thing differently: "We're to the point where they are now asking what seems like some cleanup questions. I wouldn't expect it would take them too long to come out with an order." I hoped this wasn't one of those cases where it would turn out we were both correct. In my mind, granting Cornerstone the license would lower the bar even more for what is considered educational broadcasting.

At the June 1998 meeting of WQED's board of directors, George Miles said he was looking forward to FCC approval of the WQEX sale. On August 31, 1998, the new Pax television network debuted across the country but not in Pittsburgh. Vancheri had expressed confidence that Paxson's clout would have wrapped up the case by then. Indeed, to a colleague Paxson had boasted of having the commission "in [his] pocket." Apparently the FCC still felt free to not approve his application.

I called Randi Albert at Georgetown to commemorate the occasion. The *Post-Gazette* continued to run press releases from WQED, but both local papers had stopped calling us for comment. Sally Kalson told me they were all puzzled as to why the FCC was taking so long to decide the case—presumably in favor of the transaction. Apparently it never occurred to them that our broad-based opposition and Cornerstone's serious lack of qualifications might actually deter the FCC from approving the deal. We had made the story interesting for them, but we were not supposed to win and that's the journalistic bottom line.

Around this time, the *Post-Gazette* hired a new TV reporter, Rob Owen. His photo showed a young face with very close-cropped hair, also a dark suit and tie. I called him to introduce myself. With a naïveté to match his youthful photo and voice, he wanted to know why I was opposed to losing WQEX when I would be getting four channels from WQED in a couple of years. I asked him how long he had to hear an explanation. Owen grunted with a semblance of recognition when I argued that the digital promise was still chancy, but said he could not understand why the FCC had rejected the original application to sell WQEX. He seemed impatient with the public interest arguments. His job was to inform people about TV programs and personalities, most of which were commercial. He said that Barbara Vancheri would be covering the story, but not much later Vancheri became one of the paper's movie critics and Owen was the one we had to call.

As of the September 15 WQED board meeting, Miles was saying, "I expect something to break this fall, I just don't know when." Todd Gutnick from the *Tribune-Review* called the FCC and was told that a decision could be expected "before the end of the year." He indicated that if the FCC hadn't approved the sale by October 31, WQED would have to negotiate an extension on the station's debt with Mellon Bank. It did so shortly thereafter. At the meeting, Miles announced that Jim Roddey had received the Elaine Peterson Distinguished Service Award from the National Friends of Public Broadcasting for "volunteer work that significantly contributed to local public broadcasting." We took this as another sign of how far public broadcasting had retreated from its community mission.

Early in 1999, it looked like the case was going to take a dramatic turn. On Tuesday, January 19, Randi Albert called me. FCC mass media bureau attorney Joyce Bernstein had called her to ask whether we could attend a meeting with the other parties in Washington, D.C., on Friday. Albert had told Bernstein that she and Angela Campbell were willing, but she didn't know whether her clients could make it on such short notice. Bernstein had responded that if this meeting were not possible we would have to wait until mid-February, and if that were not possible we might not be able to meet. A few hours later Bernstein called Albert back to advise her that the meeting would include lawyers only, no clients, because (get this) they didn't want there to be any "lobbying" at the meeting.

According to Albert, Bernstein said that the FCC had something to present to take back to the clients. When Albert asked her if the point of the meeting was "negotiation," Bernstein replied, "No, there is a standard for reserved licenses." She went on to say that the meeting would be in bureau chief Roy Stewart's office and include Stewart, Barbara Kreisman, Clay Pendarvis, herself, and all the attorneys.

On the afternoon of Thursday, January 21, our attorneys got a call from Kreisman advising that the meeting had to be canceled because Cornerstone had refused to attend. According to the rules, all parties had to be present or there could be no meeting. I called the story in to Sally Kalson.

The next morning the *Post-Gazette's* front page blared, "FCC Scraps

Meeting It Called on WQEX Sale." Co-bylined by Sally Kalson and Barbara Vancheri, the article stated, "It was unclear yesterday who, if anyone, refused to attend and why." It also claimed that Cornerstone had amended its application "several times." In a lengthy and sympathetic discussion of WQED finances and Miles's reforms, the article characterized the station as "a reformed spendthrift."

I whipped out a two-page letter to editor John Allison at the *Post-Gazette*, stating the facts about the canceled meeting and providing another perspective on WQED's debt, Miles's reforms, and the options available. Kalson called me. Allison was out of town and the letter had been dropped off on "Weekender" editor Scott Mervis's desk. Somehow Vancheri had gotten it, read it, and slammed it down on Kalson's desk with the statement, "Now you know why I don't call Jerry Starr."

Kalson went on to explain that Cornerstone had denied refusing to attend. Rather than run my statement and their denial, she had chosen to characterize the situation as "unclear." She also attributed the claim about Cornerstone amendments to Pendarvis. I agreed to soften the letter, but I was concerned about its appearing on the back page of Friday's "Weekender" entertainment section, which is typically reserved for letters like "Your critics suck! Spice Girls rule!" Mervis also considered this placement inappropriate. He called John Allison, who gave him what he called a "weak answer." Allison later told me it was a "non-decision." Mervis was pleasant enough but gave me a hard time on the contents of the letter. Among other things, he objected to my claim that Cornerstone had refused to attend the meeting. He insisted on independent corroboration. I said this was a citizen letter and I was testifying to the truth of my own experience. He was unmoved. At my suggestion, he called Barbara Kreisman, but reported that she refused to comment. I was finally allowed to say, "our attorneys had agreed to come."

On February 2, 1999, Owen began his column with, "To the FCC: I want my Pax TV!" He went on to say that, being young and single, he was "unlikely to watch it much," he didn't think it would be "educational," and he had doubts about the "quality" of its two original programs. However, he wanted Pittsburgh viewers to "have Pax TV as an option. To me it is a matter of choice." There it was again—the claim that a seventh commercial network channel offered viewers more choice than a second public channel.

Owen neglected to mention that Paxson is available by cable in some markets. In Pittsburgh this would achieve 80 percent coverage. Owen's column revealed that the delay in the acquisition of WQEX had caused two

Pax employees to quit and two more to be laid off. The station had stopped renting the satellite dish and the general manager was on loan to other stations. Knowing that the original license transfer agreement had expired, we dared hope that Paxson would walk away.

Owen's column provoked a letter in support of our campaign, rejected by the *Post-Gazette* but printed in the Merton Center Newsletter. Days later, Duggan, Coonrod, and Brugger sent another letter to the FCC, citing WQED's "severe financial distress" and "strongly" urging the FCC to "act on this issue without further delay."

Paxson and Friends Renew the Offensive

On March 24, 1999, Paxson announced that it was selling three stations for $40 million to Acme TV and had renewed its contract to buy Channel 40 for $35 million. The new contract included $1 million up front to WQED, to be credited against its share after the deal was concluded. One clause called upon WQED or Cornerstone to use their "best efforts" to transfer Channel 16 to Paxson if Cornerstone could not assume that license.

In April, Cornerstone filed a supplemental showing with the FCC that claimed that "almost two-thirds of Cornerstone's planned programming for Channel 16 qualifies as 'general educational' or 'instructional.'" Cornerstone argued, "The concept of 'advancement of educational program' is itself amorphous; the Commission's evaluation of the requirement seems haphazard." They also provided another tape of selected excerpts from various programs.

Science writer Mike Schneider analyzed the tapes and reported to the FCC that again "virtually every program communicates an evangelical Protestant message" and that "Cornerstone serves only a small sectarian audience in a market that is religiously and culturally diverse." Also, professor and former Catholic priest Michael Drohan provided a lengthy evaluation of Cornerstone programming that concluded, "I could not say that Cornerstone helps anyone to develop their critical faculties, which is the essence of education" and "the conception of the world that [Cornerstone] conveys is harmful." All of these letters were submitted to the FCC.

Cornerstone countered that FCC case law holds that "religious educational programming can qualify as educational" and we were wrong to suggest that "noncommercial stations must somehow . . . meet all the educational needs of the entire service area (or, at least, the religious needs of the entire Catholic community)." Two months later, Cornerstone announced the addition of two new board members. One was the chairman of the board of National City Bank of Pennsylvania, the other owner of a McDonald's franchise in the area. Both had several church affiliations and both were active in Christian outreach activities. The bank official William Roemer previously had written in support of WQED's 1996 dereservation petition. We suspected that WQED was the matchmaker here.

Apparently no longer trusting Cornerstone to defend itself adequately, WQED filed its own reply to our letter of opposition. It contained letters from four of their board members involved in the education field. School superintendent Stanley Herman praised the "positive presentation of news events reflected on the 700 Club and Christian World News." In a gratuitous aside, Herman also questioned Monsignor Charles Owen Rice's qualifications to evaluate whether Cornerstone's allegedly Catholic programming actually served that community. The other three letters, including one from Duquesne University president John Murray, argued that Cornerstone programs were educational because they teach viewers how to use religion in coping with life's problems. Miles's control of his board could certainly not be questioned.

We Oppose WQED and WQEX License Renewals

In April 1999, WQED's five-year license renewal came due and it filed the required application. On June 1, we filed a petition to deny the license renewals for both WQED and WQEX, basing our complaint primarily on WQED's simulcasting identical programming on both frequencies for some twenty months, which we called "a significant waste of a valuable and limited public resource." We argued further that this lack of a distinct program service was equivalent to WQEX going dark, which normally causes a license to expire after twelve months. We also cited a pattern of abuse in petitions still pending before the FCC, including the violation of the Communications Act in airing paid political advertising as well as other rule violations and misrepresentations.

In its reply, WQED attorney Lerman accused us of a "frivolous, meritless effort" that amounted to "constant harassment" based on "patently fanciful" claims and "scurrilous" and "untrue allegations." He claimed that there was no rule against simulcasting and that, in fact, on occasion it had been permitted. In response, we pointed out that all such examples involved partial simulcasting, AM/FM radio, or commercial stations, none of which cases were applicable to this one. The absence of a specific rule, we argued, only indicated that the commission had never encountered such an abuse; however, correcting it was well within its discretion.

To support our interpretation, we cited the fact that three cable systems within the WQED viewing area had dropped or planned to drop WQEX because of the duplication. In one case the decision was provoked by viewer and City Council complaints. Moreover, the fact that WQED had justified the simulcasting as an effort to save money violated both their 1996 pledge to the FCC that WQEX would continue broadcasting programs and the FCC prohibition against going dark for financial reasons. We argued that WQED, by its own admission, was not qualified to keep either license.

WQED claimed that viewers' needs were taken into account because it had polled them for their preferences and "incorporated the best of both" stations into their new WQED schedule. We countered that only a thousand viewers had responded (a tiny fraction of all subscribers) and that the programming decisions made had not even implemented their choices. For example, 35 percent had indicated a preference for exercise shows and 12 percent for sewing and crafts, but WQED chose to include only one exercise show and broadcast five craft shows. The other shows moved over to WQED were five British and Canadian sitcoms, two British science fiction shows, four painting shows, three cooking shows, and the "gay-oriented 'In the Life.'"

This list of programs stood as ugly testimony to WQED's total abandonment of mission. The one concession to public interest programming was *In the Life,* aired occasionally very late at night. However, the station had refused to pick up the PBS prime-time feed of *After Stonewall,* a documentary on the history of the gay rights movement since the famous confrontation with New York City police in 1972. Billy Hileman, spokesperson for Pittsburgh's Cry Out! Act Up! cited this in his complaint to the FCC in support of our petition to deny.

WQED also produced a letter signed by three members of its board of directors or community advisory board who were affiliated with organized labor. They said they didn't think the station had an obligation "to broadcast the particular labor-oriented or other programs that a handful of individual viewers, such as those whose Declarations are attached to the Petition, may prefer."

The letter, obviously constructed by station officials, listed nine programs in the past three years that had addressed labor concerns, two of which were series. Almost half of the total hours for all such programs cited were broadcasts of the series *We Do the Work,* but I was sure that none of these signers knew anything about that struggle and its great disappointments. In a footnote to our reply we referred to the 4,000 petition signers, 29 declarations, and letters supporting us from the Allegheny County Labor Council (80,000 members), United Electrical Radio and Machine Workers of America (40,000 members) and several union locals with from 10,000 to 20,000 members each.

Enter the Lobbyists

WQED's lobbyists delivered three more separate letters signed by public broadcasting heads Duggan, Coonrod, and Brugger. Duggan urged FCC chair William Kennard to "approve without further delay [this] special urgent case."

On May 5, Congressman Bill Coyne wrote to "urge the FCC to make a decision on WQED's petition in the near future." While he did not call for approval, Coyne praised WQED's "high quality of service" and did not refer to the July 16, 1997, letter in which he had strongly opposed the Cornerstone transfer.

Deeply disappointed, I later called Coyne aide Matt Dinkle. He admitted writing both letters at the congressman's instructions, insisted that Coyne still was opposed to the deal, and explained the May letter as having been written because Coyne "values WQED." I told him that a call for an FCC public hearing to finally resolve the matter would be fairest to all sides.

I also took my concerns to Coyne's most activist constituency, the Fourteenth Ward Democratic Party. The leader, Eric Marchbein, and several members also were supporters of the QED Accountability Project. Apparently, the pursuant appeals somehow turned Coyne around again. On October 15, he wrote to the commissioners to remind them of his earlier opposition and request that they refer the case for public hearing.

For later reference, please note that six weeks later—December 1, 1999 —FCC assistant general counsel John I. Riffer returned Coyne's letter to him with the instruction that, in order "to be considered by Commission decision-making personnel," he had to resubmit it "in accordance with the ex parte rules by serving copies" on all parties to the proceeding. Our attorneys, now alerted, did so on Coyne's behalf.

The Dealmakers Escalate Their Lobbying

On July 8, Lanny J. Davis of the firm of Patton Boggs sent FCC commissioner Susan Ness a lengthy letter in which he argued there could be no doubt that Cornerstone programming is " 'primarily' educational or instructional" and that objections like ours would someday lead to "government rejection" of "Jewish or Muslim or even PBS 'primarily' educational programming." In light of Cornerstone programs attacking other religions, this seemed ironic at best, hypocritical at worst. Davis, a frequent cable pundit, has been described by *Brill's Content*, a media watch magazine, as "President Clinton's point man on pre-Lewinsky damage control" and by *New York Times* reporter Christopher Drew as a "master manipulator." The firm Patton Boggs is a leading lobbyist for corporate interests from oil and telecommunications to tobacco and insurance. The firm's dominant figure is Thomas Hale ("Tommie") Boggs Jr., son of former members of Congress Hale and Lindy, brother of media pundit Cokie Roberts, and former head of the Democratic National Committee. In 1998, *George* magazine rated Boggs one of the twenty-four "most powerful" "private" persons in the nation's capital. An admiring rival noted in *George*, "He is famous for doing favors back and forth for public officials. It's a big chit."

Our attorneys were concerned that this was an effort to intimidate Commissioner Susan Ness, who expected to be renominated by President Clinton for another five-year term. Sure enough, less than two weeks later, Patton Boggs attorney Thomas Siebert sent a "Dear Susan" letter to Ness announcing that his firm had "recently been engaged by WQED" and urging her to approve the license transfer agreement. The letter cites WQED's financial problems and touts Paxson's "highly appealing family programming" but does not mention Cornerstone.

A lobbyist friend of mine estimated the cost of retaining a major firm like Patton Boggs to be at least $10,000 a month. When questioned by the *Post-Gazette*'s Sally Kalson, Miles said that the station was splitting the cost with Paxson and that "whatever it costs, it'll be less than $17.5 million."

In July, the investment started to pay off. Pennsylvania congressman Frank Mascara wrote to Chairman Kennard to "request Commission's immediate grant" of the applications in question. Citing the delay, Mascara charged "the appearance of abuse of agency discretion" that has caused "palpable harm to [his] constituents." He argued further that the U.S. Constitution, the Supreme Court, and FCC precedent support the concept of a religious broadcaster operating a channel reserved for educational use.

On August 6, Congressman Steny H. Hoyer of Maryland wrote another "Dear Susan" letter, urging approval of the applications. His letter read like a favor done by an outsider. Sentences would begin "I am told," "I understand," "I also understand," etc. In the middle of the letter, Hoyer lamented that Paxson's "popular family-oriented programming" was being shut out of the Pittsburgh market. There was no doubt now who was running the influence campaign.

On August 25 Kennard wrote back to Mascara to explain that the application was opposed by thousands and required time for all parties "to participate fully in the record of this proceeding." Kennard closed, "The item is before my fellow commissioners for a vote, and I have urged their prompt consideration of the matter."

On September 22, Mascara shot back, "Unfortunately, your letter does not ameliorate my concerns; to the contrary, it has heightened them." He accused the FCC of "threatening to apply an unprecedented standard to evaluate Cornerstone." He dismissed the opposition as "less than two hundred individual viewers" and he asserted that the Alliance for Progressive Action was the only "formal opponent to WQED's application" and, citing the NAACP, was "known to overstate its constituency."

On September 3, Representative Tom Udall (D-N.Mex.) wrote to Commissioner Tristani (who comes from his state), to argue that WQED "needs a speedy decision" because it is in "financial limbo" and unable to "attract local or government funding, or expand programming and services to the community."

Later in September, NBC completed its acquisition of a 32 percent stake in Paxson Communications for $415 million in new Paxson convertible stock, with an option to acquire 49 percent in 2002 for another $800 million. An FCC decision permitting networks to own two TV stations in cities with seven other separately owned stations had opened the door to this deal. By rights, Pittsburgh should not have been vulnerable, but somehow the FCC counted a West Virginia public station and a Maryland public station, neither of which can be seen locally, as serving our market.

Since Paxson's "rerun-heavy" programming often drew a rating of less than one, there was speculation that NBC might use Paxson's outlets to pressure affiliates into better terms, as "secondary NBC stations" to do local sports programming and/or to create a new network pitched to the teenage audience.

On September 20, Congressman Ron Klink wrote to FCC chair William

Kennard stating that approval of the applications was needed because he had "now come to believe that unless action is taken WQED will cease to exist." Although Klink had criticized WQED for its mismanagement and Cornerstone for its bigotry, privately he had complained to me about "enormous pressure" to back WQED from former KDKA and other television colleagues, some of whom now were employed by the station. The only new development was that Klink was preparing to resign his House seat to run for the U.S. Senate against Republican incumbent Rick Santorum. Given the crowded field for the Democratic nomination, Klink's Senate bid looked like an expensive quest.

Finally, on December 2, 1999, House Telecommunications Subcommittee chair Billy Tauzin himself weighed in. He referred to earlier letters from Klink, Mascara, and Santorum, added "[his] voice to the congressional chorus," and requested immediate approval of the applications.

We sought to respond with a letter from White House Chief of Staff John Podesta, who had worked on the case while a Fellow at Georgetown and was very familiar with Cornerstone's serious shortcomings as an educational broadcaster. Unfortunately, several calls and a fax to him were not answered.

The good congressmen's alarm over WQED's financial crisis seemed especially misinformed in light of public revelations over the past several months. In August 1999, the trade paper *Current* reported, WQED's debt had been cut in half and was down to "between $6.5 million and $7 million," a large chunk of which was owed to WQED's own restricted capital fund.

At the same time, we learned firsthand that WQED had turned down a substantial offer for *Pittsburgh Magazine,* valued by the Mellon Bank at $3 million or more and by Jim Roddey at up to $5 million. A September article in the *Post-Gazette* quoted WQED to the effect that it had ended the year "with a positive gain of $155,843 in excess operating revenues over operating expenses." The article also noted that the station had recently hired a new director, filled an old position, and was developing several new programs.

In an August interview, Miles stated that the station now had commitments for most of the $4.5 million needed to produce a nightly news magazine show for the next three years. On November 19, WQED announced that the show would debut on January 17, 2000. While the actual evidence of WQED's imminent collapse seemed to be immaterial to their supporters in Congress, we wrote to the FCC in hopes that the commissioners at least would attend to the contradictions.

Our Own Monkey Trial

The month of September was remarkable for a heated public debate in the local media over the scientific claims of evolution versus creationism. Taking off from the Kansas Board of Education ban on the teaching of evolution, science writer Michael Schneider and Carnegie Mellon University physicist Lincoln Wolfenstein wrote an editorial for the *Post-Gazette* criticizing Russ Bixler's *Origins* program on Cornerstone for presenting "misinformation" about geology, astronomy, radioactive nuclear decay, and Einstein's theory of relativity while dismissing the teaching of evolution as "detrimental to the development of scientific reasoning." They also expressed concern that the FCC might put its "governmental stamp of authority" on programs like *Origins* by granting an educational license to Cornerstone.

This statement led to a talk radio and cable TV appearance by Schneider and provoked a flood of letters and editorials, about a dozen of which were printed in the *Post-Gazette*. Cornerstone's Bixler, the president of a local sectarian college, a *Post-Gazette* national affairs writer, and a private citizen all argued the religious view. Officials from the Carnegie Museum of Natural History and half a dozen private citizens argued the scientific view. Many linked it to the pending license transfer.

At my request, our attorneys sent all of this material along to the FCC with special attention to Cornerstone president Bixler's published letter stating "evolution is not a science, but rather is ancient pagan religion dressed up in modern scientific language." He claimed the "theory of evolution violates at least four natural laws," and that the Kansas Board of Education's decision was based on scientific, not religious, grounds. Bixler went on to attribute the shootings at Columbine High School, along with atrocities committed by Hitler and Stalin, to "following the theory of evolution to its logical conclusion."

Schneider and Wolfenstein commented, "WQED has argued that this deal has nothing to do with politics. To say this is to be somewhere in the land of Oz. From where we sit, it looks a lot like [the WQED board is] in Kansas."

Media Buries More WQED Scandal

After more than three years of frustration, Frank Cappelli had finally been able to strike a deal with WQED. In exchange for waiving his claim to the unspent $16,000 in production money, WQED would return the rights to his children's program *Frank's Garage* and the master and submaster tapes needed to re-edit it for interested investors.

When the time came to deliver, however, WQED claimed that it could not locate the tapes. (Cappelli later called for a meeting with the WQED board of directors at which he accused WQED of looking like "the most ungrateful, arrogant group of people in the business," and asked for $150,000 in damages.)

The Cappelli story should have been newsworthy because, at the time, Jim Roddey was running for county executive and Cappelli was willing to stand behind his charges regarding the (earlier discussed) $300,000 reimbursement from WQED CEO George Miles to Roddey's Hawthorne Group for its investment in the now defunct *Frank's Garage*. Since Roddey was seeking a powerful public office, I also included documentation of Roddey's misrepresentations to city council concerning the disposition of WQEX.

Months earlier, I had gotten an anonymous complaint from someone at the station that WQED was throwing away archival materials to make room for Paxson and others. After his piece in the *Post-Gazette*, Michael Schneider got an anonymous call that specifically charged WQED with destroying their inventory of past productions and other records.

According to the second caller, WQED tried to put together a special highlight tape to celebrate *Black Horizons* as the longest-running local African-American public affairs program on public television. Unfortunately, he alleged, the production staff discovered that most, if not all the two-inch broadcast-quality masters had been thrown out. It occurred to me that this, most likely, was what had happened to Cappelli's tapes. The caller provided names of several employees and former employees alleged to be knowledgeable about this.

I also discovered that a grievance had been filed against WQED by its technicians over unpaid retirement benefits pending for more than ten years. I spoke with Bill Moore, the head of the International Association of Theatrical and Stage Employees Local 820, who confirmed that the underpayments were discovered in 1987 and the grievance filed over 1991–1992. An audit revealed underpayments or missed payments going back to 1976.

It seems that WQED's system of separate accounting by payroll and human resources was the culprit. Moreover, WQED had not changed the system in the wake of the discoveries. Over the years, according to Moore, WQED had presented several calculations. After being far apart, the station and union had recently reached tentative agreement on a $500,000 reimbursement. Moore allowed, however, that WQED had moved so slowly in rectifying this wrong that some members of the union were talking about a lawsuit to resolve the matter.

Obviously, we cared because this continuing evidence of incompetence and impropriety made it not only difficult to justify selling Channel 16, but also to be confident that such sale would end WQED's fiscal problems. Was all this newsworthy? Every editor and writer I talked with at both dailies and the *City Paper* agreed that it was, and they all claimed to have assigned these stories for investigation. After weeks of my calling back and being given the runaround, however, I realized that none of it would ever see print.

FCC Decides

On December 15, 1999, the FCC issued a press release announcing that it had approved the license transfers and resolved all other filings. We were stunned. The release added that "the order also provides additional guidance regarding the programming requirements applicable to all entities, including Cornerstone TeleVision, Inc., that hold or seek to obtain a non-commercial educational television license." Apparently the decision was controversial; four of the five commissioners had approved in part and dissented in part.

"We're thrilled and delighted with the decision but since we haven't seen the actual order yet we have no comment," said Paxson spokeswoman Nancy Udell to the *Tribune-Review*. Cornerstone president Oleen Eagle advised the *Post-Gazette*, "We're pleased that the FCC has granted the assignment . . . and we look forward to working out our future plans." In a less gracious comment to the *Tribune-Review*, Eagle said, "It's the mystery of the age why it took 2.5 years for them to come to this decision."

WQED's B. J. Leber told the *Post-Gazette*, "It's been a long wait for the right result." "We're excited," said George Miles to *Public Broadcasting Report*. The *Post-Gazette* business page rated the decision "thumbs up" and the society page reported Champaign toasts at WQED's Christmas party. I called it "a sad chapter in the decline of public broadcasting in America," adding, "Cornerstone absolutely is not qualified to be an educational broadcaster." Wambaugh said, "If this decision prevails in the long run, the real losers will be the viewing public."

None of us realized that the story was only beginning. On December 15, the day of the decision, Steve Klitzman of the FCC faxed to our attorney Angela Campbell letters from all five commissioners responding to letters from John McCain, the Arizona Senator and U.S. presidential candidate.

McCain also is chair of the U.S. Senate Committee on Commerce, Science and Transportation, which controls the FCC budget and its appointments.

Campbell subsequently got copies of McCain's letters. On November 17, McCain requested "that the Commission act on these applications at its regularly scheduled monthly meeting in December if it has not acted on them in the interim. If in your judgement the Commission cannot meet this request, please advise me of this fact in writing with a specific and complete explanation, no later than November 18."

A second letter from McCain on December 10 notes that he had previously called for "final action," but the agenda for the commission meeting of December 15 did not list the applications for consideration. He then requested that "each member of the commission advise me in writing no later than close of business on Tuesday, December 14, 1999, whether you have already acted on these applications" and, if not, to do so at the general meeting or explain why.

Both of McCain's letters concluded with what *New York Times* reporter Stephen Labaton later described as a typical "boilerplate" disclaimer that McCain is not speaking on behalf of any particular party and that the letter should be treated in conformity with the rules.

Clearly, however, McCain was calling for approval of the applications. First, the contract binding all parties to the deal was scheduled to expire on December 31. We later learned that Cornerstone and, perhaps, WQED had indicated reluctance to sign an extension if the situation was not resolved before year's end. Second, the only choice available to the commissioners was to approve the applications or refer them for public hearing, further delaying the final determination. In fact, WQED CEO George Miles later acknowledged to the press that, had the applications been referred for hearing, the deal would have been "dead in the water." Steve Labaton advised us that this was "the most aggressive intervention" he had yet witnessed on the Arizona senator's part.

Commissioners Susan Ness and Harold W. Furchtgott-Roth wrote to McCain on December 14 informing him simply that they had voted. Commissioner Michael (son of Colin) Powell, who had been nominated to the commission by McCain, wrote that he had voted to approve the transfer of the licenses.

On the other hand, Commissioner Gloria Tristani stated, "In order to preserve the integrity of our processes, it is my practice not to publicly disclose whether I have voted." Commission chair William Kennard retorted, "It is highly unusual for commissioners to be asked to publicly announce their voting status on a matter that is still pending." He said such inquiries "could have procedural and substantive impacts on the Commission's deliberations and, thus, on the due process rights of the parties."

In contradistinction to the ex parte rules that had been observed throughout, neither of these letters had been served on us until after the FCC's final decision. Consequently, we had no opportunity to reply. On December 20, Angela Campbell asked FCC general counsel Christopher Wright "to impose sanctions . . . including an order to show cause why the applications should not be dismissed or denied."

Campbell was disturbed by the decision. In our view, Cornerstone had done nothing to meet the expectations laid out by the Mass Media Bureau in March 1998. I counseled her not to give up. The next day, she informed me that her husband had done some research and uncovered at least $15,000 in contributions to McCain's campaign from Paxson, his people, and his attorneys in the past few months. Realizing that our only chance was to make McCain's heavy-handed interference a public issue, my office issued a press release to scores of papers, headlined "Sen. McCain Muscles FCC to Approve Deal." We followed up with phone calls to reporters we thought might be interested.

The decision itself still had not been released, but the *Post-Gazette* already was applauding the outcome. In an unsigned editorial it excused McCain for just "telling a federal agency to get a move on," and personally attacked me for being a "troublemaker" with a "quaint, 1960s view of public television" who was never able to demonstrate " 'community outrage' over the demise of WQEX." The editors did print my reply promptly and in full, including my quip that "the editorial is so passionate about some of [its] assertions, it is hard to tell whether the writer is ignorant or just pretending to be ignorant."

Reporters from Pittsburgh and the trade papers began calling for comment. Probably caught off guard, an aide for McCain told *Communications Daily,* the letter wasn't ex parte because "there was no formal opposition." I wondered whether McCain actually had been told that or whether she was improvising her damage control rather badly. Another staffer told *Broadcasting & Cable* that McCain didn't care about the outcome, he just wanted it to be "timely."

Mark Buse, staff director for the Senate Commerce Committee, insisted to the *Post-Gazette:* "McCain's actions were fully appropriate." Asked how McCain became aware of the pending deal, Buse admitted, "He's been made aware of this by the companies involved and by individuals in Pittsburgh."

Buse promoted McCain's position that a slow-moving federal bureaucracy was obstructing honest commerce, adding that the senator had been concerned for some time about the backlogs at the FCC. Implicitly supporting this line, the *Post-Gazette* noted that "a letter to the FCC's Wireless Bureau about pending matters produced a list of 63,000 items an inch and a half thick."

The *Post-Gazette* reporters failed to note how such "pending matters" were the obvious consequence of a Congress that had destroyed public interest protections to open the floodgates to mergers and acquisitions in every field of telecommunications. Many of the items were from giant corporations battling each other over access to the nation's consumers.

It would be up to the national press to address the question of why McCain chose to intervene in this case now. On January 5, 2000, Walter Robinson's exposé grabbed the front page of the *Boston Globe*. The next day, the story of McCain's intervention on behalf of major contributor Paxson Communications was on the front page of the *New York Times, Washington Post,* and through the Associated Press, in every major paper in the country. Angela Campbell and Andy Schwartzman were called to appear with McCain on Ted Koppel's *Nightline* and I was interviewed by CBS Radio News.

Robinson's *Globe* article revealed that the day before McCain sent the December 10 letter, he used Paxson's private jet for a trip from New York to Florida for a fund-raiser that was held aboard a yacht in Paxson's hometown of West Palm Beach. The day after the letter, McCain took the company jet from Florida to Washington. The campaign reimbursed the company at first-class airfare rates, well below the $10,000 it would normally cost to charter a jet of that size. McCain used the Paxson company jet at least two other times. Paxson's top officers and their family members gave $12,000 to McCain, and his law firm, Dow, Lohnes & Albertson, contributed $8,000 recently on a single day.

The *Washington Post*'s Susan Glaser and Dan Balz discovered that McCain's letter was written at the request of Alcade & Fay, the Washington lobbying firm retained by Paxson. They went on to report that other lobbyists believed that McCain "crossed a line." One characterized telling the commissioners "when to vote on something" as "very unusual." Glaser and Balz observed: "In many ways, the episode offers a classic example of how Washington works, intertwining campaign contributions, corporate lobbyists and a powerful committee chairman." Despite his insistence that he did nothing wrong, McCain announced that he had canceled a Florida fundraiser Paxson planned for him that very weekend.

The replies from the politicians and media moguls were revealing. Paxson complained that McCain did not take a clear position on the merits (as if he did not get his money's worth.) He pointed out that he lends his corporate jet and raises money for candidates of both parties, explaining, "I'm a political person. Why? Because I happen to be in a business that politics is very heavily involved in."

Democrat Lanny Davis defended McCain, pointing out that McCain had refused "to take a position on the merits." However, the *Boston Globe*'s Robinson reported that within the FCC, McCain's "letters were widely interpreted to favor the complicated transfer." And on January 7, the *Washington Post* editorialized that McCain "badly overstepped the rules" and his disclaimers "make it worse; the pretense of neutrality compounds the breach it seeks to mask."

To Steve Labaton, McCain said, "All citizens deserve their government to work." However Labaton's review of two thousand pages of correspondences from McCain and his staff told a different story. While he and his staff often forwarded complaints without taking a position, "in the vast majority of those particular regulatory matters where Mr. McCain himself sent a letter, the interested parties had contributed to his presidential campaigns."

The other side launched a counteroffensive. A long editorial in the *Wall Street Journal* alleged that all community opposition was a front to mask an effort to grab the "potentially lucrative" station license for nothing by political "shakedown" artists Jim Ferlo, Rosemary Trump, Allen Kukovich and me. As the reader may recall, these colleagues participated in one meeting (actually Ferlo couldn't make it and Kukovich was on speakerphone) in Fred Polner's "viable alternative" legal strategy that was over a full year before Paxson even came on the scene. Danny Schechter of the Media Channel spotted the editorial, faxed it to me, and wrote up my side for his online media news magazine.

The Decision

The decision itself was forty-five pages long and included four separate dissenting opinions. The case will be contested in the FCC, Congress, and the courts for years. First, our license renewal challenge to WQED was denied. According to the FCC, "commonly owned noncommercial educational television stations" are not required "to be separately programmed" nor "to operate on a regular schedule with a specified minimum number of hours." As for public funding, the CPB had granted "a temporary waiver." File this one under "there oughta be a law."

The commission merely "admonished" WQED for running the paid political ads and reminded it of FCC "underwriting requirements." All other documented shortcomings were dismissed. For example, the failure to make their public inspection file available on demand was termed an "isolated instance" contrary to written station policy. Likewise, WQED attorney Steve Lerman's accusation that we had made frivolous claims to delay proceedings was dismissed.

Commissioners Kennard and Tristani voted to refer the applications for public hearing. They wrote: "there are simply too many unresolved questions of fact regarding whether the proposed programming is primarily educational or primarily something else." In their view, "the right solution" would have been "not to give this applicant a free pass. The people of Pittsburgh—who are counting on the commission to preserve the integrity of channels reserved for educational use—deserve no less."

Commissioner Susan Ness, who typically votes with fellow Democrats Kennard and Tristani, voted with the two Republicans in approving the applications. The majority decision noted that Cornerstone originally identified "over 70 percent of its programming as having a religious component." It noted that Cornerstone is not a formal educational institution and affirmed that applicants for noncommercial educational television (NCETV) licenses must be used "primarily to serve the educational needs of the community."

The commission rejected Cornerstone's constitutional argument, stating: "the First Amendment does not prevent the Commission from establishing incidental restrictions on speech that are required for a broadcaster to maintain eligibility for a reserved allocation." Moreover, the commissioners acknowledged that, although Cornerstone's proposals over time had become more detailed, it is clear that it "primarily will continue to broadcast religiously oriented programs that have aired on Channel 40, albeit with some additions and modifications."

While the commission noted that NCETV licenses are expected to serve the overall public and not just "a particular political, economic, social or religious interest," it nonetheless held that the "disparaging comments" we noted, while "clearly offensive to some viewers," did not rise to a level that would warrant inquiry into whether Cornerstone "can be relied upon to administer fairly its responsibilities as a licensee." Unfortunately, the commissioners did not indicate what that "level" might be and how we could document such.

In several pages that wavered back and forth between arguments and principles, the commissioners finally decided that First Amendment concerns had moved them "to defer to the broadcaster's judgment unless that judgment is arbitrary or unreasonable." In short, despite its past intransigence, the commissioners decided to accept Cornerstone's promises regarding future programming and board membership. Regarding the latter, they state: "we fully expect that [Cornerstone] will continue to broaden the representative nature of its Board of Directors and management over the course of its operation on Channel 16." As for programming, Commissioner Ness stated: "My conclusion is based in significant part on the absence of clarity in our definition of 'general educational programming' and our guidelines for determining what is 'religious' but not 'educational.'"

Commissioner Ness then joined with Kennard and Tristani in providing additional "clarification" for the eligibility standards for NCETV licenses; specifically "more than half" of all programming hours on a reserved channel "must primarily serve an educational, cultural or instructional purpose." Moreover, in order to be "counted in determining compliance," a program must have as its "primary purpose service to the educational, instructional or cultural needs of the community."

A key statement spells out that, among other things, this provides that "programming primarily devoted to religious exhortation (e.g. preaching), proselytizing, or statements of personally-held religious views and beliefs generally will not qualify as educational programming." In a footnote, the decision states that church services normally would not qualify as "general educational" programming." Again, however, the commissioners indicated they will defer to the judgment of the broadcaster unless it appear to be "arbitrary or unreasonable." Worse, they state that the FCC's "function is not to judge the merit, wisdom or accuracy of any broadcast discussion or commentary."

Despite the continuing vagueness of the "clarified standards," the commissioners state that they will "continue, as we have in the past, to closely scrutinize all applications for assignment of noncommercial educational licenses" and "to take appropriate actions" when notified that a noncommercial educational station is "operating contrary to our rules and policies."

To us it looked like the commissioners simply had spelled out standing policy and then failed to apply it to a clearly problematic case. Worse, they failed to give us or other community groups any concrete guidelines or standards with respect to documenting noncompliance. Nevertheless, the two Republicans dissented, claiming the clarified guidelines could "open a Pandora's box of problems." Among other things, they alleged that the decision "singles out religious programming," constitutes "federal intrusion into programming," and is "unwarranted and may well be unconstitutional."

Questioned by *Post-Gazette* reporter Sally Kalson, Cornerstone president Oleen Eagle said, "Until we figure out what the FCC is saying, there's no way we can make a judgment on [transferring the license]." Revealingly, Eagle concluded, "We have a mission and we can't jeopardize it. Our mission statement says Cornerstone is called by God to serve and excel as a media ministry to bring glory to his name. Our objective now is to preserve our purpose and be able to meet the qualifications. That is what we're working on." With Cornerstone wavering, I announced that we will continue to monitor them to ensure that they "refrain from commercialism and hatemongering."

On January 4, 2000, a spokesman for the National Religious Broadcasters announced that his group was looking into the decision because "it appears to set a dangerous precedent for religious broadcasters." Conservative religious groups, like the American Family Association, spread the word through the Internet about the FCC's "dangerous decision." The Conservative News Service announced, "More than 125 noncommercial television broadcasters may be forced to drop religious programming" because broadcasts "'primarily devoted to religious exhortations, proselytizing or statements of personally held religious views or beliefs'" are "prohibited under the agency's educational programming licensees." Of course, this was not true. Such programs still were allowed. However, they could not be counted as educational in meeting the standard of an NCETV license.

It soon became clear, however, that the religious right wanted an official rollback of all educational standards. Karl Stoll, spokesperson for the National Association of Religious Broadcasters, stated, "I would think that religious services and exhortation would certainly serve the needs of the community." He later opined that, unless overturned, the "net effect" of the ruling would be "less preaching of the gospel, less programming of church services." The organization sent a letter to their twelve hundred members decrying the ruling. We realized that, given religious broadcasters' heavy reliance on such syndicated programs, this could be a problem for them.

Apparently fearing that Cornerstone might back out of the deal, Paxson himself announced on January 11 that the FCC clarified guidelines "were adopted without any notice to, or comment, from the public," that they "thrust the FCC into program content review," and that they would "immediately affect" all broadcasters, both commercial and noncommercial, and "raise serious constitutional issues." Paxson called on the broadcast industry, the religious community, elected officials, and the public to file petitions with the FCC by January 28. He also indicated that certain publicly funded legal institutions were expected to file court challenges.

At Paxson's urging, a letter was sent to FCC Chairman Kennard and Vice President Al Gore by Congressmen Michael Oxley, Steve Largeant, Charles "Chip" Pickering Jr., and Cliff Stearns demanding a reversal of the ruling. They stated, "We advise you to reverse this ruling, or stand by and see it overturned legislatively or in court." Kennard responded that the FCC granted Cornerstone's application, the NCE standards apply only when NCE certification is requested and do not apply to most religious broadcasters, and that NCE standards never prohibit particular programming from being aired based on its religious nature.

At the same time, the battle in Pittsburgh continued to heat up. Michael Schneider organized scores of clergy and educators from every major college and university in the area to denounce the deal. Supporters included Nobel Prize winner Herbert Simon and South African poet Dennis Brutus. There were TV and radio debates and many letters to the editor. Schneider e-mailed me, "I thought we were in the bottom of the ninth, but it might be only the top of the first." In terms of the larger controversies that had been unleashed, one could make such a case.

Cornerstone Quits: WQEX Is Saved

Through the week of January 17, I began to get indications that Cornerstone was wavering. I heard that Paxson was asking the parties for a ninety-day extension while he pursued a political solution to the educational guidelines obstacle. I made it known that we had recruited twenty Cornerstone monitors and were on our way to fifty. I also talked up our coalition building.

On Wednesday, January 19, Angela Campbell, Jeneba Jalloh, and the Georgetown team called to inform me that Cornerstone had notified the FCC that it was withdrawing all applications. The deal was off! On its web page, Cornerstone explained, "Our decision to terminate the transaction was forced upon us by the unprecedented December 29, 1999, Order of the FCC which would have seriously jeopardized our ability to carry out our mission." The statement went on to denounce the decision and pledge to reverse it. Eagle lamented that "a simple license exchange transaction has become so politicized in Washington that it now has nationwide ramifications."

In our scheduled conference call, Wambaugh, the attorneys, and I agreed to challenge WQED's simulcasting and any initiative to have the FCC reconsider educational license requirements. We reflected on educational options for Channel 16—say, a consortium of colleges and universities with broadcast training programs taking it over. We also did a lot of whooping and hollering. After almost four years of struggle, it appeared that Channel 16 was saved.

The next day, WQED CEO George Miles got a vote of confidence from his board and boasted (in the wake of the collapse of his one option) that he now had "eight options," none of which he was prepared to discuss publicly. Doubtless, they involve whatever private leases and paid telecommunication services WQED can get away with. Separate programming in the public interest is not currently on the table.

On January 24, Rep. Mike Oxley (R-OH) and forty-two cosponsors introduced the "Religious Broadcasters Freedom Act," seeking to overturn the additional guidelines. It immediately was referred to the Commerce Committee, where it did not figure to surface again for many weeks at best. To add to the pressure, House Telecommunications Subcommittee chair Billy Tauzin sent a letter to all the commissioners demanding that each provide a written response to thirty-two questions concerning the decision by February 4.

Seeking to give the commissioners cover for standing up for the public interest, my office in Washington began organizing the "Coalition to Defend Educational TV." In the first week we signed up seven major organizations, all of which placed action alerts on their web sites and linked them with ours so that members could be briefed on how to write to the FCC and Congress on this matter.

Diane Shust, manager of federal relations at the National Education Association, stated, "This is not discrimination against religion, but a defense of education. It is not unwarranted federal intrusion, but the FCC doing its duty to protect the public interest, convenience and necessity."

Ralph Ness, president of People for the American Way Foundation, observed, "It is clear that some religious broadcasters are not willing to be bound by standards that apply to all noncommercial educational licenses. They are asking for special privileges and claiming that the failure to grant them is discrimination. Congress and the FCC should resist right-wing pressure on this issue."

The Rev. Barry W. Lynn, executive director, Americans United for the Separation of Church and State, responded, "The FCC is attempting to apply fair and reasonable guidelines to ensure that educational TV licenses are truly educational and not extensions of somebody's religious ministry. We think the FCC is on the right track and should not cave in to pressure from powerful religious broadcasters and their political allies."

The week of January 24, a severe snowstorm shut down the federal government and most other offices for two days. Nevertheless, we continued to enlist supporters, including several major national religious groups. Unfortunately, the commissioners did not wait for this support. On January 28, the last day to file for reconsideration of the decision, commissioners Kennard and Ness "caved in." Only two weeks into the religious right reaction, they "reconsidered and vacated" the two paragraphs that spelled out what it meant for a license to be used for "primarily educational" purposes.

None of the reporters who called me for comment could ever recall the FCC revising its own decision before all interested parties had an opportunity to file their own petitions for reconsideration. Privately characterizing the action as "spineless," one reporter led his story with: "The FCC blinked."

In his original dissent to the applications, Kennard (joined with Tristani) had said that, "Standing alone, the majority's decision to grant this application would eliminate all eligibility standards for the reserved band." In her statement, Ness acknowledged that commissioners "have an obligation to provide additional guidance to FCC staff, as well as to applicants and existing licensees, if we are able to assess whether a broadcaster's judgment is reasonable."

In justifying this sudden about-face, Kennard and Ness expressed regret that their actions "have created less certainty rather than more, contrary to [their] intentions." In contradistinction, Commissioner Furchtgott-Roth commented, "It was not for lack of clarity that [critics] objected to the decision but for infringement of freedom of speech and freedom of religion— and rightly so."

Commissioner Gloria Tristani dissented, calling it "a sad and shameful day for the FCC. In vacating last month's 'additional guidance' on its own motion, without even waiting for reconsideration petitions to be filed, this supposedly independent agency has capitulated to an organized campaign of distortion and demagoguery." Among other things she stated succinctly, "In a religiously diverse society, sectarian religious programming, by its very nature, does not serve the 'entire community' and is not 'educational' to non-adherents.'" She got it.

In Tristani's words, "having stuck their head out of the foxhole and drawing fire, the majority is burrowing back in as quickly and deeply as they can." The ultimate offense is that Kennard and Ness agreed with their critics' demand for "broad comment," but then failed even to designate a rulemaking that would have permitted such.

On Sunday, January 29, the *Washington Post* revealed that Kennard and Ness had responded to pressure from Democratic presidential candidate Al Gore to vacate the guidelines. The Republican leadership had garnered seventy sponsors and lobbied Gore to muscle the commissioners into reversing themselves. Gore had positioned himself as a "born-again" Christian in his race against Bill Bradley, and Gore's advisers saw defense of the new guidelines as a liability.

Paxson Communications issued a statement proclaiming, "This is a great day in America for the First Amendment and Free Speech," but the most telling quote belonged to Rep. Oxley: "Al Gore's people saw this as a huge liability politically and they wanted to lance that boil."

After so many years of watching public interest protections eroded by big money and political intimidation, our movement finally welcomed the opportunity to represent ourselves. This betrayal by Democratic appointees deprived us of that chance. We were left with the intolerable situation described by Tristani: "The majority's mantra that we will defer to the licensee's judgment unless that judgment is 'arbitrary and unreasonable' simply begs the question—when does a licensee's judgment cross the line and become arbitrary or unreasonable?"

I decided to take the occasion of the FCC's Notice of Inquiry on the Social Responsibilities of Digital Broadcasters to propose a rulemaking on the eligibility requirements of noncommercial educational licenses. I am confident that a broad and open debate on this issue would clarify the distortions and generate public support for new and more meaningful guidelines. Since this also is known popularly as the "Gore Commission," however, I doubt that we will be given the chance. In the final analysis, a decision made under political pressure by a few powerful interests was partially unmade under political pressure by those same interests, this time with the private complicity of the apparent opposition.

Because the commissioners had possibly reopened the door for Cornerstone at the last possible moment, our attorneys were forced to work through the day to prepare filings for reconsideration that would not have been necessary. Attorney Angela Campbell delivered our papers to the FCC with one minute to spare. As she said to me the next morning, there were so many irregularities cited, at the least, it would "cloud any deal."

To the local press, WQED's B. J. Leber said it sounded like "great news" to her and WQED looked "forward to meeting with the other parties to see where it goes from here." I said, "It would be a serious mistake for Cornerstone to assume that this adjustment in language, out of concern for other stations, suddenly makes their [original] application acceptable. Their programming is still expected to be educational, and it's still expected to serve the broader community, and if necessary we're still prepared to monitor them and report."

The last word belonged to Cornerstone. Mark Dreistadt, Cornerstone's vice president of administration and finance, said the company had no plans to reenter the deal: "We feel at this point the risk is too significant. Unless and until we have strong assurance from the FCC that religious programmers would not be subject to scrutiny or our license would not be subject to any level of peril, we're not entertaining even conversations toward entering into the agreement."

Ironically, Cornerstone ultimately was willing to acknowledge what those appointed to guard the public interest were not—it is not an educational broadcaster and never had any intention to be. It is a conservative religious ministry claiming carte blanche to program whatever it wants on a reserved educational channel.

Certainly one message from this struggle is that, with enough passion and persistence, ordinary people can take on institutional power and prevail. At the same time, we must acknowledge that, in a very real sense, there is no ending to this story. The people in Pittsburgh still are confronted with an aloof management and board that continues to squander a scarce public resource by simulcasting its programs on two channels.

As for the national scene, when Cornerstone president Oleen Eagle announced her decision to withdraw from the contracts, she stated, "We went into the whole thing because fifteen or twenty full-power stations in the U.S. were already operating on reserved channels and they had the same type of programming we had." That means that there are that many communities around the country where people are being subjected to hateful harangues against those who are different on channels that are supposed to serve them. There is more work to be done.

It should be understood, moreover, that even legal or legislative victories are never the last word. New laws or regulations must be continuously defended against later noncompliance or challenges. The public interest requires constant vigilance. Fortunately, there always seem to be more passionate people willing to step up when others grow weary and drop out. The two hundred or so clergy and academic supporters that Mike Schneider rallied in the last couple months of the campaign are evidence of that.

A Moral and a New Beginning

While this may not be a Hollywood ending, I can sweeten the outcome with a moral and a new beginning. The moral of the story is that, whether NBC eats Paxson or Paxson eats Cornerstone or Cornerstone tries to eat WQEX, the media sharks will keep circling our precious few public broadcasting channels until the people put a stop to it.

And the new beginning? As I got deeper into my research I saw how many of WQED's problems, while aggravated by local arrogance and malfeasance, were endemic to the system as a whole. I recruited a working group of scholars and public broadcasting veterans to create a proposal for how to restructure the service, starting with a mechanism for permanent, independent funding.

I presented papers on this vision at several professional meetings. My colleagues and I circulated drafts of this proposal to about twenty distinguished academics and public broadcasters. In time, two leaders in public broadcasting took notice: Bill Moyers of Public Affairs Television, Inc., and Jack Willis, former CEO of Twin Cities Public Broadcasting.

Moyers is also president of the Florence and John Schumann Foundation and Willis now serves as senior fellow at the George Soros–funded Open Society Institute. After several months of discussion, these foundations agreed to subsidize the launch of Citizens for Independent Public Broadcasting, a national campaign to reform public broadcasting as an independent public trust and to empower community groups to democratize their local stations. I currently serve as the organization's executive director. Karen L. Conner is my associate director, and Alex Traugott is our office manager/outreach coordinator (see Appendix for boards and contact information).

On November 16, 1999, the Benton Foundation hosted the press conference to kick off our campaign. Speakers included former FCC commissioner Nicholas Johnson, Emmy Award–winning PBS producer Alvin Perlmutter, FAIR program director Janine Jackson, and esteemed media researcher George Gerbner. All speakers signed a Declaration of Public Broadcasting Independence calling for, among other things, a public broadcasting service "not to sell products" but "to enhance citizenship and public service." The declaration hangs proudly on a wall in our national office.

All the trade papers covered the event and C-SPAN televised it for a national audience. FAIR's *Counterspin* radio program also heralded the new organization. Whenever either of these shows played, our four telephone lines lit up with interested callers.

While the struggle in Pittsburgh goes on, it is important to note that it is not unique. It is part of a larger, longer history of citizen action to promote more community-responsive public broadcasting. My participation in this rich heritage has brought me in contact with many other activists. CIPB will be drawing on them to build a broader and more coordinated movement to put the public and the public interest back into public broadcasting.

Chapter 9

Other Fronts:
Putting the Public into Public TV

Community battles for accountable public broadcasting go back more than twenty years. The late 1970s saw movements in Boston, New York, St. Louis, and Washington, D.C. Issues included lack of diversity on boards of directors, neglect of local programming, censorship of controversial programs, underrepresentation of minorities in employment and programming, and insufficient citizen participation generally.

Out of this maelstrom there emerged the National Task Force for Public Broadcasting, organized by DeeDee Halleck and Larry Hall to serve as a resource center and clearing house for local initiatives challenging what Hall characterized as a system closed to creative staff, independent producers, and interested citizens. The task force assembled a powerful coalition of labor, consumer, and civil rights organizations.

Its campaign was a huge success. The Public Telecommunications Financing Act of 1978, also known as the (Lionell) Vandeerlin Bill, mandated the Corporation for Public Broadcasting to issue program grants directly to independent producers, local stations, and production centers. The act established public access to satellite technology, required enforcement of equal employment opportunity, and required stations to establish community advisory boards and open board meetings. In a larger sense, in Hall's words, it "recognized the rights of citizens to be involved in communications and communications policy."

Public Broadcasting Activism in the 1990s

Since 1993, I have interviewed activists in public broadcasting reform campaigns in San Francisco, Chicago, Phoenix, Jacksonville, and elsewhere. Many in these local movements learned of each other through national organizations promoting more democratic media.

A major force in this arena is Fairness and Accuracy In Reporting (FAIR), which refers to itself as a "national media watch group." FAIR focuses on how corporate ownership of the media influences media organizations to serve the establishment and marginalize women, labor, minorities, and other public interest constituencies. FAIR advocates for "greater media pluralism and the inclusion of public interest voices in national debates."

Toward these ends, FAIR conducts studies, publishes a bimonthly magazine, *Extra!*, and a newsletter, *Extra Update*, and produces a weekly half-hour media analysis program, *Counterspin*. FAIR also promotes media activism. In fact, every issue of *Extra!* lists FAIR local contacts in various U.S. cities. I am the FAIR contact for Pittsburgh and I get occasional calls from that city and other parts of the country. The introduction to FAIR's media activism kit reads, "FAIR believes that long-term citizen pressure and grass-roots action are key to media reform," whether it be "challenging mainstream media" or "promoting independent media."

In September/October 1993, FAIR published an entire special issue of *Extra!* on "The Broken Promise of Public Television." One feature in that issue cited "5 Shows to Help Balance Public TV": *We Do the Work, America's Defense Monitor, Rights and Wrongs, In the Life,* and *Street Life.* Promoting these programs became central to the strategy of several local movements, including my own.

All of the grassroots media movements that I have studied shared similar goals. Their members wanted a genuine alternative to a corporate-controlled commercial television system driven by the bottom line of selling products to targeted demographics. They wanted a local public station whose governance observed FCC rules and regulations and whose programming embodied the principles articulated in the Public Broadcasting Act. In short, they sought whatever reforms were needed to make their local stations accessible and accountable to members and viewers.

By and large, these people had no aspirations to take over the stations in their communities. In fact, I believe many would not have been so insistent about governance issues if they had been getting programming that was interesting, reflected the community's diversity, and provided a forum for its issues. This would mean programming that was truly noncommercial and included more shows that were independently and/or locally produced. Some of these shows would include space for advocates for labor, the environment, consumers, peace, human rights, and all other noncorporate public interest perspectives effectively locked out of the commercial media; some would feature creative people on the cutting edge of artistic performance, to balance the middlebrow "pledge specials" of popular artists.

Public Interest Programs

Community activists I surveyed typically advocated airing the programs promoted in the FAIR special issue, whose producers had labored on shoe-string budgets to bring the voices of the unserved and underserved to the public, hoping that active citizens and responsive broadcasters would give them a chance to be seen.

We Do the Work

Produced by the California Working Group in half-hour segments, this magazine-format on-location show covered a "wide variety of issues ranging from how working people are faring in the global economy to light-hearted commentary about making ends meet." Celebrity hosts have included Ed Asner, Ned Beatty, Will Durst, Lee Grant, Howard Hesseman, and Alfre Woodard. According to executive producer Patrice O'Neill, however, "The real stars of the show are working people. Workers are very smart, articulate and analytical about what's affecting their lives." O'Neill hoped the program would "appeal to people who don't consider themselves working-class" as well as to "opinion leaders," so that working people's perspectives would become "critical to the discussion of the important issues of our time."

Because of the constraints of PBS underwriting guidelines, *WDTW* could not accept union money for production. That made the series expensive to lease, which was the excuse WQED first gave me for not airing it. By fall of 1993, however, the producers had solved their "underwriting problem" by raising funds from various health insurance companies with union clients and workplace coverage. A major contributor was Kaiser Permanente. With the new funding, the program could be offered free, by satellite downlink, to public stations across the country. By 1996, *WDTW* could be found on eighty-five public television stations.

WDTW won the prestigious Sidney Hillman Award and the Film Arts

Foundation's Joady Award. Several individual documentaries in the series finished first in their categories at the Chicago International Film Festival, the National Educational Film and Video Festival, and the American Film and Video Festival. Nevertheless, PBS still wasn't willing to make it part of its national program service.

In 1997, the California Working Group renamed itself the Working Group and replaced *We Do the Work* with *Livelihood,* hosted by comic Will Durst. The producers describe *Livelihood* as "a new series of upbeat and entertaining theme-based specials about how our work lives relate to our families, communities, and the larger questions the country faces as a whole."

Rights and Wrongs

Emmy Award–winning network producers Danny Schechter and Rory O'Conner cofounded Globalvision in 1987. This New York–based international television and film company produced the award-winning series *South Africa Now.* In 1992 it launched a new program, *Rights and Wrongs: Human Rights Television,* hosted by Charlayne Hunter-Gault, national correspondent of the *MacNeil/Lehrer NewsHour.* Drawing on the contributions of a global network of staffers, stringers, and independent filmmakers, this weekly half-hour newsmagazine exposed human rights violations, examined problems, and honored heroes.

With help from the MacArthur Foundation and the Open Society Institute, Schechter and O'Conner produced eighteen episodes in 1993 and another fourteen in 1994. There were reports on war crimes and hate crimes, rape, racism, and other issues from all points of the globe, including "hot spots" like China, El Salvador, Haiti, Ireland, South Africa, and Sarajevo. In its first year the show was carried by eighty-five PBS stations and many cable outlets and shown in fifty-two countries.

Schechter and O'Conner found corporate money impossible to raise. Typically they were told that being identified with a human rights show would cause problems with the corporation's clients overseas—clients like China, for instance. Seeking more secure funding and a wider audience, the producers proposed the series to PBS program chief Jennifer Lawson.

Lawson rejected the proposal, saying that human rights was "an insufficient organizing principle" for a PBS series. As *New York Times* columnist Bob Herbert recalled, "It's the kind of comment that . . . is so ludicrous, you have to hear it at least one more time, just to be certain you heard it correctly." Instead, Herbert observed, PBS was putting $1.5 million into development of twenty-two episodes of a Hollywood-style prime-time quiz show.

In August 1994, the thirty-two-member Congressional Black Congress endorsed a letter by Congresswoman Eleanor Holmes Norton to PBS president Ervin Duggan asking that PBS reverse its earlier decision and fund *Rights and Wrongs*. They were joined by thirteen more members of Congress as well as by organizations ranging from Amnesty International to Reebok. Rejecting this appeal, Duggan lauded PBS for its "courageous programming" and warned about "the coercive hand of government" stifling "the free exercise of editorial choice."

By 1996, *Rights and Wrongs* could be seen on 140 PBS affiliates, covering about 75 percent of the viewing public. However, the time slots assigned were often at low-audience viewing hours—late night, midday, or early in the morning. In the summer of 1997 Schechter advised me that *Rights and Wrongs* had lost all funding and was going out of production.

America's Defense Monitor

Admiral Gene R. La Rocque founded the Center for Defense Information (CDI) in 1972. Its directors consist of retired high-ranking officials from all branches of the military, and its mission is to support "an effective and efficient defense policy." This means opposing "waste, mismanagement, and policies that increase the danger of war." The CDI serves this mission by conducting research and publishing the results in a series of easy-to-read reports.

CDI's other major project is *America's Defense Monitor* (*ADM*), an award-winning half-hour television series. The program has high production values and examines subjects in depth that are passed over by the commercial media. Its producer, Sanford Gottlieb, says the show is funded independently and he is "very scrupulous about [representing] every relevant viewpoint." According to *ADM's* promotional material, "Topics range from the social costs of military spending to nuclear proliferation, the arms trade, and the impact of the military on society, the media, and the environment."

ADM is subsidized by a broad range of public foundations and offered free by satellite downlink, or on videotape for a nominal cost. It is carried from year to year by about fifty-five PBS affiliates. Many stations in California and Nebraska have been regular broadcasters of the program; others have come and gone. The program is also distributed to public access cable channels independently through Free Speech TV.

In the Life

In the Life is the only nationally broadcast gay and lesbian television news-magazine series, presented by WNET-TV New York and distributed through the American Program Service. The series is produced by In the Life Media, Inc., with 60 percent of its budget underwritten by foundations, 20 percent from videotape sales and other services, and 20 percent from a national membership of nearly five thousand individuals who give an average of forty dollars each.

The program was conceptualized by John Scagliotti, former program director of Pacifica's WBAI-FM and producer of the gay movement documentary *Before Stonewall. In the Life* debuted in June 1992 as a musical variety show taped in front of a live audience, and only six stations carried the opener. For its second season the show switched to its present newsmagazine format. Its primary goal is "to shatter negative stereotypes of gay men and women so often erroneously presented by mainstream media," and these days the show can be found on almost a hundred PBS member stations in nineteen of the twenty top markets. Communications director John Catania estimates that the program reaches 85 percent of the nation's TV sets and is seen by about 1.5 million people. Scores of celebrities, both straight and gay, have appeared on the program and several colleges and libraries have purchased episodes.

I have enormous respect for these producers in their fight for public interest programming despite corporate indifference and PBS national program service rejection. Eli N. Evans of the Charles H. Revson Foundation added this comment to the Twentieth Century Fund Task Force report on public television: "Every success story in the past twenty-five years is a saga of personal courage, often by a remarkable individual with a special vision who succeeded in spite of the politics of the system."

Local Movements in the 1990s
San Francisco

The oldest public television reform movement is based in the City by the Bay. KQED-TV was launched in 1953 as the nation's sixth public television station. The station's bylaws were modeled after those of the Berkeley Food Co-op, which called for subscriber election to the board of directors. KQED remains the only PBS station that elects its full board.

KQED's first president, James Day, recalls that in the beginning the station had a staff of eight and its headquarters was in the back seat of a station wagon. Even with such a modest operation in terms of cost, Day soon had to persuade his board to give him an extra month to raise the money needed to keep the station going. Friends donated a few thousand dollars and an all-night telethon brought in another $6,000, but it wasn't enough.

In desperation, he hired a public relations firm, which came up with an idea that was to become a public broadcasting institution—a twenty-four-hour TV auction. The first auction featured such disparate supporters as atomic bomb physicist Edward Teller and stripper Tempest Storm and raised enough money to avert the crisis. By 1954 KQED's budget was up to almost $70,000, which seems like a speck next to its 1996 budget of $34 million, but, as Day points out, "We became part of the community."

KQED headquarters moved up to a cramped dressing room at the top of the Mark Hopkins Hotel, using a transmitter donated by a local commercial station. Next stop was a trade school "where signs in the restrooms above the studio warned, 'Don't flush during broadcasts.'" From there they moved to a $500-a-month rented truck garage, covering the walls with egg crates for better acoustics.

During this time, Day, program manager Jonathan Rice, and others produced hundreds of live programs featuring performances of small orchestras, dance and jazz groups, and lots of interesting talk by people from all walks of life—from artists, scientists, and politicians to stevedores, mechanics, cultists, and cooks.

Frank Baxter pioneered an interview show at KQED called *Kaleidoscope* that featured such guests as Buster Keaton, Eleanor Roosevelt, Aldous Huxley, Bing Crosby, Robert Kennedy, Maurice Chevalier, Ella Fitzgerald, and Ogden Nash. Day comments, "We were in a city that was wide open to new ideas. . . . People came to us, people who were able to do and say unconventional things."

Some of these programs, like *Kaleidoscope,* became popular nationally. There was the twelve-part *Conversations with Eric Hoffer,* featuring the immigrant longshoreman/philosopher who authored the book *The True Believers.* T. Mikami's *Japanese Brush Painting* inspired a national craze. Alan Watts, an English-born former Anglican priest and the often-published exponent of Zen Buddhism, had his TV debut in 1959 with the very popular program *Eastern Wisdom.*

Richard Moore, who succeeded Day as KQED president, produced *Jazz Casual* with Ralph Gleason, *Poetry USA,* Mortimer Adler's *Great Ideas,* Ansel

Adams's *Photography/The Inclusive Art*, and *Writers in America*. Moore was responsible for 110 documentaries at KQED, including *Take This Hammer* with James Baldwin, *Losing Just the Same*, on ghetto life in Oakland, and an outdoor ballet choreographed by Merce Cunningham with natural sounds arranged by John Cage. According to Jonathan Rice, "[Moore] hated anything that was familiar. He would drive me crazy wanting to do things that often didn't seem to make any sense. He didn't want to do anything typical."

In 1968, following a local newspaper strike, Moore and Rice launched the *Newspaper of the Air*, featuring reporters hired literally off the picket lines at $100 per week. *San Francisco Chronicle* reporter Mel Wax hosted the show, in which everyone sat around a long table and took turns presenting major stories. When the strike ended KQED got $750,000 from the Ford Foundation to produce a new show called *NewsRoom*.

Moore left KQED in 1972. Reflecting back in 1997, at the age of seventy-five, he saw today's managers as lacking the "educational or intellectual background . . . openness of mind or curiosity" to have a true programming vision. Indeed, KQED's artistic and financial decline seemed to start after Moore's departure: smaller ideas being produced in bigger buildings, with more attention to business dollars and less to core viewers' interests.

In 1970, KQED accepted the gift of second station KQEC, Channel 32. Within two years, however, KQED got FCC permission to suspend broadcasting on KQEC temporarily because of "unforeseen fiscal difficulties." In September 1974, employees of the station went on strike. Henry Kroll, who worked in the station's engineering department during the strike and became part of a community movement to reform the station, recalled, "The strike was a catalyst that coalesced a number of community concerns over the direction and policies of public television in the Bay Area. Prior to 1974 KQED did a lot of community programming. The cuts didn't start until that year, but then they began snowballing."

The period from 1974 to 1980 was critical. During those years, KQED phased out local programs *Bay Area Profile, World Press, Open Studio*, and the popular *NewsRoom*. Rollin Post, a political reporter on *NewsRoom*, said that station management claimed it couldn't afford a complete daily newscast. However, he observed, KQED was "now playing big-time television. Those in charge of the station felt it should be a production center for national programming." At the same time, "there was increasingly less access by community groups to local programming than there had been."

During the strike, viewers organized in support of the workers. As they became educated to the broader issues they formed a coalition called the

California Public Broadcasting Forum. When the strike ended in January 1975, the coalition tried to block KQED's license renewals on the grounds that the station was keeping second station KQEC (Channel 32) off the air just to save money.

The FCC renewed both of KQED's licenses, but warned the station that its "financial difficulties [didn't] justify [allowing] Channel 32 to lie fallow." The commission ordered KQED to return KQEC to the air with the warning "Failure to comply could result in dismissal of KQEC-TV's renewal application, depletion of call letters or other appropriate sanction."

Angry over the loss of local programming, activists challenged KQED's license renewal again in 1977. That year two members of the Committee to Save KQED, Henry Kroll and Jane Kennedy, were elected to the KQED board, having run on a platform calling for more local programming, greater community participation, and less reliance on corporate funding. As soon as they took their seats, Kroll and Kennedy were informed that their terms would be only one year, not the usual four. The KQED nominating committee chair, Rai Okamoto, claimed that two of the eight slots to be filled were for the unexpired terms of resigned members and only good for one year; since the petition candidates finished seventh and eighth, he argued, they should get the one-year terms.

Kroll and Kennedy complained that neither they nor the voting membership had been apprised of these conditions in advance. They also pointed out instances in the past where candidates had received full terms even though technically filling unexpired terms. After months of appeals to the board failed, Kroll and Kennedy filed suit in Superior Court. When the judge ruled in favor of KQED, Kroll stated to the press, "They did this to stifle criticism and retain a board without dissent." KQED board chairman Philip D. Armour III claimed it was a "complete oversight" not to have informed the candidates or members of the one-year terms, but he also acknowledged, "It would be less than honest to say that I am not pleased they will not be on the board."

Late in 1978, the KQED board hired Anthony Tiano as its new general manager and president. Despite a $500,000 to $1 million budget shortfall, Tiano implemented plans to make capital improvements, in particular to install a new master routing switcher in 1979. To keep KQEC on the air during the transition, the station would have had to move, rent, or purchase standby equipment. Depending on the option chosen, the cost would have been practically nothing to a maximum of about $5,000. Instead, Tiano decided to suspend KQEC operations temporarily.

244] Air Wars

In the ensuing months, Tiano and several of his staff discussed shutting down KQEC for a longer time to save money. According to one estimate, this would save almost $140,000 over eight months. On November 5, 1979, KQEC was taken off the air as planned. On May 29, 1980, seven months later, it was returned to the air shortly after completion of the switcher installation and just in time for KQED's annual auction. During this period, KQED informed the board and the public that KQEC had been shut down "to help reduce the station's large budget deficit"; to the FCC, however, KQED cited technical not fiscal reasons—a delay in shipment of the new switching system.

In 1980, Larry Hall, president of the California Public Broadcasting Forum, went through FCC records in Washington, D.C., and discovered the misrepresentations. He recruited New York attorney David Rice and on January 18, 1980, informed KQED that the Forum would challenge its license renewal on the grounds that it had misrepresented its reasons for shutting down KQEC to the FCC. (The real reasons were, of course, in direct contradiction to the FCC's orders to the station just five years earlier.) To the dismay of the coalition, however, the FCC renewed KQED's license without even designating the case for hearing to determine who was telling the truth.

The Forum appealed the FCC decision to the district court in Washington, D.C. Hall insisted that taking away the station's license was not really what he wanted: "We want them to become part of the community. We want fair elections there and we want an accounting of where the money is going. Less than ten percent of their money goes to programming. If this were the United Way or any other charity, giving less than ten percent of the proceeds for what they were raising the money for, there would be a big outcry."

David Rice agreed to take the appeal pro bono, and Hall contributed $15,000 of his own money and raised additional funds from the community to cover expenses. The case sat for three or four years before the court decided that the FCC had acted capriciously and ordered a hearing; it took the FCC more than two years to get around to holding it.

The attorneys at the FCC's mass media bureau presented evidence that Anthony Tiano had had many solutions to his control switcher problem that were never explored. KQED's director of administration admitted that the shutdown of KQEX was solely for financial reasons and that, in fact, it had been Tiano who had suggested to her and others that the master switch installation was a "good excuse" to give the FCC.

On December 17, 1986, the district court approved the renewal of the station's three licenses (including one for FM radio), but only for thirty months. Both the coalition and KQED appealed to the FCC's review board. KQED sought a full renewal; the coalition sought denial of all three applications. Eighteen months later, on May 2, 1988, the FCC review board revoked KQED's license to operate Channel 32, stating, "The great preponderance of the record evidence confirms that vital financial considerations, deliberately not reported, were at the heart of the decision to remove Channel 32 from the air."

In 1988, at KQED's next license renewal time, a group called the Minority Television Project (MTP) put in a bid for Channel 32. In its bid, MTP told the FCC it wanted to produce and show programs for and about blacks, with some access for other minorities also. Its eight-member board consisted entirely of African Americans. Since blacks constituted only 10 percent of the community, Judge Tierney felt that the group's mission was too narrow. The FCC overruled him and granted MTP the license. Despite initial help from the CPB and the city of San Francisco, MTP was never able to make a go of it. For a time they leased the channel for foreign language broadcasts and PBS reruns, a sad ending for all concerned.

KQED apparently learned no lesson from this experience. Tiano began making huge real estate gambles. In 1988 he put the station's headquarters on the market, expecting it to sell for $5 million. Before selling it, he built a new $19 million building large enough to house 500 employees. This became station headquarters in 1992. The old building didn't sell until a year later and then for only $1.9 million. By 1991 the station had only 350 employees. Continuing fiscal crises reduced the payroll to 200. In 1994, Mary Bitterman replaced Tiano as CEO of KQED. In 1996, KQED still owed $13.7 million on a building that was now assessed at only $12 million.

In the face of such self-inflicted debt, KQED resorted to stripping assets and increasing its reliance on commercial sponsors. In 1998, KQED sold off its books and tape division and its magazine to cover its short-term debt. It floated a twenty-five-year tax-free bond to cover its long-term debt. It now leases space in its building to other organizations. And it has introduced thirty-second commercials between programs.

The Committee to Save KQED has continued to challenge the station's management. In recent years it has been joined by the labor-oriented group Accountable Public Broadcasting. Every year, one-third of KQED's twenty-seven-member board turns over and in almost every election the activists run a slate of petition-nominated candidates for those seats. Typically, only about 10 percent of the 250,000 plus KQED members vote. In 1991, reform candidate Henry Kroll was elected to the board for the third time.

According to Kroll, the committee held monthly meetings that attracted anywhere from a handful of core members to several dozen, depending on whether they were organizing for an event or an election campaign. Likewise, they put out mailings that varied from between five hundred to several thousand. KQED challengers were especially active during the period 1991–92. By this time, KQED was down to one half-hour local show a week, *This Week in Northern California*.

During the Gulf War, in the winter of 1991, the progressive satellite video network Deep Dish petitioned KQED to air its *Gulf Crisis TV Project* to balance pro-war coverage on commercial TV. Their campaign included calls, letters, meetings with KQED personnel, a demonstration, and community showings of the program. KQED finally agreed to broadcast the program as well as Deep Dish's *Behind Censorship* series, which included a program critical of corporate influence at PBS.

During that same year PBS cancelled the documentary *Stop the Church*, scheduled for showing on the independent film series *P.O.V.* The film is critical of the Catholic Church's policies toward gays, and the San Francisco gay community protested its cancellation. KQED became one of the few stations in the country to show the film. Also, labor activists with Accountable Public Broadcasting prevailed on the station to air *We Do the Work* once a month as well as provide a full day of worker-oriented programming on Labor Day.

The station balked, however, when it came to airing *Deadly Deception*, the twenty-eight-minute documentary exposé of General Electric produced by Debra Chasnoff for INFACT, sponsors of the G.E. boycott. Chasnoff was local to the area and the film had won the 1991 Academy Award for "best documentary short." Nevertheless, KQED quoted PBS that the film violated underwriting guidelines because it was produced and funded by the same source. KQED program director Ron Santora went further, stating, "What does winning an Oscar mean? Does that make it valid? Does that mean the facts are accurate?" Santora did not actually challenge the accuracy of any of the factual claims in the film. Instead, he explained that the station simply "stays away from documentaries commissioned by groups of that nature. We use more independent producers without an ax to grind."

Paper Tiger, the progressive cable video producer, and FAIR organized a campaign to get *Deadly Deception* on KQED. They pointed out KQED's hypocrisy in the application of underwriting guidelines, citing the approved *Submarine: Steel Boats, Iron Men*, an hour-long tribute to the nuclear submarine funded by several major military contractors. They also pointed out that KQED-FM aired *Market Place*, a business news show sponsored by G.E., whose underwriting statement was not balanced by INFACT commentary. The station was not persuaded.

Reform activists held a large Accountable Public Broadcasting forum in August to "examine the conflicts between the PBS system and film and video makers." The forum featured five speakers, including Debra Chasnoff. After the discussions there were a series of house parties at which people were urged to write or phone KQED.

When WNET-TV New York became the first station to schedule *Deadly Deception*, FAIR and Paper Tiger called a demonstration in KQED's parking lot to coincide with that showing, on September 27, at which they proposed to project the film on the side of KQED's corporate headquarters because, they explained, the only way the film would ever be "shown on KQED [was] literally." This imaginative publicity stunt caused KQED to relent.

In 1992, two more "new priorities" candidates were elected to the KQED board from an alternative slate of seven. One was Sasha Futran, former director of the Mt. Diablo Peace Center. The other was Sylvia Siegel, a consumer consultant and the founder of the utility watchdog group T.U.R.N. Everyone celebrated with music and comedy at a benefit for the Committee to Save KQED.

The three petition candidates were subsequently joined by board-appointed labor representative Shelly Kessler, to establish the largest block of dissident voices in the history of the KQED board. Apparently threatened by this intrusion into their ranks, the board leadership began to manipulate the election process to handicap outside challenges.

Board leaders increased the number of signatures required for nomination by petition from fifteen to eighty-five. The three hundred words a candidate was allowed on the ballot to present his or her position was cut back to two hundred and the three minutes each was given on the air were cut out entirely. Board-nominated candidates were listed first on the ballot, followed by petition-nominated candidates. In 1993, the board put up its own slate of eight "friends of KQED" as "alternative" candidates, making for a crowded and confusing ballot; all nine board-endorsed candidates were elected by substantial margins that year.

In response, the reformers added fair subscriber elections to their concerns about better programming and public accountability. They called for candidates to be listed alphabetically or randomly, for airing of candidates' viewpoints on radio and TV, and for KQED action to create a more economically and culturally diverse board. They also objected to the scheduling of board meetings during the day, when working people cannot attend, and to the ban against board members tape-recording meetings or talking to the press.

In 1995, the three activist incumbents ran for reelection and were among the top four finishers; however, five activists failed in their bids for seats two years later, in 1997. When Kroll, Futran, and Siegel finished their terms in 1998, KQED's board, for the first time in years, was once again completely in the hands of board-nominated leadership. Moreover, even when there had been four reform-mind people on the board at the same time, their influence was limited. Sasha Futran said they were able to introduce some motions under "new business" but never succeeded in getting an item on the agenda; both Kroll and Futran researched, crafted, and lobbied for passage of some kind of program policy statement, for instance, but to no avail.

In Futran's view, their greatest contribution was occasionally being able to stop the "railroading" of certain decisions and to compel discussion. This didn't mean they were always provided documents relevant to such decisions, nor did it mean that some important decisions weren't railroaded still. After Anthony Tiano resigned in early 1993, for example, the board was faced with choosing an interim successor and then launching a national search. The chair of the board appointed committees for these purposes. None of the reformers were included and the committees carried on their work in secret. Later, in March, at the end of a regular board meeting, the full board was unexpectedly presented with a nominee for interim CEO. According to Futran, board members were given copies of the candidate's resumé and asked for a vote of approval before they even had time to read it. Several members had already left. The four activists on the board protested in vain. Perhaps their concerns were noted, however, because Henry Kroll reports he was included on the search committee for the permanent CEO and participated actively in the process and the choice.

In such a situation it is little wonder, perhaps, that despite the ban on talking to the press, activist members sometimes used the media to expose questionable actions by the board. The most publicized example of this was in 1996, when Sasha Futran revealed that KQED was proposing a one-hour documentary in praise of wine mogul Robert Gerald Mondavi, to be funded largely by Mondavi money. Internal KQED documents revealed that the station's marketing department had pitched the project to the winery as a documentary that would "pay tribute to a remarkable man." KQED accepted $50,000 in development money from a foundation created and chaired by Mondavi and arranged to get another $150,000 from the same source if work on the film met with its approval. Mondavi also provided KQED with a "lead list" of people to help raise another $400,000 to finish the program. Mondavi asked to meet with the prospective executive producer and got agreement on content guidelines, including censorship of any mention of their family's well-publicized feuds.

When the story broke, KQED tried to characterize the program as being about the vibrant culture of the Napa Valley rather than a profile of Mondavi. It also insisted that despite the source of its funding, the station retained "editorial control." The board voted twenty-two to two that it had done nothing wrong, weakly comparing this case to the general practice of commercial media accepting money from sources they also cover (as when newspapers print both motion picture listings and reviews). When all that failed to persuade the press and public, the station dropped the project, apologized profusely in print to the Mondavi family for any embarrassment, and blamed the whole fiasco on Futran.

The debate wasn't just about a Mondavi documentary, of course, but about the mission and future of public broadcasting in San Francisco and the country. At the height of the controversy, *San Francisco Chronicle* columnist Jon Carroll likened the documentary to a "tasteful infomercial." According to Futran, one KQED board member said the station should be making "more deals for infomercials" and was applauded by others for his statement.

At last word, the Accountable Public Broadcasting Project was cosponsoring a campaign to ban advertising and promote regular labor and environmental programming on National Public Radio.

Phoenix

When Tom Blazier founded the Arizona Media Action Committee (AMAC) in Phoenix in 1992, his vision was to forge a more cooperative relationship between public interest groups and the media. At the second Media and Democracy Congress, in New York in October 1997, Blazier advised colleagues, "Every progressive organization has a gripe about the media, wants their point to be heard and wants more access," and this makes media activism "unique," with great opportunities for success. "You can appeal to them," Blazier proposed, "in terms of what you can do for them; why you are an asset to their group." Practicing what he preaches, Blazier and his associates set up literature tables wherever sympathetic souls were likely to gather—

bookstores, libraries, co-ops, campuses, and especially major events like Earth Day celebrations, peace fairs, and concerts by artists like Jackson Browne.

I first interviewed Blazier by phone in 1993. A year later my wife and I were in Phoenix and had dinner with Blazier and AMAC members Sam Insana of the National Lawyer's Guild and Margaret Grannis of Amnesty International. AMAC clearly had enabled various public interest groups to cooperate around a common problem. They told me how their educational sessions for members helped build cohesion and increase effectiveness. I was presented with ample documentation of the group's accomplishments.

Blazier contributed to an alternative monthly, *Current,* writing, drawing cartoons, and helping build circulation. The paper, which now includes sixty-five member organizations and has a circulation of 14,000, features a regular "Media Watch" column from AMAC. In issues I reviewed, FAIR activist David Winkler advised readers of the "highs" and "lows" in media coverage around the nation and in the community. Cleverly written, his column schools its readers in media literacy, and its "highs" segment applauds investigative journalists who do good work. Blazier has also contributed commentary and interviews.

Blazier and his colleagues worked hard to cultivate relationships with editors, reporters, and radio talk show hosts. Phoenix is served by the *Arizona Republic,* the nation's sixth largest newspaper in terms of circulation. Blazier noted that the paper regularly published conservatives like Cal Thomas, former public relations director for the Moral Majority, but had no alternative voices from the left. In spring 1993, Blazier wrote to the editorial page editor with a number of suggestions and included samples of "On the Media Beat," the column by FAIR's Jeff Cohen and author Norman Solomon. Cohen and Solomon began running in the *Arizona Republic* in August and two to three times a month thereafter. AMAC members wrote appreciative letters to the editor to reassure staff of interest in the column as well as to promote it to other readers. The *Arizona Republic* carried the column (in later years by Solomon alone) until a new editor took over in 1998.

AMAC also made certain to build media coverage around any events they organized. The group debuted in July 1992 with a forum on "Racism in the Media," held at Arizona State University and featuring eleven panelists from minority communities and the media. About eighty people attended the panel, which was covered by the *Phoenix Gazette,* and followed by a seventy-minute radio interview with Blazier and another panelist. In February 1993, KPNX-TV hosted about twenty-five minority community leaders, along with Blazier and Winkler, to discuss how the station could improve its coverage of minority community issues. AMAC members also arranged two radio interviews for Carl Jensen, founder of Project Censored, whose distinguished panel of journalists and scholars select and bring to public attention the ten most important news stories of the year neglected by the major media.

To build interest in its movement, AMAC organized events around popular speakers and award-winning films. In March 1993, it hosted FAIR executive director Jeff Cohen, and in April 1994, author and columnist Norman Solomon. Both speakers were booked at Arizona State University (before audiences of up to two hundred) and Mesa Community College before moving on to the University of Arizona, and both did interviews with the alternative weekly *New Times,* local radio shows, the local NPR affiliate, and a public access television program. Three days after the Cohen appearance, AMAC cosponsored the Academy Award–winning and PBS-banned *Panama Deception* at the Valley Art Theatre in Tempe for a two-week run, including a special benefit showing featuring Jacqueline Sharkey, a professor and journalist who had served as a resource during production of the documentary; about 130 people attended, and the film received excellent reviews in the two major papers in town.

To kick off the summer, the committee sponsored the showing of *Manufacturing Consent: Noam Chomsky and the Media,* also at the Valley Art Theatre, where it ran for a week. A Thursday night opening drew about seventy people to hear guest speaker Mark Lowenthal from Project Censored. The *Arizona Republic* did a feature on the film, which was given a favorable review by *New Times.* While in town, Lowenthal also spoke at Mesa Community College and did several radio interviews. One of the interviews played as a local segment on NPR's *Morning Edition,* another included national television news personality and Project Censored panelist Hugh Downs by telephone from New York.

Whenever AMAC found a receptive outlet, it worked with it as often as possible. For example, the Jeffrey Gale AM radio show devoted seven programs over a six-month period to AMAC-sponsored speakers, including *Rights and Wrongs* producer Rory O'Conner and James Bush from the Center for Defense Information, producer of *America's Defense Monitor.*

AMAC employed this same cooperative approach in trying to make PBS affiliate KAET-TV Phoenix more responsive to the public interest community. On June 11, 1993, AMAC members Tom Blazier, David Winkler, and Louis Porter and *Current* editor Ferd Haverly met with KAET-TV station manager Charles Allen, program director John Wilson, and members of the station's community advisory board. AMAC presented two general concerns: (1) the station's board included too many corporate representatives and was not sufficiently reflective of the broader community, and (2) there was not enough diversity in the station's weekly and nightly news and issues programming.

In mid-September, AMAC mailed copies of a special issue of *EXTRA!* to KAET-TV management and advisory board members. The issue featured a critical study of prime-time PBS programming by academics William Hoynes, David Croteau, and Kevin Carragee. The mailing included a letter urging KAET-TV to "be more inclusive of public interest voices" and specifically recommending the weekly human rights series *Rights and Wrongs*. AMAC also promoted a radio interview for Hoynes, to spread word of the study; at AMAC's urging, the station was able to recruit Arizona senator John McCain to join the interview. Blazier advises activists to seek out and use such empirical data in their public outreach and education.

The following month, AMAC members Blazier, Haverly, and Jean Chauduri met with the station's advisory board, station manager Beth Vershure, and John Wilson. The group repeated its concerns about the lack of diversity on KAET's board and in its programming. Chauduri suggested a Native American representative should be on the board. AMAC also recommended the station run *Rights and Wrongs, America's Defense Monitor,* and *We Do the Work.* Four AMAC members met again with Vershure and Wilson in February of 1994 for updates on the programs that had been discussed. The news was good. *Rights and Wrongs* was scheduled to debut on April 5, 1994. The station subsequently put on all fourteen episodes and then went into reruns. On August 9, Wilson said viewer response was favorable and the station might air the program the next year; *We Do the Work* was said to be still "under consideration." Blazier described the meeting to me as "upbeat." On Labor Day 1994, the station aired several hours of the series.

In 1994, Blazier moved from Arizona to Oregon to attend graduate school and the work of AMAC was carried on under the leadership of Dave Winkler, Mary Richards, and Gray Cavender. When I interviewed Winkler in September 1999, he had more successes to report. The AMAC core group continued to meet occasionally, sometimes showing a video to be considered for KAET-TV broadcast. Also, Winkler still made suggestions to program director Joe Campbell and wrote columns and letters to the editor to increase the pressure. Sometimes this effort was supplemented by supporters sending e-mails to the station and, on one occasion, by threat of a boycott. As a result, in 1997 KAET-TV ran all twelve episodes of *We Do the Work* and now carries *Livelihood*. The station has also programmed several controversial documentaries, including *Father Roy: Inside the School of the Assassins* (1998), *Fear and Favor in the Newsroom* (1999), and the *Just Solution* series of four one-hour documentaries on human rights, produced and distributed by Human Rights Watch and Free Speech TV (1999). It must be acknowledged that the station refused to program *Tell the Truth and Run*, despite Winkler's offer to contribute $500 of the $1,000 license fee.

In Winkler's experience, "[KAET-TV] will ignore you as long as it can until you force the issue." It took a year to get the station to show *Fear and Favor in the Newsroom*. Nevertheless, persistence pays off. Looking back in 1997, Blazier advised those interested in similar work to network actively and to be persistent but not confrontational. "It doesn't take a lot of people to make a difference. In many cases I was working alone or maybe with one or two other persons."

Chicago

Up until 1992, reform activists had been frustrated in their appeals to Chicago public station WTTW-TV. In 1991, after the president of the Chicago Federation of Labor, Robert Healy, requested *We Do the Work*, WTTW's vice president for programming, Richard Bowman, told him the station "had concerns about the evenness of quality and the fairness of certain segments." At around the same time, Bob Cleland, the founder of Illinois Peace Action, asked the station for *America's Defense Monitor* (*ADM*) and was similarly dismissed.

In 1992, filmmaker Scott Sanders and activist Melissa Sterne began building the Chicago Media Watch (CMW), a local offshoot of FAIR, into the Coalition for Democracy in Public Television (CDPTV). As with its counterparts around the country, CDPTV came to include a great diversity of endorsers and members. Its stationary lists the Coalition for New Priorities, which itself includes one hundred groups, as well as more than twenty other organizations.

The CDPTV's steering committee included Sanders and Sterne, filmmaker Allan Siegel, and a number of concerned citizens. In the beginning, filmmaker Gordon Quinn provided meeting space and support. Sanders was elected to handle press relations and to represent the group to WTTW. One of his first projects was to publicize WTTW's refusal to air *Deadly Deception*, the Oscar-winning documentary critical of General Electric, which happened to be WTTW's top corporate contributor. CDPTV's stated mission was to "respond" to "WTTW's lack of public openness and narrow programming spectrum" through educating the viewing public and pressuring the station's management.

On June 9, 1993, coalition representatives attended the quarterly meeting of the WTTW board's programming committee. Scott Sanders spoke from a prepared text. He first commented on the "anti-democratic" restrictions that governed communications between the station and the public: inadequate public notice, limits on who could attend and speak, minutes and agendas denied, even letters on public file not available for inspection. "This is the last time we will meet under these ground rules," Sanders said. "They are anathema to the spirit of public broadcasting."

The lack of diversity on the "self-perpetuating" board, he continued, was reflected in parallel gaps in station programming: "No trade unionist on the board, no labor-oriented series. No community-level peace organizer on the board, no serious peace program." On the other hand, Sanders noted, corporations were well represented on the board and five of six public affairs discussion series were hosted by "avowed pro-corporation conservatives"; likewise, despite its noncommercial status, WTTW aired "commercials for the likes of realtors, utilities, car manufacturers and insurance companies." (The public broadcasting trade paper *Current* later noted that WTTW was "one of the most aggressive private-sector fundraisers in public TV." Indeed, in 1984 the station was one of the first to offer corporate donors on-air acknowledgements that resembled commercial advertising.)

Sanders then announced that CDPTV was seeking the airing of four programs on WTTW: the original version of the censored Republican Convention episode of *The 90's*, *We Do the Work*, *The Panama Deception*, and *Deadly Deception*. In his closing remarks, he suggested that the station's subscribers should elect the WTTW board. Soon after Sanders's presentation, WTTW added two members to its forty-five-member board, the first Latino and another African American.

Less than two months later, on July 28, thirteen CDPTV representatives met with WTTW's Richard Bowman and Bruce Marcus, vice president of corporate marketing and communications. The discussion covered better access for local independent producers, showing the two Oscar-winning films, and running *We Do the Work*, *America's Defense Monitor*, and *Rights and Wrongs*. At the meeting, the station agreed only to run public service announcements from the Coalition for New Priorities. In September 1993, however, WTTW launched a Sunday afternoon series called *Viewpoint* and used it to alternately air episodes of *We Do the Work* and *America's Defense Monitor*. In February 1994, WTTW's *Eleven* magazine started to run letters to the editor "for the first time in over fifteen years." Finally, in April 1994, WTTW scheduled *Rights and Wrongs* for early morning broadcast on Saturdays.

In contrast to the tone of the accountability campaign in Phoenix, however, both station officials and activists in Chicago were reluctant to give each other much respect. Bruce Marcus said the coalition "played a role" in the decision to launch "a viewpoint program," but the decision to air the two alternative shows was "not in response to [the] meeting." He added that while *Deadly Deception* might run, *Panama Deception* contained "charges totally without confirmation" and would never be shown. Bob Cleland, who had fought for the latter, then referred to the program concessions made as "a couple of bones" to cover for the refusal of the two "deception" films. Nevertheless, on August 26, 1993, he wrote to 320 members of Illinois Peace Action, urging them to watch the two scheduled segments of *America's Defense Monitor* and send an appreciative response to station officials; Cleland later was named to the station's community advisory board.

The gains made by CDPTV seemed to be tenuous. By the end of April 1994, both Scott Sanders and Robert Healy were writing to Bowman to protest the moving of *We Do the Work* to 7:30 A.M. on Thursday mornings. Sanders complained to me that station officials said they only liked some of the *We Do the Work* programs and sometimes held segments for a month before showing them. Despite these obstacles, CDPTV organized a public event on May 2, 1994, that featured keynote speaker Lewis Lapham, editor of *Harper's*, and included panelist Bruce Marcus of WTTW along with filmmaker Gordon Quinn and representatives of Operation PUSH and the Mexican Fine Arts Museum.

The relationship between CDPTV and WTTW-TV ruptured on July 7, 1994, when the coalition filed a complaint with the FCC in response to what it called WTTW's "home shopping" broadcasts. For two weeks in October 1993, WTTW had displaced regularly scheduled programming on weekend afternoons and weeknights late to run about forty-five hours of "The Holiday Gift Exchange," in which the station peddled products and showcased the latest offerings from other cultural institutions in the community, like the Field Museum and the Lincoln Park Zoo. Most items were priced between $35 and $100, including such things as a Chicago Symphony Orchestra silk scarf and a Picasso poster from the Art Institute; most of the revenue went to the cultural institutions.

WTTW's Marcus insisted that the program was "educational and entertaining" and "didn't break any rules." Another spokesperson added later that "The Holiday Gift Exchange" had been "an experiment" and the station had no plans to repeat it. Gigi Sohn of the Media Access Project called it "an outrage" and called for FCC punishment: "They used the public airwaves, which were set aside for public education, to sell commercial goods. Don't they know that making money and the public interest are mutually exclusive?"

The CDPTV's seventeen-page complaint condemned the broadcasts as "setting a bad precedent." The Media Access Project and the Georgetown University Law Center provided legal counsel for the filing. Sanders stated in their press release, "Sometimes giving praise to WTTW is appropriate. But WTTW is just trying to sell us all a bill of goods with its home shopping broadcasts." Marcus countered by characterizing the challengers as "a few individuals trying to get an elected board here in Chicago and are grabbing onto every issue they can."

Throughout 1995, CDPTV promoted meetings with David Kohn, chief legislative aide to Congressman John Porter, to protest the Republican assault on public broadcast funding. For the CPB annual meeting in Chicago later that year, Melissa Sterne designed a leaflet which Sanders and others passed out, calling for PBS "democracy" and for "permanent trust funding for public broadcasting."

On October 23, 1995, almost sixteen months after the filing of the complaint, the FCC found no violation of the rules against commercialism on public broadcasting. The commission explained that it does not regard promotional announcements for nonprofits as advertising because technically the merchandise is not sold "for profit." On the other hand, it said, the station was wrong in changing its regular programming to raise funds for other nonprofits without a waiver from the FCC. And it admonished WTTW "to use care to comply with the Commission's noncommercial rules and policies in the future."

Commenting on the decision, *Current* editor Steve Behrens called it "a light slap on the wrist." Andy Schwartzman of the Media Access Project said he was pleased that the FCC had made a distinction between stations selling products for their own support and selling them for others: "We cannot save noncommercial broadcasting by commercializing it." He said his clients were ready to put this behind them and would like to "start off on a clean slate with WTTW."

When I talked to Sanders in February of 1996 he was rather melancholy about it all. "We haven't met as a group in several months," he said. "The problem is that we were not permitted to talk to the station while the suit was pending." Thinking about the future, Sanders said that he felt his group had "sufficient legitimacy to be represented on the [station's] board of directors," but he confessed to being "perplexed about how to reopen communication." "I would like to be perceived as having made a legitimate point and deserving of respect and not just [as] an adversary," he mused. "My real aspiration is for the station to offer programs which make it a public forum on important issues confronting the city."

Apparently the CDPTV complaint put WTTW on the FCC's radar. Late in 1997, the commission cited November 1996 underwriting spots for Zenith, Amoco, Prudential Securities, and Sun America Insurance as violating FCC rules and imposed a $5,000 fine. The FCC said their action was prompted by a "confidential" complaint. WTTW conceded that the Zenith spot that promoted "images more realistic than ever before" should not have been aired, but it claimed that the FCC was changing the ground rules with respect to the other complaints. WTTW and PBS said they would seek a meeting to get a clearer understanding.

On January 2, 1998, WTTW filed a response to the FCC's "notice of apparent liability." WTTW executive vice president Bob Mauro took the position that this was "a system-wide issue, going beyond the walls of Chicago." *Electronic Media* called it "ground zero in the battle over [the] commercialization of public television." As of this writing, the fine remains unpaid. Sanders suggests that WTTW might be considering a court challenge, perhaps joined by PBS or by other individual stations.

In recent years Scott Sanders has become a librarian as well as a filmmaker, still interested in public broadcasting. In 1997, CMW and FAIR sponsored a full-day conference on "Media and Disinformation," featuring David Barsamian, Janine Jackson, and Ron Daniels. After a lapse, the *Viewpoint* series at WTTW was revived. In August 1999 it presented *It's Elementary,* a controversial Debra Chasnoff documentary on sexual preference.

The Chicago Media Watch has carried on under the leadership of Liane C. Casten and colleagues. The group puts out a quarterly newsletter, *Chicago Media Watch Group Report,* featuring media criticism and stories on issues like pollution in South Chicago that are not covered by the corporate press. The group also hosts a monthly series of speakers presenting news stories not covered by the mainstream media.

Jacksonville

Since 1982, Jacksonville, Florida, had been served by a WJCT public radio program that aired from 4 to 5 P.M., hosted by Landon Walker and called *The Metro*. Walker played bass in a jazz trio and read beat poetry; with his wire-rimmed glasses and long white beard, he also looked like a true bohemian spirit.

The Metro was an eclectic mix of live interviews, jazz, world pop, blues, and comedy skits, along with a bulletin board for the cultural community. Most importantly, to quote one reporter, "[It was] a one-of-a-kind platform for area artists and arts organizations interviews." In fact, the Arts Assembly of Jacksonville had given Walker their 1992 award for outstanding individual achievement. *Folio*, the city's weekly entertainment magazine, called Walker the area's number one radio personality.

In June of 1993 Walker was advised that *The Metro* was being moved to 11 P.M. and his new work shift would be 7 P.M. to midnight—his old time slot would be filled by a new show called *90 in the Shade*. Station manager Gene Napier claimed that Walker's sagging ratings and the need to build "a broader audience" had dictated the schedule change.

Walker was concerned that the new show just "wouldn't look anything like the old *Metro*, because live interviews won't happen." He later reflected, "It became clear I was not welcome." On August 2 at 11 P.M., Walker broadcast a show that he called "The Last Metro," featuring a lot of farewell-type songs. The next day Napier asked Walker for his resignation and had him escorted to his desk and out of the building.

In the first few weeks after the change, the station received more than 300 phone calls and 220 letters. Those opposed to the change outnumbered those in favor by nine to one. About three-fourths of those who called or wrote said they were canceling financial support for the station. The Florida *Times-Union* also reported "dozens of letters and telephone calls" complaining about the change. In response, Bob White, executive director of Theatre Jacksonville, joined with attorney Andy Goshen to form a citizens group called Members for the Metro. Their goal was to have the station reinstate Walker and his show at its old time slot. Within days of the announcement about fifty protestors showed up in the station's parking lot at 4 P.M. to picket, shout, and bang on drums.

Rob McKnight, the station's vice president for marketing, came out of the building to tell the crowd that the decision to move the program was final; Arbitron ratings indicated that *Metro* listeners had declined by 25 percent over the past eighteen months, he said. Undaunted, the protestors were back a week later, three times as strong, tooting horns, blowing whistles, and banging on pots and pans.

A third rally on July 8 drew 400 of the show's faithful. Andy Goshen set up an escrow fund to which people could pledge money to the station, contingent on the show's reinstatement by August 31, after which all moneys would be returned unless otherwise authorized by the contributor. By the end of the third rally, some 260 supporters of Members for the Metro had contributed more than $16,000 in donations and thousands more in pledges.

On July 9, Members for the Metro met with Gene Napier and William Birchfield, chairman of the station's board of trustees. They demanded evidence of the poor ratings Napier and McKnight claimed were behind the decision; Napier said the station was bound not to release its Arbitron survey numbers. Calls to the CPB and the Radio Research Consortium itself revealed that public stations are free to release ratings numbers, and on July 23, Goshen wrote to the station that refusing to do so was a breach of the public trust.

Meanwhile, when Goshen researched case law on the matter he found that the courts typically ruled against plaintiffs trying to get them to order a station to air a particular program. He decided against an FCC complaint because he had heard that "they are pretty complacent." Goshen settled instead on using what he called "a fairly liberal Florida law that holds that public agencies or their contractors must divulge their records to the public." A twenty-minute hearing was held on August 3 and another three-hour hearing three days later. On August 10, Judge Brad Stetson ruled that WJCT was obliged to make available certain public records.

Instead of appealing, on August 17 Birchfield reached a consent agreement with Goshen that required the station to open its records, including membership and donor lists, and provide up to two thousand pages of such records to Goshen at no cost. The station was also required to add an editorial page to its program guide, with content under the control of Members for the Metro. More important, the station's twenty-five-member community advisory board had to be expanded by twenty-five, with ten members, including the chair, to be elected by CAB members. Five candidates from Members for the Metro were appointed to new seats and ten were elected. Finally, station manager Gene Napier was directed to apologize at the annual board meeting and in the program guide for not responding to the repeated letters, telephone calls, and other requests for information.

In a November 1993 movement newsletter, Andy Goshen called Members for the Metro "a grassroots watchdog group" and suggested that they consider reorganizing under a new name to pursue broader station reforms. Noting that the trustees used to be elected by the members of the station, he suggested "a return to membership voting privileges would be a step in the right direction!" At a late December 1993 business meeting and "bash" with "terrific food and great bands," Members for the Metro accepted nominations for a name change and elected officers. Thirteen of fourteen positions were filled, including Andy Goshen as president and Myrtice Craig as newsletter editor.

On January 27, 1994, Napier resigned from WJTC effective September 30, 1994. (Craig reported that Napier said he would be working as a PBS consultant!) Members for the Metro met again in March 1994 under their old name; however, when I spoke briefly with Craig and Goshen in August 1997, the movement had come to an end. Much of its passion had been focused on Landon Walker, Goshen explained. Nonetheless, the group had made its point with station management: the community would not be taken for granted again.

Lessons for the Future

These are just some of the battlefronts upon which citizen activists have challenged public broadcasting stations to be more responsive to their communities. In every case, despite the prevailing constraints, they got results: members of minorities added to the board, conflicts of interest being exposed, member concerns given a broader airing, and/or public interest programs put on the air. In the case of San Francisco, the community's demonstrated persistence moved the station to voluntarily agree to air certain "controversial" programs without having to be prodded by protest actions.

Changes in the structure of the national system to support more public participation would make the goals of local public interest advocates even more easily attainable. In the final chapter we will consider what forms such changes might take.

Chapter 10

Public Broadcasting
in the Public Interest:
Toward a Democratic Alternative

In 1996, Harvard political scientist Robert Putnam presented considerable evidence that in all arenas of life civic participation was disappearing in America: in fact, as he put it, people were even "bowling alone." After determining that this historical pattern could not be explained by standard variables, Putnam concluded that the culprit was television. In his view, the many hours spent at home in front of the tube have removed people from participation in social life.

The *American Prospect* magazine invited a host of distinguished scholars to debate Putnam's proposition. Some found fault with his measures, others pointed to structural explanations for the phenomenon. No one questioned why television should be assumed to discourage rather than encourage civic participation.

Yet in my youth, Edward R. Murrow's CBS presentation of *Harvest of Shame* opened my eyes to the plight of migrant workers in America. Television coverage of Bull Connor's assaults on civil rights demonstrators moved me to join that movement. As an organizer I have solicited television coverage of various events in order to motivate the participation of others. Some who have responded have advised me, "I saw you on television." I was thrilled when in the hour following the Pittsburgh broadcast of *Defending*

Our Lives, about a hundred people with domestic violence problems phoned counselors at WQED for help.

It cannot be denied that political participation in America has declined drastically. A 1996 *Washington Post* poll found that two-thirds of Americans did not know the name of their representative in Congress and half could not identify his or her party. In that year's presidential election, voter turnout fell below 50 percent for the first time since 1924. This put the United States at 139th in terms of voting rate, which averages 80 percent in other industrial democracies.

A series of surveys by the Freedom Forum Media Studies Center found that for the 1996 presidential campaign five times as many viewers got their political information from TV as radio, more than three times as many from TV as from newspapers. The clear conclusion is that America needs and deserves television programming that informs as well as distracts, that encourages rather than discourages civic participation. In the words of media scholar Patricia Aufderheide, public broadcasting could be "a public project executed through broadcasting . . . using mass communication as a tool of public life."

This kind of public television would be dedicated to serving the public interest, that is, it would consider all those things that are essential to community and nation. There is a public interest in crime-free streets, good schools, safe roads, economic opportunity, just workplaces, clean air and water, reliable transportation, adequate health care, and all that makes for a good society.

According to the distinguished educator John Dewey, it is the media's job "to interest the public in the public interest." These things are of a different order than celebrity gossip or home shopping, no matter how many individuals might be interested in such things. The same can be said for typical PBS fare, like how to cook, garden, paint, sew, or make money in the stock market. Such subjects do not address the public interest.

"In a democratic society," Douglas Kellner further advises, "the public's interest is to further democracy." This means providing each individual, and certainly each group, "with an equal opportunity to participate in the political process and to advance economically and socially. This version of the public interest requires equal access to education, information and the media of public debate."

Whither Public Broadcasting?

Clearly public broadcasting in America is at a crossroads. The road it now travels—modest federal support with close political supervision and increasing commercialization—is a dead end in terms of preserving its founding mission and any semblance of editorial independence. Two events in the summer of 1999 laid this crisis bare for all to see.

For one, there was the way in which the Public Broadcasting Service responded to pressures to shrink the system by eliminating stations with "overlapping" signals. Almost three-fifths of Americans have access to two or more public television channels. There are twenty-nine markets where station signals "substantially" overlap and forty markets with some degree of overlap.

Two or three separate public television channels are common in Europe, while U.S. markets feature dozens of commercial channels each. Any community should be able to make good use of a second or third noncommercial channel. Nevertheless, many in public broadcasting argue that public broadcasting channels should be cut to one per market.

The managers of large-market stations have long complained about secondary (usually smaller and often newer) stations paying less for industry programming, fragmenting their audiences, and competing for their subscriber dollars. In 1989, PBS commissioned a systematic evaluation of the question. Surprisingly, researchers found duplication of programming to be "very low"; in a composite week, an average of 85 percent of all programs were shown on only one station, and even "additional airing of a program brought in almost a totally new audience." Not only did viewers not see program duplication as a problem, they often appreciated the opportunity to see a program on one station that they might have missed on the other. The researchers also found secondary station program schedules to be "more diverse" and secondary station managers "to be more responsive to local audience needs." In fact, they concluded, "secondary stations appear to have remained more faithful to the vision of service to local communities through diverse program offerings [as] advocated by the 1967 Carnegie Commission."

In 1995, still undeterred, a coalition led by the big-city stations proposed reducing PBS member stations to one per market, selling off several, and using the proceeds to support surviving stations. The Corporation for Public Broadcasting's Andy Russell argued that this could save the industry $100 million. The Association of America's Public Television Stations proposed that second stations sell their expected ATV allocations and put their programming on the first station's allocation.

While neither of these plans was enacted, a proposal was passed to effectively reduce the size of the CPB community service grant to the second station in a duopoly (the latter is defined as two stations owned by the same company). The following year, PBS established an overlap market fund to encourage station colaboration. The money actually comes from from the community service grants of the overlapping stations themselves; however, stations may apply for grants from the fund to subsidize talks and collaboration.

In August 1999, Indianapolis station WFYI and Butler University's WTBU announced a joint operating agreement that was facilitated by some $400,000 from the PBS overlap market fund. The agreement consolidates their program selection, fund-raising, and master control functions at the larger entity, WFYI, under a five-year contract.

In June 1999, a bill proposed by House Telecommunications Subcommitee leaders Billy Tauzin (R-LA) and Ed Markey (D-MA) included provisions limiting federal funds to one broadcast license per market and selling or leasing broadcast stations that serve overlapping markets, with the money to be invested in other stations. In November 1998, PBS imposed a one-year moratorium on admission of new members while it studied whether to permanently close or restrict its membership.

Regardless of the hyperbolic claims for the possibilities of multi-stream digital broadcasting, we should not give up any of the frequencies currently reserved for noncommercial public broadcasting. To the extent that duplication of programming is a legitimate concern, a far superior approach, along the lines of the overlap market fund, would be to provide incentives and disincentives for "overlapping" stations to coordinate and differentiate their programming.

Seeking a less draconian solution to the alleged duplication problem, PBS hired commercial broadcasters Hope Green and Derk Zimmerman to draft a centralized plan for overlapped stations. In late May of 1999, after four months of work, Zimmerman unveiled PBS-2, a plan that foresees a three-night-a-week service consisting of programs acquired from such sources as BBC, Buena Vista, Columbia, Tri-Star, Twentieth Century Fox, Warner Brothers, and CBS. These older, cheaper programs can be purchased for $20,000 an hour, on average. They include old episodes of *Sixty Minutes, On the Road with Charles Kuralt,* and CBS war documentaries, along with a series about a "pet emergency room," one about a "daily soap opera inside a police station," and one about "reality in a small English village." The target audience is males from twenty-five to fifty-four years of age, "an audience that has enormous disposable income and [is] highly desired by prestige advertisers."

Bill Moyers commented, "This plan is about business, period. It has nothing to do with mission. . . . This is the lingo of merchandisers and advertisers, not educators or public broadcasters." Moyers proposed that PBS offer instead "programming that is vital to the life of the country and the lives of viewers, not programming whose only aim is to offer people more passive ways to spend their leisure time."

Bill Baker, CEO of WNET New York, looked at the plan and commented, "It has the feeling of public television losing its soul." Then he added, "There's a million ways they can differentiate themselves, all tied to mission." Despite these concerns, Mel Rogers, president of KOCE Los Angeles, opined that either PBS-2 "will happen fairly quickly" or overlapped stations "will create something that will ultimately marry to the PBS-2 concept down the road."

In August 1999, a scandal erupted over PBS stations selling and trading donor lists. At the time, House leaders of both major parties had endorsed a reauthorization bill that would boost CPB's annual appropriation 40 percent, to $475 million in fiscal year 2002, and also provide nearly all of public broadcasting's $770 million request for digital conversion aid. While Virginia Republican Thomas Bliley still deplored the "government handouts," several House members referred to public broadcasting as the "jewel" or "treasure" of the nation. "What a difference a few political seasons make," commented California Democrat Anna Eshoo.

During hearings on this bill, the friendly atmosphere was suddenly exploded by the revelation that WGBH Boston had exchanged the names of several thousand public broadcasting donors for a comparable list of political contributors to Boston-area members of the Democratic National Committee. (Actually, this information had been available months earlier, but Republicans on the committee chose this moment to make of an issue of it.) Predictably, several Republicans reacted by claiming liberal bias, and various House members called for a station sanction, criminal penalties, or reduced funding for the whole system.

An in-depth investigation later found that almost half of all public TV licensees had rented fund-raising lists from political groups. (Interestingly, lists from Republican organizations outnumbered those from Democratic organizations.) However, only 53 of 591 CPB grantees (9 percent) had provided lists to political groups, all of which were Democratic groups. However, Kenneth Konz, CPB inspector general and author of the report, added, "I saw no evidence that Republican organizations had ever *requested* names from stations."

Tauzin spokesman Ken Johnson commented, "To those who argue that less than 10 percent engage in that activity, that's 10 percent too many." Ed Markey's aide, Colin Crowell, reported to me that his boss also was angry over the affair.

While some might consider it an invasion of privacy, the trading of lists has become common practice in the nonprofit world; underfunded and urged to be ever more entrepreneurial, PBS stations had simply followed suit. Nevertheless, a familiar degradation ceremony was reenacted: a Republican congresswoman twice called for giving these stations "a good hard wack," a conservative media critic called for eliminating all federal funding, and CPB issued new rules against trading lists and launched an internal investigation of 575 stations.

Embattled PBS chair Ervin Duggan commented that this was not about politics but reflected "the sometimes frenetic and desperate search for names that sometime represent contributions." He vowed to carry on the fight for federal funding for PBS, even though it represented only 14 percent of PBS's budget and even if it meant "nasty political scrapes."

Many both inside and outside the system have argued that public broadcasters should give up federal funding altogether and replace it with commercial revenue. However, as we have seen, this would only mean trading corporate for government control. In fact, Republican Congressman Steve Largeant has publicly endorsed federal defunding as a strategy to reduce support for public affairs programs such as the gay-sympathetic documentary, *It's Elementary.*

Practically speaking, to make the system more commercial would jeopardize the whole enterprise. A 1995 Lehman Brothers study for the CPB concluded that more advertising would cause subscriber contributions and federal appropriations to decline, resulting in "a net loss" for public television. Leslie Peters of public radio's Audience Research Associates has confirmed that forty-four percent, or nearly half, of public radio's audience is anxious about underwriting. People . . . have told us that, in the future, they may contribute less if there are more underwriting spots from businesses on the air."

While it might work out financially for some stations, a more commercial option would be a disaster for many others. Some state-owned networks prohibit such commercialism by law. Stations in smaller markets have limited commercial opportunities and depend significantly on federal funding. During the 1994 Newt Gingrich–led assault on federal funding for public broadcasting, Duggan speculated that if funding were stopped, as many as eighty-five smaller stations, who rely on CPB for 20 to 40 percent of their budgets, would have to fold.

There is an even greater danger. In 1999, some big-market station leaders proposed that the social contract for PBS be changed from "noncommercial" to "nonprofit." Duggan responded, "All of my instincts tell me that our non-taxable status, our copyright concessions—all of the advantages that we enjoy because we're noncommercial—would be lost, would be taken away, if we went commercial in that way."

In the final analysis, it may be that all this talk about removing federal support for public broadcasting is just a bluff to keep the system's leaders responsive to conservative pressures. In 1995, Speaker of the House Newt Gingrich threatened to "zero out" federal funding for public broadcasting. Nevertheless, he accepted an invitation from Atlanta's WPBA to participate in their pledge drive. Gingrich praised Ken Burns's documentaries and *Sesame Street* and advised viewers, "Tell them Newt Gingrich told you that it's important that PBS stays on the air."

After the flurry of 1995 self-sufficiency proposals had become a memory, Sharon Percy Rockefeller, president of WETA-TV D.C., mused, "It was a good idea that the trust fund got as far as it got; it's got in people's heads. But I don't see much chance that Congress will want to relinquish control of the annual appropriations. Keeping control is safer for them."

Public Television: A Vision for the Future

There is an obvious alternative to the present course as well as to the path to total commercialization, and that is to de-commercialize public broadcasting. The time has come to restructure the public broadcasting service as an independently funded public trust. This would take it off the federal dole, remove corporate advertising, stop the "frenetic and desperate search" for money, and free public broadcasting to pursue its mission without the constant threat of censorship.

"The first step toward defining a truly different community service television," says independent producer Larry Daressa, "must be . . . to stop looking at audiences as 'viewers' or a demographic group and start thinking of them as citizens, parents, workers, with a life beyond television. We need to conceive of them . . . as people intentionally joined together to shape the future: preserving their families, fighting discrimination in city services, caring for the elderly, educating the young."

Daressa calls for a truly social public television that stages "community events," in which "people could congregate via television to explore shared concerns." The Twentieth-Century Fund Task Force has suggested that public broadcasting adopt the model of "an electronic town square" in which stations "take the lead in attempting to solve community problems by putting their resources at the disposal of community groups and agencies that are addressing these problems." In the 1990s, exploiting the flexibility in the system, a group of fifteen big-city stations formed a network within PBS, the Nitty Gritty City Group, to produce and distribute programs about urban problems.

This kind of public television would be diverse, complex, and open-ended, like the democratic process and the publics it creates. At its best, today's public TV is still trapped in the model of "educational" television, which presumes to provide a complete and authoritative statement on a subject. This leads to the ritualistic preoccupation with political "balance" and "objectivity" that often disserves the truth. As Robert Hughes advises, balance should mean "the clash of opinion over a span of time," not "self-canceling programs that won't offend anyone."

All knowledge is grounded in some social location. Facts never speak for themselves—they must be interpreted. This inevitably invokes values. People can be trained to utilize methods to strive for fairness and accuracy, but truly disinterested "objectivity" is never really possible in human affairs, and it cannot be simulated by a pose of noninvolved neutrality. In fact, to address certain issues dispassionately is to devalue them. In the final analysis, we can come closer to the truth if we take into account the interests and values that bias all who participate in any discussion.

Certainly the pretense of a debate format does not always serve the truth. Credible disagreement does not exist about every issue. Two sides are not always equal and often there are more than two points of view. Daressa suggests a deliberate "mix" of "points of view and artistic approaches." He characterizes this as a "prismatic" public television that "would emphasize that what we see is not as important as how we see it" and demonstrate that "we can invent a future different from the past." Such television would conceive of its audience as participants not just consumers, as discrete publics not just part of the mass.

Indeed, PBS has shown that it can build participation into its programming. In December 1995, PBS presented *Leona's Sister Gerry,* a documentary about Gerri Santoro, a young mother whose death from an illegal abortion made her a symbol of the pro-choice movement. It was one of a series of *P.O.V.* broadcasts designed to promote dialogue between "reasonable" people who disagree about abortion. The program featured tags encouraging viewers to share their reactions through e-mail, fax, voice-mail, or video letters. About 85 percent of the more than one thousand responses came through an 800-number voice-mail setup. Calls were sifted for the best material, visuals were created to complement the voice recordings, and within a week a follow-up reaction program was on the air.

This intense effort was rewarded by a very positive response. KCET Los Angeles broadcast director Jackie Cain said, "Every single person involved in it was very touched and moved by this whole thing." Anticipating trouble, KCTS in Seattle hired a security guard; a *Seattle Times* story reported that the guard "would have been of more service had he been handing out Kleenex." James Steinbach, production director for Wisconsin Public Television said, "I was really happy to be involved in it because this is precisely the thing we ought to be in the business of—encouraging this kind of dialogue."

Unfortunately, today's PBS rarely approaches this participatory vision. Programs like the *NewsHour* show public affairs to be the preserve of "experts," not active citizens, who are almost never invited to participate. And "scream TV" programs like the *McLaughlin Group* do not encourage viewers to think that political discussion can lead to understanding, let alone solutions, with regard to the issues at hand. Longtime McLaughlin panelist Jack Germond has said that a show where "people repeatedly interrupt each other, shout for attention, deliver ad hominen attacks on one another and deride the moderator" should not be taken seriously. Another panelist, Eleanor Clift, laments, "You don't have time to express the ifs, ands, or buts." In the analysis of linguist Deborah Tannen, "Viewers conclude that if the two sides are so far apart, the problem can't be solved, so why try?"

As an alternative, Ervin Duggan has suggested that PBS coverage of politics could include "deliberative polls." Instead of taking a snapshot of public opinion, public television could take a "sustained X-ray of a representative sample of Americans as they learn and change their minds." Such presentation would do much to affirm the role of reason in the formation of public opinion.

I am not suggesting that the PBS schedule should be exclusively concerned with public affairs. I would want to see high-quality children's programs offered during daytime hours, and certainly there is still a place for how-to and nature shows.

Personally, I would also welcome more programming on the arts. While middlebrow pledge specials like *Cats, Lord of the Dance,* and *The Three Tenors* apparently draw large audiences, some artistic presentations, I think, should reach beyond mere diversion to raise questions about society and challenge the individual to reflect on his or her own choices in life. I would love to see original drama and comedy on public broadcasting, especially new productions by American playwrights and screenwriters, with American directors and actors. It is not that I am xenophobic about such matters; it is just that I think U.S. public broadcasting has the privilege and responsibility to nurture and exhibit indigenous talent—to make a contribution to the growth of the performing arts in America.

And—most important—we must not forget the mandate to serve the local community. *Harper's Magazine* editor Lewis Lapham, a onetime PBS program host, suggests that PBS "forget about costly entertainment production values" and take a lesson from C-Span on the art of eavesdropping: he would bring PBS cameras into campus debates, state legislatures and city halls, town meetings, university lecture rooms, and plays and poetry readings.

Media scholar Marilyn Lashley suggests that local stations might offer "forums on local issues, showcasing local artists, and other topics unique to the coverage area." The gain in stimulating content would more than compensate for the marginal sacrifice in production values.

Remembering the Mission

As organizational development guru Peter Drucker explains, a nonprofit institution does not measure its performance by financial return; rather it "has to judge itself by performance in creating vision, creating standards, creating values and commitment, and increasing human competence."

The Twentieth-Century Fund Task Force considers the following to be "of much greater importance" than ratings to public television: "filling gaps in overall media coverage, giving prominence to ideas or viewpoints that might not otherwise be seen or heard, providing programs for minorities and minority opinion, encouraging new talent, and courageously taking on controversial issues."

Even PBS's own advice to programmers suggests that in addition to ratings, underwriting, and pledge dollars, program evaluation might recognize an "award," a "positive press review," a "higher than average number of positive calls and letters," "significant outreach and education efforts," and/or "significant local community service."

There was wisdom to defining public broadcasting's mission as a service that "could help us see America whole, in all of its diversity [and] know what it is to be many in one." Media scholar George Gerbner explains that the modern theory of community holds that "competing interests can live more or less side by side, freely pursuing their conflicting interests by virtue of their power to tell stories from their own points of view." In other nations, this concept is institutionalized in public service broadcasting.

Peter Moore, commissioning editor for documentaries for Britain's Channel Four states, "We were expressly ordered by Parliament, if you like, to make programs for gays and for blacks and for communists." The Dutch broadcasting system is open to all significant "voices" in the society; the system's board of governors is chosen from a diverse range of political and social groups, and groups that can demonstrate a sufficient number of members are allowed proportionate access to the system. All significant constituencies of taxpaying U.S. voters deserve to be addressed by and represented on U.S. public broadcasting. Our willingness to provide a forum for voices that challenge the conventional wisdom might be considered a measure of our maturity as a democracy. At the least, hearing others' stories in their own words can broaden our understanding of our common citizenship and humanity.

Overcoming the Obstacles

Despite such wonderful possibilities, there is considerably less government support and protection for public television in the United States than exists anywhere else in the modern world. In other industrialized countries the amount spent on public television far exceeds that spent in the United States. In 1995, the governments of the United Kingdom spent almost $39 per capita, Canada more than $32, and Japan almost $18. In the United States, federal government support barely exceeded $1. Support from all sources in the United States amounted to less than $7 per person.

With such modest funding for production and promotion, public television cannot compete with the $40 billion a year commercial broadcasting industry. On an average evening, barely more than 2 percent of the American television audience is tuned in to public TV, as compared to commercial TV ratings of 13 percent or higher. In contrast, the BBC attracts 44 percent of its country's television audience, PSB Australia 16 percent, and CBC in Canada 14 percent.

Public broadcasting advocates in the United States have long known that the system is fundamentally flawed by its lack of financial independence. For more than thirty years they have sought to establish a mechanism for independent and permanent funding. In 1966 the Ford Foundation proposed financing by an innovative domestic satellite system. This was followed shortly by the Carnegie Commission's proposal for a federal trust fund based on a manufacturer's excise tax on the sale of television sets.

The Communications Act of 1978 proposed that public broadcasting be supported by spectrum fees on commercial broadcasters. The Communications Transfer Act of 1987 called for the creation of a "Public Broadcasting Trust Fund," to be financed by a 2 percent tax on the sale price (to be paid by seller) on the transfer of television and radio licenses. In 1988, the Senate Commerce Committee sought to create a trust fund based on a 2 to 5 percent fee levied on the transfer of all properties licensed by the FCC. Also in 1988, the Working Group for Public Broadcasting advocated a tax of 2 percent on factory sales of consumer electronic products and broadcast equipment. The new revenues were to be used to create a $600 million fund to ensure more diverse high-quality programs on public broadcasting. In 1993, the Twentieth-Century Fund Task Force called for independent funding for public broadcasting based on a share of spectrum auctions or spectrum usage fees.

Through the years, despite congressional sponsors, all such proposals have been defeated by a combination of forces—a powerful National Association of Broadcasters (NAB), timid politicians not willing to confront commercial broadcasters or risk independent voices in the public arena, a divided public broadcasting community, and the narrow base of reform movements.

Predictably, commercial broadcasters vigorously opposed the 1988 Senate proposal. The bill's sponsor, Senator Ernest Hollings, challenged public television officials in the Senate hearing. "Where was their constituency?" he asked. "Why couldn't they fight a corporate lobby with numbers—viewers who would ring their legislators' bells to preserve and defend noncommercial programming?" Patricia Aufderheide reports, "No one answered him. And no one on the panel was there—from organized labor, community groups, supporters of children's television, issue-oriented groups, or the educational community—to say that public television mattered to them one way or the other." Unfortunately, too many public television officials show interest in the public only at pledge time.

In 1994, proposed GATT treaty–related legislation included an annual broadcasters' tax of 1 percent of gross advertising receipts. The NAB defeated it: during the hearings, it argued that many stations were unprofitable, that broadcasters already pay conventional business taxes, and that they "pay" again for the use of the airwaves by providing free programming, including news, weather, and other public service programming.

Chicago Tribune columnist Eric Zorn has observed that an extension of such logic would conclude that government should supply free timber land to newspapers to support their similar services to the public. More importantly, the NAB neglected to mention that from seven to nine minutes of every thirty-minute mainstream news program consists of paid commercial messages. The average profit margin on local TV news is 40 percent. Neither did broadcasters mention that the advertisers' costs for these commercials are passed on to consumers, who pay about $1,000 more per household per year in increased product prices. That's right, *we* pay the advertisers who pay the networks for our allegedly free TV.

Over 1995–96 conservative members of Congress again criticized the system of annual federal appropriations to fund public broadcasting and challenged the industry to produce proposals for "self-sufficiency." One was submitted jointly by the Association of America's Public Television Stations (APTS), PBS, NPR, and Public Radio International (PRI). The CPB submitted another. Congressman Jack Fields, then chair of the House Telecommunications Subcommittee, submitted one of his own.

The joint proposal suggested auctioning off public broadcasting's share of the noncommercial analog spectrum after FCC allocation of the digital spectrum. In March 1996, APTS president David Brugger acknowledged that this "funding mechanism" was proposed because it was the only one "that would sufficiently capitalize the trust fund that does not have the opposition of the commercial media." The proposal also suggested that if commercial spectrum fees and revenue from spectrum sales and auctions were also included, commercial broadcasters should be compensated with relief from children's programming and other public interest obligations, except for equal time for political candidates.

This afterthought brought a sharp rebuke from NAB president Edward Fritts, who stated that the NAB would "vigorously oppose this proposal with every means at our disposal." Added Fritts, "[The] public broadcasting system should be funded through public means, not through taxes on commercial broadcasters and advertising, and if not the entire system should be reevaluated."

The NAB does have a stake in preserving as many noncommercial stations as possible. It makes their commercial licenses more valuable. The NAB also has an interest in seeing that public broadcasting is adequately funded, if only to stop PBS stations from competing with local commercial stations for advertiser revenue. In 1995, John Hendriks, then running both Discovery and the Learning Channel, argued for continued federal aid to public TV, admitting that advertising on PBS would be his "worst nightmare." And in 1997, David Donovan of the Association of Local Television Stations stipulated that before his members agreed to any subsidy, he wanted assurances that public TV would stop actively seeking commercial revenue. If the subsidy were adequate, such a requirement would be reasonable.

Although it has an interest in stopping the commercialization of public broadcasting, the NAB will put up formidable opposition to any effort to improve public broadcasting by taxing the profits of its own members. Such opposition would mean a veritable blackout of the issue on most commercial media. This would still leave hundreds, perhaps thousands of public radio and television stations as a vehicle for the campaign. Unfortunately, we cannot expect a solid front on the part of public broadcasters. Many of them identify with their "commercial brethren." More importantly, there are serious divisions within public broadcasting.

According to a 1996 report from BMR Associates, a firm hired by APTS to help improve public TV's decision-making process, "Stations distrust their national organizations, which earn distrust by fighting among themselves and operating with 'unclear mandates and fuzzy lines of authority.' As a result, public TV is neither a single institution nor a community, but a 'pluralistic society' whose members have different and often conflicting goals."

The CPB and member stations seem always to be in dispute about the size of member dues and amount of PBS common carriage programming member stations are expected to broadcast. As we have seen, there are also conflicts between large-market community-owned stations and small-market and state-owned stations over the increasing commercialization of public broadcasting and the cutting of "overlapped" secondary stations.

The Trust Fund Is on the Table

The most recent bill for permanent, independent funding of public broadcasting was the handiwork of House Telecommunications Subcommittee leaders Billy Tauzin and Ed Markey. Now withdrawn, the bill would have created a nine-member blue-ribbon commission to recommend changes in the "operation, funding, and mission" of public broadcasting. Commission members were to have been appointed by the president and the leadership of both parties.

The legislation called for the commission to consider a wide range of possible reforms, including the creation of a permanent PBS trust fund, abolishing the CPB, and cutting commercial underwriting; funding was to have come from a "fee-for-exception" program, relieving commercial broadcasters of specific public service obligations in exchange for payments into the PBS trust fund.

At about the same time, the Presidential Advisory Committee on Public Interest Obligations for Digital Television issued a final report. Otherwise known as the Gore Commission, its work was launched with a proclamation from the vice president: "We are here today to begin serious study of one of the most important questions of our time: how to ensure that one of our most precious public properties continues to serve the public's needs—a forum not just for entertainment, but for education, enlightenment, and civic debate as well."

While public interest advocates far outnumbered commercial broadcasters, only "broad consensus" recommendations were featured in the report. According to one member, "The [commercial] broadcasters played hardball and threatened to walk out if we voted to recommend, as most of us wanted to, that digital TV be given major and specific public interest obligations."

Nevertheless, the report strongly recommends that Congress should create a trust fund for public television and that, if it does so, public stations should eliminate "enhanced underwriting," which "closely resembles full commercial advertising." While no strategy was recommended for financing the fund, the report does recommend that the broadcast frequencies that public television now uses not be auctioned off for commercial purposes, but be retained for noncommercial educational programming.

Among the options for paying for the channels, the commission does mention spectrum auctions, the fees that the FCC is already empowered to collect from "ancillary and supplemental services" on digital channels, and new proposed fees on digital multicasting.

The Public Broadcasting Trust: A CIPB Proposal

To make the founding mission of public broadcasting a reality would require restructuring the system as an independently funded public trust, comparable to the Red Cross or Little League Baseball. To support innovative, diverse programming for both national and local audiences, an independent public broadcasting service would require at least $1 billion in insulated annual program funds, in addition to current levels of operational support from state governments, individual subscribers, and foundations.

Such a trust would liberate public broadcasting from dependence on congressional appropriations and corporate program underwriting and their accompanying censorship and commercial pressures. In fact, corporate donations should be restricted to general system support and given brief and dignified acknowledgements on a randomly rotating basis. This is the way it always has been done with respect to support for community arts groups. When a corporation gives to a symphony orchestra or an opera company it does not tell the conductor what to play or the diva what to sing.

The newly established Public Broadcasting Trust (PBT) would replace the politicized Corporation for Public Broadcasting, and it would also take over the satellite distribution systems now administered by PBS and NPR. In contrast to that of the CPB, the PBT's board of trustees would be insulated from direct political pressure.

Following the recommendations of the 1988 Working Group for Public Broadcasting, headed by John Wicklein, the PBT would have nine members, with appointments made by representatives of the public broadcasting community (three), educational community (three), and President's Commission on the Arts and Humanities (two). The PBT's managing director would be the ninth member of the board, selected by the original eight. All members would serve staggered six-year terms. Participants in the nominating process would include representatives of public television and radio stations, independent producers, and associations for school administrators, teachers, academics, librarians, and school boards.

One-half of the PBT's funds would go into commissioning, producing, and distributing programs as part of a national service to local stations. The national television service's share would be administered through a television program department, itself divided into a division of news and public affairs and a division of cultural and educational programming.

This programming, with funds for promotion, would be offered to local public stations free of charge. Thus the program department would provide for a daily in-depth news program, documentaries, specials, and coverage of special events as well as arts, entertainment, dramatic, and children's programming. Aided by proper oversight, this structure should ensure that public affairs programs are scheduled in prime time on a regular basis.

Within the program department, there would be a national independent program laboratory, with a director and its own advisory board. This laboratory would support independent productions for consideration by both local stations and the national service.

The other half of the PBT's funds would be passed through to local television and radio stations to produce and acquire programs of interest to their specific communities. Since local program production is disproportionately costly, this part of the fund would support productions that few stations now undertake for their communities. (In fact, over the past twenty years, the percentage of stations' broadcast hours produced locally has declined from 11.4 percent to 4.6 percent. Only 17 out of 349 stations nationwide offer a local news program every night.)

In addition, there would be a radio department to distribute funds to national programming services, like NPR and PRI, as well as independent producers. The radio department could commission new programs as well as support existing ones, all of which would be offered to local stations via satellite. The radio department would also make grants to local radio stations to produce national programs and program segments. These would be offered to local stations for their own choosing.

Funding Options

Even though the vast majority of the American public continues to support federal funding for public broadcasting, a vocal minority still clamors for its elimination, claiming that people should not be taxed to support programs they don't approve of or watch.

This proposition takes libertarianism to the extreme of misanthropy. Fortunately, taxpayers do not have a line-item veto, nor does the government guarantee satisfaction or your money back. The unexamined premise of the extreme libertarian position is that we are not a community, only a marketplace of individual contractors. To extend this logic, people without children should not be taxed for schools, people who don't like football should not be taxed for stadium construction, and so on and on. Curiously, these critics rarely complain about corporate welfare, like subsidizing McDonald's to sell hamburgers in Europe. They also fail to acknowledge that the government heavily subsidizes commercial broadcasting through protecting their channel assignments and allowing them tax deductions; in fact the authority of the taxpayer-subsidized FCC is what makes it possible for broadcasters to monopolize frequencies in order to make their huge profits.

The question to ask is what do we require as a democratic society in order to prosper? The answer to that question is that we cannot afford not to have a well-funded and robust public broadcasting service. Moreover, in these days of a $1 trillion federal surplus (not to mention a $2 trillion Social Security surplus), there is no good reason why the federal government should not put 2 percent of the surplus ($20 billion) into a trust fund (at 5 percent interest) to provide at least $1 billion in annual revenue for public broadcasting in perpetuity. This would still amount to much less than the level of support it enjoys in other democracies around the world.

Many argue that commercial broadcasters must also pay their fare share. Former PBS and NBC News president Lawrence Grossman has commented, "Broadcasting is the only industry in America where you can make money off a public resource and not pay a thing for it. If you drill for oil on a public land, you pay a fee. If your cattle graze on a public land, you pay a fee." Extending this last comparison, former FCC chair Reed Hundt has referred to the new digital spectrum being given free to broadcasters by the federal government as "beachfront property on the Cyber Sea."

Any proposal for funding a public broadcasting trust must respect the following criteria: Is it fair? Is it sufficient? Is it reliable? Our group, Citizens for Independent Public Broadcasting, generally favors proposals that tax corporate profits rather than citizens and consumers for public broadcasting services; however, it should be understood that we would not approve of a quid pro quo in which commercial broadcasters were relieved of all their public interest obligations in exchange for such payments. That is a totally separate question and must be examined on its own merits.

A December 1998 poll by Lake, Snell, Perry, and Associates found that only 19 percent of the public knew that broadcasters pay no fee to use the public's airwaves. Once advised of this fact, almost two-thirds of those with an opinion favored charging broadcasters for any additional airwaves, including airwaves for digital TV. This poll also found an overwhelming 79 percent of the American public favoring a proposal to require commercial broadcasters to pay 5 percent of their revenues into a fund to support public broadcasting programming.

Over the past several years, the FCC has conducted fourteen spectrum auctions, raising more than $23 billion for the federal treasury. The value of remaining unsold channels is estimated at between $70 billion and $100 billion. If placed in appropriate interest-bearing instruments, $20 billion in spectrum auction proceeds (20 to 30 percent of the total) would provide $1 billion in annual trust revenue.

Others have proposed a tax on the sale or transfer of commercial broadcast licenses. A 5 percent tax (to be paid by the seller) on the sales of television and radio licenses transferred in 1997 would have generated the billion dollars needed. Such a method of financing public broadcasting would be fair and sufficient. The major problem with this mechanism is that since station sales fluctuate in response to economic conditions, the flow of money would be less reliable than that from certain other sources.

Advertising in the United States is a $200 billion a year business. In 1997 advertisers spent almost $50 billion just on television and radio. Since broadcasters and corporations realize huge profits from using the public's airwaves, it would be fair to expect them to help support a public, noncommercial system. A 2 percent tax on broadcast advertising would generate $1 billion for a public broadcasting trust fund. This amount would likely grow by at least 5 percent annually.

An annual spectrum fee on the revenues of commercial broadcasters may be the one device that is most fair, sufficient, and reliable. In 1993, the Twentieth-Century Fund Task Force estimated that a 2 percent spectrum fee would produce $1 billion in annual revenue. Given the profit potential of digital broadcasting, such revenues could be expected to increase with time.

Underwriting Reform

Permanent independent funding is a necessary condition for reforming the system, but it is not sufficient. In the present context, such funding would simply be regarded as more discretionary money for the system's managers. Funding would have to be part of a larger reform effort designed to reduce control by public broadcasting's other money masters—corporations, state politicians, and wealthy contributors.

Clearly, a major target of any reform must be the hypocritical underwriting guidelines that turn a blind eye to the self-interest of profit-seeking corporations and conservative foundations, but shut out public interest membership groups with an educational message.

In the wake of PBS's withdrawal of support for *Out at Work*, writer James Ledbetter asked PBS official Barry Chase if this meant that a labor union could never fund any program on public television that had to do with issues of the workplace. Chase replied, "Yes, that's exactly what I'm saying." This represents an abandonment of mission. The role of public television is not to simply reflect the power structure, but to reflect on it.

For too many years, PBS has been failing the underwriting "perception test" miserably with a "significant number" of "reasonable" people. There are only two ethically consistent alternatives to this dilemma. One alternative, in the words of TV critic Marc Gunther, is to "accept the reality that all donors have an interest in what they finance and open the door to unlimited giving from business, labor and public interest groups."

The first advantage of a new openness, Gunther points out, would be that "more programs would be made." Moreover, PBS still would have the opportunity and responsibility "to make its own journalistic and programming decisions about what to air," and it could protect fairness, accuracy, and truth through various kinds of editorial procedures (including peer review) involving knowledgeable judges considering the merits of each case. Such a process would not discriminate against a submission merely because the work was partly funded by a public interest group with a point of view on the subject. This would enable such work to be done in the first place, and it would do away with the hypocritical pretense that corporations and right-wing foundations do not have their own quite explicit political agendas.

In our view, the disadvantage of this alternative would be that it would do nothing to address the problem of programs being driven by funding rather than mission. Moreover, since the resources of labor unions and public interest groups are miniscule when compared to those of the corporations and their foundations, the imbalance in perspectives would still be heavily biased toward establishment views.

Our alternative would be to ban outside underwriting for programs altogether, at least for public affairs programs. Instead, we could solve the problem through an adequately funded trust. Stations and independent producers would all have access to funds for national and local productions. Such funds would be provided through a system of grant review designed to ensure both fair distribution and quality.

State-Level Censorship

Under the proposed plan, public broadcasters would still depend on state governments for operational support. In fact, many stations are state-owned, and it must be acknowledged that state politicians have also exploited the power of the purse to censor public broadcasting. Fortunately, the general public has usually been way ahead of them.

The Watergate hearings did much to restore public broadcasting's image for editorial independence at the time; however, a bare majority of PBS stations approved of the decision to broadcast the hearings and nearly a third did not carry them. *Steambath*, the black comedy that garnered an 8.5 rating in Los Angeles in 1973 and has since become a benchmark of daring programming, was originally carried by only about two dozen PBS stations.

A Recent Case in Point

In 1994, PBS's *American Playhouse* presented *Tales of the City* by Armistead Maupin. Broadcast in January over three consecutive nights, the six-hour drama looked at San Francisco culture in the 1970s, featuring both straight and gay characters. *Tales of the City* was widely praised by critics, but scenes of two men kissing and fondling each other in bed provoked bombastic denouncements from conservative politicians in Georgia, Oklahoma, South Carolina, and Tennessee.

In Georgia, Republican candidate for governor John Knox held a press conference calling on Georgia Public Television (GPTV) to "stop running X-rated movies" and cancel *Tales of the City*, and state representative Charlie Watts threatened to oppose GPTV's $19.6 million budget request for a new Decatur production facility if they did not do so. Republican Congressman Grover Campbell vehemently rebuked Oklahoma's ETV for showing "obscene" material and warned of retaliatory legislation that would restrict the state's network programming, cut its state funding in half, and transfer its authority to the State Department of Education. South Carolina ETV banned the show on the grounds that it had been given only three days to preview it and needed a month; vice president for communications Kathy Gardner-Jones said they wanted to screen the program first because "we are in a very conservative state." In Tennessee, the *Chattanooga Times* ran an inflammatory article headlined "Nudity and Profanity Will Be Viewed on TV 45." WTCI's vice president, Kelley Wilde, said the station had gotten "hundreds of negative phone calls," including a bomb threat. The board's executive committee screened the offending portion of the series and decided to pull the program one hour before it was set to air.

In most cases, the pressure to censor *Tales of the City* was later shown to reflect only a small, vocal minority. In Georgia, the series attracted a "well above average" 2.8 rating/7.0 share. Letters supporting the decision to broadcast the program ran three to one in favor, and more than seven hundred phone calls ran five to one in favor. In addition, the Atlanta *Journal-*

Constitution ran a strong editorial blasting opponents for their ignorance and hypocrisy. In Oklahoma, the station received about eight hundred calls, "mostly favorable," toward the decision to air the program. Arkansas's ETV received more than eight hundred calls, with 80 percent supporting the decision to broadcast the program. In fact, many viewers were surprised to find that the second two evenings had been "edited" and called in to protest. In Chattanooga, some contributors vowed to pull funding in protest of the censorship.

Overall, *Tales of the City* was a huge success. Viewership in Nielson's twenty-five metered markets averaged a 4.3 rating and a 7 share, about twice the PBS prime-time average. Five major market stations on both coasts got average ratings of 5 to 6. In San Francisco itself, the series had a 14 rating and a 21 share. It went on to receive several Emmy Award nominations.

Given this, many people felt profoundly betrayed when PBS announced it would not fund the sequel to *Tales of the City*. Questioned by the press, Ervin Duggan claimed that the show's British coproducers had asked PBS to pay ten times more for a second series than it had paid for the original. *Post-Gazette* TV critic Robert Bianco reports that Duggan was then asked "whether that argument wasn't disingenuous, as PBS admittedly paid close to nothing for the original. Duggan said [that] they like shows that cost nothing."

At the time, Duggan refused to say whether he personally liked the show. His evasions left little doubt that he had bowed to conservative pressure, a conclusion reinforced by his *ad homonym* accusation: "The people who are clamoring 'censorship' and 'banning' are disgruntled authors and directors." *Tales of the City* was subsequently booked on Showtime, another contribution to the potentially self-fulfilling prophecy that cable makes public television redundant.

Who Shall Set the Standards?

This episode and others described in previous chapters make it clear that ways must be found to protect public service broadcasting from censorship by hostile politicians at the state and local levels. When his film *Tongues Untied* was banned from more than two-thirds of PBS stations, filmmaker Marlon Riggs responded, "Whose community? When they say community standards won't abide by such work, they're reflecting their myth of what that community is about and not the tremendously diverse community as it exists." Certainly, the local culture in Atlanta or New Orleans is significantly different than that in rural Georgia or Louisiana, but as we have seen, the good news is that citizens can and do challenge prevailing myths regarding "what the community is about" by communicating their support for independent programming and their opposition to censorship to their station managers and public officials. To the extent that such support is organized, it will be even more effective.

Promoting Community Participation

Unfortunately, many stations have done little to involve the local community. Near the end of the 1970s, public television veteran Jack Willis remarked, "Today what we have is a series of stations that, with few exceptions, are nothing more than minor bureaucracies who represent only a small part of the public, who have very high overhead, who do not see their job as producing programs, nor fostering talent, nor representing the diversity in our society."

Toward the end of the 1990s, *Harper's* editor and former PBS producer Lewis Lapham characterized the PBS system as "the Holy Roman Empire during the last days of its decaying hegemony—351 petty states and dukedoms, each with its own flag, court chamberlain and trumpet fanfare."

The culture that governs the system has been years in the making, and without structural intervention it will persist. New measures are needed to ensure that local stations' boards of directors are truly diverse, have a clear sense of mission, and recruit and reward station managers for measurable public service rather than profit-making ventures.

To ensure minimal accountability, there would have to be some mechanism to require stations to observe existing FCC rules and regulations. This would include posting board and committee meetings widely and making them open to the public. This would also include providing members of the public with easy access to complete public inspection files, including financial reports and correspondence with viewers and listeners. In addition, a properly functioning Public Broadcasting Trust would supervise random accountability audits. There would be procedures to identify noncompliance and facilitate compliance on threat of loss of funding.

Beyond that, the question of how to make station governance and programming responsive to the community is complex. Managers are afraid, often with reason, of boards that infringe on their professionalism and try to "micro-manage" affairs. At the same time, few board members have sufficient commitment, knowledge, or resources to provide proper oversight of management.

Some feel that subscriber election of board members would, at the least, empower them to monitor management in the name of their constituencies. Of course, election procedures would have to be as fair and open as possible. Candidates should be adequately presented through station media so that voters can make informed choices. Since many stations have magazines and all have regular mailings, balloting subscribers would be relatively cheap and easy.

Board nominating and election procedures can and should be designed to ensure diversity by race, gender, age, and community affiliation. Diversity should also be served by assigning seats for different constituencies—banking and business, education, government, health and sciences, organized labor, public interest, and so on. A diverse board would make policy discussions broader and more inclusive, better survey the interests of public constituencies, and provide easier access for station promotion efforts. Such diversity should not be difficult to achieve in a board of twenty to thirty persons.

Another way to ensure true responsiveness to the community would be to empower community advisory boards to actually perform their designated function. Advisory board members should have routine access to active program proposals, ongoing production schedules, and alternative program sources. They should also be engaged in active outreach to the community to solicit evaluations and assess needs. All of this would be guided by a program policy developed by the station's board of directors. And of course all of this would be subject to final approval by professional management and staff. Finally, the PBT would provide financial incentives for local program development.

To foster an open public sphere, public broadcasting must provide a forum for the diverse publics that form around different issues. We recognize that in different communities, on different issues, this would encompass a broad range of groups typically excluded from public affairs broadcasting as being too extreme. However, citizenship is meaningless if you have a right to speak but not the right to be heard. What might emerge from inclusive discussions of the public interest by active citizens has to be more interesting than the plodding fare of the *NewsHour* or the bombastic punditry of the *McLaughlin Group*. And it would be more democratic.

Finally, the proposed Public Broadcasting Trust would be accountable to the federal government. The General Accounting Office would conduct a biennial financial audit to ensure fiscal responsibility. Every ten years there would be an investigation, hearings, and a report, with suggested legislative changes, prior to renewal of the mandate. Both an ongoing presidential commission and Congress would be involved in the process.

Activism Works

It is clear that to create the public sphere that would enable real publics to emerge, we ourselves must first become a public for public broadcasting. Those of us who understand the significance of the struggle and are alert to the weapons that might be used need to take the initiative and set the example. By accepting this challenge, we will be joining a well-established tradition in communications history.

In past years commercial television has been a battleground between network executives and various constituencies over programming. Groups representing racial and ethnic minorities, gays and lesbians, women, conservative Christians, antiviolence advocates, family planning advocates, and others have brought pressure to bear on the commercial networks and their affiliates. Such groups have used a wide range of tactics—threats of sponsor boycotts, pressure on network affiliates, national letter-writing campaigns, press conferences and staged events, petitions to Congress, lawsuits, FCC complaints, and lobbying of the television industry. To be sure, some of these have been censorship campaigns. Even there, however, sometimes the target has been graphic and gratuitous violence or racial and ethnic stereotypes in the media. Other campaigns have promoted a more in-depth examination of complex social issues like homosexuality, abortion, and euthanasia.

These days more than 150 organizations actively lobby television producers with ideas for stories, characters, or props designed to communicate their message to TV viewers. Nearly one-fourth of all American teens, for example, have indicated that they learned about birth control from TV and the movies. To cite another, the 1988 "designated driver" campaign was the brainchild of a Harvard professor and was inserted into the story lines of 160 prime-time shows. Surveys indicate that only one year later, two-thirds of U.S. adults had gotten the message and more than half of those under thirty had in fact served as designated drivers on occasion.

In 1999, a large coalition of minority civil rights groups organized to protest the lack of ethnic diversity on the major networks' fall prime-time lineups. The share of black characters on all entertainment series for the four leading networks had declined from 17 percent to 10 percent over the period from 1992–93 to 1998–99. Of the twenty-six new comedies and dramas premiering in fall 1999, not one featured a member of a minority in a leading role. The National Latino Media Council launched a fall "brownout" of ABC, NBC, CBS, and Fox. The NAACP and several Asian-American groups joined in the protests.

Suddenly the networks were seized with an urgent need to add minority characters. *Family Law, 7th Heaven, Safe Harbor, E.R., Judging Amy, Suddenly Susan, Dawson's Creek,* and the pilot for *Wasteland* all added black, Latino, or Asian characters. CBS announced a new series about several generations of a Mexican-American family living in New York; ABC ordered the development of a one-hour series based on the exploits of a black detective.

Citizen action made a difference in public television as well. For example, during the Nixon assault on public broadcasting, the proposed cancellation of *Washington Week in Review* provoked 15,000 complaints, which resulted in the reinstatement of the program. When funds were cut for *Tony Brown's Journal,* a hundred black viewers picketed outside a CPB board meeting and funding was restored.

Past efforts to establish a trust fund for public broadcasting did not achieve their primary goal, but they did lead to significant reforms. Over 1977–78, the National Task Force for Public Broadcasting, led by DeeDee Halleck and Larry Hall, helped to craft legislation that opened up community advisory boards, increased opportunities for minorities and women, provided more support for independent producers, and increased access to PBS's satellite system for national distribution. This initiative was supported by a broad coalition of national organizations, including the AFL-CIO's executive committee, the American Federation of Television and Radio Artists (AFTRA), the Consumers Federation of America, the National Citizens Communications Lobby, the National Black Media Coalition, and the National Organization for Women, among others.

The Independent Television Service

In 1987, members of the Association of Independent Video and Filmmakers presented testimony to Congress that independent producers faced an increasingly "closed system" in gaining access to PBS. At the same time, more stations were broadcasting commercial network reruns like *Lassie, Ozzie and Harriet,* and *Star Trek.*

In response, Congress directed the CPB to establish "an independent production service" by 1989. This became the Independent Television Service (ITVS), funded by a "set-aside" from CPB and charged to "provide increased access to the public broadcasting system for independent producers and promote greater innovation and diversity . . . in the programming supported by the CPB and made available to the public." Particular emphasis was placed on "programs by and about minorities" and "programming addressing the lives and concerns of the American worker." The CPB's Multiracial Programming Fund became a statutory requirement.

Over the years, conservative lawmakers and the CPB itself have tried to kill off or hold up ITVS funding, but it has always survived. By 1997, the ITVS subsidy had grown from about $6 million to $7.6 million and the organization had funded more than two hundred projects. Unfortunately, PBS has felt no obligation to broadcast the programs; former PBS vice president of programming Kathy Quattrone said she regarded ITVS as just one of several competing suppliers from which she hoped she could "pull the best for the national schedule."

Despite occasional showings of ITVS productions, in 1997 its director, Jim Yee, conceded, "The PBS schedule has not really changed in the last several years. There is very little room for original programming. We need to find other models." Lately Yee has signed deals for cable distribution in an effort to provide more airtime for ITVS productions. One new sponsor is the Sundance cable channel for independent films.

Yee remains hopeful. He says it took only about two hundred hardworking people and good timing to get Congress to create ITVS. While it will take a more sustained effort to make it work, we are starting with a legislative mandate and congressional appropriation thanks to activism in the past.

Micro Broadcasting or Pirate Radio?

The broadcasting battlefront has even extended to the homes, basements, and garages of neighborhood activists operating unlicensed "micro radio" stations. These "radio pirates" use shoebox-sized FM transmitters to broadcast on unused frequencies over areas that extend for a few square blocks or several square miles. (The typical major radio station broadcasts at about 50,000 watts, allowing a much larger range.) These low-watt stations are illegal because the FCC stopped issuing licenses to stations under 100 watts nearly twenty years ago, although it does allow exceptions for a large number of low-power travelers' advisory broadcasts.

As far back as 1989, activists began to defy the FCC ban with low-watt citizen radio. Springfield, Illinois saw the first confrontation, when Mbanna Kantako broadcast a daily show, *Black Liberation Radio,* to members of his housing complex. Served notice by the FCC to cease broadcasting immediately and fined $6,000, Kantako refused to pay the fine and continued to operate.

Stephen Dunifer started Free Radio Berkeley out of his home in 1993. By 1996, Dunifer and about ninety-five volunteers were running the station on 50 watts of power out of a commercial office building near the Berkeley-Oakland border. Everyone pitched in $10 a month to help cover the rent and operating costs. The station offered a twenty-four-hour schedule of clearly alternative programs. There were music shows, from "punk" to "Latin and Irish folk" to "hardcore blues and rap," and spiritual shows, and programs featuring alternative politics from labor activism to anarchism.

Dunifer became the Johnny Appleseed of micro broadcasting. His International Radio Action Training Education project (IRATE) supplied equipment and trained operators in cities across the country. By mid-1998, Dunifer estimated that he had built and distributed between three hundred and four hundred low-power transmitters. Dunifer called it "an all-out, no-holds-barred movement of electronic civil disobedience."

Under pressure from the NAB, the FCC fined Dunifer $20,000. In response, Dunifer compared the "overlapping control of the FCC and the NAB" to that of "the Pentagon and the defense industry." He stated simply, "If people can't communicate, they can't organize. And if they can't organize, they can't fight back." Since start-up costs under the current regulatory structure run $100,000 or more, the poor are left out of public interest broadcasting, whereas with micropower broadcasting a community FM station can be put on the air for $1,000 or less.

Dunifer challenged the law in court. His attorney, Peter Franck from the National Lawyer's Guild, said the "real pirates of the airwaves" are the "billionaire commercial interests that control the airwaves as if they own them." In an era when even "public broadcasting is told to get its money from corporations," Franck argued, "micro radio may be our last best hope for democracy on the airways."

Throughout 1997, the FCC staged armed raids on micro broadcasters, making arrests, seizing equipment, and imposing fines. By the end of the year, the FCC crackdown had led to the closure of about 250 stations. Nevertheless, by 1998 the FCC estimated there were between 300 and 1,000 unlicensed stations still operating across the country, and these broadcasters had organized in mutual support. Between 1993 and 1998 there were five conferences, each larger than the last. At a 1998 conference in Las Vegas, the micro radio community called on the NAB to support their proposal for a low-power radio FCC rule-making that would democratize the airwaves.

The NAB is opposed to any such reform on the grounds that it would cause interference with the larger stations. National Public Radio has joined this position. However, research in Canada has documented hundreds of lower-power stations operating without causing problems even in the most densely populated areas.

Despite his concern for maintaining control of the allocation process, FCC Commissioner William Kennard was moved by these acts of civil disobedience. In 1998, he proposed squeezing new stations operating at between 100 watts and 1,000 watts onto the dial where interference standards permit. The FCC sought comments about whether it could loosen interference standards for low-power stations and about the merit of creating licenses for stations using 1 to 100 watts of power. (Signals from a 10-watt station can reach about two miles, a 100-watt station about four miles). On January 20, 2000, the FCC approved low-power FM.

Troubled Waters at Pacifica

Founded in 1949 by pacifist Lewis Hill, Pacifica Radio owns and operates stations in Berkeley, Houston, Los Angeles, New York, and Washington, D.C. It also distributes programming to about seventy stations via Pacifica's own satellite. Over the years, Pacifica programs have actively promoted civil rights, civil liberties, and global peace initiatives. Accordingly, powerful conservative forces from the McCarthy era to the present have tried to drive it from the air.

While Pacifica's strong community base enabled it to survive such frontal assaults, a backdoor strategy engineered by Congress and the CPB has thrown the network into turmoil. In 1998, the CPB made federal funding for public radio contingent on a minimum audience size or level of fund-raising. Moreover, no credit was given for the value of volunteer labor. In response, Pacifica's Mark Schubb complained that the resources needed for long-term growth were being exhausted in meeting these legislated goals, and he questioned the continued pressure for higher ratings: "To me, the diversity of public radio is one of its strongest points. We need more stations not less."

In 1999, the situation changed dramatically. The CPB insisted that Pacifica centralize decision making or lose its funding. At a meeting in February, the national board's composition was changed from ten appointees of local advisory boards and six at-large members to sixteen at-large members, all nominated by the board's governance and structure committee. Except for one hour allowed for public comment, the national board then closed its meetings. Important deliberations were subsequently carried on in executive session.

Citing stale programming and the need to expand the network's audience, the new board began to dismiss old-time program hosts. Many listeners and volunteers complained about the perceived abandonment of Pacifica's mission to more "yuppie" shows on personal investing, cooking, health, and spirituality.

In March, the Pacifica Foundation's executive director, Lynn Chadwick, declined to renew the contract of KPFA Berkeley station manager Nicole Sawaya on the grounds that she wasn't "a team player." Sawaya had questioned the increasing share of KPFA's budget that was going to subsidize the national board. She had also brought home a pledge drive $40,000 above its goal and was a popular leader with workers at the station.

In April, longtime programmer Larry Bensky used his show to protest the board's action and was dismissed. A network-wide gag rule was implemented. Six staff members were disciplined for reading a statement on the air opposing Pacifica's dismissal of Sawaya. Listeners issued thousands of calls, letters, and e-mails to protest the termination of her contract. In June, activists who staged a sit-in at Pacifica's offices were arrested and charged with trespassing.

In July, Pacifica veteran Dennis Bernstein was physically removed by guards in the middle of a broadcast. Some four hundred listeners and programmers hurried to the station and staged a peaceful sit-in. Management called the police, and fifty-three people were arrested. Programs like *Counterspin* and *Democracy Now!* were pulled for violating the gag rule. A July 19 concert "to take back KPFA," featuring Joan Baez and others, drew thirty-five hundred supporters. Protests by organized labor and other groups followed.

The battle over Pacifica now raged in every progressive journal and wherever media activists gathered. In the midst of this, an errant e-mail message revealed board plans to sell Pacifica's New York Station WBAI, valued at up to $100 million. The board denied such intentions, but it no longer had any credibility.

On the last day of July, some ten to fifteen thousand people rallied in

Berkeley in support of KPFA and its employees. Progressive leaders, including San Francisco's mayor, Willie Brown, called for Pacifica board chair Mary Frances Berry to resign. Seventeen California legislators proposed auditing Pacifica's tax-exempt status. A lawsuit was filed.

On August 5, the Pacifica board lifted the lockout and the gag order and invited all the programmers they had dismissed back to resume their broadcasts. The board now disclaimed any plans to sell off WBAI or any other station in the network.

Future decisions about Pacifica management or programming remain unresolved. The CPB directive that pressured stations into sacrificing autonomy and localism to professionalism and ratings remains in place. However, as we have seen, community action gets results. As this and the following cases make clear, boards and management will find selling off a station or even changing its mission to be very difficult if the station's community of listeners make their collective will known and are persistent.

Other Community Actions

Because of rising prices, some noncommercial licensees that operate on commercial frequencies have put their licenses up for sale. Washington, D.C., lost WDUC-FM, their jazz radio station, and New York City lost WNYC-TV, with its many programs for ethnic minorities. Other licenses going to market include Oklahoma City, Albany/Schenectady, and Buffalo.

But even these changes have been stopped or modified by community opposition. In the 1995 case of WNYC, its owner, New York City, received FCC permission to sell the station to ITT and Dow Jones for $207 million. WNYC had been providing programming for eighteen different ethnic and community groups. The city was also considering options for its two public radio stations, which had a combined estimated value of $40 million to $50 million. The Coalition of Ethnic Broadcasters petitioned the FCC to stop the sale of WNYC. While this petition failed, the strength of the community support it had received persuaded the city to transfer the licenses of its two public radio stations at a bargain price to the foundation that already covered most of their costs.

In 1997, the University of the District of Columbia (UDC) put WDUC-FM up for sale to close out a $10 million deficit. UDC accepted a bid of $13 million from Salem Communications, one of the nation's biggest religious radio chains. The citizen's group Save Jazz 99 secured representation by the

Media Access Project and prepared to file an FCC challenge, questioning the nonprofit credentials of the corporation Salem had set up to purchase the station. NPR considered filing its own challenge and CPB demanded that WDUC's licensee return the $1 million in grants it had awarded the station since 1991. The issue was publicly debated and covered by local and national media. Eventually, C-SPAN, a nonprofit owned by the consortium of cable TV systems, stepped forward and assumed Salem's bid for the station. While it looked like the end of jazz on WDUC, the new radio service promised no underwriting, no ratings services, and a full schedule of public service programming.

Finally, in 1999 our attorney from the first round of the Save Pittsburgh Public Television campaign, David Honig, called to ask my help in finding plaintiffs in Buffalo to challenge WBED's plan to sell off second station WNEQ to the Sinclair Broadcasting Group. I phoned several organizations and eventually found the right contact through the Institute for Alternative Journalism (IAJ). I was proud to see our successful opposition to WQED's 1996 dereservation petition cited as a precedent.

An Outline for a New Campaign

As established, any attempt to restructure public broadcasting will have to overcome opposition by forces within the public broadcasting establishment, the commercial broadcasting lobby, and Congress. The only force with such potential is the people themselves.

Our challenge is to put independent public broadcasting on the action agenda of public interest groups across the country: labor, environmental, consumer, and human rights groups generally. Public interest groups must recognize the great potential and responsibility of public television and radio to amplify their educational outreach, starting with more programs that address social problems and feature the voices of public interest advocates. In addition, local stations can run public service announcements for community meetings and events.

Currently, Citizens for Independent Public Broadcasting (CIPB) is forging partnerships with a broad range of national public interest and educational organizations. These groups consult to us on educational films and program series that deserve to be broadcast on public television and radio. Such recommended programs (annotated and with awards and contact information) are one of the many items on our web site (www.cipbonline.org).

Through these national offices, we are recruiting local members to participate in the building of community chapters of Citizens for Independent Public Broadcasting. Such chapters are working to reform local stations while pressing for the national legislation that would transform the system.

CIPB has produced an instructional video and training manual to advise members who wish to improve their local public broadcasting service. For example, most people do not realize that public broadcasting is a membership organization, not an affiliated network. The requirements for common carriage of the national program service are only seven hours a week, no more than two hours a day. In fact, a station can use the PBS name and logo by subscribing to as little as 10 percent of the national program service.

In addition, stations get substantial community service grants from the Corporation for Public Broadcasting to produce and/or acquire supplementary programming. This means that local program directors and station managers largely determine the content of public broadcasting in any community. Since their legislative mandate is to serve the full diversity of their local communities, concerned citizens have a right to approach stations officials to nominate programs and volunteer for service on their boards of directors and/or community advisory boards.

The specific advantage of this grassroots strategy is that many small battles can be won while the war for a reformed system is being waged. As citizens become empowered and begin to recognize the larger system's problems and possibilities, we can build a national grassroots movement to reform public broadcasting into an independent and publicly accountable trust, free of undue government and corporate influence.

Such a campaign must also include the many institutions concerned with public education and culture: libraries, schools, museums, and relevant professional associations. These institutions are the cornerstones of modern civilization and have also been subject to gratuitous criticism and reckless budget cutting. Their leaders understand the vital role that public broadcasting could and must play in advancing the arts as well as a healthy democratic society.

Along with this national grassroots base, we must create an active network of allies within the public broadcasting industry. Happily, there still are people in the system trying to keep the original spirit of public broadcasting alive despite the pressures that threaten it. In September 1995, eighty-five top station executives signed a letter to Congressman Jack Fields opposing advertising as "antithetical to our guiding principles" and "economically unsound." In April 1997, fourteen state networks and twenty-four other public TV licensees signed a pledge to reject thirty-second underwriting "spots," and a 1999 poll has found that half of all PBS stations are opposed to such spots.

The Media and Democracy Congresses

In recent years, the Institute for Alternative Journalism has organized conferences that have revealed the growing strength of the many movements for media democracy. In March 1996, the IAJ attracted more than seven hundred journalists, media makers, and activists representing more than three hundred organizations to San Francisco to participate in the first Media and Democracy Congress. The event was cosponsored by more than thirty organizations spanning thirty-two states, and included three full days of workshop presentations, followed by a business meeting to launch projects and plan for the future.

The congress's attendees endorsed an "Information Bill of Rights," which begins with a preamble criticizing the increasing concentration of communications resources, the erosion of regulatory policies to protect the public interest, and the decline of mass participation and calls for "a more just, equitable, participatory, and accountable media system." The IAJ worked hard in the aftermath of this first event to facilitate networking among the participants, establishing a directory and an Internet listerv.

In October 1997, an even larger Media and Democracy Congress was held in New York City. More than 1,200 people attended, traveling from thirty-eight states and seven countries. Thanks to the efforts of the organizers, the second gathering was even more diverse than the first had been. Women constituted 50 percent of the attendees and 40 percent of the speakers, people of color 20 percent of the attendees and 30 percent of the speakers, and there were 150 college and high school students in attendance.

All sessions are available on audiotape and some on video. An important source book, *We the Media*, has since been published. A "Pledge of Journalistic Integrity" was prepared for media owners, demanding a public commitment to not interfere, or let their advertisers interfere, with reporters and correspondents following stories wherever they lead. Former CBS news anchor Walter Cronkite signed the letter and hundreds of other signatures are being solicited.

The second congress featured an "activist roundtable" event, with nearly thirty tables, including Citizens for Independent Public Broadcasting, We Interrupt This Message, Paper Tiger Television, Free Speech TV, the Center for Campus Organizing, ITVS, the People's Video Network, and the Media Education Foundation.

The highlight for many was a bus tour of New York's media monopolies: Viacom, Disney, Fox, NBC, Time Warner, and CBS. Participants were bused to each location, where they disembarked and cheered speeches denouncing the "moguls" and calling for "noncommercial, truly public space on the airwaves." Media coverage of the congress was noted on AP, CNN, NPR, and Reuters.

Within a couple of weeks of the first Media and Democracy Congress, the Cultural Environmental Movement (CEM) held its founding meeting in St. Louis. As CEM founder George Gerbner explains, "Our children are born into a cultural environment created mostly by a small group of conglomerate storytellers who have little to tell but a great deal to sell." The meeting drew more than 150 organizations and supporters "united in working for freedom, fairness, diversity, responsibility, respect for cultural integrity, the protection of children, and democratic decision-making in the cultural mainstream." A second meeting of CEM took place at Ohio University in March of 1999; at that meeting delegates officially endorsed the Citizens for Independent Public Broadcasting campaign.

A Last Word

In a mass society we need the mass media of communications to create a social space or "public sphere" out of which publics can emerge. We cannot expect this of the profit-driven corporate media, who offer chewing gum for the eyes so that they can sell those eyeballs to advertisers. However, we must expect this of public media. To truly serve the public interest, public broadcasting must not be bound by the imperatives of profit or power.

Imagine surfing through a sea of commercials and coming to rest on an oasis of pure programming. Imagine in-depth investigations of major issues, well beyond the headline service that passes for news these days. Imagine hearing the voices of citizen activists and public interest advocates in addition to those of the usual government and corporate officials.

Imagine theater for those who love it, in addition to theater for people who rarely go. In addition to *Cats,* there would be workshops, showcases, experiments, and premiers of original drama and comedy with an edge.

Imagine great minds from great universities talking about great ideas, in addition to the paperback author of the week telling you how to manage your money or your emotions or decorate your house.

Imagine children's programs dedicated to teaching those you love about language, numbers, science, and relationships without exposing them to consumer pitches. Imagine how-to shows that go beyond home economics to teach people about their rights and responsibilities as members of society. Imagine services like workforce education and retraining, job placement bulletin boards, literacy training, and electronic classrooms in schools, prisons, county buildings, and rural areas.

We need a public broadcasting service that serves publics, not just markets. To accomplish this we need to form coalitions among public interest, educational, cultural, and other groups to press for basic structural reform of the present system.

We have seen that the system is responsive to pressure. If pressure comes only from corporate and reactionary political forces, an already compromised system will continue to decline. The place to start is in our own communities, with our own public broadcasting stations, who are pledged to serve us and are supported by our taxes and contributions. By rallying those who should care—those who have the most to gain—we can make a difference.

Appendix: Citizens for Independent Public Broadcasting

1029 Vermont Avenue, NW, Suite 800, Washington, DC 20005
(202) 638–6880; FAX (202) 638–6885
http://www.cipbonline.org
Executive Director: Jerold M. Starr, Ph.D.
Associate Director: Karen L. Conner
Outreach Coordinator: Alex Traugott

Board of Directors

Nolan Bowie is a senior fellow and adjunct lecturer in public policy at the Kennedy School of Government, Harvard University. From 1986 to 1998, he served on the faculty of Temple University. Bowie has an extensive record of government and public service as an attorney and an expert on telecommunications policy.

Daniel del Solar is the proprietor and operator of Solar Imaging, a media production company. Del Solar has served as general manager of WYBE-TV Philadelphia (1992–95) and general manager KALW-FM San Francisco (1985–92). Earlier in his career, he was director of training and development for the Corporation for Public Broadcasting. Del Solar has been development director of the Mission Cultural Center for Latino Arts and a consultant to the Mexican Museum, both in San Francisco.

George Gerbner is Bell Atlantic Professor of Telecommunications at Temple University. From 1964 to 1989, he was dean of the Annenberg School of Communication at the University of Pennsylvania. Gerbner's pathbreaking research on violence in television has been supported by many organizations, including the President's Commission on the Causes and Prevention of Violence. He is also the founder of the Cultural Environment Movement. Gerber's many publications include *Invisible Crises: What Conglomerate Media Control Means for America and the World*.

Janine Jackson is program director for Fairness & Accuracy In Reporting (FAIR), the national media watch group. She is also host/producer of FAIR's nationally syndicated radio show *CounterSpin* and the host of CUNY-TV's monthly cable TV program *Labor at the Crossroads*. Jackson coedited *The FAIR Reader: An EXTRA! Review of Press and Politics in the '90s*.

Nicholas Johnson is a professor at the University of Iowa College of Law, specializing in mass media law, and the chair of the National Citizens Communication Lobby. Johnson also served as a commissioner of the Federal Communications Commission (1966–73) during the years of public broadcasting's creation. He has been a Supreme Court law clerk to First Amendment defender Justice Hugo Black, a nationally syndicated columnist, and the author of *How to Talk Back to Your Television Set*.

Alvin H. Perlmutter (chair) is president of Alvin H. Perlmutter, Inc., a television production company, and chair and CEO of Sunrise Media LLC, a television and educational newsfilm archive. Perlmutter has originated more than a hundred PBS documentaries. He has been the recipient of numerous awards, including six Emmys. Prior to his work in public broadcasting, Perlmutter served as program manager of WNBC-TV New York and as a vice president for NBC News.

Jerold M. Starr (executive director) is a professor of sociology at West Virginia University. A Fulbright and National Endowment for the Humanities fellow, Starr is founder and past president of many local and national organizations, including the Association for Humanist Sociology. He has authored six books and numerous articles.

Barbara Trent is a filmmaker, teacher, author, and lecturer. Since 1983 she has been codirector of the Empowerment Project (which she cofounded), producing documentary films and videos as tools for social change. From 1983 to 1992, Trent produced six documentaries. *The Panama Deception* (1992), which she also directed, won several awards, including the Oscar for Best Documentary Feature.

National Advisory Committee

Robert K. Avery is a professor of communication at the University of Utah, where he works with KUED-TV and KUER-FM. A former public broadcasting executive, he is a past chairman of the National Association of Educational Broadcasters. Avery is also founding editor of the scholarly journal *Critical Studies in Mass Communication*. The most recent of his many writings appear in the 1999 edition of *A History of Public Broadcasting*.

Jeff Cohen is a regular commentator on Fox *News Watch* and former columnist for *Brill's Content*. He is the founder and former executive director of Fairness & Accuracy In Reporting (FAIR). Cohen is a former syndicated columnist and coauthor of four books, including with Norman Solomon, *Wizards of Media Oz: Behind the Curtain of Mainstream News*.

Jannette Dates is dean of the School of Communications at Howard University. She is chair of the Black College Communications Association and a member of the board of directors of the Broadcast Education Association. Earlier, Dates served as anchor and executive producer at Baltimore's WBAL-TV (NBC) and as a public affairs panelist at Baltimore's WJZ-TV (ABC). Her latest work is *Split Image: African Americans in the Mass Media*.

Barbara Ehrenreich is an award-winning political essayist, columnist, and social critic. Her commentaries have appeared in *Time* magazine, *The Nation, Harper's, Z Magazine*, and *Mother Jones*. Ehrenreich is a Guggenheim fellow and author of several books, including *Blood Rites: Origins and History of the Passions of War, Fear of Falling: The Inner Life of the Middle Class, The Worst Years of Our Lives: Irreverent Notes from a Decade of Greed*, and a novel, *Kipper's Game*.

Henry Geller served as communications fellow with the Markle Foundation from 1989 through 1998. From 1981 to 1989 Geller was director of the Washington Center for Public Policy Research. From 1964 to 1981 his positions included assistant secretary of commerce for communications and information and general counsel at the Federal Communications Commission. Geller has served on the faculties of Northwestern University and Duke University.

David Honig is a communications attorney with offices in both Washington, D.C., and Miami Beach. He is founder and president of the Minority Media and Telecommunications Counsel, an organization that coordinates FCC rule-making and policy litigation on behalf of national minority organizations. Honig has published widely on communications issues and teaches civil rights litigation at the University of Miami School of Law.

William Hoynes is chair of the sociology department of Vassar College. His book *Public Television for Sale: Media, the Market and the Public Sphere* was awarded the 1996 Goldsmith Prize from Harvard University's Shorenstein Center. Hoynes is coauthor of *Media/Society: Industries, Images and Audiences* and *By Invitation Only: How the Media Limit Political Debate*.

Bill Kovach is curator of the Nieman Foundation's journalism fellowships at Harvard University. His forty years in journalism include eighteen with the *New York Times*. From 1979 to 1986, Kovach headed the *Times*'s U.S. Washington bureau. Previously he was editor of the *Atlanta Journal-Constitution*. Over the years Kovach has supervised reporting projects that have won four Pulitzer Prizes. In 1999 he coauthored (with Tom Rosenstiel) *Warp Speed: America in the Age of Mixed Media*.

Nancy Kranich is president of the American Library Association and associate dean of libraries at New York University. A freedom of information advocate, she sits on the advisory board of the National Security Archive in Washington, D.C. She has made more than 150 presentations and written more than 50 articles on media and democracy and related policy issues.

Jerry M. Landay is a professor emeritus in journalism at the University of Illinois, where he still teaches "Issues in Television" to Chancellor's Honors students. Landay is a former news correspondent for ABC and CBS. He writes frequently on media and democracy issues for major national publications.

Lewis H. Lapham is an award-winning essayist, as well as editor of *Harper's Magazine*, where he writes a monthly essay called "Notebook." Lapham has been a syndicated newspaper columnist and speaker at the nation's leading universities, as well as a commentator on NPR and CBC radio. He hosted and authored a six-part documentary series broadcast on public television and was the host and executive editor of *Bookmark*, a weekly PBS series.

Edward L. McClarty is emeritus dean of telecommunications at Modesto College and a former

California State University professor of communication. For ten years, McClarty served as chair and member of the California Public Broadcasting Commission. He also served nine years on the board of directors of KVIE-TV Sacramento.

Henry Morganthau III is an author and television producer. In twenty years at WGBH-TV Boston, he created and produced many documentaries and talk shows for the national network, winning Peabody, Emmy, UPI, EFLA and Flaherty awards. Earlier, Morganthau worked as a television producer for ABC, CBS and NBC and was acting program manager at WNYC.

Alvin Poussaint is director of the Media Center of the Judge Baker Children's Center in Boston. He is also clinical professor of psychiatry at Harvard Medical School. An expert on race relations, Poussaint has authored many publications, including *Raising Black Children*. In 1997, he received a New England Emmy as co–executive producer of *Willoughby's Wonders*.

Danny Schechter is cofounder and executive director of Globalvision, an international television and film company. Through Globalvision, Schechter created and produced the series *South Africa Now* and also *Rights and Wrongs*. An Emmy Award winner with ABC's *20/20*, he has directed seven independent films and is author of *The More You Watch, the Less You Know*.

Jack Willis is senior fellow with George Soros's Open Society Institute. Most recently, he was president and CEO of Twin Cities Public Television. Before that, he was vice president of programming and production for CBS Cable, CBS, Inc., and director of programming for Metromedia Producer's Corporation and WNET-TV New York. Willis's productions have won many awards, including seven Emmys.

Notes

Chapter 1: Trouble in Three Rivers City

1–11   The story of WQED is based on personal field notes and interviews; WQED records distributed to members of the corporate governance committee, board of directors and community advisory board; internal records both shared by WQED staff and held in WQED's FCC Public Inspection File; press accounts by the Pittsburgh *Post-Gazette,* the Pittsburgh *Tribune-Review, In Pittsburgh Newsweekly, City Paper,* the *Wall Street Journal, Current,* and *Public Broadcasting Report;* FCC petitions and reponses; and occasional references in the literature on public broadcasting history (see References).

Chapter 2: Corporate Media's Threat to Democracy

12–13   Figures on concentration of media ownership are based on Ben Bagdikian, *The Media Monopoly* (Boston: Beacon Press, 2000); Robert W. McChesney, *Corporate Media and the Threat to Democracy* (New York: Seven Stories Press, 1997); Robert W. McChesney, "The Global Media Giants: The Nine Firms that Dominate the World," *Extra!* November/December 1997, 11–12; Mark Crispin Miller and Janine Jacquet Biden, "The National Entertainment State," *The Nation,* 3 June 1996, 23–27; Mark Crispin Miller, "Free the Media," *The Nation,* 3 July 1996, 9–15; Mark Crispin Miller, "The Crushing Power of Big Publishing," *The Nation,* 17 March 1997, 11–18; and Mark Crispin Miller, "Who Controls the Music?" *The Nation,* 1 September 1997, 11–16.

13   Figures on bookstore concentration from Institute for Alternative Journalism, "Media and Democracy: A Blueprint for Reinvigorating Public Life in the Information Age," working paper, December 1996, 4.

13   *Publisher Andre Schiffrin comments.* Quote from Schiffrin, "The Corporatization of Publishing," *The Nation,* 3 June 1996, 29–32.

13   Data on newspaper chains from Jack Bass, "Newspaper Monopoly," *American Journalism Review,* July/August 1999, 64–86; data on "clustering" of small newspapers from the Project on the State of the American Newspaper, *American Journalism Review,* May 1999. Comment on its consequences from Neil Hickey, "Money Lust: How Pressure for Profit Is Perverting Journalism," *Columbia Journalism Review,* July/August 1998, 28–36.

13   *Even the small arena.* Ben A. Franklin (ed.), "More News Monopolies," *The Washington Spectator,* 15 September 1999, 4.

13   *"The success of the alternative press."* Jay Walljasper, "Do We Still Need the Alternative Press?: The Changing Role and Uncertain Future of Independent Print Media," quoted in Don Hazen and Larry Smith, eds., *Media and Democracy: A Book of Readings and Resources* (San Francisco: Institute for Alternative Journalism, 1996), 142–44.

13   Alternative press chains are discussed in Jay Walljasper, "Age of the Mega-Alternatives," *Utne Reader,* July/August 1997, 11.

14   *Carly Berwick . . . asked.* Quote from Berwick, "The New Harmonics in Hartford: When the Daily Buys the Weekly, Where's the 'Alternative'?" *Columbia Journalism Review,* July/August 1999, 12–13.

14   *In just three years.* See Kevin McNulty, "Adding Low-Watt Stations to the FM Dial," *American Journalism Review,* September 1999, 12.

15   *On September 8, 1999.* Lawrie Mifflin, "Viacom to Buy CBS, Forming 2nd Largest Media Company," *New York Times,* 8 September 1999, 1, C-13; and Alex Kuczynski, "CBS Chief Wanted His MTV: How Mel Karmazin Sold Viacom on the Merger," *New York Times,* 8 September 1999, C1.

15   Information on NAB and Fritts from Common Cause's report *Channeling Influence: The Broadcast Lobby and the $70 Billion Free Ride* (Washington, D.C.: Common Cause, 1997), 23.

15   Information on House campaign media spending from Common Cause, *Channeling Influence,* 29. Figures on media money to political parties and members of Congress from Tom Goldstein, "Does Big Mean Bad?" *Columbia Journalism Review,* September/October 1998, 52–56.

15   Figures on telecommunications industry campaign contributions are from Thomas Ferguson, "Bill's Big Backers," *Mother Jones,* November/December 1996, 60–66.

16   Projected figures on 2000 campaign spending by the telecommunications industry are from Jessica Brown, ed., "Broadcasters Expect Big Profits from Election Ads," *The Forum Connection,* 1 October 1999.

16   Figures on commercials from Mary Jane Kuntz and Joseph Weber, "The New Hucksterism," *Business Week,* 1 July 1996, 1, 30.

16   Report on layoffs and effects from Hickey, "Money Lust."

16   Figures on press and PR releases are from McChesney, *Corporate Media,* 15.

16   *In 1996, only 14 percent.* Joanmarie Kalter, "Burnout," *Columbia Journalism Review,* July/August 1999, 30–33.

16   *A new commercialism.* Jeremy Iggers, "Get Me Rewrite," *Utne Reader,* September/October 1997, 46–48.

16   Marquette University survey data from Ann Marie Kerwin, "Advertiser Pressure on Newspapers Common: Survey," *Editor & Publisher,* 16 January 1993.

17   *The top one hundred advertisers.* George Gerbner, "The Stories We Tell," *Media Development,* April 1996, 13–17.

17   *Their concern to avoid.* Serling quote from Stan Opotowsky, *TV—The Big Picture* (New York: Collier, 1962).

17   *A study of . . . reporters and editors.* Lawrence Soley, "The Power of the Press Has a Price: TV Reporters Talk about Advertiser Pressures," *Extra!* July/August 1997, 11–13.

18 *Sociologist David Crouteau's 1998 survey.* David Croteau, "Challenging the 'Liberal Media' Claim," *Extra!* July/August 1998, 4–9.

18 *As one network executive.* Charlotte Ryan, *Prime Time Activism: Media Strategies for Grassroots Organizing* (Boston: South End Press, 1991), 204.

18 *"The evening news."* Gralneck quoted in Mark Hertsgaar, *On Bended Knee: The Press and the Reagan Presidency* (New York: Farrar, Strauss, Giroux, 1988), 80.

18 *In the 1940s.* William J. Puette, *Through Jaundiced Eyes: How the Media View Organized Labor* (Ithaca, New York: 1992).

19 *Bruce Nussbaum explains.* Nussbaum, "The Myth of the Liberal Media," *Business Week,* 11 November 1995, 34–35.

19 *Los Angeles Times poll.* "The Media Poll," *Los Angeles Times* poll No. 94, April–June 1985.

19 *David Moberg reports.* Peter Perl story in Moberg, *"Washington Post* Labor Struggles," *Extra!* May/June 1989, 1, 12–13.

19 *When Senate Republicans.* "The Striker Replacement Bill," *Washington Post,* 12 July 1994.

19 *According to studies.* Paul Kleit, Robert A. Bardwell, and Jason Salzman, *Pavlov's TV Dogs: A Snapshot of Local TV News in America 9/20/95* (Denver, Colorado: Rocky Mountain Media Watch, 1995).

19 *Sally Wiggin confesses.* Wiggin, speaking at a workshop sponsored by United Way of Allegheny County, spring 1996.

20 *According to George Gerbner.* Gerbner, "The Stories We Tell," 16.

20 *In Lewis Lapham's view.* Lewis H. Lapham, "I'm Just Curious: How Do You Propose to Carry on the Struggle against the Disney Co.?" *Current,* 28 August 1995, 16–17.

20 *Many have argued.* Figures on cable system concentration from Douglas Kellner, *Television and the Crisis of Democracy* (Boulder, Colorado: Westview, 1990), 211.

20 *The FCC cleared the way.* Stephen Labaton, "Ownership Rules in Cable Industry Loosened by F.C.C.," *New York Times,* 9 October 1999, 1.

21 Figures on cable network ownership provided by the Project on Media Ownership, 34 Stuyvesant Street, Suite 503, New York, NY 10003; (212) 992–9494.

21 *In 1952.* Fred Powledge, *Public Television: A Question of Survival* (Washington, D.C.: Public Affairs, 1972).

21 *The Carnegie Commission issued.* Carnegie Commission on Educational Television, *Public Television: A Program for Action* (New York: Bantam, 1967), 98–99.

21 *Robert McChesney points out.* McChesney, *Corporate Media,* 45–46.

22   *As Browne explains.* Allan Browne, "Public Service Broadcasting in Four Countries: An Overview," *Journal of Media Economics*, 1996, 76–81.

22   *McChesney asks.* McChesney quoted in *Monthly Review*, December 1995, 17.

22   *Bill Moyers has advised.* Moyers quote in Pat Aufderheide, "A Funny Thing Is Happening to TV's Public Forum," *Columbia Journalism Review*, November/December 1991, 63.

22   *Les Brown informs us.* Brown, "Broadcasting's Vanishing Species," *Channels*, 1985, 16.

22   *For a nation torn.* Carnegie Commission, *Public Television*.

22   *A broad diversity of conflicting interests.* Ralph Engelman, *Public Radio and Television in America: A Political History* (Thousand Oaks, California: Sage Publications, 1996), 164.

23   *President Johnson declared.* *Public Papers of the Presidents of the United States* (Washington, D.C.: National Archives and Records Service, 1969), Lyndon B. Johnson, 1967, vol. 2, 996.

Chapter 3: The Broken Promise of PBS

24   *In 1997, Ron Hull.* Karen Everhard Bedford, "Hull Dived into the PBS Archives, Found Himself Among Old Friends," *Current* (12 May 1997).

25   *In Europe.* Patricia Aufderheide, *The Daily Planet: A Critic on the Capitalist Culture Beat* (Minneapolis, Minnesota: University of Minnesota Press, 2000).

25   *James R. Killian Jr. argued.* Killian quote from Carnegie Commission on Educational Television, *Public Television: A Program for Action* (New York: Bantam, 1967).

25   *Rather, it has made.* Marilyn Lashley, *Public Television: Panacea, Pork Barrel, or Public Trust?* (Westport, Connecticut: Greenwood Press, 1992).

25   *The CPB would act as a "heat shield."* Twentieth-Century Fund Task Force on Public Television, *Quality Time?: The Report of the Twentieth-Century Fund Task Force on Public Television* (New York: The Twentieth-Century Fund Press, 1993), 84.

25   General information on public broadcasting structure and funding from the Corporation for Public Broadcasting.

26   *"The 'lemon socialism' of mass media."* Patricia Aufderheide, "Public Service Broadcasting in the United States," *Journal of Media Economics*, 1 September 1996, 65.

28   *In her very revealing look.* B. J. Bullert, *Public Television: Politics and the Battle over Documentary Film* (New Brunswick, New Jersey: Rutgers University Press, 1997), 14.

28–30 "A Short Political History" is based on several sources, including "The Story So Far," in *Quality Time?*, 81–100; "Public Television," in Ralph Engelman, *Public Radio and Television in America: A Political History* (Thousand Oaks, California: Sage Publications, 1996), 135–218; James Day, *The Vanishing Vi-*

sion: The Inside Story of Public Television (Berkeley, California: University of California Press, 1995); Fred Powledge, *Public Television: A Question of Survival* (Washington, D.C.: Public Affairs, 1972); James Ledbetter, *Made Possible by . . . : The Death of Public Broadcasting in the United States* (New York: Verso, 1997); Lashley, *Public Television;* William Hoynes, *Public Television for Sale: Media, the Market, and the Public Sphere* (Boulder, Colorado: Westview Press, 1994); Carnegie Commission, *A Public Trust: Report of the Carnegie Commission on the Future of Public Broadcasting* (New York: Bantam, 1979).

28   *An immediate goal.* Jon Rose, statement of 15 October 1971, quoted in Day, *The Vanishing Vision,* 236.

29   *Marilyn Lashley considers.* Lashley, *Public Television.*

29   *"The greatest force for blandness."* James Day, quoted in Fred Powledge, *Public Television: A Question of Survival,* 15.

29   *It wasn't until 1989. Quality Time?,* 95.

30   General figures about viewership, education, and income are drawn from following sources in order: Neil Hickey, "Public TV: Why Reports of Its Death Seem Premature," *TV Guide,* 4 December 1982, 12–18; Molly Ivins, "For Sale: PBS," *Funny Times,* April 1995; Jacqueline Conciatore "Gore Assails 'All-out Attack' on Enrichment for Kids," *Current,* 6 March 1995; Patricia Aufderheide, "The Corporatization of Public TV: Why Labor's Voice Seldom Is Heard on PBS," *Union,* October/November 1991, 11–13.

30   *A recent survey.* Information on education of public TV viewers from Ken Mills, "Confessions of a Former Public Television Member," *Current,* 20 September 1999, B–5.

30   *In the view of . . . Willard Rowland.* Willard D. Rowland Jr., "Public Involvement: The Anatomy of a Myth," in *The Future of Public Broadcasting,* ed. Douglas Cater and Michael J. Nyhan (New York: Praeger, 1976), 118.

30   *The check writers are.* Patricia Aufderheide, "A Funny Thing Happened to TV's Public Forum," *Columbia Journalism Review,* November/December 1991, 60–3.

30   *As one WGBH-TV producer advised.* Producers quoted by Hoynes, *Public Television for Sale,* 113.

30   *In 1992.* Heritage Foundation, *Making Public Television Public* (Washington, D.C.: Heritage Foundation, 1992).

31   *The industry trade paper.* Jacqueline Conciatore, *Current,* 28 February 1994.

31   *"New York Times TV critic."* Quoted in Jacqueline Conciatore (above).

32   *Series on "the gender wars."* Materials, including program and letter quotes, provided by Jennifer Pozner, FAIR.

33   National Desk *executive.* Karen Everhart Bedford, "Strong Op-Ed from the Right Draws Strong Feminist Response," *Current,* 13 December 1999, 16–17.

33   *It should be noted.* Mick Martin and Marsha Porter, *Video Movie Guide 2000* (New York: Ballantine, 1999), 215.

34 Discussion of *Dark Circle* from Bullert, *Public Television: Politics and the Battle.*

34 Material regarding *Building Bombs,* including quotes, courtesy of Mark Mori, of the group Hollywood Coalition vs. PBS Censorship.

35 Material regarding *Deadly Deception,* including quotes, courtesy of INFACT.

35 Material regarding *The Panama Deception* courtesy of the Empowerment Project and PBS.

35 Material regarding *Out at Work* from Deidre McFadyen, "Public Television's Double Standard," *In These Times,* 28, July 1997, 10.

36 *The official justification.* Quotes in the following discussion are from *PBS National Program Funding Standards and Practices,* 1990.

38 *As described by.* Patricia Aufderheide, "What Makes Public TV Public? It Gets Harder and Harder to Tell," *The Progressive,* January 1988, 36.

40 *Already by the mid-1970s.* John Weisman, "Public TV in Crisis: How to Make It Better," *TV Guide,* 8 August 1987, 22–36.

40 *Marc Gunther elaborates.* Gunther, "Public Relations: Are Corporate Sponsors Influencing What PBS Viewers See?" *Detroit Free Press,* 7 July 1993.

40 *In his study of WGBH-TV.* Hoynes, *Public Television for Sale,* 122.

40 *Robert MacNeil acknowledged.* Quoted in Ron Weiskind, "PBS Isn't Elitist or Liberal, MacNeil Asserts," *Pittsburgh Post-Gazette,* 28 March 1995.

41 *Glass's "one vow."* Ira Glass, quoted in Marshall Sella, "The Glow at the End of the Dial: Ira Glass Is, Um (Pause, Delete) . . . Listening," *New York Times Magazine,* 11 April 1999, 68–77.

41 *A senior public affairs producer.* Quote from Kurt Anderson, "How Necessary Is PBS?" *Time,* 26, July 1993, 75.

41 *A group led by Stanley Aronowitz.* City University of New York Committee for Cultural Studies, *PBS and the American Worker* (New York: CUNY, 1990). The study's findings were reported in both the commercial daily and union press. Organized labor later lobbied Congress, resulting in language inserted in the 1991 Public Telecommunications Act calling for more "programming which addresses the lives and concerns of American workers and their families, in documentaries, dramas, and public affairs programs."

41 *Former PBS official Barry Chase.* Quoted in Martin A. Lee and Norman Solomon, *Unreliable Sources: A Guide to Detecting Bias in News Media* (New York: Carol Publishing Group, 1992), 89.

41 *A 1992 study.* Hoynes and Croteau's studies are detailed in David Croteau and William Hoynes, *By Invitation Only: How the Media Limit Political Debate* (Monroe, Maine: Common Courage Press, 1994).

42 *In 1991.* MacNeil quoted from 1991 broadcast of WNET-TV, *The Eleventh Hour;* Lehrer quoted in Lee and Solomon, *Unreliable Sources,* 88, and Engelman, *Public Radio and Television in America,* 207.

42 *In December 1998.* William Hoynes, *The Cost of Survival: Political Discourse and the "New PBS,"* Vassar College, unpublished research paper, June 1999.

43 *As might be expected.* Engelman, *Public Radio and Television in America,* 102–3.

43 *One NPR news staffer.* Quoted in Lee and Solomon, *Unreliable Sources,* 85–86.

43 *Charlotte Ryan's 1991 study.* Ryan, "A Study of National Public Radio," *Extra!* April/May 1993, 18–21.

43 *Worse yet.* David Stewart, "The Pimp Show Turned Out to Be Rare Error. Thank God," *Current,* 29 November 1999, 16.

44 *By 1998, the list.* Jacqueline Conciatore, "The Amazing Shrinking 'Dis List': All but Six Stations Avoid Losing CPB Grants," *Current,* 16 March 1998.

44 Marty Durlin writing in *Current.*

45 *Considering the evidence.* Ruder and Finn poll cited in Lee and Solomon, *Unreliable Sources,* 92.

45 *Even some.* Buchanan and Krystol quotes from Norman Solomon's, syndicated column, "On the Media Beat," 25 July 1996.

45 *Noam Chomsky has suggested.* Cited in Robert W. McChesney, *Corporate Media and the Threat to Democracy* (New York: Seven Stories Press, 1990), 59.

46 *CPB board member.* Victor Gold quoted in *Current,* 16 January 1995.

46 *PBS chief.* Duggan comments from *Quality Time?,* 53–55.

47 *Moderate Democrats.* Al Gore quoted in Jacqueline Conciatore, "Gore Assails 'All-out Attack on Enrichment for Kids,'" *Current,* 6 March 1995.

47 *Also in February.* Statement of Richard W. Carlson, president and CEO, Corporation for Public Broadcasting, on the Christian Coalition's Contract with the American Family, 17 May 1995, unpublished news release.

48 *The encroachment.* The Schmertz saga is told in many sources, including Engelman, *Public Radio and Television in America.*

48 *A masterful strategy.* Timothy Brennan, "*Masterpiece Theatre* and the Uses of Tradition," *Social Text,* fall 1985, 111.

48 *Barnouw observed.* Erik Barnouw, *The Sponsor: Notes on a Modern Potentate.* New York: Oxford, 1978.

49 *The payoff.* Steve Bass quote from *Fortune Magazine,* 22 April 1991, 17. Aufderheide quote from *In These Times,* 17 October 1994.

49 *In 1984.* John Witherspoon and Roselle Kovitz, *The History of Public Broadcasting* (Washington, D.C.: Current, 1987), 56.

49 *Other big business interests.* Sources on corporate sponsorship include Engelman, *Public Radio and Television in America,* 196–97, and Hoynes, *Public Television for Sale,* 100.

49 *While individual supporters.* Discussion of corporate underwriting in *Current,* 12 May 1997, 6.

50 *TV writer Les Brown.* Brown, "Broadcasting's Vanishing Species," *Channels,* 1985, 15–16.

50 *Between 1982 and 1991.* Drop in corporate support reported in *Public Broadcasting Report,* 11 November 1993.

50 *"A welcome infusion."* Duggan quoted in *Extra!* February 1995.

50 *In 1997.* Information on PBS courting of advertisers from Steve Behrens, "How Will PBS Make Underwriting 'User Friendly'?" *Current,* 4 July 1994, 1, 8. Duggan quoted in *Current,* 12 May 1997, 6.

51 *Former PBS president.* Grossman's PTV plan is discussed in Lawrie Mifflin, "Ads on Public TV? Stations Are Tempted," *New York Times,* 5 June 1997, B1–2. See also, "Critics Arise as PTV Weekend Plan Gets Some Ink," *Current,* 23 June 1997, 1, 23A.

51 *The Community Station Resource Group.* Information on stations selling spots reported in *Current,* 7 July 1997, 7.

51 *In 1996, PBS entered.* James Ledbetter, *Made Possible By . . . : The Death of Public Broadcasting in the United States.*

52 *This escalating commercialism.* PBS record deals reported in *Current,* 4 August 1997.

52 *A nine-member jury.* Steve Behrens, "Nesmith Wins $47 Million in Video Suit against PBS," *Current,* 8 February 1999, 1, 14. See also Lawrie Mifflin, "Judge Rules That PBS Must Pay Video Distributor $47 Million," *New York Times,* 3 February 1999, C-4; and Robert N. Wold, "PBS and Nesmith Settle Dispute, Mum about Price," *Current,* 19 July 1999, 1.

53 *Communications scholar.* Gerbner remarks at press conference announcing launch of Citizens for Independent Public Broadcasting, Benton Foundation, Washington, D.C., 16 November 1999.

53 *To address the question.* Duggan "station equity model" discussed in *Current,* 12 May 1997, 6.

53 *In the middle 1990s.* Report on Store of Knowledge and Learningsmith in *Current,* 23 June 1997.

54 *Reader's Digest chairman.* Rich Breitenfeld, report on Reader's Digest partnership, *Current,* 23 June 1997, 9B.

54 *In 1999, Duggan.* Robert G. Ottenhoff, "Programs Do Migrate: The Question Is How We Respond," *Current,* 8 June 1998, B-1, B-6.

54 Steve Sherman, "Plenty Enter the Big Store, Most for Just One Product," *Current,* 3 July 1995, 16–17.

55 *"Many program decisions."* Kathy Quattrone quoted in *Current,* 6 November 1995, 14. Bruce Christensen quoted in Elizabeth Jensen, "Barney and Friends: Public TV Prepares for Image Transplant to Justify Existence," *Wall Street Journal,* 13 January 1994, A-4.

55 *In September 1999.* Steve Behrens and Karen Everhart-Bedford, "Duggan Withdraws from 'Head-Butting' Arena," *Current,* 20 September 1999, p. A1,

A16; Lawrie Mifflin, "Public Broadcasting Head, Noted for Fund-raising, Quits," *New York Times*, 10 September 1999, A13.

55 *Despite his success.* "Remarks of Ervin S. Duggan, President and CEO, PBS to the 1999 PBS Development Conference," Loew's Miami Beach Hotel, Miami, Florida, September 25, 1999, unpublished.

Chapter 4: The Battle to Reform WQED

56 *Richard Mellon Scaife.* Sources on Scaife include: Joel Bleifuss, "Building Plans," *In These Times*, 10 July 1995, 12–13; Steve Rendall and Jill Steinberg, "Heritage of Extremism," *Extra!* July/August 1996, 11; Joe Conason, "The Right Connections: The Starr in Richard Scaife's Eyes," *Washington Post*, 17 March 1997; Dan Smith, "IRS Looks at Backer of Stories on Foster," *Sacramento Bee*, 29 March 1997; and Howard Kurtz, "Shake-up at the Spectator," *Washington Post*, 20 October 1997.

57 *First, the one exception.* Harvey Molotch and Marilyn Lester, "News as Purposive Behavior: On the Strategic Use of Routine Events, Accidents, and Scandals," *American Sociological Review*, 1974, 107–25.

57 *It also helped.* Ben Bagdikian, *The Media Monopoly* (Boston: Beacon Press, 1992), 216.

58 *Since the media.* Charlotte Ryan, *Prime Time Activism: Media Strategies for Grassroots Organizing* (Boston: South End Press, 1991), 32.

58 *As Charlotte Ryan explains.* Ryan, *Prime Time Activism*, 68–70.

60 *As communications scholar.* Daniel C. Hallin, *We Keep America on Top of the World: Television Journalism and the Public Sphere* (New York: Routledge, 1994), 21.

61 *When talk radio calls.* On talk radio and other tactics, see Jason Salzman, *Let the World Know: Make Your Cause News* (Denver, Colorado: Rocky Mountain Media Watch, 1995).

63 *"Banned by PBS."* See Susan Kimmelman, "Frame by Frame: Debra Chasnoff Has Scripts for Political Change," *In These Times*, 31 May 1993, 10–11; Amal Kumar Naj, "Oscar for Film Lambasting GE Cheers Activists," *Wall Street Journal*, 1 April 1992.

Chapter 5: Old Wine in New Bottles

80 *As Richard Ingram advises.* Ingram, *The Ten Basic Responsibilities of Nonprofit Boards* (Washington, D.C.: National Center for Nonprofit Boards, 1988).

81 *Bob Norman's assessment.* Sources include Bob Norman's meeting notes, interviews with Bob Norman, committee meeting minutes, and newspaper accounts.

82–85 Sources on George Miles and WNET include interview with and columns provided by *New York Newsday* TV critic Marvin Kitman; and Ron Weiskind, "Taking Charge: Miles Clears QED's 'Weeds,' " Pittsburgh *Post-Gazette*, 6 November 1994, M-1, M-3.

93 *"There is nothing more embarrassing."* Peter Drucker, *Managing the Nonprofit Organization: Principles and Practices* (New York: HarperBusiness, 1990).

95 *The various broadcasters.* Jacqueline Conciatore, "NPR Election Project Puts the People's Voice on the Air," *Current,* 31 October 1994, 1, 6, 15.

96 *WQED's paucity.* In perhaps his most disingenuous spin on the subject, Miles complained to *In Pittsburgh*'s Richard Wexler about the high cost of local programming and added, "to me *MacNeil/Leherer* is a local Pittsburgh program." Miles said that Pittsburghers want to know more than their own community; thus to describe such national programs as other than local "doesn't give the people of Pittsburgh enough credit." Richard Wexler, "QED: Where the Medium Is the Massage," *In Pittsburgh,* 1–7 September 1994, 18.

99 *PBS had rejected.* "PBS Rejects Another Oscar-Winning Documentary," *Extra!* July/August 1994, 21.

99 *At a press conference.* Duggan quoted in Robert Bianco, "New PBS President Defends Programming," *Pittsburgh Post-Gazette,* 27 July 1994.

106 *With WQED not willing.* See Christine Triano and Patrice O'Neill, "Not in Our Town: A Success Model for Media Collaboration and Community Organizing," in *Media and Democracy,* ed. Don Hazen and Larry Smith (San Francisco, California: IAJ, 1996), 137–40.

Chapter 6: What Am I Bid?

121 *He was also an outspoken.* Rich Lord, "Just What the Doctor Ordered?" (Pittsburgh) *City Paper,* 6–13 October 1999, 20–23.

122 *In 1999, activists revealed.* James O'Toole, "Activist Questions Roddey's Record in Human Services," *Pittsburgh Post-Gazette,* 5 October 1999, B-7.

132 *In 1946.* Kathryn C. Montgomery *Target: Prime Time—Advocacy Groups and the Struggle over Entertainment Television* (New York: Oxford University Press, 1989), p. 221; William Hoynes, *Public Television for Sale: Media, the Market, and the Public Sphere* (Boulder, Colorado: Westview Press, 1994), 39.

132 *In subsequent years.* William Hoynes, *Public Television for Sale,* 93.

132 *Unfortunately, the FCC.* Ibid., p. 40.

132 *In the 1980s, Reagan-led.* Douglas Kellner, *Television and the Crisis of Democracy* (Boulder, Colorado: Westview Press, 1990), 92.

132 *In 1984 the FCC abolished.* Ben H. Bagdikian, *The Media Monopoly* (Boston: Beacon, 2000).

133 *Restrictions on children's.* Douglas Kellner, *Television and the Crisis of Democracy,* 196.

133 *The most significant step.* Kathryn C. Montgomery, *Target: Prime Time,* 223.

137 *Roddey told the City Council.* From transcript of tape recording of City Council hearing, 17 May 1996.

140–145   Background on Russell Bixler from Sally Kalson, "The Answer to Corner-
           stone's Prayers," *Pittsburgh Post-Gazette*, 22 July 1996, C1–3; Erik Rosen,
           "Godsend or Ungodly: An Interview with Reverend Russ Bixler, CEO of Cor-
           nerstone TV, *In Pittsburgh*, 28 November–4 December 1996.

141–145   The discussion of Cornerstone programs is based on notes from campaign
           participants assigned to watch and record.

    143   *In August 1996.* Adrian Rogers-Melnick, "Host of Lightmusic Leaving TV Sta-
           tion," *Pittsburgh Post-Gazette*, 10 August 1996, B-2.

    143   Information on Cornerstone and the religious right from "Religious/Far
           Right Organizations," *Rethinking Schools*, spring 1996; Adele M. Stan, "Power
           Preying," *Mother Jones*, November/December 1995, 35–45; Isaac Kramnick
           and R. Lawrence Moore, "Is God a Republican?" *The American Prospect*, Sep-
           tember/October 1996, 51–55; Danita Pfeiffer, "Inside the 700 Club: Pat Rob-
           ertson's Former Co-Host Speaks Out," *Extra!* March/April 1998, 17–19; James
           A. Haught, "Today's Far-Out Religious Right Comes Out of a Crazy Mold,"
           The Washington Spectator, 15 September 1995.

    146   *At the 1986 . . . convention.* "Must Carry: Fairness Doctrine Tackled at NRB
           Convention, *Communications Daily*, 1986.

    146   *Ron Kramer noted.* Kramer, "Lucky to Get Reserved Spectrum, We May Now
           Have to Work to Keep It," *Current*, 6 October 1997, 25–26.

Chapter 7: Round Two, The Battle over WQEX

    164   *KQED San Francisco.* George Raine, "KQED Turns Five-Year Loss Around,"
           San Francisco Examiner, 20 March 1997, D-1. "KQED Sells Books Division in
           Bid for Fiscal Recovery," *Current*, 8 July 1996.

165–167   Information about the transition to digital technology from David B. Liroff,
           "ATV: If You Work in Television, You Can Sit This One Out," *Current*, 25
           March 1996; Stephen E. Nevas, "DTV Opens the Door to New Media for Pub-
           casting," *Current*, 20 January 1997, 20; Steve Behrens, "FCC Gives Public 6
           Years to Go Digital," *Current*, 14 April 1997; Steve Behrens, "Sought: 45% of
           DTV Cost," *Current*, 6 October 1997, 1,22; Joel Brinkley, "PBS Makes Digital
           Plans," *New York Times*, 20 October 1997; David B. Liroff, "On the Eve of DTV,
           Public TV Is Not Yet Ready to Cope," *Current*, 3 November 1997, 20; Mitch
           Gitman, "Sharpening TV's Focus," *New York Times*, 10 January 1998; "CPB to
           Review Strategies for a Digital Future That's Different and Better: A Current
           Interview with Bob Coonrod," *Current*, 16 March 1998; Bruce Jacobs, "High-
           Def: Too High-Quality, Too High-Cost," *Current*, 7 June 1999; Karen Everhart
           Bedford, "Federal Aid Merely Trickles for DTV Transition." *Current* 18, 22
           (November 29, 1999), 1,12.

    165   *In October 1999.* Joel Brinkley, "Stations Challenge Digital-TV Standard,"
           New York Times, 11 October 1999.

    167   *Pendarvis said.* Notes of meetings recorded by Sana Coleman and Charles
           Blackburn, Institute for Public Representation, Georgetown University
           Law Center.

Chapter 8: The Killing of WQEX and the Final Showdown

215   *Davis, a frequent cable pundit.* Jeff Pooley, "The Perils of Spin," *Brill's Content,* July/August 1999, 46; Jeff Cohen and Norman Solomon, "Journalists Fail to Follow the Money in Washington," in *Through the Media Looking Glass: Decoding Bias and Blather in the News* (1995), 12–13.

216   On NBC's acquisition of Paxson stock, see Bill Carter, "NBC Completes Acquisition of 32% Stake in Paxson," *New York Times,* 17 September 1999; Seth Sutel, "Struttin' Their Stuff," Associated Press, 17 September 1999; Rob Owen, "WQED President Likes Peacock-Pax Partnership," *Pittsburgh Post-Gazette,* 17 September 1999.

Chapter 9: Other Fronts in the War

235   *Community battles for accountable.* Ralph Engelman, *Public Radio and Television in America: A Political History* (Thousand Oaks, California: Sage Publications, 1996), 178–80, 183.

240–249   Discussions of KQED and the Committee to Save KQED are based on my interviews with activists Henry Kroll, Sasha Futran, Shelly Kessler, Art Persyko, and Steve Zeltzer over the years 1993 to 1999; David Kalson's insightful 1993 report on his interviews with KQED acting director Marshall Turner, station manager Kevin Harris, director of communications Mark Powelson, and several board members, including Sasha Futran; campaign materials provided by activists; and on numerous press accounts.

241   *KQED's first president.* David Stewart, "KQED Made Its Mark by Making Programs," *Current,* 3 February 1997, 19–21; James Day, *The Vanishing Vision: The Inside Story of Public Television* (Berkeley, California: University of California Press, 1995).

242   *The period from 1974 to 1980.* Charles Linbarger, "The FCC Pulls the Plug on KQED's Channel 32," *San Francisco Bay Guardian,* 18 May 1988; Robert Levering, "The Hidden Issues in the KQED Elections '78," *San Francisco Bay Guardian,* 1978.

243   David Armstrong, "KQED on the Rocks," *San Francisco Examiner,* 3 March 1996, A1, A12.

245   Kim Deterline and Steve Rhodes, "Bay Area Activists Target Public TV," *Extra!* December 1992, 23.

246   "Board Slate Sweeps Election at KQED," *Current,* 13 December 1993.

247   "How Low Can Public TV Go? KQED's Adventures in the Infomercial Business," *Extra! Update* February 1997, 3; Norman Solomon, "Ethics and Leadership at KQED," *San Francisco Chronicle,* 27 November 1996; Jon Carroll, "Getting Straight at KQED," *San Francisco Chronicle,* 2 January 1997, C-12.

249–253   Discussion of AMAC based on interviews with Tom Blazier; meetings with Blazier, Insanna, and Grannis; and campaign materials and press accounts provided by Blazier.

253–257   Discussion of Chicago's WTTW and CDPT based on interviews with Scott

Sanders, Allan Siegel, and Liane C. Casten; correspondence with Ira Shorr and Robert Cleland; and campaign materials and press clippings provided by Sanders.

254 *In September 1993.* Liz Stevens, "More Public Television: WTTW Makes Room for Point-of-View TV," *New City,* 2–8 September 1993.

255 *The relationship between CDPTV.* Michael Stoll, "FCC Asked to Investigate Public-TV Sale of Non-Profit Groups' Merchandise," *The Chronicle of Philanthropy,* 26 July 1994, 23; Ted Shem, "Media: Hi! You're Shopping Channel 11!" *Reader,* 3 December 1993; "FCC Is Asked to Fine a Public TV Station over Shopping Show," *Wall Street Journal,* 8 July 1994.

256 *WTTW's Marcus insisted.* "FCC Petitioned to Ban Shopping Shows on PTV," *Current,* 1 August 1994, 18.

256 *The CDPTV's seventeen-page complaint.* "Home Shopping Trial Broke Rule; FCC Admonishes WTTW to 'Use Care,'" *Current,* 6 November 1995, 3.

258 *Since 1982.* Discussion of Members for the Metro based on interviews with Myrtice Craig and Andrew Goshen; campaign materials provided by both; and press clippings provided by Craig, including the following: "From the Editor," Jonathan Rogers, "Live 'Metro' No More," *Florida Times-Union,* 1993; Jonathan Rogers, "'Metro' Time Change Raises Listeners' Ire," *Florida Times-Union* 1993; *Folio Weekly,* 6 July 1993; Jonathan Rogers, "'Metro' Fans Protest, Raise Funds," *Florida Times-Union,* 8 July 1993; Jonathan Rogers, "Stereo 90: Public Airs Complaints that Go beyond 'Metro,'" *Florida Times-Union,* 18 July 1993; Jonathan Rogers, "Stereo 90 Producer Landon Walker Fired," *Florida Times-Union,* 4 August 1993; Joe White, "Radio Waves," *Folio Weekly,* 24 August, 1993; Bill Holland, "Mr. Tapioca Speaks," *Folio Weekly,* 31 August 1993; Jonathan Rogers, "Listeners Cool to '90 in the Shade,'" *Florida Times-Union,* 5 August 1993; Jonathan Rogers, "Personality Clash Behind 'Metro' Tiff Says Memo, Figures," *Florida Times-Union,* 5 September, 1993.

Chapter 10: Public Broadcasting in the Public Interest

261 On the topic of civic participation in general, see Robert D. Putnam, "The Strange Disappearance of Civic America," *American Prospect,* Winter 1996, 34–48; Michael Schudson, "What If Civic Life Didn't Die?" *American Prospect,* March/April 1996, 17–20; Theda Skocpol, "Unraveling from Above," *American Prospect,* March/April 1996, 20–25; Richard M. Valelly, "Couch Potato Democracy?" *American Prospect,* March/April 1996, 26–28; William A Galston, "Won't You Be My Neighbor?" *American Prospect,* May/June 1996, 16–18; Katha Pollitt, "For Whom the Ball Rolls," *The Nation,* 15 April 1996, 9; Everett Carl Ladd, "We Are So Bowling Together," *Pittsburgh Post-Gazette,* 20 July 1996.

262 *A series of surveys.* "The Media and Campaign' '96 Briefing," from the Freedom Forum Media Studies Center, 580 Madison Avenue, 42nd floor, New York, New York 10022.

262 *Public broadcasting could be.* Patricia Aufderheide, "Public Television and the Public Sphere," *Critical Studies in Mass Communication,* 1991, 168–81.

262 *"In a democratic society."* Douglas Kellner, *Television and the Crisis of Democracy* (Boulder, Colorado: Westview Press, 1990), 185.

263 *In 1989, PBS commissioned.* John Fuller and Sue Bomzer, "Anything You Can Do, I Can Do Better: Friendly (and Not So Friendly) Competition in the PTV Overlapped Markets," PBS Research Department, 19 June 1990.

263 *In 1995, still undeterred. Current,* 16 January 1995.

264 *While neither of these plans.* Karen Everhart Bedford, "Proposal for TV: 3-Year Transition to 'One Grant Per Market,'" *Current,* 15 January 1996, 10.

264 *In August 1999.* Steve Behrens, "Once-Wary Stations Take Their Vows in Indianapolis," *Current,* 30 August 1999, 1, 19.

264 *Seeking a less draconian.* Hope Green and Derk Zimmerman, "PBS-2 Business Plan," unpublished, 19 May 1999.

265 *Bill Baker, CEO of WNET.* Bill Baker and Mel Rogers quotes in *Current,* 24 April 1998.

265 *A scandal erupted.* Steve Behrens, "Duggan Postlude: Wear 'Noncommercial' as Badge of Honor," *Current,* 4 October 1999, 3. See also Lawrie Mifflin, "Public Broadcasting Head, Noted for Fundraising, Quits," *New York Times,* 10 September 1999, A-13; Steve Behrens and Karen Everhart-Bedford, "Duggan Withdraws from 'Head-Butting' Arena," *Current,* 20 September 1999, A-1, A-16–17.

265 *During hearings.* Steve Behrens, "Congress Reacts Hotly to List Swaps with Dems," *Current,* 19 July 1999; Steve Behrens, "CPB Bans List Dealing with Politicos," *Current,* 2 August 1999; Steve Behrens, "List Probe: 9% of Stations Swapped with Pols," *Current,* 20 September 1999, A-1, A-15.

265 *An in-depth investigation.* Steve Behrens, "List Probe 9% of Stations Swapped with Pols," *Current 18,* 20 September 1999, A1, A14.

266 *Practically speaking.* Data from CPB programming surveys cited in Gary O. Larson, *Fulfilling the Promise: Public Broadcasting in the Digital Age* (Washington, D.C.: Center for Media Education, 8 July 1998), 39. Leslie Peters quoted in *Current,* 21 June 1999.

267 *"All of my instincts."* Ervin Duggan, quoted in *Current,* 13 September 1999.

267 *"It was a good idea."* Rockefeller quoted in *Current,* 14 October 1996, 8.

267 *The first step.* Daressa quoted in *Current,* 12 February 1996, 20; also in Pat Aufderheide, "Public TV's Public Sphere," 1991, 179–80.

268 *"An electronic town square."* *Quality Time? The Report of the Twentieth-Century Fund Task Force on Public Television* (New York: The Twentieth Century Fund Press, 1993), III.

268 For information on the Nitty Gritty City Group, see *Quality Time?,* p. 172, and Ralph Engelman, *Public Radio and Television in America: A Political History* (Thousand Oaks, California: Sage Publications, 1996), 214.

268 *As Robert Hughes, advises.* Hughes, "Television: Who Needs It?" *New York Review of Books,* 16 February 1995, 42.

269   *PBS has shown.* Information on *Leona's Sister Gerry* in *Current,* 4 December 1995.

269   *Longtime McLaughlin panelist.* Jack W. Germond, "Confessions of a Mc-Laughlin Group Escapee," *Brill's Content,* September 1999, 84–87.

270   *Forget about costly entertainment.* Lewis H. Lapham, "Adieu Big Bird: On the Terminal Irrelevance of Public Television," *Harper's,* December 1993, 35–38.

270   *Media scholar Marilyn Lashley.* Lashley, *Public Television: Panacea, Pork Barrel or Public Trust* (Westport, Connecticut: Greenwood Press, 1992), 128.

270   *As . . . Peter Drucker explains.* Drucker, *Managing the Non-Profit Organization: Principles and Practices* (New York: HarperBusiness, 1990), 112.

270   *"Of much greater importance." Quality Time?,* 18.

271   *George Gerbner explains.* Gerbner, "Fred Rogers and the Significance of Story," *Current,* 13 May 1996, 1, 34–36.

271   *Peter Moore.* Quoted in Karen Everhart Bedford, "The Inspiration: Channel Four Supports Its Mission with Ads," *Current,* 25 January 1996, 1, 6, 18.

271   *The Dutch broadcasting system.* See Kellner, *Television and the Crisis of Democracy,* 204; also Dennis McQuail, *Media Performance: Mass Communication and the Public Interest* (London: Sage, 1992), 62.

271   *Less government support.* Figures on comparative national spending on public broadcasting from *Quality Time?,* 152.

271   *On an average evening.* Ratings discussed in Patricia Aufderheide, "Public Service Broadcasting in the United States," *Journal of Media Economics,* 1996, 71.

272   *The Ford Foundation proposed.* Ford report in Ralph Engelman, *Public Radio and Television in America,* 150; *Quality Time?,* 150–52; William Hoynes, *Public Television for Sale: Media, the Market, and the Public Sphere* (Boulder, Colorado: Westview Press, 1994), 170–71.

272   *Hollings challenged.* Hollings quoted in Patricia Aufderheide, "What Makes Public TV Public? It Gets Harder and Harder to Tell," *The Progressive,* January 1988, 38.

273   Chicago Tribune *columnist.* Eric Zorn. "If Government Owns the Airwaves, Where's Our Cut?" *Chicago Tribune,* 25 June 1995, 1.

273   *Neither did they mention.* See Ben Bagdikian, *The Media Monopoly* (Boston: Beacon Press, 1992), 148.

273   *Over 1995–96.* Corporation for Public Broadcasting, *Common Sense for the Future,* May 2, 1995, unpublished report to Congress; *The Public Broadcasting Trust Fund: The Road to Self Sufficiency: Public Broadcasting Meets the Congressional Challenge,* Legislative Proposal of America's Public Television Stations, National Public Radio, Public Broadcasting Service, and Public Radio International, May 2, 1995, unpublished report to Congress; Elizabeth Rathbun, "Public Broadcasters Seek Trust Fund," *Broadcasting and Cable,* 8 May

1995, 78–79; Karen Everhart Bedford, "Now a Flurry of Options," *Current*, 6 March 1995.

273 *A sharp rebuke.* Fritts quoted in *Communication Daily*, 12 September 1995.

274 *Donovan . . . stipulated.* Donovan quoted in *Current*, 23, June 1997, 23A.

274 *A 1966 report.* BMR report in *Current*, 11 November 1996.

274 *The most recent bill.* Steve Behrens, "Bill Would Boost CPB 60%, Restrict Underwriting Credits and Launch Funding Study, *Current*, 22 June 1998, 1; "Key Lawmakers Unveil Plan to Reform, Reauthorize PBS," Congress of the United States, House of Representatives, Washington, D.C., 15 June 1998.

275 *The Gore Commission.* Steve Behrens, "Gore Panel Endorses Adding Educational DTV Channels," *Current*, 21 December 1998, 1, 100.

278 *Grossman has commented.* Lawrence Grossman quoted in *Quality Time?*, 152.

278 *FCC chair Reed Hundt.* Hundt quoted in Neil Hickey, "Beachfront Property on the Cyber Sea," *Columbia Journalism Review*, September/October 1999, 47.

278 *A December 1998 poll.* Lake, Snell, Perry, and Associates, *Television in the Digital Age: A Report to the Project on Media Ownership and the Benton Foundation* (Washington, D.C.: December 1998); Steve Behrens, "Poll: 8 in 10 Say Commercial TV Should Aid Public TV," *Current*, 25 January 1999, 1, 19.

279 Funding mechanisms are discussed in *Electricity Journal*, December 1997; "Cable TV and New Media," *Law and Finance*, August 1997; *Investor's Business Daily*, 8 December 1997; *Variety*, 12 January 1998; and *Forbes*, 12 January 1998.

279 *Ledbetter asked.* Speech by James Ledbetter at the Media and Democracy Congress, sponsored by the Institute for Alternative Journalism, October 1997.

280 *One alternative.* Marc Gunther, "Public Relations: Are Corporate Sponsors Influencing What PBS Viewers See?" *Detroit Free Press*, 7 July 1993.

281 *American Playhouse presented.* State censorship reported in *Current*, 31 July 1994; *Public Broadcasting Report*, 28 July 1994.

282 *Questioned by the press.* Robert Bianco, "New PBS President Defends Programming," *Pittsburgh Post-Gazette*, 27 July 1994.

282 *Marlon Riggs responded.* Riggs quoted in B. J. Bullert, *Public Television: Politics and the Battle over Documentary Film* (New Brunswick, New Jersey: Rutgers University Press, 1997), 104.

283 *Jack Willis remarked.* Willis, "Discussion of Draft Proposal on the Issue of Independents and Public Television," unpublished (16 October 1979), quoted in Engelman, *Public Radio and Television in America*, 172.

283 *Lapham characterized.* Lewis H. Lapham, "Adieu Big Bird: On the Terminal Irrelevance of Public Television," *Harper's*, December 1993, 37.

283 *To ensure minimal.* Federal Communications Commission, *The Public and Broadcasting Manual*; Revised and Released June 7, 1999.

285 *In past years.* Katherine C. Montgomery, *Target: Prime Time: Advocacy*

Groups and the Struggle Over Entertainment Television (New York: Oxford University Press, 1989).

285 *These days more than 150.* See Craig Cox, "Prime Time Activism: These Days, TV Sells Sex, Soap, and Social Change," *Utne Reader,* September/October 1999, 20–22.

285 *A large coalition.* Associated Press, "Panel: TV Regressing on Minorities," 13 April 1999; Greg Braxton, "Minorities Join to Protest Exclusion by Network TV," *Los Angeles Times,* 27 June 1999; Bernard Weinraub, "Stung by Criticism of Fall Shows, TV Networks Add Minority Roles," *New York Times,* 19 September 1999.

287 *Director Jim Yee conceded.* James Yee, speech at Media and Democracy Congress II, sponsored by the Institute for Alternative Journalism, New York, October 1997.

287–289 On micro broadcasting, see Greg Milner, "Micro-Radio: A Little Static and a Big Stick," in *Media and Democracy,* edited by Don Hazen and Larry Smith (San Francisco: IAJ, 1996); Jacqueline Conciatore, "FCC Wins Injunction Against Microradio Leader Dunifer," *Current,* 10 August 1998, 5, C1; Matt Richtel, "FCC Takes a Harder Look at 'Microradio' Stations," *New York Times,* 20, August 1998; Gloria Tristani, "Keeping the Local in Local Radio," unpublished speech, 3 September 1998; William Kennard, speech to the National Association of Broadcasters, (unpublished), 16 October 1998; Rona Kobell, "Warrant Wrenches Radio Rebel Off the Air," *Pittsburgh Post-Gazette,* 8 November 1998; Stephen Labaton, "FCC Offers Low-Power FM Stations," *New York Times,* 29 January 1999; Jacqueline Conciatore, "Public Radio Wary of Interference from New Low-Power FM Stations," *Current,* 19 April 1999; "Microradio Stations Fight for Their Lives" (unpublished), 30 April 1999; Americans for Radio Diversity, "FCC Proposes Low-Power FM Radio Service" (unpublished), 18 May 1999; Danny Schechter, "(Low) Power to the People," *The Nation,* 24 May 1999, 10; Kevin McNulty, "Adding Low-watt Stations to the FM Dial," *American Journalism Review,* September 1999, 12–13.

289 Peggy Noton, "Independent Radio's Problems and Prospects: An Interview with Peter Franck, Former President of Pacifica Radio," *Z Magazine,* 1994, 51–57; Jacqueline Conciatore, "Tempers Rise as Pacifica Board Decides to Select Its Own Members," *Current,* 8 March 1999; Jacqueline Conciatore, "Pacifica's Heated Conflict Boils Over at KPFA," *Current,* 22 April 1999; Jacqueline Conciatore, "KPFA Staff Continues Siege of Pacifica," *Current,* 5 July 1999; Jacqueline Conciatore, "Hundreds Protest for KPFA after Tussle on the Air," *Current,* 19 July 1999, 1, 13; Venise Wagner, "Huge Berkeley Rally Calls for Local Autonomy at KPFA," *San Francisco Examiner,* 1 August 1999; Jacqueline Conciatore, "Pacifica Opens KPFA's Doors, Staffers Continue Protest," *Current,* 2 August 1999, 1, 11; A. Clay Thomas, "Air War," *In These Times,* 22 August 1999, 7; Laura Flanders, "Pacifica Imperiled?" *In These Times,* 5 September 1999, 8; Phillip Connors, "Mixed Signals," *In These Times,* 5 September 1999, 19; Larry Everest, "KPFA Back on the Air," *Z Magazine,* September 1999, 9–10.

291 Information on WNYC-TV from Steve Behrens, "Compromise at WNYC: Radio Stays Public, TV Goes Commercial," *Current,* 13 April 1995; Steve Behrens, "Ethnic Programmers Petition FCC against Sale of WNYC-TV," *Cur-*

rent, 23 October 1995; Jacqueline Conciatore, "Suddenly a Great Sense of Possibilities: WNYC's Walker: 'We Need to Be More New York,'" *Current,* 25 November 1996.

291–292 Information on WUDC-FM from Mark Fisher, "One Last Request for Jazz 90, NPR Protest Is Unlikely to Halt Station's Sale," *Washington Post,* 1 July 1997, D7; Alan Kline and Samuel Godreich, "C-SPAN to Enter Radio by Buying UDC Stations; Jazz Fans Want Time Amid Public Affairs," *Washington Times,* 14 August 1997, A1; Kristan Trugman, "Jazz Fans Sing Blues in Protest at C-Span's Plans for WDCU," *Washington Times,* 4 September 1997, C4; David Hatch, "Public Radio Sale in D.C. Raises Concern," *Electronic Media,* 6 October 1997, 6.

292 *Finally, in 1999.* David Earl Honig, *Comments, Counterproposal, and Proposal to Reserve All Channels Used by Noncommercial Television Stations,* 16 November 1998 (unpublished).

293 *In September 1995.* Steve Behrens, "Reaffirming a Noncommercial Public TV Service," *Current,* 28 April 1997, 15; Steve Behrens, "Investor Backs Talks on Grossman's Commercial Network Plan," *Current,* 12 May 1997; "Opponents Say Advertising Is 'Antithetical to Principles and Economically Unsound,'" *Current,* 25 September 1995, 6; Karen Everhart Bedford, "The Question of Length Is Really Settled," *Current,* 17 February 1997; Steve Behrens, "Public TV Evenly Split on 30-Second Underwriting Credits," *Current,* 5 April 1999.

References

Aronson, James. *Deadline for the Media: Today's Challenges to Press, TV, and Radio.* New York: Bobbs-Merrill, 1972.

Aufderheide, Patricia. "Cable Television and the Public Interest." *Journal of Communication* 42, no. 1 (winter 1992): 52–65.

———. *Communications Policy and the Public Interest: The Telecommunications Act of 1996.* New York: Guilford Press, 1999.

———. "The Corporatization of Public TV: Why Labor's Voice Is Seldom Heard on PBS." *Union,* October/November 1988: 11–13.

———. "A Funny Thing Happened to TV's Public Forum." *Columbia Journalism Review,* November/December 1991: 60–63.

———. "Public Service Broadcasting in the United States." *The Journal of Media Economics* 9, no. 1 (1996): 63–76.

———. "Public Television and the Public Sphere." *Critical Studies in Mass Communication* 8 (1991): 168–83.

———. "What Makes Public TV Public? It Gets Harder and Harder to Tell." *The Progressive,* January 1988: 35–36, 38.

Bagdikian, Ben H. *The Media Monopoly.* Boston: Beacon Press, 2000.

Barnouw, Erik. *The Sponsor: Notes on a Modern Potentate.* New York: Oxford, 1978.

Berelson, Bernard, "Democratic Theory and Public Opinion." *Public Opinion Quarterly* 16 (Fall 1952): 313–20.

Blumer, Herbert. "The Mass, the Public, and Public Opinion." In *Public Opinion and Communication,* eds. Bernard Berleson and Morris Janowitz. New York: The Free Press, 1966.

———. "Public Opinion and Public Opinion Polling." *American Sociological Review* 13 (October 1948).

———. "Social Movements." In *Social Movements: Critiques, Concepts, Case-Studies,* ed. Stanford M. Lyman. New York: New York University Press, 1995.

———. "Social Problems as Collective Behavior." In *Collective Behavior and Social Movements,* ed. Russell L. Curtis Jr. and Benigno E. Aguirre. Boston: Allyn and Bacon, 1993.

Boardman, Anthony E., and Aidan R. Vining. "Public Service Broadcasting in Canada." *The Journal of Media Economics* 9, no. 1 (1996): 47–61.

Bogart, Leo. "No Opinion, Don't Know, and Maybe No Answer." *Public Opinion Quarterly* 31, no. 3: 331–45.

Branscomb, Anne W. "A Crisis of Identity: What Is Public Broadcasting?" In *Public Television: Toward Higher Ground,* ed. Douglas Cater. Palo Alto, California: Aspin Institute Program on Communications and Society, 1975.

Brennan, Timothy. "Masterpiece Theatre and the Uses of Tradition." *Social Text*, fall 1985: 102–112.

Brown, Les. "Broadcasting's Vanishing Species." *Channels* 5, no. 3 (1985): 15–16.

Browne, Allan. "Economics, Public Service Broadcasting, and Social Values." *The Journal of Media Economics* 9, no. 1 (1996): 3–15.

———. "Public Service Broadcasting in Four Countries: An Overview." *The Journal of Media Economics* 9, no. 1 (1996): 76–81.

Browne, Allan, and Catherine Althaus. "Public Service Broadcasting in Australia." *The Journal of Media Economics* 9, no. 1 (1996): 31–48.

Bullert, B. J. *Public Television: Politics and the Battle over Documentary Film.* New Brunswick, New Jersey: Rutgers University Press, 1997.

Cancian, Francesca. "Conflicts between Activist Research and Academic Success: Participatory Research and Alternative Strategies." *The American Sociologist* 24, no. 1: 92–106.

Carnegie Commission on Educational Television. *Public Television: A Program for Action.* New York: Bantam, 1967.

Cave, Martin. "Public Service Broadcasting in the United Kingdom." *Journal of Media Economics* 9, no. 1 (1996): 17–30.

Cirino, Robert. *Power to Persuade: Mass Media and the News.* New York: Bantam Pathfinder, 1967.

Clark, Carroll. "The Concept of the Public." *Southwestern Social Science Quarterly* 13 (March 1933): 311–20.

Cohen, Jeff, and Norman Solomon. *Adventures in Medialand: Behind the News, Behind the Pundits.* Monroe, Maine: Common Courage Press, 1993.

Common Cause. *Channeling Influence: The Broadcast Lobby and the $70 Billion Free Ride.* Washington, D.C.: A Common Cause Report, 1997.

Croteau, David. "Challenging the 'Liberal Media' Claim." *Extra!* July/August 1998: 4–9.

Croteau, David, and William Hoynes. *By Invitation Only: How the Media Limit Political Debate.* Monroe, Maine: Common Courage Press, 1994.

Curtin, Michael. *Redeeming the Wasteland: Television Documentary and Cold War Politics.* New Brunswick, New Jersey: Rutgers University Press, 1995.

Daressa, Larry. "Television for a Change: To Help Us Change Ourselves." *Current,* 12 February 1996: 20.

Day, James. *The Vanishing Vision: The Inside Story of Public Television.* Berkeley, California: University of California Press, 1995.

Downton, James, and P. E. Wehr. "Peace Movements: The Role of Commitment and Community in Sustaining Member Participation." *Research in Social Movements, Conflicts, and Change* 13: 113–34.

Drucker, Peter F. *Managing the Non-Profit Organization: Principles and Practices.* New York: HarperBusiness, 1990.

Engelman, Ralph. *Public Radio and Television in America: A Political History.* Thousand Oaks, California: Sage Publications, 1996.

Epstein, Edward Jay. *News from Nowhere.* New York: Random House, 1973.

Friedland, Lewis A. "Public Television and the Crisis of Democracy: A Review Essay." *The Communication Review* 1, no. 1 (1995).

Fuller, Linda K. "Saving Stories: A Goal of the Cultural Environment Movement." *Gazette: The International Journal for Communications Studies* 60, no. 2 (1998): 139–54.

Gamson, William A. "Constructing Social Movements." In *Social Movements and Cultures,* ed. Hank Johnston and Bert Klandermans. London: UCL Press, 1995.

Gans, Herbert J. *Deciding What's News: A Study of CBS Evening News, NBC Nightly News, Newsweek, and Time.* New York: Vintage Books, 1980.

Garnham, Nicholas. *Capitalism and Communication: Global Culture and the Economics of Information.* London: Sage Publications, 1992.

———. "Comments on John Keane's 'Structural Transformations of the Public Sphere.'" *Communication Review* 1, no. 1 (1995): 23–26.

———. "The Media and the Public Sphere." In *Habermas and the Public Sphere,* ed. Craig Calhoun. Cambridge, Massachusetts: MIT Press, 1996.

Gerbner, George. "Fred Rogers and the Significance of Story." *Current,* 13 May 1996: 32–36.

———. "Introduction: Why the Cultural Environment Movement?" *Gazette: The International Journal for Communications Studies* 60, no. 2 (1998): 133–38.

———. "The Stories We Tell." *Media Development,* April 1996: 13–17.

Gitlin, Todd. *The Whole World Is Watching: Mass Media in the Making and Unmaking of the New Left.* Berkeley, California: University of California Press, 1980.

Gore, Al. "Remarks as Prepared for Delivery by Vice President Al Gore, Presidential Advisory Committee on Public Interest Obligations for Digital TV," Wednesday, 22 October 1997.

Green, Hope, and Derk Zimmerman. *PBS 2 Business Plan.* 19 May 1999.

Gunther, Marc. "Public Relations: Are Corporate Sponsors Influencing What PBS Viewers See?" *Detroit Free Press,* 7 July 1993.

Habermas, Jurgen. "Further Reflections on the Public Sphere." In *Habermas and the Public Sphere,* ed. Craig Calhoun. Cambridge, Massachusetts: MIT Press, 1996.

Hallin, Daniel C. *We Keep America on Top of the World: Television Journalism and the Public Sphere.* New York: Routledge, 1994.

Hazen, Don, and Julie Winokur, eds. *We the Media: A Citizens' Guide to Fighting for Media Democracy.* New York: The New Press, 1997.

Herman, Edward S., and Noam Chomsky. *Manufacturing Consent: The Political Economy of the Mass Media.* New York: Pantheon Books, 1988.

Hickey, Neil. "Money Lust: How Pressure for Profit Is Perverting Journalism." *Columbia Journalism Review,* July/August 1998: 28–36.

————. "Public TV: Why Reports of Its Death Seem Premature." *TV Guide* 11 (4 December, 1982): 12–18.

Hondagneu-Sotelo, Pierrette. "Why Advocacy Research? Reflections on Research and Activism with Immigrant Women." *American Sociologist* 24, no. 1: 56–68.

Hoynes, William. *Public Television for Sale: Media, the Market, and the Public Sphere.* Boulder, Colorado: Westview Press, 1994.

————. *The Cost of Survival: Political Discourse and the "New PBS."* Vassar College, June 1999, unpublished.

Hughes, Robert. "Television: Who Needs It?" *New York Review of Books* 42, no. 3 (16 February 1995).

Iggers, Jeremy. "Get Me Rewrite: How the New Market-Driven Journalism Is Turning Our Stories into Industrial Waste." *Utne Reader,* September–October 1997: 46–48.

Ingram, Richard T. *The Ten Basic Responsibilities of Nonprofit Boards.* Washington, D.C.: National Center for Nonprofit Boards, 1988.

Jensen, Elizabeth. "Barney & Friends: Public TV Prepares for Image Transplant to Justify Existence." *Wall Street Journal,* 13 January 1994: A1, A4.

Johnston, Hank. "The Cultural Analysis of Social Movements." In *Social Movements and Cultures,* ed. Hank Johnston and Bert Klandermans. London: UCL Press, 1995.

Kalter, Joanmarie. "Burnout." *Columbia Journalism Review,* July/August 1999: 30–33.

Keane, John. "A Reply to Nicholas Garnham." *Communication Review* 1, no. 1 (1995): 27–32.

————. "Structural Transformations of the Public Sphere." *Communication Review* 1, no. 1 (1995): 1–22.

Kellner, Douglas. *Television and the Crisis of Democracy.* Boulder, Colorado: Westview Press, 1990.

Kerwin, Ann Marie. "Advertiser Pressure on Newspapers Is Common: Survey." *Editor & Publisher,* 16 January 1993.

Lake, Snell, Perry, and Associates. *Television in the Digital Age: A Report to the Project on Media Ownership and the Benton Foundation.* Washington, D.C.: December 1998.

Lapham, Lewis H. "Adieu, Big Bird: On the Terminal Irrelevance of Public Television." *Harper's,* December 1993: 35–38.

————. "'I'm Just Curious: How Do You Propose to Carry on the Struggle against the Disney Co.?'" *Current,* 28 August 1995: 16–17.

Larson, Gary O. *Fulfilling the Promise: Public Broadcasting in the Digital Age: A Report for the Center for Media Education.* Washington, D.C.: 8 July 1998.

Lashley, Marilyn. *Public Television: Panacea, Pork Barrel, or Public Trust?* Westport, Connecticut: Greenwood Press, 1992.

Ledbetter, James. *Made Possible By . . . : The Death of Public Broadcasting in the United States.* New York: Verso, 1997.

Lee, Martin A., and Norman Solomon. *Unreliable Sources: A Guide to Detecting Bias in News Media*. New York: Carol Publishing Group, 1992.

Marx, Gary T., and Douglas McAdam. *Collective Behavior and Social Movements: Process and Structure*. Englewood Cliffs, New Jersey: Prentice-Hall, 1994.

Mazzocco, Dennis W. *Networks of Power: Corporate TV's Threat to Democracy*. Boston: South End Press, 1994.

McAdam, Doug, and Ronnell Paulsen. "Specifying the Relationship between Social Ties and Activism." In *Social Movements: Readings on Their Emergence, Mobilization, and Dynamics*, ed. Doug McAdam and David A. Snow. Los Angeles: Roxbury Publishing Company, 1997.

McAuliff, Kevin. "No Longer Just Sex, Drugs, and Rock 'N' Roll: The Alternative Weeklies Go Mainstream—and Thrive." *Columbia Journalism Review*, March/April 1999: 40–45.

McChesney, Robert W. *Corporate Media and the Threat to Democracy*. New York: Seven Stories Press, 1997.

———. *Telecommunications, Mass Media, and Democracy*. New York: Oxford University Press, 1994.

McQuail, Denis. *Media Performance: Mass Communication and the Public Interest*. London: Sage Publications, 1992.

Molotch, Harvey, and Marilyn Lester. "News as Purposive Behavior: On the Strategic Use of Routine Events, Accidents, and Scandals." *American Sociological Review* 24, no. 1 (1974): 107–25.

Montgomery, Kathryn C. *Target: Prime Time—Advocacy Groups and the Struggle over Entertainment Television*. New York: Oxford University Press, 1989.

Morris, Aldon D. "Black Southern Sit-In Movement: An Analysis of Internal Organization." In *Social Movements: Readings on Their Emergence, Mobilization, and Dynamics*, ed. Doug McAdam and David A. Snow. Los Angeles: Roxbury Publishing Company, 1997.

Nussbaum, Bruce. "The Myth of the Liberal Media." *Business Week*, 11 November 1995: 34–35.

Oliver, Pamela E. "'If You Don't Do It, Nobody Else Will': Active and Token Contributors to Local Collective Action." In *Social Movements: Readings on Their Emergence, Mobilization and Dynamics*, ed. Doug McAdam and David A. Snow. Los Angeles: Roxbury Publishing Company, 1997.

PBS National Program Funding Standards and Practices. Washington, D.C.: PBS, February 1990.

Petras, Elizabeth McLean, and Douglas V. Porpera. "Participatory Research: Three Models and an Analysis." *American Sociologist* 24, no. 1: 107–25.

Phillips, Mark, Tom Griffiths, and Norman Tarbox. *PTV Overlapping Service Survey of Station Managers*. Washington, D.C.: PBS Research, 1990.

Pollock, Friederich. "Empirical Research into Public Opinion." In *Critical Sociology*, ed. Paul Connerton, 225–36. New York: Penguin, 1976.

Powledge, Fred. *Public Television: A Question of Survival.* Washington, D.C.: Public Affairs, 1972.

A Public Trust: The Report of the Carnegie Commission on the Future of Public Broadcasting. New York: Bantam Books, 1979.

Raboy, Marc. "Public Broadcasting and the Global Framework of Media Democratization." *Gazette: The International Journal for Communications Studies* 60, no. 2 (1998): 167–80.

Ryan, Charlotte. *Prime Time Activism: Media Strategies for Grassroots Organizing.* Boston: South End Press, 1991.

———. "A Study of National Public Radio." *Extra!* April/May 1993: 18–21.

Salzman, Jason. *Let the World Know: Make Your Cause News.* Denver, Colorado: Rocky Mountain Media Watch, 1995.

Schechter, Danny. *The More You Watch, The Less You Know.* New York: Seven Stories Press, 1997.

Schiffrin, Andre. "The Corporatization of Publishing." *The Nation*, 3 June 1996: 29–32.

Schiller, Herbert I. *The Mind Managers.* Boston: Beacon Press, 1973.

Snow, David A., E. Burke Rochford Jr., Steven K. Worden, and Robert D. Benford. "Frame Alignment Processes, Micromobilization, and Movement Participation." In *Social Movements: Readings on Their Emergence, Mobilization, and Dynamics*, ed. Doug McAdam and David A. Snow. Los Angeles: Roxbury Publishing Company, 1997.

Snow, David A., Louis A. Zurcher Jr., and Sheldon Eckland-Jones. "Social Networks and Social Movements." In *Social Movements: Readings on Their Emergence, Mobilization, and Dynamics*, ed. Doug McAdam and David A. Snow. Los Angeles: Roxbury Publishing Company, 1997.

Soley, Lawrence. "The Power of the Press Has a Price: TV Reporters Talk about Advertiser Pressures." *Extra!* July/August 1997: 11–13.

Speier, Hans. "Historical Development of Public Opinion." *American Journal of Sociology* 55, no. 4 (1950).

Starr, Jerold M. "The Challenges and Rewards of Coalition Building: Pittsburgh's Alliance for Progressive Action." *Contemporary Justice Review* 2, no. 2 (1999): 197–217.

———. "Cultural Politics and the Prospects for Radical Change in the 1980s." In *Cultural Politics: Radical Movements in Modern History*, ed. Jerold M. Starr. New York: Praeger, 1985.

———. "The Public Impact of Sociology: Public Broadcasting and the Public Interest." In *The Student's Companion to Sociology*, ed. Chet Ballard, Jon Gubbay, and Chris Middleton. Oxford, England: Blackwell, 1997.

———. "Taking Sides: The War at Home." In *The Lessons of the Vietnam War*, ed. Jerold M. Starr. Pittsburgh: Center for Social Studies Education, 1988.

Swidler, Ann. "Cultural Power and Social Movements." In *Social Movements and Cultures*, ed. Hank Johnston and Bert Klandermans. London: UCL Press, 1995.

Tuchman, Gay, ed. *The TV Establishment: Programming for Power and Profit.* Englewood Cliffs, New Jersey: Prentice-Hall, 1974.

Turner, Ralph, and Lewis M. Killian. *Collective Behavior.* Englewood Cliffs, New Jersey: Prentice-Hall, 1987.

Twentieth-Century Fund Task Force on Public Television. *Quality Time? The Report of the Twentieth Century Fund Task Force on Public Television,* with background paper by Richard Somerset-Ward. New York: Twentieth-Century Fund Press, 1993.

Victor, Kirk. "Airwaves." *National Journal,* 8 October 1994.

Walljaspar, Jay. "Age of the Mega-Alternatives." *Utne Reader,* July/August 1997: 91–94.

———. "Do We Still Need the Alternative Press?" In *Media and Democracy: A Book of Readings and Resources,* ed. Don Hazen and Larry Smith. San Francisco: Institute for Alternative Journalism, 1996, 142–44.

Walter, Victor E. "Mass Society: The Late Stages of an Idea." *Social Research* 31 (winter 1964): 391–410.

Weisman, John. "Public TV in Crisis: How to Make It Better." *TV Guide,* 8 August 1987: 26–30, 34–40.

Wirth, Louis. "Consensus and Mass Communication." *American Sociological Review* 13 (February 1948): 1–15.

Wolff, Robert Paul. "Beyond Tolerance." In *A Critique of Pure Tolerance,* ed. Robert Paul Wolff, Barrington Moore Jr., and Herbert Marcuse. Boston: Beacon Press, 1969.

Zorn, Eric. "If Government Owns the Airwaves, Where's Our Cut?" *Chicago Tribune,* 25 June 1995: sec. 2, p. 1.

Acknowledgments

The Florence and John Schumann Foundation (Bill Moyers, president) subsidized a leave of absence to complement my sabbatical from West Virginia University. The beneficence of both institutions made it possible for me to complete the first draft of this book. Holly Ainbinder generously advised me on fund-raising strategy.

By late summer 1999, I was again indebted to the Schumann Foundation and to Jack Willis, senior fellow, and his colleagues at the Open Society Institute, for funding the launch of Citizens for Independent Public Broadcasting, with me as executive director.

Micah Kleit of Beacon Press encouraged me to write, advocated my proposal, and then invested a great deal of time, talent, and energy into showing me how to make this a better book. My agent, Gerry Thoma, always pleasant, responsive, and informative, represented my interests well.

I am very pleased to acknowledge the following esteemed scholars for reading earlier drafts of this manuscript and sharing suggestions for its improvement: Pat Aufderheide, American University; Jeff Cohen, FAIR; Bill Hoynes, Vassar College; and Bob McChesney, University of Illinois.

From July 1996 to the submission of the final draft of this book, the Pittsburgh community and I were blessed to enjoy pro bono representation by outstanding legal talent, including Angela Campbell, Randi Albert, Karen Edwards Onyeiji, and Jeneba Jalloh (Institute for Public Representation, Georgetown University Law Center); David Honig (Minority Media and Telecommunications Council, in Washington, D.C.); Fred Polner (Rothman, Gordon, in Pittsburgh); and Andy Schwartzman (Media Access Project, in Washington, D.C.). In addition, I wish to acknowledge the legal support provided by students at the Georgetown University Law Center: Jennifer Bier, Charles Blackburn, Erin Brown, Juina Carter, Sana Coleman, Ken Itralto, Nicole Lemire, Melissa Lin, Alan Marzilli, and Anana Mazumdar. Without the philanthropy of these attorneys and students and their institutions there would be no story to tell.

The following Pittsburgh-area citizen activists are just a few of the many who gave selflessly to the QED Accountability Project and the Save Pittsburgh Public Television campaign: Rick Adams, Rob Bellamy, Benita Campbell, Russ Gibbons, Mark Ginsberg, Fred Gustafson, Ann Sutherland Harris, Bonita Johnson, Allen Kukovich, Charlie McCollester, Andy Newman, Bob Norman, Barney Oursler, Rick Peduzzi, Glenn Plummer, Keith Powell, Joni

Rabinowitz, Monsignor Charles Owen Rice, Brian Rieck, Molly Rush, Mike Schneider, Pete Shell, Mary Alice Shemo, Dick Siegler, Carol Stabile, the late Paul Stackhouse, Elayne Tobin, Rosemary Trump, Mike Vargo, Linda Wambaugh, Bill Wekselman, Gina Wilson, and Mark Wirick. I hope that anyone I have overlooked will forgive me my lapse and know that their contributions were and are valued.

I was privileged to spend the winter term of 1998 as a visiting scholar in the Department of Communications of the University of California at San Diego. I am grateful to Herb Schiller and Dan Hallin for making such arrangements on my behalf. While working on this book, I was helped enormously by DeeDee Halleck's memories and materials from past struggles for a more democratic public broadcasting service. Others who gave me encouragement and insights include Robert Horwitz, Dan Schiller, Michael Schudson, and Fred Turner.

Index